Social Cognition

Social Cognition

An Integrated Introduction

Second edition

Martha Augoustinos, Iain Walker and
Ngaire Donaghue

SAGE Publications

London ● Thousand Oaks ● New Delhi

SAGE Publications Ltd
1 Oliver's Yard
55 City Road
London EC1Y 1SP

SAGE Publications Inc.
2455 Teller Road
Thousand Oaks, California 91320

SAGE Publications India Pvt Ltd
B-42, Panchsheel Enclave
Post Box 4109
New Delhi 110 017

British Library Cataloguing in Publication data

A catalogue record for this book is available
from the British Library

ISBN-10 0-7619-4218-1   ISBN-13 978-0-7619-4218-4
ISBN-10 0-7619-4219-X   ISBN-13 978-0-7619-4219-1

Library of Congress Control Number: 2005935759

Typeset by C&M Digitals (P) Ltd, Chennai, India
Printed in Great Britain by The Alden Press, Oxford
Printed on paper from sustainable resources

Contents

List of Figures

List of Tables

List of Textboxes

Preface

The first edition of this book was published more than a decade ago. In that time a lot has changed in the world and in social psychology; a lot remains the same too. Looking at the first and the second editions of the book, one can similarly see that a lot has changed, and a lot remains the same. Among the most notable changes are the addition of Ngaire Donaghue to the authorial team, and a complete restructuring of the whole book. Among the constancies are the intellectual aim of producing a text which integrates significantly different social psychological approaches to a small number of topical areas, and of writing a book which is simultaneously a textbook to be used for teaching and a monograph which develops a unique social psychological viewpoint which challenges and stimulates our colleagues.

The writing of this second edition has benefited greatly from the contributions and suggestions of a great many people. All whose contributions were acknowledged in the preface to the first edition continue to have had an influence in this edition. More directly, though, Michael Carmichael and his editorial team at Sage have been helpful and patient. Two anonymous reviewers of a draft manuscript provided detailed, thoughtful commentary which we have tried to incorporate. Colleagues who have used the first edition as a text in their courses have offered many suggestions and requests over the years, as have a great many students from around the world. Closer to home, members of the Discourse and Rhetoric Unit (DARU) at Adelaide have read and commented on various parts of the draft manuscript. At Murdoch, Tim Kurz and other colleagues and students in the Social Psychology Reading Group have debated at length several draft chapters, and Tammy Geddes, Maureen Mankoo and Sarah Miller have provided individual support. Our biggest debts, of course, are to our families and friends, to whom we dedicate this book in recognition of, and with thanks for, all your support: Dave and Dylan; Jane, Alex, Joel and Patrick; and James.

Acknowledgements

Figure 1.1 is from Michael Leunig, *Ramming the Shears*, 1985, with permission from Penguin Books Australia Ltd.

Table 2.1 is adapted from Tajfel et al., 1971, p. 157, with permission from John Wiley & Sons Ltd.

Figure 3.1 is adapted from Fiske & Neuberg, 1990, with permission from Elsevier.

Table 5.1 is adapted from Jones & Harris, 1967, p. 6, with permission from Elsevier.

Table 5.4 is adapted from Hunter et al., 1991, p. 263, with permission from the *British Journal of Social Psychology* © British Psychological Society.

Table 5.5 is adapted from Furnham, 1982a, p. 315, with permission from Adrian Furnham and the *British Journal of Social Psychology* © British Psychological Society.

1 Introduction

Michael Leunig's cartoon, *The Understandascope*, captures the essence of something profound and, in this case, paradoxical. We see a lone figure, peering through a telescope-like device at a mass of people interacting below. In the background there is a city of buildings, with a plane flying by. Although the cartoon predates September 11, 2001, it is hard to avoid seeing the plane as though it is flying towards one of the skyscrapers. The people in the foreground are all interacting with one another, presumably arguing, telling jokes, chatting up, deciding whether to go to a lecture or what to have for dinner, and all the other things people do in everyday life. High on the hill, the lone figure peering through the Understandascope observes all this and, aided by the wonderful contraption, understands it all. If only it were so easy.

The aim of social psychology is to understand the social nature of being human. Social cognition is an area of social psychology, with the narrower aim of understanding how humans come to understand the social world and their position in it. In many ways, the social psychologist is the solitary figure in Leunig's cartoon, trying and hoping to understand humanity with the aid of some theoretical and methodological contraptions. Unfortunately, that endeavour and hope are thwarted by the paradox within Leunig's cartoon.

The solitary figure is separated from the mass below, set apart as though unafflicted by being human and unaffiliated with anything human. In peering through the Understandascope, the figure fails to recognize that he (and the figure does seem to be drawn as 'he', and that only highlights the point we are making here) is inseparable from those below, and indeed that any understanding that comes through the Understandascope is not given to him as if divinely, but rather depends on his interpretation of the information provided. His understanding is the joint product of the Understandascope and himself. Furthermore, if the Understandascope genuinely does provide understanding of what it is to be human, it ought to provide that understanding regardless of which group of humans it is focused on, and even – perhaps especially – when it is focused backwards on the viewer.

In all these ways, Leunig's cartoon neatly captures the nature of social psychology as an intellectual discipline, and says something about social

Figure 1.1 *The Understandascope* **by Michael Leunig**

psychologists as well. The technology of social psychology, impressively built up over more than a century, is like the Understandascope – capable of providing insightful information, but not insight itself. Unfortunately, social psychology over the past century has focused its technology almost solely on just one group of humans, the ubiquitous psychology undergraduate student, as though such people can represent all of humanity. Even more unfortunately, social psychology has rarely put itself and its practitioners in front of the Understandascope. It has proceeded on the 'God Trick' assumption, that we social psychologists can, by standing on a hill and observing from a distance, remove ourselves from the realm of what it is we are trying to understand. This is clearly absurd.

The solitary figure in Leunig's cartoon seems dismayed. It is not clear, though, whether that dismay is because of what he sees through the Understandascope (a sea of mostly angry-looking people) or because of his understanding of what those mostly angry-looking people are angry about. Is it the anger itself, or the understanding that there is little or no alternative to the anger, that is dismaying? Once again, Leunig's cartoon captures nicely a common characteristic of social psychology and social psychologists. The index of any standard social psychology textbook is replete with references to the nasty, brutish aspects of humans. There is, in stark contrast, little about the upbeat, the stuff that might put a smile on the face of the solitary figure. The same is true of this book. That is not to say that the upbeat is less important. Rather, it is more a reflection of the urgency of understanding humans' propensity to be nasty to one another. But, lurking quietly in the background of social psychology is an often tacit assumption that by understanding the nasty and the brutish, we can better go about producing social change for the better. We share this view, and wish that social psychology more explicitly wrestled with an agenda for social change rather than being content with trying to understand.

In this book, we set out to examine what we see as the primary ways in which social psychologists have gone about building a systematic understanding of how humans come to understand the social world. Although social psychologists are all largely concerned with understanding the same social phenomena, there are remarkable divergences in how they describe, and certainly in how they understand, those phenomena. These divergences mark the boundaries between four major perspectives we cover in this book – social cognition, social identity theory, social representations and discursive psychology. In the book, we attempt to demarcate those perspectives, and then consider how each perspective understands phenomena such as attitudes, identity, and prejudice. Our position is that an adequate social psychological account of *any* phenomenon – from the perception of the ordinary and mundane routine of everyday life to the genocidal behaviours of members of one group against another – must incorporate and integrate perspectives that range from the cognitive and intraindividual to the societal and ideological. Throughout, we try to turn the Understandascope on the discipline itself, and ultimately try to sketch how to focus it a little more sharply through the development of a broader, more integrative understanding, for the benefit of the discipline and for those we study.

Defining *Social* Psychology

Social psychology is an odd discipline. Born in the social sciences baby-boom of the late 19th century, it traces its genealogy directly to parental disciplines in psychology and sociology, and more distantly to the ancient Greek philosophers. Embedded within the family tree are notable as well as disreputable ancestors: the Enlightenment movement was central in enabling contemporary western conceptualizations of the self-contained, independent individual; two world wars provided fertile grounds for the development of a technological hardware able to be applied in peacetime for other purposes; without the rise of liberalism a discipline such as social psychology would be inconceivable; and social psychology's concern with groups and the crowd is largely attributable – along with much of the discipline of sociology – to the worries of middle-class sensibilities about the rise of the masses consequent upon rapid industrialization in the 19th century.

Perhaps stretching the birth metaphor too far, social psychology is something of a bastard discipline. Its parents – psychology and sociology – have never had much of a relationship with one another, and both often disavow their progeny, perhaps because of guilt about their flirtation with something they each rejected, and perhaps because of a lingering, wistful attachment to what might have been. As a bastard discipline, social psychology has had to find its own way in the world, to work hard to establish its own identity, to develop its own ways of understanding the world and its place in it, and to work hard not to be tarnished with the same ill-repute that sometimes afflicts its parents. In finding its own way, it has made some wrong turns, traveled down some blind alleys, and flirted with some dangerous characters.

Definitely stretching the metaphor well beyond breaking point, we might continue by claiming that social psychology is still a developing, adolescent discipline, still hung up about some of its earlier, still unresolved, complexes, and still struggling with a confusing array of possibilities. Social psychology has still not established its own mature identity. Struggling with identity conflicts about theory and method that are the legacy of its bastard heritage, it still wrestles with multiple 'possible selves'. Multiplicity is not necessarily a bad thing – indeed, we would argue that it is a virtue. But some of the possible selves claim they cannot exist beside others, that they are mutually incompatible. Perhaps they can be sorted, with some effort and imagination, into a coherent, integrated whole self; perhaps they just need to learn how to engage in parallel play in the same sandpit; perhaps they need a divorce or a restraining order.

Somewhat oxymoronically, social psychology has never fully grasped what *social* encompasses. Early influential social psychologists defined social psychology in such a way that the *social* was always separated from the individual. For example, Gordon Allport defined social psychology as:

> The attempt to understand how the thought, feeling, and behavior of individuals are influenced by the actual, imagined, or implied presence of others. (1985, p. 3)

This definition establishes the individual and the social as separate, antinomical, and sometimes even antithetical. Such a definition allows, and even encourages, a focus on *either* the individual *or* the social, and sometimes a focus on how one affects the other. What such a definition disallows is a conceptualization in which the individual and the social are inextricably inseparable, in which the individual constitutes and is simultaneously constituted by the social.

Considering the individual and the social as fundamentally inseparable radically alters the understandings of human experience that are developed by social psychologists. This also constitutes, or rather *ought* to constitute, the unique, interstitial position of social psychology – unifying the individualism of psychology and the 'institutionalism' of sociology.

The Crisis in Social Psychology

As with all adolescents, social psychology experienced a 'crisis'. Almost four decades ago, Kenneth Ring (1967) published a provocative article taking to task the social psychology of his time for being frivolous, and for being more concerned with demonstrating a cute, clever experimental manipulation of the latest theoretical toy than with making serious progress in the task of building a body of worthwhile knowledge. Ring's article heralded the start of what came to be known as the 'crisis' in social psychology (Cartwright, 1979; Elms, 1975; Gergen, 1973; McGuire, 1973; Pepitone, 1976, 1981; Sampson, 1977, 1981; Tajfel, 1972; Taylor & Brown, 1979). The enthusiasm with which an earlier experimental social psychology was met became dampened by critics who described a general feeling of discontent with the discipline's direction. While experimentation deliberately and purposively controls for the 'contaminating variables' of the real world, it was argued that the artificiality of this contrived environment did not and could not adequately simulate human social experience. Furthermore, experimentation led to its own class of problem, such as demand characteristics (Orne, 1969) and experimenter bias (Rosenthal, 1969). Other possible sources of bias were identified, such as the political, ideological, cultural and biographical backgrounds of researchers (Innes & Fraser, 1971).

Expressions of discontent were not only directed at the fetishism of laboratory experimentation. On a more epistemological level, Gergen (1973) claimed that social psychology could never be a science because the subject matter with which it deals (human social behaviour) is largely culturally and historically specific, and is itself changed because we social psychologists study it. Unlike the physical sciences, general laws of human behaviour cannot be established definitively, because these fluctuate with changing cultural and historical circumstances. Social psychology is, therefore, predominantly a 'historical enquiry'. For some, the location of the crisis was in the unchallenged epistemological assumption that the individual is 'the centre of all things', and thus should be the principal unit and focus of research and analysis. In particular, Hogan and Emler (1978), Pepitone (1976, 1981) and Sampson (1977, 1988) argued that most of social psychology's theories (dissonance theory, game theory, equity theory, attitude theories, and theories of personality and socialization) are imbued with the thesis of self-contained individualism.

The individualization of social psychology is largely attributed to the joint forces of experimentation and positivism which came to dominate the discipline and cloak it in scientific respectability. These forces also led to the demise of interest in collective phenomena in which early psychologists such as Wundt and McDougall had been interested (Farr, 1989). Along with the sociologist Durkheim (1898), these early psychologists believed that cultural phenomena such as language, myths, religion and nationalism could not be reduced to the individual level of analysis. In particular, Wundt believed that such higher cognitive processes could not be adequately studied by the experimental tradition which he founded.

The conflict and tension between the individual (psychological) and collective (sociological) levels of analysis has had a long history and is documented in the famous debate between Tarde and Durkheim (Doise, 1986). Those who have provided a critical history of social psychology are in agreement that the dominance of the former tradition over the latter can partly be attributed to the behaviourist views of Floyd Allport, who was highly critical of collective concepts such as McDougall's notion of 'group mind' (Cartwright, 1979; Farr, 1989; Graumann, 1986; Pepitone, 1981). Allport's methodological individualism is obvious in his famous statement: 'There is no psychology of groups which is not essentially and entirely a psychology of the individual. Social psychology ... is a part of the psychology of the individual' (1924, p. 4). Allport was insistent that collective phenomena such as crowd behaviour and public opinion were nothing more than the sum of the actions and attitudes of the individuals who comprise the collectivity. His methodological individualism was a powerful force which helped shape the subsequent nature of the most dominant theories and methods in North American social psychology.

Little has been written of the 'crisis' since the late 1970s. For some, it was a minor distraction and little more than a 'dummy-spit' in the normal course of business. Jones (1985), for example, calls it a 'minor perturbation' in the development of the science of social psychology. For others, it has brought to the fore the limitations of social psychology's methods, its epistemology, and even its research questions (Gergen, 1985; Manicas & Secord, 1983). One of Ring's criticisms was that debates and issues in social psychology are never really resolved. Rather, they just fade away from centre stage because people lose interest in them, not because we now know more than before. Indeed, in many ways, the crisis itself faded from centre stage not because the questions being raised about the enterprise of social psychology received any satisfactory answers, but simply because the discipline lost interest. We believe that the crisis was of epistemology, not just confidence, and that the epistemological problems of the 1960s and 1970s are just as problematic in the early part of the 21st century, particularly with respect to the most dominant perspective of the moment – social cognition.

Social Cognition

Social psychology has always prided itself on never succumbing to the behaviourist revolution which so debased and derailed the rest of psychology. During the heydays of behaviourism, social psychologists continued researching internal mental constructs such as attitudes, values and stereotypes. But in avoiding the excesses and pitfalls of behaviourism during the 1950s and 1960s, social psychology became increasingly drawn to the information-processing metaphor of the person which came to dominate cognitive science. Just as with behaviourism, cognitivism is associated with its own excesses. Today, the dominant perspective in North American social psychology is known as *social cognition*. Some have argued that the 'social' is a misnomer and that the only thing social about social cognition is the objects of its study – people, groups, events. It has an impressive armament of mini theories, concepts and experimental procedures borrowed from cognitive psychology. But despite all its hardware, for many it has been unable to satisfy the doubts and the questions that the crisis raised.

Currently, research and theory in social cognition are driven by an overwhelming individualistic orientation which forgets that the contents of cognition originate in social life, in human interaction and communication. Unfortunately, the information processing models central to social cognition focus on cognitive processes at the expense of content and context. As such, societal, collective, shared, interactive, and symbolic features of human thought, experience, and interaction are often ignored and forgotten. Contemporary social cognition research is individualistic because it searches within the cognitive and perceptual domain of the person to understand social phenomena such as attitudes, attributions, and identity. Social cognition will never explain adequately the totality of human experience so long as it remains at the individual level of analysis alone. However, unlike some critics, we also argue that mainstream social cognition research is not completely irrelevant and does have much to offer alternative social psychologies which have emerged and gained momentum more recently. Indeed, we will argue that a reconciliation and integration of individual and social accounts can lead to a fuller, more reflexive, and dynamic understanding of human experience.

What is this 'social' with which we suggest social cognition ought to be integrated? It comes largely from three other approaches, each of which had their origins in European social psychology. First is the approach provided by social identity theory (SIT; Tajfel & Turner, 1986). SIT provides an analysis of identity based on group belongingness. In contrast to North American social psychology, the group has been more valorized than the individual in European social psychology. People are conceptualized first and foremost as social beings, deriving from their group memberships a sense of who they are, how they should behave, and what they should believe. Society, as a collectivity, is comprised of the complex web of intergroup relations which characterize any socio-historical period. As social identity theorists are so keen to emphasize, social identity theory reinstates the social (or group) within the individual.

The second of the European perspectives we discuss, social representations theory (Moscovici, 1984), also emphasizes the centrality of social group membership, but focuses more upon how this membership shapes and constitutes an individual's consciousness. Social representations refer to the stock of common-sense theories and knowledge people have of the social world. The theory is interested not only in mapping the contents of this common sense and how this may differ between different social groups, but also in studying how representations are used by individuals and groups to understand and construct a common and shared reality.

Third, and most recent of the predominantly European perspectives, is discursive psychology. Having its origins in the postmodern and social constructionist critique of positivist science, discursive psychology emphasizes the centrality of discourse and rhetoric in human interaction. By focusing on what people say rather than on what people think, discursive psychology challenges the cognitivist assumptions underlying not only the social cognition mainstream, but also social identity theory and the theory of social representations.

Aims of this Book

Our aim in this book is to examine some of the different theoretical and methodological accomplishments of our bastard discipline, to examine some of the different possible selves competing to define the identity of social psychology, and to begin to try to sort all these into some sort of coherent, integrated whole. This is no easy task, but we see a mature, integrated identity, rather than a divorce, as something worth working for.

We draw upon the four major and influential perspectives which have contemporary currency in social psychology – social cognition, social identity, social representations, and discursive psychology. These perspectives have largely developed in parallel, rarely considering one another. However, they each deal, in their own ways, with the same phenomena. Throughout this book, we attempt to articulate a consideration of how these approaches might be integrated into a perspective which spans levels of analysis from the intraindividual to the societal. It should be noted at the outset that the four perspectives are not equivalent. Two of them – social identity and social representations – are systematized into formal theories. The other two are not systematized much at all, and are each best thought of as perspectives.

Organization of this Book

Following this brief introduction, the book is organized into three main parts. The first comprises a large chapter (Chapter 2), in which we present four foundational perspectives – social cognition, social identity, social representations, and discursive psychology. These are presented fairly independently of one another and fairly uncritically in their own terms. Our presentation sets out the major defining features of each perspective, and illustrative examples of research done within that perspective. These four perspectives set the foundations, and the tone, for the remainder of the book. Some students may find this chapter in its entirety a heavy slog and too much material to take in at once. If so, then we recommend that each theoretical perspective is read as a 'stand alone' section serving as a background to the corresponding section in each of the topic chapters in Part Two of the book. Indeed, we have written and structured the book with this kind of cross-referencing in mind. Chapter 2 also provides definitions of key terms that are associated with each theoretical perspective. We hope that this list of keywords will facilitate students' understanding of the central tenets of each approach.

In Part Two of the book, we present chapters on six major topics in social psychology from the point of view of each perspective in turn. These topics include social perception (Chapter 3), attitudes (Chapter 4), attributions (Chapter 5), self and identity (Chapter 6), prejudice (Chapter 7), and ideology (Chapter 8). The first five of these topics are central and defining areas in the field, and are invariably included in most social psychology textbooks. The last topic – ideology – has been less central but it is one which we believe is of great significance to how we understand human experience and social life. In all these chapters, we aim to provide an account of how each perspective addresses the topic, and to point to commonalities and divergences across the perspectives. This is handled somewhat differently in each of the chapters, partly because the topics themselves and the research that supports them lend themselves differently to integrative coverage. Unlike many other textbooks, we do not attempt to provide a comprehensive coverage of all that has been written on any one of these topics – this is not an encyclopedia. Rather, we present research and theory because of its illustrative power. In doing so, we hope to sketch some sort of initial integrated perspective. Throughout all the chapters, an over-riding aim is to re-establish the primacy of the *social* in social psychology. Again, each of these chapters is designed to be self-contained, although some cross-referencing with theoretical principles in Chapter 2 may be necessary, especially for perspectives which are less mainstream, such as social representations theory and discursive psychology.

Chapter 3 deals with social perception. Categorization processes are central to almost all theorizing in social psychology, regardless of perspective. However, different perspectives conceptualize categorization in starkly different ways. The social cognitive perspective has a considerable theoretical investment in the notion of schemas, and has amassed a vast array of empirical evidence demonstrating the operation of schematic thought. Much of the recent empirical attention in this area has focused on the unconscious operation of schematic, or categorical, thinking. We make the case that social cognitive research conceptualizes schemas in markedly similar ways to the conceptualizations of a representation by social representations researchers. Categorization is also a central premise of social identity theory – it is impossible to think of identity without some sense of how self is categorized as the same as, and different from, others. Finally, discursive psychology also considers categorization, and category memberships, as critically important. It differs from the other perspectives, though, in seeing categories as something achieved through talk-in-interaction.

Chapter 4 addresses possibly the most theorized and researched concept in social psychology – attitudes. In this chapter we detail the way in which the attitude construct has traditionally been defined and theorized within social psychology. We consider the functional approach to attitudes, and discuss how various theoretical perspectives have dealt with one of the most problematic issues in the field – the relationship between attitudes and behaviour. Following this, we discuss research which has investigated the cognitive organization of attitudes, including how attitudes are activated and accessed. We criticize traditional attitude research for its very individualized and asocial treatment of the attitude construct. In light of this, we present research on attitudes as social identity phenomena and attitudes as social representations. Finally, we consider the discursive approach to the contextual variability and linguistic construction of attitudes.

Another central and dominant topic within cognitive social psychology, attributions, is the subject matter of Chapter 5. We outline the three major theoretical contributions to attribution theory: Heider's (1958) pioneering work, Jones and Davis's (1965) theory of correspondent inferences and Kelley's (1967) covariation model. We detail the various attributional biases documented within the literature and canvass various explanations of these biases. We then describe research on intergroup attributions. These clearly highlight the role of social identities in the construction of explanations for positive and negative behaviours performed by ingroup and outgroup members, and also show clearly why attributions must be considered as social and cultural phenomena, not just as individual cognitive phenomena. This ties closely to a social representational view of attributions as shared world-views. Our treatment of the interactive construction of explanations in talk, and of the inseparability of description and explanation, rounds off this chapter.

The 'self' almost defines the focus of psychology as an intellectual enterprise, and 'the self in social context' almost captures the focus of all of social psychology. We consider four different approaches to 'self and identity' in Chapter 6. Social cognitive approaches focus especially on the self as a knowledge structure (i.e., as a schema), and, within this framework, on different sorts of 'selves' and the discrepancies between them (real self, positive ideal self, etc). This individualized sense of self is challenged by the social identity perspective, which forces a consideration of the necessary social context of self, of the relationships between self and group, and of the unavoidable politics of self and identity. Social representations research reminds us that 'self' is a historical and cultural construction, and that what we in the West take to be obvious in the way we think about ourselves is actually quite unusual. The constructed and contingent nature of 'self' as an interactional category is also the focus of discursive approaches.

Chapter 7 applies many of the constructs dealt with in earlier chapters to the study of prejudice and intergroup relations. We start by reviewing theory and research that locates the source of prejudice in the functioning of the abnormal personality. This is followed by two other prolific social cognitive traditions which approach prejudice as an attitude and as a schema, respectively. The relatively asocial focus on individuals as the origin of prejudice is criticized by the social identity perspective, which argues for a radically different conceptualization of stereotyping and intergroup differentiation. The social representation approach draws attention to the shared, political, and cultural construction of group identities, embedded in which are valorizations, descriptions, and explanations of self and other. Finally, discursive approaches emphasize how the processes taken to be relatively fixed by the other approaches are, in fact, highly contingent on local interaction.

The final chapter in this part is on ideology. Ideology is one of the most contested concepts in the social sciences, and is arguably social psychology's greatest challenge. We define the social psychological study of ideology as the study of the social psychological processes and mechanisms by which certain representations and constructions of the world serve to legitimate, rationalize and reproduce the existing institutional, social and power relations within any society. Given the reluctance of social psychological theories to consider collective and societal explanations for a range of cognitive phenomena, we claim that the system-serving and justificatory functions of certain values, beliefs, stereotypes, representations and attributions have been seriously neglected. Ideology, however, should not be viewed solely as a cognitive construct. More recently, ideology has been located in linguistic and discursive repertoires as well as in certain material and behavioural practices. This chapter reviews different approaches to the study of ideology within social psychology, examining in turn ideology as (false) consciousness, ideology as discourse, and ideology as material practices. We focus especially on an analysis of individualism and liberalism, two ideologies which are central to modern western democracies and also central to modern western social psychology.

Many readers – students and colleagues – may find it odd to find a chapter on ideology in a social psychology textbook. It is indeed odd – not odd that it should be included, but odd that it is always excluded. Ideology, we contend, is of central significance to how we understand human experience and contemporary social life. It is also critical to *any* social psychological enterprise, equally those which attempt to engage with the world in order to change it, and those that abstract themselves from the world in an attempt to understand the world 'objectively'. Social psychologists of almost all persuasions have prided themselves – rightly so – on wanting to change the world, not just understand it. Any theory of, or attempt at, social change is necessarily ideological. Any attempt to be objectively distant from the world is likewise ideologically based, as well as politically conservative.

In Part Three of the book we conclude with some brief thoughts and reflections regarding our attempts to bring together what are often perceived to be disparate traditions of research within the discipline. Finally we consider the future trajectory of social psychology as a discipline in light of recent developments in the field.

Concluding Comments

Since the publication of the first edition of this book in 1995 there has been a veritable explosion in research coming under the rubric of 'social cognition'. This has been equally matched by a proliferation of work in the social identity/self-categorization tradition and in social representations and discursive psychology. Our dilemma has thus been how to adequately cover all this material in a way that is accessible and representative of the current 'state of play' in the discipline. In doing so, we have needed to change the structure of the book from the first edition so that we can do justice to the four theoretical approaches. We hope that the new topic structure that we have adopted for this edition lends itself to better coverage of each area while at the same time maintaining the integrity of the different approaches to studying these social psychological concepts.

As with the previous edition, some of our colleagues from different theoretical camps will be horrified to see critical perspectives jointly included in a book purportedly about 'social cognition'. After all, many of these researchers have been at pains to differentiate themselves from one another. All perspectives contained in this book, however, have one fundamental thing in common: they all attempt to understand how we orient ourselves in the social world we inhabit, how we come to understand and construct our world, and what consequences these understandings and constructions have for us. Moreover, more critical approaches have themselves developed in response to the crisis in social psychology which we described earlier. While many in the discipline largely ignored the crisis, others have been busily developing alternative conceptual and methodological frameworks. In presenting an attempt at integration, we hope to preserve the value of all approaches, and hope to avoid the peril of destroying them all in the process of creating a drab grey admixture of everything. Ultimately, we hope that this book ignites student interest and enthusiasm in our discipline and encourages wider intellectual debate about what social psychology is and should be.

Part One

2   Theoretical Foundations

It is sometimes noted that social psychology is a discipline with a short history but a long past (see Allport, 1985; Farr, 1996; Graumann, 1996; Jones, 1998). The short history is often dated to an early experiment by Triplett (1898) showing that cyclists cycle faster with an audience than when alone; the long past to the thinking of the ancient Greek philosophers. Either way, there has always been a focus on how people make sense of the world. This is also a defining feature of social cognition – understanding how people understand themselves, the worlds (physical, social, environmental) around them, and their relationship with those worlds. Understanding the world is a central theme throughout this book and the different perspectives contained therein, and hence social identity, social representations, and discursive perspectives are all subsumed within the broad category of social cognition. However, this broad category fails to differentiate what is commonly referred to as social cognition from those other perspectives, and fails to capture important metatheoretical differences between them. The aim of this chapter therefore is to lay bare the core defining principles of each of these approaches so that they can inform our understanding of central social psychological topics such as social perception, attitudes, attributions, self and identity, prejudice, and ideology.

Introduction to Social Cognition Models

It was only as recently as the 1970s that social psychology started using the label 'social cognition'. It is now the dominant, mainstream approach within social psychology, especially in North America. Research and theorizing in social cognition flow from earlier work on person perception, attribution, and attitudes. It draws heavily from the methods and concepts of cognitive psychology. 'Social cognition' is now a label given to textbooks (such as this one), journals, units in psychology courses, and handbooks, marking progress in the area as well as a perspective. In many ways, social cognition has indeed become sovereign in social psychology (Ostrom, 1994).

What is social cognition?

There are many different attempts to define social cognition – Thomas Ostrom (1994) estimated there are more than 100, and that figure has no doubt increased considerably in the years since. It is probably impossible to find a single-sentence definition that would capture all that is contained within the category 'social cognition' or that would satisfy all the researchers who apply the label to themselves. None the less, Ostrom suggests the following:

> At the heart of social cognition is the conceptual orientation that has emerged from the information-processing perspective in cognitive psychology, a perspective that recently has expanded to include cognitive science. The social cognition approach is based on the conviction that constructs relevant to cognitive representation and process are fundamental to understanding all human responses, regardless of whether those responses are social or nonsocial in nature. Cognitive psychologists have applied these concepts to the analysis of a wide range of phenomena, such as text comprehension, recall, recognition, classification, reasoning, vision, and audition. Social cognition researchers share this theoretical perspective, differing solely in the phenomena to be understood. (1994, p. ix)

Ostrom's paragraph-definition is an exemplar of many such definitions (e.g., Fiske, 2004, pp. 127–128; Fiske & Taylor, 1991, p. 14; Hamilton, Devine, & Ostrom, 1994, pp. 2–5; Leyens & Dardenne, 1996, p. 111), and has the added virtue of baldly stating the close ties between social cognition and cognitive psychology, the premise that cognition underlies all important human phenomena, and that the sole difference between cognitive psychology and social cognition is in the phenomena being understood. Not all social cognition researchers agree fully with these views, especially with the last point, but at least the major issues are out in the open.

Let us accept, then, that social cognition is an approach or a perspective, not a theory *per se*, and that it draws heavily from the methods and concepts of cognitive psychology. What makes it social? Why do we need the adjective at all? Ostrom's definition above simply asserts without elaboration that social cognition and cognitive psychology differ 'solely in the phenomena to be understood'. We need to elaborate more clearly what is social about social cognition.

What's so social about social cognition?

Susan Fiske and Shelley Taylor suggest that social cognition research has '… at least some concern with real-world issues' (1991, p. 14), and give examples of such issues as including the study of attitudes, person perception, stereotyping, and small groups. But this still leaves unclear the fundamentally important issue of whether these 'real-world issues' can be reduced to, or understood fully in the terms of, cognitive psychology which is, according to Fiske and Taylor, 'unabashedly mentalistic and oriented toward process' (p. 14). It does indeed appear to be the case that social cognition, as a perspective, rests on a tacit assumption that 'real-world issues' can be understood in more basic, individualistic, cognitive, 'mentalistic' processes.

Fiske and Taylor elaborate further the ways in which social cognition is *social*. Starting from the apparently trite observation, which rapidly becomes not at all trite or obvious on analysis, that 'people are not things', Fiske and Taylor enumerate nine 'important differences between people and things' (1991, pp. 18–19). We can add to this list features offered by other researchers (e.g., Leyens & Dardenne, 1996), subtract some points of overlap, and suggest the following points as critical meanings of *social* in social cognition:

- people intentionally influence their environment;
- people, as objects of perception, perceive back ('social cognition is mutual cognition'), and joint perception is negotiated;
- social cognition implicates the self as subject as well as object;
- social objects may change upon being the target of cognition;
- the accuracy, or veracity, of cognitions about people is harder, or impossible, to assess than for non-social objects;
- social cognition involves social explanation;
- social cognition is shared.

Each of the points in this list of the ways in which people are not things is undoubtedly important. But it is not clear beyond assertion that social cognition, as a perspective which is 'unabashedly mentalistic' and which relies on the methods and concepts of cognitive psychology, can provide an adequate understanding of 'social' phenomena. It is not at all clear that intentionality or reciprocal perception, for example, can be reduced to mentalistic processes.

Instead, it can be argued, especially by the other perspectives covered in this book, that a full understanding of these phenomena (and indeed, all the phenomena of interest to social cognition) requires an approach that is non-reductionistic. This view underpins the integrative approach of this book. This view does not, though, mean that social cognitive research is 'wrong' or value-less. Rather, it indicates a different meaning of social cognitive research.

A prototypical study

Before we detail the defining principles of social cognition research, we will describe two studies by Macrae, Milne, and Bodenhausen (1994) that are proto-typical of research in this tradition. These studies serve as good exemplars of the underlying principles that define this work. The studies were designed to examine the cognitive processes implicated in stereotyping, and whether, as is often claimed, thinking stereotypically frees up cognitive resources for other tasks which otherwise would have had to be spent processing information about the objects of the stereotype in a piecemeal fashion. Specifically, these studies were designed to test the long-held assumption that stereotypes are essentially 'energy-saving' devices (Chapters 3 and 7 consider these processes more fully).

In the first experiment Macrae et al. used a dual-task paradigm to get their participants to form an impression of several target persons from trait terms presented on a computer screen while also doing another unrelated task (listening to a passage of prose played on a tape recorder). Participants were told that after the tasks they would be asked about the impressions they had formed as well as about the prose they had listened to. The prose passage consisted of a series of facts about the economy and geography of Indonesia, a subject the Welsh undergraduate participants knew nothing about. The person impression task consisted of a target person's name being presented to participants on the upper half of a computer screen, with a trait word presented on the lower half. There were four target persons, and each was described throughout the experiment by ten adjectives. For half of the participants, the target person was also introduced with a category label (either doctor, artist, skinhead, or estate agent). For each target person, half of the ten adjectives were stereotype-consistent (for example, caring, honest, reliable, upstanding and responsible for the doctor, and rebellious, aggressive, dishonest, untrustworthy and dangerous for the skinhead) and half were stereotype-neutral (for example, unlucky, forgetful, passive, clumsy and enthusiastic for the doctor, and lucky, observant, modest, optimistic and curious for the skinhead).

The first result to note from this study is that those participants provided with category labels for the target persons subsequently recalled twice as many stereotype-consistent adjectives as did the participants not provided with the labels, but the two groups of participants did not differ in their ability to recall the stereotype-neutral adjectives. This indicates that the stereotypes were functioning schematically by facilitating either encoding or recall of stereotype-consistent information.

The second result shows that those participants provided with, and presumably using, a stereotype label remembered more facts about Indonesia's geography and economy than did those participants not provided with such a label. Thus, the stereotype apparently functioned to free up some of the participants' cognitive resources so they could better attend to the second, but simultaneous, experimental task.

In a second experiment, Macrae et al. repeated the procedure of the first experiment, but presented the stereotype labels to participants subliminally. This was achieved by showing the label for 30 milliseconds (ms), and then masking the label with a neutral stimulus. The effect of the stereotype label was still apparent, even though participants could have had no conscious access to the label. Participants in the stereotype-present condition remembered more of the targets' traits than did those participants in the stereotype-absent condition, and they also recalled more information about Indonesia. Thus, the schematic consequences of stereotype activation – facilitated encoding and recall of information about the target person, and the liberation of attentional resources for deployment on other tasks – do not depend on the conscious awareness of the stereotype label.

Using these two experiments as exemplars of the social cognition tradition, we can now outline the core principles that define this approach to furthering our understanding of real-world issues.

Textbox 2.1

Implicit cognition

The idea of implicit attitudes has received a great deal of research attention in social psychology in the last few years. When such attitudes are directed towards social groups, they become known as prejudice (see more on this in Chapter 7). Implicit attitudes can be assessed via fairly simple computerized tasks. You can assess your own implicit attitudes to a variety of social categorizations based on gender, race, age, ethnicity, religion, weight, sexuality, and even US presidential candidates, by visiting the following site:

https://implicit.harvard.edu/implicit/

(Continued)

> **Textbox 2.1   (Continued)**
>
> Undergo one or more of the computerized tasks honestly and faithfully. Having completed each task, a score will be provided to you, and an indicated position within a typical range of scores. Consider whether you accept that the score provided to you fairly reflects what you think are your 'attitudes' to the particular social category in question. If not, does the discrepancy indicate something about how well you understand yourself (or not), or about how well the computerized task assesses your 'attitude'? How might the discrepancy be explained theoretically?

Core principles of social cognition

Experimentation   As is plainly evident in the Macrae et al. studies above, a central, perhaps defining, methodology used in the social cognition approach is experimentation. Often, the sorts of experiments conducted in social cognition research rely on the controlled presentation of stimuli to participants via a computer, and often for a time so brief that participants cannot be aware of it, in order to observe the effects of those stimuli on participants' responses. Those effects are often judgements made about another stimulus, or the time taken to make such a judgement. Experimentation is a significant point of difference as well as similarity between the social cognition tradition and the other three traditions: social identity research often, but certainly not always, uses experimentation, but of a different style; social representations research sometimes uses experimentation, but usually in combination with other methods; and experimentation is anathema to most researchers in discursive psychology.

Metaphorical models   Aside from a commitment to experimentation as the method of research *de rigueur*, the social cognition perspective has adopted a number of metaphors over the years to understand how people perceive and make sense of the world. A dominant and underlying metaphor that underpins social cognition models is that of the person as an information glossary   processor. This ***information-processing model*** of the perceiver flourished of course with the advent of computers. People's cognitive processes have been compared to the ways in which computers receive, recognize, store and program information. Another metaphor that has been invoked is that of the glossary   person as a ***naïve scientist*** (Fiske & Taylor, 1984). Within this view, people attempt to make sense of the world around them in the same way a scientist does, by observing systematic variations in the relationships between antecedent conditions and consequent behaviours, and making inferences about the nature of the people involved in the interaction. This metaphor underlies much of attribution theory (see Chapter 5), and again is nicely represented in Leunig's cartoon in Chapter 1.

A third metaphor, following from that of the naïve scientist, and recognizing that people often fail to think or act in the 'rational' manner putatively used by scientists, is that of the person as *cognitive miser* (Fiske & Taylor, 1991). This view contends that thinking scientifically is enormously taxing, and that if people were to think in such a way they would rapidly become overwhelmed by the profusion, confusion and complexity of social stimuli to be attended to. Rather than pay attention to all the stimuli constantly bombarding them, people instead ignore a lot of information, make rapid inferences about information, chunk stimuli into discrete categories and then think categorically rather than piecemeal, and generally take whatever cognitive shortcuts they can find to reduce the enormity of the information-processing tasks everyday life presents to them. In this view, people are cognitively slothful, expending the minimum amount of cognitive energy and resources to get by.

glossary

The metaphor of the cognitive miser goes a long way to describing the heuristic nature of much of our thinking, but there are important exceptions to this miserliness. There are many occasions on which we do devote considerable energy to thinking deeply about people and things, when we do treat information in a piecemeal way rather than categorically, and when we are cognitive spendthrifts. To accommodate this (at least, as it has manifested itself in experimental results), social cognition has come to adopt yet another metaphor – that of the *motivated tactician* (Fiske, 1992). In this view, the considerable cognitive resources we each possess can be brought to bear upon any situation requiring us to process information, but we only do so when we are motivated to do so. In other words, we can be both cognitive sloths and spendthrifts, and switch comfortably between the two depending on our context-specific motivations.

glossary

The study by Macrae et al. (1994) shows clearly the application of the motivated tactician metaphor (and equally well the cognitive miser). When participants were busy working on a demanding task (trying to comprehend information about Indonesia), they formed impressions of target persons by using category labels that provided other information about those people. They performed better on the demanding task when they had labels to use than when there were no such labels. They also remembered more stereotype-related characteristics about the target persons. In terms of the metaphor, participants appeared to have limited mental resources to devote to the two different tasks, and they reduced the total demand on their limited resources by strategically exploiting the category labels provided about the target persons.

Constructivism and realism The naïve view of perception, of how we each apprehend the world around us, is that our senses detect information in the world, that that information is transferred veridically into our consciousness, and that the whole process is fairly passive, verisimilous, and realistic. This view could be described as a kind of naïve realism. The view of cognition within the social cognitive paradigm is that it is active, not passive, and constructive, not veridical. Indeed, constructivism is sometimes hailed as one of the defining features of the social cognitive paradigm (e.g., Ross & Nisbett, 1991). There are countless examples – including just about all the research we describe in this book – of how perception and cognition are constructivist.

Although social cognition rests on a constructivist premise when building models of human perception, it itself rests on the realist premise that underpins most models of psychology as 'science'. In other words, in terms of building theories of how social cognition works, social cognitive researchers strive to uncover 'truth' through the systematic and experimental investigation of cognitive processes. Paradoxically and implicitly, social cognitive researchers exempt themselves and their theories from the constructivist principles they apply to the subjects of their research and theorizing. The full meaning of this will become more apparent later in the chapter, when we consider alternative views (especially the social representations and discursive psychology perspectives) which are explicitly constructivist not only in how they view social cognition *per se* but also in how they view their own methods and theories.

Perceptual cognitivism Strongly related to the naïve realist assumptions underpinning social cognitive models, is a perceptual-cognitive metatheory. At the

glossary core of *perceptual-cognitivism* is the view that 'reality' is directly perceived by our senses and that this input is then subsequently worked upon by internal cognitive computational processes in the mind. Ultimately, these internal computational processes produce outputs in the form of mental representations which are stored in the mind as templates that can be used to understand and make sense of the world. This perceptual cognitive metatheory therefore has made it necessary to posit the existence of internal cognitive constructs, such as 'categories', 'schemas', 'attitudes', 'attributions, and 'stereotypes', all of which are hypothesized to represent particular aspects of psychological reality and experience.

Mental representations The notion of ***mental representation*** is therefore a glossary central tenet of social cognition models. Categories, schemas, attitudes, attributions, identity, and stereotypes are theorized as mental structures which organize our knowledge, evaluations, and expectations about particular social objects in the world. These mental representations of the world are learned and developed over time through our direct and indirect perception and experience. They allow us to interact with the world without having to treat every object individually. Such mental templates help guide what we attend to and what we ignore, how we encode information and experience in memory, what we remember and what we infer, and how we feel and respond in specific situations and interactions. Categorization is a critical process within social cognitive models: how we categorize a particular stimulus – how we represent it cognitively in our mind – ultimately shapes our attitudes, attributions, and behaviour towards the object.

Unconscious operations Although the idea of unconscious mental processes has largely disappeared from much of psychology, at least partly because of the strong reaction against Freudian psychodynamism, it remains a part of the social cognitive orientation. 'Unconscious', though, does not have the same meaning in social cognition that it has in psychodynamic theory.

Social cognitive researchers have demonstrated unconscious operations in several different ways. The first capitalizes on the logic of experimentation. It is a fairly simple matter to design an experiment in which one group of people is exposed to a particular environmental stimulus – loud noise outside the laboratory, for example – and another group is not, and to show that the experimental group behaved differently from the control group, even though the extraneous noise does not figure in the explanations people in the experimental group give for their behaviour (e.g., Nisbett & Wilson, 1977). A second way in which social cognitive research demonstrates unconscious operations is through subliminal perception. The second study by Macrae et al. (1994) is a good example. Recall that participants had to form an impression of target persons while also engaging in a demanding task. When a category label was provided for the target person, participants performed better on the demanding task, and recalled more stereotype-relevant material about the target person. Importantly, this effect was obtained even when the category label was presented for just 30 ms, which is so brief that participants could not have been aware of its presence – that is, the category label influenced cognitive operations unconsciously.

A final way in which social cognitive research employs unconscious operations is through the concept of ***automaticity***. A cognitive process or effect is glossary considered to be automatic if it satisfies one of several criteria (Bargh, 1984,

1989; Hasher & Zacks, 1979; Schneider & Shiffrin, 1977). It must not require conscious intention, attention, or effort; or it must be resistant to intentional manipulation; or it must happen beyond any awareness. Automatic processes and effects happen rapidly, and do not use cognitive processing capacity. If a process or effect fails to satisfy these criteria, it is said to be *controlled*. **Controlled processes** are susceptible to conscious intervention, require cognitive effort, and are amenable to consciousness. Once again, we can use the Macrae et al. (1994) study to demonstrate an automatic effect. Participants' performance on the two demanding tasks confronting them was aided by the presentation of a category label. Whether they were aware of the label or not, its effect on subsequent recall of information about the target person and about the economy and geography of Indonesia was automatic. It did not require conscious intervention, attention, or effort. The effects of the label on cognitive processes were beyond awareness. And the effect of the category label did not require cognitive processing capacity – indeed, the label liberated capacity. This is a nice demonstration of the cognitive miser principle in social perception, in which perceivers rely on limited and schematic representations such as stereotypes in order to process information quickly and without much deliberation. We will see in Chapter 3, though, that a category label does not invariably produce an automatic effect. Rather, automaticity is conditional, and subject to the goals of the person in interaction. In such instances, the social perceiver is a motivated tactician rather than a cognitive miser.

glossary

Summary

The social cognitive approach is a foundational approach within social psychological theory and research addressing how we understand the world around us and our place in it. Social cognitive research is experimental, and focuses on intraindividual mental processes. Emphasis is placed upon the structure of knowledge into mental schemas, which direct attention, facilitate encoding of information into memory, and facilitate recall of information. Schemas are activated, often unconsciously, by situated environmental stimuli. Activation makes it more likely that other related schemas will also become activated, and also makes less likely the activation of other, competing schemas.

Introduction to Social Identity Theory

The question of identity is one of the most central questions facing people throughout their lives. The ways to answer the question are close to infinite, but, at least in contemporary western societies, there are just a few, reasonably consistent ways of thinking about who we are.

It is useful to distinguish between *personal identity* and *social identity*. *Personal identity* refers to those qualities and characteristics we see in ourselves which are strictly individual. Statements such as 'I am bored', 'I worry a lot' and 'I am highly strung', reveal aspects of what would normally be called personal identity. On the other hand, statements such as 'I am a psychology student', 'I am Australian' or 'I am in group A in this experiment', reveal aspects of social identity. *Social identity* is defined as 'that *part* of the individual's self-concept which derives from his [sic] knowledge of his [sic] membership of a social group (or groups) together with the value and emotional significance of that membership' (Tajfel, 1981a, p. 255, original emphasis). Social identity normally locates an individual in relation to a social category, social position or social status. Our social identities are normally attached to, and derive from, the groups to which we belong (these are called membership groups). But we can also identify with groups to which we do not belong (called reference groups), and with particular individuals. Roger Brown's 'test of being a fan' (of the Boston Celtics or the soprano Renata Scotto, in his examples) is simple: your own self-esteem must rise and fall with the successes and failures of the object of your admiration (1986, pp. 555–556). The same test applies more generally as a test of social identity. Social identity is always attached to some social referent, usually a social group. If your psychological fortunes wax and wane with the fortunes of that social referent, then you identify with the referent.

glossary

glossary

Contemporary social psychology has tended to be over-enthusiastic and uncritical in viewing the self from the standpoint of the individual and individualism, and some writings on the subject relegate social identity to a minor position in the analysis of self (see Brewer, 1991, for an extension of this argument). Social identity is *not* just another aspect of individual identity. Social identity is not reducible to personal identity, or any other form of identity. Indeed, strictly speaking, the notion of 'personal' identity is a fiction – all identity, all forms of self-construal, must be social. Even apparently asocial self descriptions subtly depend on particular forms of social organization. The notion of a solely personal identity is fictional, as is the distinction between personal and social.

One further preliminary point must be made before we proceed to consider social identity theory. When we say that the distinction between personal and social is forced and fictional, we mean that the social is forever and always reproduced within the individual. The distinction between personal and social, between individual and group, has been problematic throughout the history of social psychology. Early on, debates were waged over the issue of whether the idea of a 'group mind' was sensible. On the one hand were those who argued that all groups, and all group psychology, were ultimately reducible to the individuals constituting those groups and to their individual psychology (e.g., Allport, 1924). On the other were those who argued that such reducibility was impossible, that as individuals were aggregated into groups, properties emerged from that aggregation which were not reducible to the constituent elements (e.g., McDougall, 1921). Our position is that social psychology is genuinely *social* (Hogg & Abrams, 1988, pp. 10–14; Taylor and Brown, 1979), that the phenomena social psychology seeks to understand are not explicable in terms of subsidiary, individual, elemental properties.

The most all-encompassing approach to the study of social identity is known as social identity theory or SIT (Abrams & Hogg, 1990a; Brewer & Brown, 1998; Brown, 2000; Hogg & Abrams, 1988, 2003; Tajfel & Turner, 1986). SIT has been developing since Henri Tajfel's first formulations in the early 1970s, and represents both a *movement* in European social psychology away from the individualistic excesses of North American social psychology (Jaspars, 1986) and a more narrowly defined set of postulates and explanatory principles.

SIT is explicitly a theory of *intergroup behaviour*. A distinction is commonly drawn between *interindividual* behaviour and *intergroup* behaviour (Tajfel & Turner, 1986, p. 8*). **Interindividual behaviour** involves individuals interacting with one another solely on the basis of their respective qualities as individuals. Any groups they may belong to are irrelevant to the interaction. Just as there are no forms of identity which are strictly personal (asocial), there are no forms of strictly interpersonal behaviour. **Intergroup behaviour** is exemplified by interactions among people which are governed primarily by their respective group memberships and not by any individual qualities they may display. All behaviour is seen as falling somewhere on a *continuum* from interindividual to intergroup.

An early experiment

Prior to SIT, the dominant theory of intergroup behaviour was realistic conflict theory or RCT (Sherif, 1966). RCT is premised on the appealing notion that intergroup conflict is always based upon *real* competition between groups over scarce resources. There is ample evidence (e.g., Brewer & Campbell, 1976; Campbell, 1967; Sherif, 1966; Sherif, Harvey, White, Hood & Sherif, 1961; Sherif & Sherif, 1956) to support this simple premise. But there are examples where real competition is neither a necessary nor a sufficient cause of intergroup conflict (see, e.g., Tajfel & Turner, 1986) – although undoubtedly it is a major and prevalent cause.

To investigate the unique individual effects of each of the many possible causes of intergroup conflict it would be ideal to create a 'minimal' group in an experimental laboratory – a group which is stripped of all that we take as normally characterizing what it is to be a group, such as real social and economic relations, interaction among ingroup members, structural divisions within the group to create different roles, interdependency among ingroup members, and so on.

The aim of the original *minimal group* experiment was to create a 'baseline' experimental condition in which there was *no* intergroup differentiation, on to which could be layered differential characteristics of 'groupness' to evaluate the effects of each characteristic on intergroup differentiation (Reynolds & Turner, 2001). This is the research programme that Henri Tajfel initiated in his now famous minimal group experiments, and which led directly to the development of SIT (Tajfel, 1970; Tajfel, Billig, Bundy & Flament, 1971).

glossary

To create a minimal group, experimental groups were created in which group members were alone and anonymous. Subjects were 14- and 15-year-old schoolboys in a state school in Bristol, England. Each estimated the number of dots which were projected quickly on a screen in successive clusters. After doing so, subjects were allocated to either a group of 'overestimators' or 'underestimators' (the allocation was done randomly, though). While the first experimenter was apparently marking the answer sheets, another experimenter announced that a second experiment was also going to be conducted, involving rewards and penalties, and that the existing groups of over- and underestimators would continue to be used. Participants were then seated in a cubicle, and asked to complete a series of 'payoff matrices' which appeared in a booklet. They were told that they were about to allocate points to two people. Sometimes the two people would be from the same group, sometimes the two would be from different groups, and sometimes there would be one person from each group. At the end of the experiment, the number of points allocated by all the participants to each person would be added up, and that person would receive an amount of money proportional to the number of points. To eliminate self-interest, participants never made an allocation decision involving themselves. The booklet consisted of one payoff matrix on each of its 18 pages. Each matrix had two rows of numbers, as shown in Table 2.1. What is of interest is what happens when the two recipients belong to different groups.

Suppose that a participant had been told he was an overestimator, and was faced with the matrix in Table 2.1. He knows that one of the recipients is also

Table 2.1 *Example of an 'intergroup differential' payoff matrix used in a minimal categorization experiment*

Member 26 of the overestimators	7	8	9	10	11	12	13	14	15	16	17	18	19
Member 17 of the underestimators	1	3	5	7	9	11	13	15	17	19	21	23	25

Source: Tajfel et al., 1971, p. 157

an overestimator. This group is, then, the ingroup. The other recipient is an underestimator, and hence belongs to the outgroup. How would the participant decide which allocation to make? He could follow a strategy of maximizing joint profit, and choose the 19:25 response. He would also choose the 19:25 response if he followed a strategy of maximizing ingroup profit. Or he could follow a strategy of maximum difference in payoff to the two groups, and choose the 7:1 response. Different payoff matrices can be constructed to assess the relative strengths of each of these allocation strategies.

What did the schoolboy participants do in the original minimal group study? For the matrix in Table 2.1, participants who were told they were overestimators settled, on average, on the 12:11 response choice. What does this mean? It means that participants did not follow a communal strategy of maximizing joint profit. Nor did they attempt to maximize ingroup profit, and neither did they allocate strictly fairly. Rather, they seemed to resolve a conflict between a fairness strategy and a maximum ingroup profit strategy by choosing the fairest response which also allowed the ingroup to receive more points than the outgroup – even though doing so meant that the ingroup member received fewer points than had the participant followed a maximum joint profit strategy.

Later research with the minimal group paradigm shows that the results are obtained when participants are categorized according to their putative preferences for abstract paintings by Klee or by Kandinsky (Tajfel et al., 1971, experiment 2) and even when the categorization is made explicitly random by tossing a coin (Tajfel & Billig, 1974). Research has also shown that the results are not just due to something about English schoolboys, with the effect being obtained (albeit with varying strength) with Maori and Polynesian children (Vaughan, 1978a, 1978b; Wetherell, 1982), and with adults in the United States (Brewer & Silver, 1978; Locksley, Borgida, Brekke & Hepburn, 1980) and in Switzerland (Doise & Sinclair, 1973). A review of 137 tests of the ingroup bias phenomenon in 37 different studies concluded that the effect is robust (Mullen, Brown & Smith, 1992).

It appears, then, that the results of the Tajfel et al. (1971) experiments, and those of many other minimal group studies since, constitute a genuine intergroup phenomenon. But how can the results be explained? Realistic conflict theory can't explain the results, since there is no real competition between the groups – participants could easily have followed a maximum joint profit strategy, for example. These minimal groups lack all the characteristics normally associated with groups. There is no history or culture within and between the groups, there is no interaction among group members, there is no intragroup structure, there is no common fate among group members, there is nothing. The groups are truly minimal. In a sense, there are no 'groups' at all. Yet participants still acted in a way which is inexplicable in terms of solely intrapersonal or interpersonal processes. The participants acted as though the groups were real for them, and the way in which they acted – to create positive intergroup differentiation – can only be thought of as intergroup behaviour in search of an explanation.

SIT was developed largely to account for the minimal group phenomenon. We outline here the three core principles of the theory.

Core principles

Categorization   It is an undeniable fact that the social world is carved up into many social categories. Some of these are large, such as class, race, religion, ethnicity and gender. Others are smaller, more localized, more transient, and perhaps more idiosyncratic, such as hobby groups, minor political groups and groups created by an experimenter in a laboratory. For any person, though, some of these categories will be ingroups, or membership groups, and some will be outgroups. Most, but not all, social categories stand in real status or power relation to one another. *Social categorization*   glossary refers to the process of identifying an individual as belonging to a particular social group.

The simple act of categorization has important cognitive consequences (McGarty, 2002). The *accentuation effect* asserts that when stimulus objects   glossary are categorized, similarities among members of one category are perceived as greater than they actually are, and differences between members of different categories are perceived as greater than they actually are – in other words, intercategory differences and intracategory similarities are accentuated. The accentuation effect has been demonstrated in the judgement of lines as well as in the judgement of social stimuli. Tajfel and Wilkes (1963) showed that when eight lines of different length were presented to subjects who had to estimate their length, and when the four shortest lines were always presented with a letter A and the four longest lines were always presented with a letter B, subjects overestimated the difference between the A lines and the B lines. Some evidence, though not statistically significant, was also found that subjects overestimated the similarity of lines within each group. The accentuation effect has been demonstrated using all sorts of physical stimuli (see Doise, 1978; Doise, Deschamps & Meyer, 1978; McGarty, 2002; and McGarty & Penny, 1988, for reviews).

The accentuation effect also operates in the judgement of social stimuli. One set of studies, for example, showed that white subjects in the United States who were asked to rate the degree of 'negroness' of a series of pictures of faces, imposed their own classification on to the faces so that some were judged to be 'white' and others were judged to be 'black'. Once so classified, the similarities among the faces within one category and the differences between categories were accentuated (Secord, 1959; Secord, Bevan & Katz, 1956). Other examples of categorization effects with ethnicity are provided by Tajfel, Sheikh & Gardner (1964) and Doise (reported in Doise et al., 1978). One can begin to see how the basic, and probably unavoidable, perceptual process of categorizing the social world can lead to the formation of stereotypes. However, not all categorizations produce accentuated judgements. The accentuation effect is only to be expected when the categorizations are salient to the person judging the stimuli and when the categorizations are useful to the person in the judgement task (McGarty & Penny, 1988).

To sum up, then, the most elemental part of SIT is the simple and obvious proposition that the social world is perceived in categories which are socially constructed. We each belong to some categories and not to others. In the minimal group experiments, the categorizations available for participants are, literally, minimal. Any meaning they have for participants, who always are assigned to one or the other category, is imposed by the participants themselves. Despite being empty categories, the act of categorization reliably produces systematic effects on perception and behaviour.

Identity Identity is central to SIT. One of the most basic categorizations – perhaps *the* most basic – is the distinction between *self* and *other,* and its more social corollary, the distinction between *us* and *them.* The acquisition of the disjunction between self and other is an early and necessary part of socialization. Some – notably the symbolic interactionists – argue that the distinction only arises through social interaction, and that a necessary consequence is the distinction between self as subject and self as object (see Mead, 1934/1962; Stryker & Statham, 1985).

A powerful and perhaps universal motive is the motive to think well of one's self, to have a positive evaluation of identity; or, in the parlance of pop psychology, and also in a vast amount of research in individual psychology, to have a positive self-esteem (e.g., Tesser, 1986, 1988). Failure to enact this motive successfully is often considered psychologically unhealthy. But the motive operates at the social as well as the individual level. There is as strong a motive to evaluate one's social identity positively as there is to evaluate one's personal identity positively. This motive for a positive social identity propels much social behaviour, and is expressed as a tendency to evaluate one's ingroup memberships, the social categories one belongs to, positively.

A person's social identity is constituted by the vast number of social identifications that person has with various social categories. Not all those identifications are primed, or activated, or salient, at any one time. Rather, social identity at any one time is made up of a few identifications selected to suit the particular social context (Ellemers, Spears, & Doosje, 2002).

We have more to say about identity in Chapter 6. For now, it is enough to note that knowledge of social identifications on its own is not sufficient to form an evaluation of those identifications. For a person to know he or she is Australian, or a psychology student, or a parent, is not enough, and inherently can never be enough, on its own for that person to evaluate those category memberships. Evaluation of category memberships can only be made through processes of social comparison.

Comparison In evaluating self on any dimension, an implicit social comparison with others is necessary. So it is also, only perhaps more so, with the evaluation of social identifications of self with social categories. Any particular social category membership can inform a positive social identity only through social comparison between the ingroup and some relevant outgroup. The value of being Australian, or a psychology student, or a parent, can only be evaluated through comparison with other social categories. How people evaluate personal and social attributes through social comparison has been theorized and studied since the 1950s. The theory of social comparison processes, which forms the backbone of this last part of SIT, has undergone major changes over the years.

The original version of the theory was formulated by Festinger (1954), and was largely a theory of how people evaluate individual qualities. It suggested that people prefer to evaluate self and its qualities against some 'objective' criterion or other. When such objective criteria are unavailable, people turn to social comparison – comparison with others – for evaluative standards. Festinger distinguished between comparison of abilities and comparison of opinions, and suggested that the motives driving comparisons of each were different: accuracy and self-improvement in the case of abilities; gaining social consensus in the case of opinions. In the case of abilities, Festinger proposed a *universal drive upward,* in which a person selected as the comparison referent someone who displayed a greater amount of the ability in question. The principle of *similarity* asserts that, all other things being equal, a person will select as a comparison other someone who is more similar than dissimilar. Joining the universal drive upward with the similarity principle leads to the prediction that, when evaluating abilities, a comparison other will be selected who is only slightly better than the comparer.

The motive underlying all comparisons, according to Festinger, is the

glossary desire for an accurate *self-evaluation.* Plenty of evidence has amassed since the 1950s that this is not the case. Rather, people appear to engage in social

glossary comparisons mostly for reasons of *self-enhancement.* The proposition that people compare upwards to evaluate their self and their abilities conflicts with much research on self-esteem, which suggests that people selectively attend to information which bolsters their self view. Self-evaluation and self-enhancement are usually conflicting and competing motives, and, usually, people follow a self-enhancement strategy. This is the position taken by SIT, and is the cornerstone of SIT's use of social comparison.

To make a social comparison between an ingroup and outgroup two problems must first be resolved. First, the ingroup member must decide which outgroup of the many available should be chosen as the comparison other. This is known as the problem of *referent selection.* And second, along which dimension should the comparison be made? This is the problem of *dimension selection.* These twin problems have plagued social comparison theory for four decades (Brown, 2000; Kawakami & Dion, 1993, 1995; Pettigrew, 1967; Wheeler, 1991).

Regardless of *how* people engage in social comparisons between ingroups and outgroups, it is the *consequences,* rather than the mechanisms, of such comparisons that are most important to SIT. Undoubtedly it is the consequences of social comparison that are of prime importance to those doing the comparing too, in as much as people select referent targets and dimensions according to the anticipated (positive) outcome of the comparison.

SIT proposes that people are motivated to achieve a positive social identity, just as they are motivated to achieve a positive self-esteem (Hogg, 2000). Most of the time, social category memberships, on their own, can neither enhance nor degrade social identity. Category memberships are only of value in relation to other categories. It is only the relative status positions of an ingroup and an outgroup on a comparison dimension of value to the ingroup member which affect the social identity of that member. SIT proposes the axiom that there is a motive to evaluate group memberships positively so as to enhance social identity, and that this positive differentiation of ingroup from outgroup is achieved through comparison of the ingroup to an outgroup. An important difference between this approach to social comparison and that of Festinger is that Festinger articulated comparison processes at an individual level, between individuals as individuals, where individual characteristics are evaluated and self-esteem and self-knowledge are affected. SIT discusses social comparison processes at a group level, where group memberships are evaluated and social identities are shaped and valorized. When making comparisons, especially when evaluating the fairness of outcomes, people often engage in comparisons between an ingroup and some referent outgroup. The consequences of invidious intergroup comparisons are articulated in relative deprivation theory (Walker & Smith, 2002). For now, all we need to note is that group behaviours are more strongly linked to *intergroup* glossary *social comparisons* than they are to interindividual comparisons.

Another important difference between Festinger's approach to social comparison and that of SIT concerns the core function of social comparison, and is best seen in research by Gartrell (2002). Gartrell notes that in social comparison theory people, as social comparers, are treated as 'isolated social atoms', unrelated to one another and free to engage in one-directional comparisons with any other isolated social atom. In contrast, Gartrell's research shows that people are embedded in a social network and engage in multidirectional comparisons with related, not disconnected, others. Further, social comparisons are engaged in – or avoided – to preserve social relationships. Gartrell's approach to social comparisons is consistent with that of SIT, in emphasizing the *social* processes, consequences, and functions of social comparisons.

Intergroup differentiation

Recall that, in the minimal group experiments, participants acted on the basis of a trivial or even explicitly random classification by discriminating between an ingroup and an outgroup member. This is an enigma from the point of view of realistic conflict theory. Participants in a minimal group experiment are confronted with an almost empty situation. They are allocated to one of two groups on the basis of some trivial or random act, they are separated from anyone other than the experimenter, and they are asked to allocate points to other participants who are identified only by a number and their group membership. What meaning does – or even can – such an empty situation have for them? According to SIT, the participants recognize their group membership. They are also motivated to enhance their social identity. The situation is so minimal and empty that there is only one avenue open to do this. Participants can only enhance their social identity by striving to differentiate their group from the other group, and by elevating their group relative to the other group. Doing so puts their group in a superior position relative to the other group, and, hence, through social comparison, their own group becomes positively valorized, which in turn, and through their identification with that group, enhances their social identity.

SIT, formulated in such stark and minimal terms, does not claim to be able simply to generalize its explanation of intergroup differentiation in a minimal group experiment to situations of intergroup conflict and hostility between 'real' groups. At the least, the history of intergroup relations and the economic and social positions of the conflicting groups must be considered. However, the principles of SIT are claimed to undergird all intergroup contexts. One example of the way in which minimal groups are not the same as real groups is provided by Brown (1986), who notes that participants in minimal groups are free to enhance their social identity by discriminating in their point allocations between ingroup and outgroup members. There is nothing in the experimental setting to prevent them from doing so. But members of real groups, with real status and power differences between the groups, are not so free. It is not so easy, and often not possible at all, for members of minority groups in society to assert their group's superiority by inventing flattering comparison dimensions or comparison others. This raises the issue of the consequences of threats to social identity, and these are covered in some detail in Chapter 7 on prejudice.

glossary   It is important to note that ***intergroup differentiation*** is a complex and multifaceted phenomenon (Hewstone, Rubin, & Willis, 2002). Generally it can occur as either ingroup favouritism or as outgroup derogation, but these two aspects are not necessarily tied closely to one another – that is, ingroup favouritism does not necessarily also entail outgroup derogation, and conversely, although, to be sure, they are often to be found together (e.g., Mummendey & Otten, 1998). Ingroup favouritism can vary with strength of ingroup identification, ingroup size relative to the outgroup, and perceived group threat (Hewstone et al., 2002). Either or both of ingroup favouritism and outgroup derogation can represent prejudice, about which we have more to say in Chapter 7.

Self-categorization theory

Tajfel and Turner (1986) based SIT upon the interpersonal–intergroup dimension. But how and why is a situation construed by an individual as 'interpersonal' or 'intergroup' or in between? Partly in response to this, and other, problems, John Turner and his colleagues (1985, 1999; Turner, Hogg, Oakes, Reicher, & Wetherell, 1987; Turner & Oakes, 1989) developed self-categorization theory (SCT).

In SCT, social identity and personal identity are not qualitatively different forms of identity, but, rather, represent different forms of self-categorization. Self-categorization can occur on three broad levels: the *superordinate level* (e.g., defining self as part of humanity), the *intermediate level* (e.g., defining self by particular group memberships) and the *subordinate level* (e.g., defining self in individual, personal terms). Naming these levels superordinate, intermediate and subordinate is not intended to convey any greater value in one than the other. They are so-called because of their relative inclusiveness: Higher-order categories include within them all lower-order categories. The ordered structure of categories used by SCT comes from influential work on the categories used by people in the cognitive representation of the physical world (Rosch, 1978).

glossary
glossary
glossary

Because self-categorization is context-specific, and self can be variously categorized in individual or group terms, the distinction between personal and social identity originally made in SIT is no longer justified. Rather, personal and social identities represent different levels of self-categorization. The personal is social, and the social personal. As self-categorizations become more social, self is said to become *depersonalized*. This is not meant in a pejorative sense, but, rather, just in the sense that the self-categorization is relatively less imbued with personalistic connotations. When self is categorized it is also stereotyped. As will be discussed later in Chapter 7, stereotyping is usually thought of as a process applied to outgroups in which outgroup members are ascribed the same traits or qualities because of their group membership. SCT suggests that self-perception operates in the same way – self is judged stereotypically on the basis of self-categorizations; to *self-stereotype* is to perceive identity between self and the ingroup.

glossary

glossary

Self-categorization theorists insist that SCT is not intended to supersede SIT. It is an extension of it, developing the construct of identity and the process of categorization, reconceptualizing the distinction between personal and social identity, and providing a mechanism for predicting when and how people will self-categorize in one way or another. Whereas SIT is primarily a motivational theory, SCT is primarily cognitive. SCT has been applied to several traditional problems in social psychology, such as stereotyping (e.g., Oakes, Haslam, & Turner, 1994), group polarization and crowd behaviour (e.g., McGarty, Turner, Hogg, David, & Wetherell, 1992; Turner et al., 1987), and leadership (Haslam, van Knippenberg, Platow, & Ellemers, 2003).

Summary

Social identity theory provides a systematic account of the links between personal and social identity, and between interindividual and intergroup behaviours. It focuses on the nature of social categorization, especially into ingroups and outgroups, the primacy of social identity and positive social differentiation, and on social comparison processes as the main means for evaluating the valence of social identifications. Self-categorization theory is a development which extends SIT into a fuller examination of the cognitive processes underpinning the contextual fluidity of personal and social identities.

Introduction to Social Representations Theory

The theory of social representations, originally developed by Serge Moscovici (1981, 1984, 1988, 2000), reinstates the primacy of collective concepts such as culture and ideology in social psychology. As such, it seeks to understand individual psychological functioning by placing the individual in his or her social, cultural and collective milieu. The theory views psychological experience as being mediated and determined by the individual's belongingness to a collectivity of others who share similar views, experiences, and a common environment and language. Unlike the atomistic notion of the individual which underpins many theories in social psychology, social representations theory begins with the premise that the individual is primarily a social being whose own existence and identity is rooted in a collectivity. It therefore attempts to understand how social processes impinge upon and influence the social psychological functioning of individuals and groups. Social representations theory, however, does not juxtapose or separate the individual and society, but, rather, sees both in a dialectical relationship, in which the individual is both a product of society (its conventions, norms and values) and an active participant who can effect change in society.

What is a social representation?

glossary   Moscovici defines *social representations* as the ideas, thoughts, images and knowledge which members of a collective share: consensual universes of thought which are socially created and socially communicated to form part of a 'common consciousness'. Social representations refer to the stock of social knowledge which people share in the form of common-sense theories about the social world, and are comprised of both conceptual and pictorial elements (Moscovici, 2000). Social representations shape our beliefs, attitudes, and opinions, and are the processes by which we construct social reality (Philogène & Deaux, 2001). Moscovici has defined social representations thus:

> Social representations ... concern the contents of everyday thinking and the stock of ideas that gives coherence to our religious beliefs, political ideas and the connections we create as spontaneously as we breathe. They make it possible for us to classify persons and objects, to compare and explain behaviours and to objectify them as parts of our social setting. While representations are often to be located in the minds of men and women, they can just as often be found 'in the world', and as such examined separately. (1988, p. 214)

Social representations range from hegemonic structures that are shared by a society or nation, to differentiated knowledge structures that are shared by subgroups within a collective (Moscovici, 1988). The individualistic conception of the person as the centre of cognition, action, and process is an example of such a collectively shared representation which permeates most aspects of thinking within western industrialized societies (Lukes, 1973).

The concept of 'representation' has a long history and spreads across a number of interrelated disciplines in the social sciences. Moscovici (1989) draws on diverse sources when explicating the theory of social representations, but relies primarily on Durkheim's (1898) notion of 'collective representations'. Durkheim used this concept to differentiate collective thought from individual thought. Collective representations were seen by Durkheim to be widely shared by members of a society, to be social in origin and generation, and to be about society. Although he regarded representations as emerging from a 'substratum' of individuals, he maintained that they could not be explained at the individual level. Instead, collective representations such as myths, legends and traditions were phenomena with their own distinctive characteristics, independent from the individuals who expounded them, which required explanation at the sociological or societal level (Lukes, 1975).

Moscovici's concept of *social* representations is differentiated from Durkheim's *collective* representations in that the former emphasizes the dynamic and changing nature of representations ('social life in the making') and also takes into account the array of differentiated knowledge shared by subgroups within contemporary western societies (Moscovici, 1988, p. 219). It is through shared representations that social groups establish their identities and come to differentiate themselves from other groups within society. Like Durkheim, Moscovici argues that social psychology's primary task is to study the origins, structure and inner dynamics of social representations and their impact on society; that is, to study the nature of a 'thinking society' (Moscovici, 1984). Just as society can be considered to be an economic and political system, so also it should be viewed as a thinking system (Moscovici, 1988). Social psychology should therefore concern itself with the nature of a thinking society and become an 'anthropology of the modern culture' (Moscovici, 1989, own translation).

The role of representations is to conventionalize objects, persons and events: that is, to locate them within a familiar context. Representations are prescriptive and generative: determined by tradition and convention, representations impose themselves in our thinking. Often we are unaware of these conventions, so that we remain unaware of the social determination of our thought, preferring to view our thoughts as 'common sense'. Indeed, Moscovici has likened the study of social representations to the study of common sense:

> By social representations we mean a set of concepts, statements and explanations originating in daily life in the course of inter-individual communications. They are the equivalent, in our society, of the myths and belief systems in traditional societies; they might even be said to be the contemporary version of common sense. (1981, p. 181)

In addition to their consensual nature, what makes representations social is their creation and generation, through social interaction and communication by individuals and groups. Social representations originate from social communication. They construct our understanding of the social world, enabling interaction within groups sharing the representation. The theory's clear imperative is the need to study social communication and interaction as the *sine qua non* of social cognition.

Unlike Durkheim, whom Moscovici argues has a rather static conception of representations, Moscovici emphasizes the plasticity of representations, characterizing them as dynamic structures: ' ... there is a continual need to reconstitute "common sense" or the form of understanding that creates the substratum of images and meanings, without which no collectivity can operate' (1984, p. 19). Once created, representations behave like 'autonomous entities' or 'material forces': ' ... they lead a life of their own, circulate, merge, attract and repel each other, and give birth to new representations, while old ones die out' (1984, p. 13).

Two processes are central to the generation of representations: *anchoring* and *objectification*. These are the processes by which unfamiliar objects, events, or stimuli are rendered familiar. The purpose of all representations is to make the unfamiliar familiar. Moscovici accords primary importance to the need for individuals to make sense of, to grasp the nature of, an unfamiliar object: that which is foreign and alien is threatening and frightening, and compels comprehension. People make sense of that which is unfamiliar by giving it meaning, and the role of representations is to guide this process of attributing meaning. People search for meaning among what they already know and with which they are familiar.

> ... the images, ideas and language shared by a given group always seem to dictate the initial direction and expedient by which the group tries to come to terms with the unfamiliar. Social thinking owes more to convention and memory than to reason; to traditional structures rather than to current intellectual or perceptual structures. (Moscovici, 1984, p. 26)

Anchoring

Anchoring refers to the classification and naming of unfamiliar objects or [glossary] social stimuli by comparing them with the existing stock of familiar and culturally accessible categories. In classifying, we compare with a prototype or model, and thus derive a perspective on the novel stimulus by determining its relationship to the model or prototype. When we compare, we either decide that something is similar to a prototype (that is, we generalize certain salient features of the prototype to the unfamiliar stimulus), or we decide that something is different (that is, we particularize and differentiate between the object and the prototype). If we favour similarity, the unfamiliar acquires the characteristics of the model. In cases when discrepancy exists, the object is readjusted so as to fit the defining features of the prototype. Thus classifying and naming always involve comparisons with a prototype.

Moscovici refers to the assignment of names and labels in our culture as a 'nominalistic tendency'. The process of naming something takes on a solemn significance. It imbues that which is named with meaning, and thus locates it within a society's 'identity matrix'. Only then can the object be represented. 'Indeed representation is, basically, a system of classification and denotation, of allotting categories and names' (Moscovici, 1984, p. 30). Thus, representations are reflected in the way we classify and allot categories and names to stimuli because, by classifying or categorizing, we are, in essence, revealing our conceptual frameworks, 'our theory of society and of human nature' (Moscovici, 1984, p. 30). By classifying and naming an object, we are able not only to recognize and understand it but also to evaluate it, either positively or negatively, or as normal or abnormal. Thus 'naming is not a purely intellectual operation aiming at a clarity or logical coherence. It is an operation related to a social attitude' (Moscovici, 1984, p. 35).

Objectification

glossary   *Objectification* is the process by which unfamiliar and abstract notions, ideas and images are transformed into concrete and objective common-sense realities. It refers to the human tendency to simplify or distil complex information into a core or 'figurative nucleus' of both pictorial (iconic) and cognitive elements. 'To objectify is to discover the iconic quality of an imprecise idea or being, to reproduce a concept in an image' (Moscovici, 1984, p. 38). Many scientific and technological concepts undergo such a transformation as they disseminate into everyday lay usage and discourse. Moscovici's (1961) own research on the diffusion of psychoanalytic concepts throughout sections of French society was essentially a study of the objectification process. Moscovici was able to show how laypeople adopted Freudian notions such as 'complexes' and 'neuroses' and used them to explain their own and others' behaviour. In the process of this usage, these conceptual and analytic categories are transformed into objective entities with properties rendering them with an independent existence. So, abstract constructs such as 'mind' or 'ego' are perceived as physical entities, and 'complexes' and 'neuroses' are construed as objective conditions that afflict people. This process of objectification is akin to that of the metaphor, whereby any new phenomenon may be accommodated in terms of its similarity to the already known (Lakoff & Johnson, 1980). As Moscovici and Hewstone (1983) point out, the diffusion and popularization of scientific concepts throughout society is occurring at a rapid rate through the mass media. The increasing proliferation of scientific 'knowledge' throughout all sectors of society has made the lay public 'amateur' scientists, 'amateur' economists, 'amateur' psychologists, 'amateur' doctors, etc. Ordinary people with little expert training discuss issues such as the greenhouse effect, damage to the ozone layer, inflation and the current accounts deficit, stress-related ailments, familial and relationship problems, cancer prevention diets, etc. Most of this knowledge becomes an integral part of mass culture and, ultimately, what will come to be regarded as 'common sense'.

Moscovici and Hewstone (1983) describe the three external processes by which knowledge is transformed into common sense or a social representation: the personification of knowledge, figuration, and ontologizing. First, glossary the *personification of knowledge* links the idea, theory or concept to a person or group – for example, Freud and psychoanalysis or Einstein and the theory of relativity. The association of an idea with a person gives the idea a glossary concrete existence. Second, *figuration* is the process by which an abstract notion is embodied or dominated by a metaphorical image so that, again, what is conceptual is made more accessible or concrete. For example,

Hewstone's (1986) study of social representations of the European Community found that people used metaphorical language and images which had originated in the media, such as milk 'lakes' and butter 'mountains' when referring to food surpluses of the community. In covering the first Gulf War (1990–91), the media generated graphic metaphors such as the description of hostages in Iraq before the onset of the war as Saddam Hussein's 'human shields'. Third, *ontologizing* is the process by which a verbal or conceptual construct is imbued with physical properties – for example, abstract concepts such as 'mind' or 'neurosis' become construed as material phenomena. These three processes all contribute to making highly specialized and technical knowledge more accessible to the lay community so that communication about this knowledge is able to take place.

glossary

The consensual and reified universes

Moscovici suggests there are two distinct and different types of reality: the *reified universe*, which is the world of science, and the *consensual universe*, which is the world of common sense. The transformation of expert knowledge into common sense marks the distinction between the reified and consensual universes. The consensual universe is comprised of social representations which are created, used, and reconstituted by people to make sense of everyday life. The reified universe is one which the expert scientist inhabits – one in which the scientist subjects reality to rigorous scrutiny and experimentation. The laws of science govern the reified universe in which human thinking takes a logical and rational form. Moscovici argues that it is the consensual universe in which social psychologists should be interested: how ordinary people create and use meaning to make sense of their world.

glossary

In distinguishing between the forms of thinking that characterize the reified world of science, and the social representations that constitute common sense, Moscovici (2001) is not suggesting that everyday thinking (as opposed to scientific reason), is full of distortions, biases, illusions, and misperceptions. This has become a central tenet of the social cognition tradition, that human perception and cognition is 'faulty' or 'inferior' to scientific reason. On the contrary, Moscovici (2001) suggests that by understanding the underlying social representations that constitute common sense, social psychologists will begin to understand the social glue that derives from shared values and beliefs. Likewise, any delineation between expert scientific thought and lay everyday thinking becomes blurred when one considers the work in the sociology of science showing that scientific knowledge is not immune from social representations. Scientists also rely on social representations to construct reality and to imbue their activities with meaning (e.g., Gilbert & Mulkay, 1984; Latour, 1991). What this delineation between the reified and consensual universes does, however, is emphasize the increasing significance of expert knowledge in constituting contemporary social knowledge.

The increasing proliferation of science and expert knowledge endows the reified universe with considerable significance in the modern world. This expert knowledge is transformed or represented and appropriated in the consensual universe so that it is made more accessible and intelligible. This re-presented version eventually takes form and contributes to the stock of common-sense knowledge which people draw upon to understand social reality. Laypeople reduce complex ideas and theories to a *figurative nucleus* of images and concepts to re-present this knowledge in a more simplified and culturally accessible form.

glossary

The case of psychoanalysis has already been discussed. Moscovici and Hewstone (1983) also discuss the transformation which the theory of hemispheric specialization underwent when popularized in the consensual universe. Most laypeople, through the popular press and media, have been introduced to the notion that the left hemisphere specializes in logical, rational and analytic thinking, while the right hemisphere is said to engage in more intuitive, emotional and subjective functions. This cerebral dualism, which originated in the reified universe of neuroscience, was used by people and the popular press to explain a wide range of opposing cultural tendencies in human behaviour, such as femininity vs. masculinity, and rational vs. intuitive thought. The split brain view has proliferated so widely that it is now endowed with an objective reality and has become part of common-sense knowledge: a social representation.

> Once a society has adopted a paradigm or figurative nucleus it finds it easier to talk about whatever the paradigm stands for, and because of this facility the words referring to it are used more often. Then formulae and clichés emerge that sum it up and join together images that were formerly distinct. It is not simply talked about but exploited in various social situations as a means of understanding others and oneself, of choosing and deciding. (Moscovici, 1984, p. 39)

Core and periphery

A social representation is an organized, coherent, socially shared set of knowledge about an object or domain of objects. Implicit in this conceptualization is the notion of *structure* – the set of knowledge that constitutes the representation consists of a range of elements, some more important, or central, than others to the whole representation. Abric (1976) was the first to distinguish between what he called the ***central core*** and the ***periphery*** of a glossary social representation (see also Abric, 1984, 1993).

The central core of a representation is the *sine qua non* of the representation. It is defined, at least partly, by the object of the representation and by the relationship of the group holding the representation to the object of the representation. Writing this way of the core implies a separation between the object of a representation and the representation itself. This separation is antithetical to social representations theory, though, since the object and the representation are always mutually defining. The core of the representation is *generative*, in the sense that it determines reactions to novel information and orients a representation to its object in an ever-changing environment. The core is also relatively stable, persisting across situational contexts. And the core is organizational, in that other, peripheral, elements are structured around the core. Peripheral elements are malleable in a way that core elements are not. If a core element is changed, so too is the representation. On the other hand, a representation (and its core) persists despite changes to peripheral elements.

The structural approach to social representations, and indeed the focus within social representations theory on anchoring and objectification, and consensual and reified universes, all tend to imply a static view of shared knowledge which is at odds with Moscovici's original theorizing. This is not necessarily the case, though, as recent research demonstrates. The theory of social representations does not require in any way that core elements must be consistent with one another. Rather, they must simply be, together, related and coherent around the object of the representation. This allows for contradictory and dilemmatic relationships among core elements. Theoretically, this provides for much greater explanatory utility, since now *change* can be better conceptualized and understood.

Inconsistent elements within a representation's core are still related to one another, joined in what Moscovici has conceptualized as ***themata*** glossary (Moscovici, 1994; see also Markova, 2000). These inconsistent elements often together constitute a *dialectical* relationship: the elements are not just inconsistent, but mutually antagonistic, mutually defining, and together in a state of tension which propels change and seeks resolution in a synthesis of the antagonism. Moloney, Hall and Walker (2005) reported research on social understandings of organ donation which helps explicate some of this abstract theorizing. Moloney et al. examined word associations with a variety of linguistic elements broadly related to organ donation and transplantation (defined in earlier research by the same authors). A clear structure underlying the pattern of associations was discernible, in which two core elements were prominent – *life* and *death*. These elements were stable across situational and experimental manipulations. They are also clearly in an antagonistic relationship, and it is this dialectic tension which determines how people understand and orient to a variety of different stimuli all related to organ donation.

Empirical research in the social representations tradition

A strong feature of the empirical work in the social representations tradition is its emphasis on the *content* of social knowledge rather than the underlying cognitive processes associated with this knowledge (Moscovici, 2001). Farr (1990) also points out that many topics studied under the rubric of social representations tend to be social issues which have attracted extensive media coverage and controversy. Most recently, this has included work on the social representations of 'risk' (Joffe, 2003), human rights (Doise, 2001; Doise, Spini & Clemence, 1999), organ donation and transplantation (Moloney & Walker, 2002), and biotechnology (Durant, Bauer & Gaskell, 1998). As a paradigmatic example of research in the social representations tradition, in this section we present an overview of the research that has been conducted in Europe on emerging representations of biotechnology.

The daily reporting in the media of rapid advances in genomics and biotechnology has led to widespread public debate and discussion about the social, moral, and ethical implications of these scientific advances. Many of these advances are presented as being full of opportunity and having enormous potential to enhance our well-being through the alleviation and prevention of a range of illnesses and medical conditions. For example, the recent completion of the mapping of the human genome was reported as being one of the most significant scientific advances in history. Graphic metaphors were employed both by scientists and the media in presenting this scientific knowledge for public consumption. The mapping of the human genome was depicted, for example, as a search for 'the essence of human life' and as the decoding of the 'book of life' (Nelkin & Lindee, 1995; Nerlich, Dingwall & Clarke, 2002; Petersen, 2001). Graphic religious metaphors such as the 'Book of Life' and the 'Hand of God' served to anchor the public's understanding of this scientific milestone to already existing cultural knowledge. At the same time, though, there has been increasing public concern and resistance to some of these developments, particularly with regard to the potential uses (and abuses) of genetic information and genetic interventions.

During this period of rapid scientific advances in genomics a group of European social psychologists has investigated the European public's representations of biotechnology. This consisted of a large-scale longitudinal study designed to assess public perceptions and understandings of biotechnology in several European nations, utilizing both quantitative and qualitative research methods. These methods included survey questionnaires (the Eurobarometer Survey 1996 and 1997), the qualitative analysis of media stories and policy statements on biotechnology (1984–96), and focus group discussions with members of the public (1999–2000).

Textbox 2.2

Public debates about technology

Find an example in the media of a public debate about the application or implementation of new technology. Some examples might be: the introduction of genetically modified food into local food production practices; allowing medical researchers to engage in stem cell research; therapeutic cloning; genetic screening of embryos; or implanting devices to allow people who have been unable to hear since birth to hear.

Track how the debate evolves over time. What triggered the debate? Who are the various parties to the debate? How do the terms of the debate shift in response to points raised by others? How is the debate resolved (if indeed it is resolved rather than just fading away)? What is assumed by the various parties to the debate in constructing their positions, and how do these assumptions differ from the assumptions made by others? To what extent are you able to detect processes of anchoring and objectification? Are the core and peripheral elements in the shared understandings being constructed? How do you identify elements as core or peripheral?

The Eurobarometer Survey The Eurobarometer Survey (Durant, Bauer & Gaskell, 1998) found that in 1996 the European public displayed considerable ambivalence towards biotechnology. Although there was considerable support for biotechnological advances in medicine, especially in the area of genetic testing, there was, in contrast, significantly less support for genetically modified (GM) foods, and even less support for laboratory research on GM animals and xenotransplants (transplanting organs for non-human to human animals). Opposition to the latter two applications was primarily associated with moral objections to this kind of experimental research. The survey also concluded that public concern was linked to a lack of trust in national bodies and institutions to 'tell the truth' about biotechnology and to adequately regulate it. The study also contradicted claims that increased public knowledge of biotechnology should lead to greater support; rather, people with greater knowledge were found to have stronger opinions about biotechnology, but these could be positive or negative.

Qualitative research   Although such quantitative surveys as the Eurobarometer on biotechnology reveal interesting trends, they merely scratch the surface of complex public representations and understandings of biotechnology. Surveys are not designed to answer questions about the representations that shape and underlie ambivalent responses to questionnaire items. Although survey data can tell us that the public finds some forms of biotechnology morally unacceptable or 'risky', they do not reveal the precise nature of these moral concerns and how they are framed by the public. For these reasons, a series of focus group discussions in ten of the participating countries were conducted to provide a richer and detailed understanding of the public's perceptions of biotechnology (Wagner et al., 2001). Although there were local variations in the issues that emerged in focus groups across the participating countries, there were none the less common concerns and understandings that were shared across the entire sample. Overall, as the previous survey studies had suggested, Europeans were ambivalent about biotechnology: although recognizing its potential benefits, it was also represented as potentially risky and unsafe because of its unknown trajectory and development. The metaphor of a 'runaway train' was used to represent biotechnology as an accelerating force that the public could not keep up with, and which institutional authorities struggled to adequately control. This representation of the inevitability and uncontrollability of scientific progress, as embodied in biotechnology, resonates with Wagner and Kronberger's (2001) proposition that the public's efforts to understand these rapid advances, to re-present them in their own 'imaginings', can be described as a form of 'symbolic coping' (see Wagner, Kronberger and Seifert, 2002).

Scientific progress, then, was perceived as dilemmatic: providing, on the one hand, future advantages, but on the other, possible risks and unknown adverse consequences. The idea of an 'uncertain future' was also found to be a pervasive theme across the groups, despite the fact that these concerns were non-specific and lacked detail. These projected fears about future delayed effects of biotechnological advances such as GM foods and the cloning of animals and humans were frequently anchored to past mishaps such as the scare surrounding the outbreak of 'mad cow' disease and its human variant BSE in the UK and the nuclear accident in Chernobyl. Both of these incidents were used to cast doubt on the trustworthiness of regulatory authorities, governments, and the scientific community to be completely honest with the public about possible risks associated with biotechnology. Furthermore, participants expressed considerable mistrust of what they described as powerful commercial interests associated with the increasing globalization and industrialization of food production. Participants argued that ordinary consumers and democratic institutions were relatively powerless in controlling and regulating these commercial interests. As one British participant put it:

> too many things have gone wrong in the past, all the things that we've eaten and taken and then suddenly they've come up with something that's got a problem, and you've thought to yourself well I thought that was tested, that's why I took this pill. (cited in Wagner et al., 2001, p. 90)

Representations of 'Nature' Together, the Eurobarometer Survey and the focus groups give us a clear indication of what we might refer to as the European public's ambivalent 'attitude' towards biotechnology. Importantly, however, Wagner et al.'s (2001) qualitative research was able to identify the underlying *representations* that give rise to this attitudinal ambivalence. Opposition to biotechnology and projected fears about its potential risks were shaped primarily by underlying representations of 'Nature' and 'Life' that the public invoked in their arguments. One pervasive construction represented Nature and Life as spiritual forces that should be respected and venerated at all costs. This representation of Nature-as-a-spiritual-force was sometimes anchored to religious beliefs, so that common expressions such as 'playing God' or 'tampering with God's Creation' were recurring moral warnings about the uses and abuses of biotechnology. This contrasted to a more secular, but none the less spiritual, representation of Nature that also perceived life as sacred and not to be interfered with. A third representation of Nature was essentially a scientific one that represented Nature as a highly complex interrelated and delicately balanced system. Human intervention in this delicately balanced system (in particular in the complex process of evolution and adaptation), was seen to be potentially hazardous, producing unintended and irreversible effects.

Thus, some applications of biotechnology were perceived as tampering or interfering with Nature, and such interference would likely wreak retribution further down the track. In these formulations, biotechnology was commonly represented as being against or opposed to Nature. This dichotomy between biotechnology on the one hand, and Nature on the other, was used as a basis for arguing against some applications of biotechnology, in particular the cloning of human beings and animals (though the cloning of specific cells for medical purposes was deemed acceptable). Likewise the use of genetic screening for 'designer babies' or for identifying life that was deemed 'unworthy' was strongly rejected. Concerns about eugenics therefore also featured in the focus groups. Again this fear was anchored to historical events, in this case, Hitler's Aryan project in Europe.

Strong opposition to biotechnology in food production was also associated with representations that contrasted GM foods with foods which were described as 'natural', 'organic' or 'healthy'. Moreover, the daily preparation of food and its consumption were viewed as significant markers of culture and identity. Food therefore was symbolically representative of local cultural identities: the increasing commercialization and industrialization of food production were seen as threats to identity and cultural practices. As Wagner et al. (2001, p. 23) argue, opposition to GM foods 'is a manifestation of a rejection of the industrialisation of food production, a re-discovery of the significance of food to healthy life styles and of its social and cultural meanings'.

This research, then, suggests that representations of biotechnology are grounded in culturally shared meaning-making practices that lend understanding to complex phenomena. Importantly, both secular and religious representations of 'Nature' and 'Life' are central in shaping the public's views of biotechnology. Moreover, the public's anxieties and fears about technology are also grounded in past experiences, in which scientific and expert reassurances to the public about their safety have been found wanting. It is not surprising then that the public is so ambivalent about scientific advances in genomics and biotechnology.

Summary

Social representations refer to the ideas, thoughts, images, and knowledge structures which members of a society or collectivity share. These consensual structures are socially created though communication and interaction between and among people. Representations conventionalize or anchor social objects, persons and events within a familiar categorical context – they give the unfamiliar meaning. Representations are reduced or objectified into both cognitive and pictorial elements which together form a core or figurative nucleus stored in memory and accessed during communication and interaction. Many of our social representations come from the world of science communicated to us through the mass media and elaborated upon by ordinary people to help make sense of everyday life.

Introduction to Discursive Psychology

All three theoretical approaches we have considered thus far – social cognition, social identity and social representations – adhere to the notion of internal mental representation. The basic philosophical presupposition underlying this notion is that an internal cognitive machinery drives human understanding and experience, and that it is the task of psychology, especially social psychology, to study and analyse this underlying cognitive architecture. From this perspective, cognition is conceptualized as prior to language, and language is viewed as a communication medium through which cognition finds expression. Although all three approaches emphasize the constructivist nature of human thought, all none the less subscribe to a *realist epistemology*: a | glossary | belief that there is a knowable domain of facts about human experience and consciousness which can be discovered through the application of reason and rationality (science) or through hermeneutic interpretative methods. The emergence of critical perspectives such as poststructuralist and postmodernist social theory across several disciplines has challenged this realist epistemology. This challenge can be attributed to the increasing interest in the role and function of language as a socially constitutive force in consciousness and experience. The 'turn to language' is reflected in the burgeoning development of discourse analytic research within social psychology. In this section we will consider this tradition of research and the radical critique it has directed towards many of the central concepts taken for granted in social psychology.

Critical social psychology

The social constructionist movement (Gergen, 1985, 1999) was among the first of the 'schools' of psychology to embrace the postmodernist critique of positivist-empiricist science and its conception of truth and knowledge. Representing a loose association of critics from differing intellectual backgrounds (feminists, hermeneuticists, Marxists and critical theorists), *social* | glossary | *constructionism* regards psychological knowledge as socially constructed via negotiated socio-cultural meanings, which are historically prevalent. Deconstructing this knowledge by elucidating its cultural and often political foundations has been a major concern for social constructionism. For example, feminist critics have highlighted the androcentric bias implicit in many psychological theories and practices, which, in turn, have justified and reproduced patriarchal forms of oppression within the discipline as well as in society in general (Hare-Mustin & Maracek, 1988; Wilkinson & Kitzinger, 1996).

Increasingly, these critical approaches to psychological knowledge are being referred to collectively as 'critical social psychology' (Hepburn, 2003; Ibanez & Iniguez, 1997; Tuffin, 2005). As Hepburn (2003) explains, critical social psychology is 'critical' in two ways. First, it is critical of psychology, its theories, models and practices, arguing that, as a discipline, psychology has produced asocial, decontextualized and dehumanizing models of the person. Second, by explicitly engaging with social and political issues central to society, it is particularly critical of psychology's role in the maintenance, reproduction and legitimation of oppressive relations and practices. As a tradition of research, discursive psychology represents one of these critical approaches, but, as we will see, there are a number of discursive approaches that differ philosophically from each other.

The publication in 1987 of *Discourse and Social Psychology: Beyond Attitudes and Behaviour,* by Jonathan Potter and Margaret Wetherell, represents a significant milestone in the development of discursive psychology as a distinct tradition of social psychological research, offering a fundamentally different way of *doing* social psychology. At that point in time, and for some time later, this new way of doing social psychology was referred to as 'discourse analysis', having as its central concern the study of situated *discourse* (both written text and talk) and its role in constructing social reality. Discourse analysis, or 'DA' as it was commonly known, proved to be an unsuitable description of this approach as the name implied that it was merely a method that perhaps could be 'tacked-on' to other methods in psychology. The use of discursive psychology or 'DP' from 1992 onwards (Edwards & Potter, 1992), emphasized that the epistemology underpinning this work was fundamentally different from the positivist and realist epistemology of mainstream social psychology. Specifically, DP is social constructionist and non-cognitivist, and fundamentally 'reworks' topics central to traditional social psychology: topics such as self and identity, attributions, attitudes, prejudice and racism.

Today, discursive psychology has proliferated as a distinct tradition of psychological research, especially in Britain. It is important however to emphasize that discursive psychology does not represent a unified approach. As with all intellectual traditions, a number of 'schools' have developed, differing from each other in important ways. Although somewhat simplifying this diversity, it is none the less useful to present discursive work as a continuum that is represented by two distinct and influential approaches at either end.

The first of these can be broadly identified by the work of Jonathan Potter and Derek Edwards who have developed an approach that is significantly influenced by conversation analysis and its focus on the local, interactional and sequential nature of everyday talk and conversation in its natural settings (Edwards, 1997; Edwards & Potter, 1992; Potter, 1996). In contrast, at the other end, there is critical discursive psychology, which is perhaps best exemplified by Ian Parker's (2002) work. This latter approach specifically calls itself *critical* to emphasize its explicit political agenda and its critical realist and materialist epistemology. While this work is informed by social constructionism, emphasizing the difficulty in ascertaining a 'true' version of reality, it none the less maintains that it is possible to arrive at a veridical version that cuts through the mystifying layers of ideology. This is in contrast to Potter and Edwards' work which maintains a relativist epistemology that questions the notion of a fixed and knowable reality (Edwards, Ashmore & Potter, 1995). Discursive work in general can be located anywhere along this continuum. For example, prominent figures in the field such as Margaret Wetherell (1998; Edley & Wetherell, 1995) and Michael Billig (1991, 1999), whose work borrows from the insights of conversation analysis but also attends to the ways in which discourse (and rhetoric) is shaped by the sense-making practices and discursive resources that are pervasive in a particular society or culture, can be located somewhere in between these two contrasting approaches. Throughout this book we will be using the generic category 'discursive psychology' when referring to all approaches. We will, however, predominantly rely on discursive research that explicitly addresses the reframing of central topics in social psychology using the empirical analysis of discourse.

Intellectual influences on discursive psychology

Discursive psychology has drawn on several intellectual influences, not the least of which has been the social contructionist movement and its critique of traditional psychology. While we cannot do justice to the full range of influences in this brief introduction, we mention three influences that are central in understanding some of the basic tenets of discursive work.

Philosophical linguistics The recent 'turn to language' that many areas of the humanities and social sciences have experienced, is in part due to the increasing interest in Wittgenstein's later philosophical writings (*Philosophical Investigations*, 1953), which emphasized the interactive and contextual nature of language. In contrast to conventional theories that theorized language to be an abstract and coherent system of names and rules, Wittgenstein viewed language as a social practice. While the former treats language as a 'mirror of reality', reflecting a world 'out there', Wittgenstein argued that words and language do not have independent objective meanings outside the context and settings in which they are actually used. Moreover, Wittgenstein challenged the view that language was merely a medium through which people expressed and communicated inner mental phenomena such as feelings and beliefs. Wittgenstein rejected the conventional and dominant understanding in both psychology and philosophy, that there are two separate and parallel systems – cognition and language – one private, the other public. Rather, Wittgenstein argued that 'language itself is the vehicle of thought' (1953, p. 329).

This emphasis on language as a social practice is central to discursive psychology, which seeks to analyse empirically how language is used in everyday activities and settings by participants. The action orientation of talk or situated discourse is associated with another important influence in discursive psychology: John Austin's speech act theory (1962). Speech act theory emphasizes how people use language 'to do things', to achieve certain ends. Words are not simply abstract tools used to state or describe things: they are also used to make certain things happen. People use language to persuade, blame, excuse and present themselves in the best possible light. Thus language is functional, it 'gets things done' (Potter & Wetherell, 1987).

Ethnomethodology and conversation analysis Conversational analysis (CA) is one particular strand of sociology that has systematically examined the ordinary everyday use of talk, which has practical consequences for participants. CA has become increasingly influential in discursive psychology. CA is an ethnomethodological approach, which studies the use of language and conversation in its everyday natural settings. In contrast to cognitive science and sociolinguistics that treat language as an abstract system of rules and categories, CA begins with people's actual talk in social interaction – '*talk-in-interaction*', as it is commonly known. Central figures in the development of CA, such as Harvey Sacks, Emanuel Schegloff, and Gail Jefferson have demonstrated through the close analysis of conversational materials, that everyday conversation is orderly and demonstrates reliable regularities in its sequential turn-by-turn organization (Sacks, 1992; Sacks, Schegloff & Jefferson, 1974). The most obvious examples of patterned regularity in conversation include sequences known as 'adjacency pairs' – questions are usually followed by answers, greetings are commonly reciprocated, and invitations are followed by either an acceptance or refusal. CA attends to the ways in which participants' talk is oriented to the practical concerns of social interaction; how, for example, descriptions, accounts, and categories in

glossary

conversation are put together to perform very specific actions such as justifying, explaining, blaming, excusing, etc. For example, Edwards (1997) has emphasized that a pervasive feature of everyday talk and conversation is that participants attend to their own stake and accountability.

Social psychology has typically treated talk-in-interaction as primarily inconsequential to social life (see Textbox 2.3). Moreover, as a source of natural data, everyday talk is viewed as 'messy', containing hesitations, pauses, interruptions, self-corrections, etc. CA, however, emphasizes how such features of talk may be highly relevant in interaction, which has led to very specific requirements regarding the level of transcription recommended for recorded materials in CA work. It is typical in CA to include details in transcripts such as the length of pauses, overlapping talk, intonation, hesitations, emphasis and volume. Moreover, CA is fundamentally concerned with how participants themselves treat the interaction, what participants treat as relevant, how they display understanding, disagreement, etc, in their talk. Analysts should not impose their own categories of understanding on the conversational materials, nor should they infer underlying motivations or cognitions for participants' talk. The talk itself and its action orientation is the focus of analysis (Schegloff, 1997).

Textbox 2.3

Talk is cheap?

A sorely neglected area of empirical research in psychology has been the everyday use of language. Instead of analysing actual talk or natural conversation to understand how people construct meaning in everyday life, argue, cooperate, persuade, attribute blame, evaluate, etc., psychologists have tried to get at these psychological phenomena in indirect ways that measure underlying cognitions. Indeed, psychology has assumed that you cannot reliably access these psychological phenomena by relying on what people say. People's 'true' feelings and opinions are assumed to reside within an inner cognitive realm that is private, and that may not be publicly accessible.

Below we have listed a number of everyday sayings that devalue talk. What assumptions do these sayings or idioms make about the status of talk?

– *Talk is cheap*
– *Actions speak louder than words*
– *Walk the talk*

Do these common-sense idioms still hold if we reconceptualize talk as a kind of social practice – an activity that has practical consequences for participants? What kind of work or activity might these particular idioms perform in social interaction?

Postsructuralism and Foucault Another important influence in discursive work is postsructuralism and, in particular, the work of Michel Foucault. Despite the enormous impact and influence that Foucault's work has had in the humanities and social sciences generally, psychology as a discipline has remained largely impervious to his prolific writings on the nature of knowledge and subjectivity. This is no surprise given the subject matter of Foucault's writings, which challenged traditional notions of truth and knowledge (Foucault, 1972).

Foucault was interested in the historical emergence and development of various disciplines of knowledge, particularly the social sciences, and how this body of 'scientific' knowledge exercises power by regulating the behaviour and subjectivities of individuals throughout all layers of society. Foucault argued that modern power is achieved largely through the self-regulation and self-discipline of individuals to behave in ways which are largely consistent with dominant discourses about what it is to be human. These discourses shape and mould our subjectivities, the people we ultimately become. For example, dominant psychological discourses about the self for a large part of this century have extolled the virtues of logical, rational thought, cognitive order and consistency, emotional stability and control, moral integrity, independence and self-reliance. These humanist discourses are powerful in that they have contributed to the shaping of certain behavioural practices, modes of thought and institutional structures which function to produce people possessing these valued qualities. Moreover, institutions and practices have emerged which rehabilitate, treat and counsel those who fail to become rational, self-sufficient, capable and emotionally stable individuals. Thus, psychology, as a body of knowledge and a 'scientifically' legitimated discipline, shapes and prescribes what it is to be a healthy and well-adjusted individual (Rose, 1989).

Changing the Subject: Psychology, Social Regulation and Subjectivity, by Henriques, Hollway, Urwin, Venn and Walkerdine (1984, 1998), was among the first books within psychology to directly engage with Foucault's writings on modern forms of subjectivity and psychology's role in producing subjects and identities shaped by the dominant discourses of individualism and cognitivism. As we will see below, discursive psychologists who draw from this tradition of work, and in particular from Foucault, understand and use the term 'discourse' rather differently from those who use this term to refer to everyday talk and conversation. Foucault's influence on discursive psychology, however, cannot be overestimated, especially on the development of critical discursive psychology.

Core principles in discursive psychology

There are several defining principles in discursive psychology but in this brief introduction we would like to emphasize at least four of these: (1) discourse is constitutive, (2) discourse is functional, (3) discourse is put together by discursive resources and practices, and (4) discourse constructs identities in talk.

Discourse is constitutive   Discursive research is primarily interested in how people use language to understand and make sense of everyday life. Discourse is viewed as reflexive and contextual, constructing the very nature of objects and events as they are talked about. This emphasizes the constructive nature and role of discourse as it is used in everyday life. This is fundamentally different from the approach taken in social cognition, social identity theory and, to a lesser extent, social representations theory. These theoretical approaches have at their core a perceptual-cognitive metatheory (Edwards, 1997) that treats objects in the world or 'reality' as an unproblematic given. 'Reality', in this view, is directly perceived and worked upon by cognitive computational processes, which is then, finally, reflected in discourse. This relationship can be summarized by the following representation (Potter, 2000):

Reality → perception → discourse

Perceptual cognitivism treats discourse as merely reflecting a stable and presupposed world 'out there'. In contrast, discursive psychology inverts this traditional approach and treats discourse as analytically prior to perception and reality (Potter, 2000):

Discourse → perception → reality

Discursive psychology begins with discourse itself, with descriptions and accounts of events and issues that are produced in talk. Discourse is therefore constitutive – objects, events, identities, social relations are constructed by the specific words and categories we use to talk about them. This is in stark contrast to psychological approaches that treat language as neutral, a transparent medium that merely reflects the world (Wetherell, 2001). The dominant metaphor of language as a picture that reflects or mirrors reality views language as passive and as 'doing nothing' (Edwards, 1997; Wetherell, 2001). In discursive work, language is viewed as actively constructing and building versions of the world.

Discourse is functional   Another central principle in discursive work is that discourse is functional; talk is a social practice that accomplishes social actions in the world. What people say depends on the particular context in which it is spoken and the functions it serves. In the ebb and flow of everyday life the context within which talk occurs and its function continually shift and change. As people are engaged in conversation with others, they construct and negotiate meanings, or the very 'reality' that they are talking about. In contrast to most traditional approaches in social psychology which look for stability and consistency in people's cognitions, discursive psychology stresses the inherent variability of what people say, as content is seen to reflect contextual changes and the functions that the talk serves. So, for example, people's accounts or views about a particular issue are likely to vary depending on how the talk is organized and what it is designed to do: for example, is it organized in such a way as to justify a position, attribute blame, present oneself positively? Discursive research, then, is interested in analysing why a particular version of social reality is constructed in a particular way and what it accomplishes in that particular context. Thus 'the focus is on the discourse *itself*: how it is organized and what it is doing' (Potter & Wetherell, 1987, p. 4, original emphasis). We will pick up on this theme again in Chapter 4 on attitudes, to demonstrate more specifically how this functional aspect of discourse challenges traditional cognitive approaches to the attitude construct in social psychology. Related to this is the observation that discourse is often organized rhetorically to be persuasive. People orient to the availability of multiple and different versions of the world in their discourse by building specific constructions in ways that undermine alternative accounts. Billig's (1991) work on the argumentative and rhetorical context of discourse has been influential in the development of discursive psychology and we will outline in subsequent chapters the rhetorical features of everyday talk and discourse.

Discursive resources and practices   If discourse is constitutive of social reality and functional, how are text and talk put together to accomplish this? Discourse is put together with *discursive resources* and *practices*. Traditional cognitive constructs such as attitudes, beliefs, opinions, and categories have been replaced within discursive psychology by an emphasis on identifying the resources and practices that are drawn upon in everyday talk when people express opinions, argue and debate (Potter, 1998). These discursive resources include *interpretative repertoires* – defined as a set of metaphors, arguments and terms – which are used recurrently in people's discourse to describe events and actions (Potter & Wetherell, 1987). They also include the identification of specific discursive strategies and devices that people mobilize in

glossary

their talk to build their accounts as factual, objective and disinterested (Potter, 1996). For example, a common device to warrant a particular view or argument is to claim that there exists a consensus on a particular issue; that everybody knows or agrees something to be true. This specific device is known as a 'consensus warrant'. Other discursive resources or tools include rhetorical commonplaces (Billig, 1987), or clinching arguments that participants mobilize in their talk. The use of idiomatic expressions such as clichés or proverbs, for example, has been shown to be difficult to argue against because of their vague but common-sense qualities (Drew & Holt, 1989). We will detail some of these discursive resources and practices throughout subsequent chapters to illustrate how discursive psychology reframes traditional topics through the detailed analysis of text and talk.

Discursive resources that are drawn upon to construct meaning in everyday talk are shaped by social, cultural and historical processes (Wetherell, 2001). People's sense-making practices and ways of understanding the world may vary and shift depending on the particular context, but these are none the less constrained by the cultural and linguistic resources that are shared within a particular language community.

Discourse and identity Discourse not only constructs objects and versions of the world but also constructs identities for speakers. Instead of seeing the self and identity as an inner psychological essence possessed by individuals, as in traditional accounts, discursive psychology argues that identities or 'subject positions' are brought into being through discourse. Different ways of talking invoke different subject positions for speakers, such as 'mother', 'daughter', 'lover', professional woman', 'friend', etc., so that specific patterns of talk are recognizable for the work they do in discursively constituting identity (Wetherell, 2001). For example, the identity of a 'parent' can be worked up in a variety of ways by the use of culturally recognized narratives in talk regarding parental rights, responsibilities and moral obligations. Unlike the traditional notion of a stable, cognitive self, discursive psychology emphasizes the shifting and multiple identities that speakers actively construct in talk (some of which may even be contradictory) to accomplish a range of interactional goals. Discourse is constitutive of identity, that is, people can be positioned by particular ways of talking, but at the same time people can make active choices about the identities they mobilize in particular settings. People are 'constituted and reconstituted through the various discursive practices in which they participate' (Davies & Harré, 1990, p. 263). This account of identity is more in keeping with postmodern and postsructural theories which emphasize the multiple, dynamic, and interactive nature of subjectivity.

We will elaborate further on the discursive construction of identity in Chapter 5, but now we will turn to an empirical study in the discursive tradition and consider how this study elaborates on the four central issues we have outlined thus far in discursive psychology.

Empirical discursive research: unequal egalitarianism

Gender inequality and discrimination is a central topic of relevance and interest in social psychology. Theories in social psychology have attributed gender discrimination to underlying sexist attitudes, and to the pervasiveness of traditional stereotypes and representations of women. An early study which sought to understand how gender inequalities are socially reproduced in discourse, despite significant challenges to traditional understandings of gender, was that of Wetherell, Stiven and Potter (1987). Instead of measuring attitudes to women or asking respondents to select trait descriptions and adjectives to determine their stereotypes of gender, Wetherell et al. (1987) analysed what university students had to say about gender, employment opportunities, careers and child rearing during semi-structured interviews. Their analysis demonstrated how speakers provided predominantly individualistic and psychological accounts of gender inequities in work, career, and parenting responsibilities. In these accounts individuals were constructed as possessing a set of inherent and stable traits and abilities that they brought with them to the job market. Social change in the status of women was seen as being the primary responsibility of individual women who needed to 'prove themselves' to employers as being just as capable and worthy as their male counterparts. Thus an *interpretative repertoire* of individualism and meritocracy featured largely in explanations for existing gender inequalities.

Although most respondents explicitly endorsed the principle of equal opportunity for men and women, at the same time they provided detailed accounts about the practical constraints that prevented this from becoming a reality: constraints such as the biological inevitability of women bearing children and the attendant responsibilities of child care. These practical considerations were deployed in ways that justified the existing gender inequities in work, career and parenting. Wetherell et al. demonstrated how the deployment of these contradictory repertoires constituted a form of 'unequal egalitarianism' that, on the one hand, appeals to the ideals of equality but, on the other, justifies the practical difficulties in realizing equitable gender relations. Such competing and contradictory themes are evident in the following response from a male participant in their study (cited in Wetherell et al., 1987, p. 63).

Interviewer: So if it was a decision between you and your wife as to who was to stay at home, you would rather go to work rather than stay at home?

Respondent: Well, no, that would have to be a unanimous decision, in other words if my wife was adamant that she wanted to go out to work, uh and if I were 90 per cent convinced that I wanted to go out to work, then it is possible that I would look after the children. But I would say that it's unlikely that I would marry a person who would be so closeted in her views anyway. So you know, it's not really likely to happen. I will be going to work.

In this extract we can see how the respondent describes the decision about who would stay at home to take care of their children and who would go out to work as a 'unanimous decision' that would be negotiated between husband and wife. This account reflects the principle of equality in decision-making between partners and allows the respondent to manage and present a particular view of himself as fair and egalitarian. Note, though, how he then sidesteps this egalitarianism by describing a wife who would insist on working as 'closeted in her views' and that he is unlikely to marry someone of this nature in any case. Moreover, he finishes his turn by categorically stating 'I will be going to work'!

Such discursive research demonstrates how people utilize a range of discursive resources to construct particular versions and accounts, and do so in ways that serve important functions in social interaction. In terms of the four themes in discursive research that we identified above, we can see how this piece of talk is constitutive: it constructs issues and objects in very specific ways, such as, how decisions are made between partners about work and parenting, and the characteristics of women who insist on working. This discourse or talk is also functional in that it attends to self-presentational goals, in this particular case, presenting oneself positively as egalitarian. Thus it also attends to the identity of the speaker who is positioning himself as a certain kind of person or potential partner. Importantly, too, in this talk we can see the workings of an enduring enigma within traditional social cognitive approaches to attitudes: how people manage to maintain what may appear to be contradictory positions. In this particular study, for example, Wetherell et al. (1987) were able to identify a pervasive discursive resource or practice that participants used to manage such inconsistencies, which they called the principle/practice dichotomy. While on the one hand participants invariably espoused egalitarian principles and ideals, on the other, they were undermined by practical considerations. Such 'practical talk' was deployed in ways that justified and legitimated existing gender inequities in society. Thus in more naturalistic conversational settings, people articulate a complex set of positions which blend egalitarian views with discriminatory ones. Discursive research of this kind is therefore able to explicate how existing gender inequities are maintained and reproduced in society despite claims that traditional attitudes and stereotypes of women have changed dramatically – findings which tend to be produced by traditional quantitative surveys and questionnaires. In Chapter 4 we will be elaborating further on how discursive research has re-theorized traditional attitude research and what insights it can throw on how attitudes are organized rhetorically when they are produced in their more natural context of everyday discourse.

Critical discursive psychology

Unlike discursive research that is primarily influenced by the ethnomethodological approach taken in conversation analysis, *critical* discursive psychology emphasizes how discursive practices or ways of talking about particular issues are shaped by influences outside of the immediate interactional context of speakers. Specifically, these influences are the historical, political and cultural context within which speakers live their lives (Wetherell, 1998, 2001). Critical discursive psychologists have argued that certain ways of talking or constructing objects and events become pervasive and dominant in particular historical moments, which make them more culturally available and thus more powerful in constructing social reality. If we take the study above by Wetherell et al. (1987) as an example, a strict conversation analysis would limit itself to the interaction between the interviewer and the respondent alone, focusing only on what the participants themselves orient to and make relevant in the interaction (Schegloff, 1968). Thus in the above extract, while the respondent states categorically that he 'will be going to work', he at the same time clearly attends to his self-presentation as someone who is reasonable and fair, as someone who would negotiate with his partner about such matters. This is probably as far as the analysis would go. In contrast, critical discursive psychology would look outside this specific interaction and comment upon the social and historical context of gender relations within western liberal democracies. What does this socio-political context say about power relations between men and women, and how do various institutions within the wider society propagate and reproduce particular constructions that come to dominate our subjective experience and our very identities as men and women (Edley, 2001; Henriques et al., 1998; Wetherell, 1998, 2001)?

As already noted, critical discursive psychology draws heavily on poststructuralist theory and, particularly, on Foucault's writings on discourse, but again there is no unified approach to this tradition of discursive psychology.

While major exponents such as Wetherell (1998, 2001) adopt this critical framework, her work is largely empirical and still shares important similarities with more conversation-analytic inspired discursive work. In contrast, Ian Parker (1990) eschews empiricism, is less interested in everyday talk and conversation and more concerned with identifying and describing hegemonic 'discourses' which proliferate within society and which inform, shape and construct the way we see ourselves and the world. It is to this construction of 'discourse' that we now turn.

Discourse as a coherent meaning system

Parker and others inspired by postsructuralist writings use the term *discourse* to refer to a recurrently used 'system of statements which constructs an object' (1990, p. 191). So, for example, within western societies there exist a number of dominant discourses which inform and shape various aspects of our lives. We have a medical discourse which informs our understanding of anything to do with health and illness; we have a legal discourse which provides us with certain codes of conduct and rules for behaviour; we have a familial discourse which buttresses views about the sanctity and importance of the family, etc. While Parker defines discourses as 'coherent systems of meaning', contradictions and inconsistencies within discourses are common, as are alternative discourses which compete with dominant ones for recognition and power. Often discourses are related to or presuppose other discourses or systems of meaning. Discourses primarily function to bring 'objects into being', to create the status of reality with which objects are endowed. As already discussed above, they also position us in various 'subject positions' so that discourses invite us, even compel us, to take on certain roles and identities. For example, an advertising discourse positions us in the role of 'consumer'. Often, however, this is achieved by addressing us by virtue of our status and identity as a woman, a parent, a worker, etc. Parker does not restrict discourse to just spoken and written language. Discourses can be found in all kinds of 'texts', such as in advertising, popular and high-brow culture, non-verbal behaviour and instruction manuals.

As coherent meaning systems, Parker argues that discourses have a material and almost 'physical presence'. Like social representations, discourses, once created, proliferate within society. Importantly, however, Parker does not view discourses in idealist terms but sees them as grounded in and shaped by historical and political (material) 'realities'. Thus he does not subscribe to the linguistic and political relativism which is associated with some discursive approaches. Parker and other discursive researchers (e.g., Willig, 1999, 2001) position themselves as 'critical realists' who are committed to developing an approach to discourse which is sensitive to the material and socio-structural conditions from which discourses emerge and take shape. The political edge to this discursive approach is that it emphasizes how some discourses function to legitimate existing institutions, and to reproduce power relations and inequities within society (Parker, 1990).

Parker's notion of 'discourses' has been criticized for its reified and abstract status. For him, discourses, as entities, exist independently from the people who use them. In contrast, approaches that are located at the other end of the continuum of discursive work are attuned to the context-specific and functional ways in which talk or discourse is mobilized in specific situations. These approaches define discourse as a 'situated practice' and thus provide a more social psychological focus to discursive research (Potter, Wetherell, Gill & Edwards, 1990). Moreover, this social psychological focus on how participants use language in specific interactional contexts does not preclude a critical and political analysis of how pervasive and recurring patterns of talk justify and legitimate inequitable relations and practices. Indeed, we shall demonstrate in Chapter 7 how Wetherell and Potter's (1992) systematic analysis of contemporary racist discourse functions precisely in this way.

Discourse and cognition

Not surprisingly, discursive psychology and its radical critique of cognitivism and positivist methods of enquiry have attracted considerable criticism from other theoretical approaches in social psychology, including cognitive psychology (Conway, 1992), social identity theory (Abrams & Hogg, 1990b), and social representations theory (Moscovici, 1985). At the same time, however, some of discursive psychology's methods and concepts have been enthusiastically embraced by prominent social psychologists working in other traditions such as social identity theory (Condor, 2000; Reicher & Hopkins, 2001) and the social psychology of prejudice and racism (Verkuyten, 2005). Despite its increasing acceptance in British social psychology, discursive psychology's strong anti-cognitivist epistemology continues to attract considerable antipathy from the mainstream. Discursive psychology and its qualitative research methods are often derided as lacking scientific objectivity and precision. The irony, of course, is that such criticisms fail to critically reflect upon the questionable assumptions that are built into the very fabric of quantitative research methods, and their claims to scientific objectivity. As we progress through each chapter and deal with social psychology's central topics, we will discuss discursive psychology's criticisms of the cognitive assumptions underlying these central constructs and their empirical investigation in laboratory environments.

None the less, it is perhaps not difficult to understand the objection that many social psychologists have to discursive psychology. For many of us, the experience of consciousness and thought furnishes us with the self-evident 'reality' of internal cognitive representation, and the very idea that our experiences and practices are not cognitively mediated may seem absurd. Cognitivism is indeed a 'discourse' that is dominant, not only within the scientific realm but also in the everyday world where people live out their lives. Cognitive concepts such as attitudes and beliefs are part and parcel of our everyday language and most people talk of their 'attitudes', 'beliefs' and 'opinions'. Shouldn't this experience alone be taken as evidence that these things really do exist? As we will see, discursive psychology treats these constructs as 'talk's topics': topics that participants themselves attend to in their talk in order to perform the important business of everyday social interaction (Edwards, 1997). The categories of the mind are therefore treated as topics of conversation rather than actual mental states that have an independent existence.

Mainstream critics have found this position – that there is nothing beyond discourse (text and talk) – and the resistance to speculating about any internal psychological realm highly problematic. Indeed, some have referred to the absence of any psychological model of the person as a 'black box' approach, reminiscent of the kind of criticism that radical behaviourism attracted long ago. Indeed, some discursive psychologists themselves have found this 'discursive reductionism' unsettling, and have looked to other theoretical frameworks to provide a more satisfying account of individual subjectivity. As Parker (1991, p. 83) puts it, discursive ' … research repeatedly begs the question: what is going on inside human beings when they use discourse?' More recently, poststructuralist theory on embodiment has argued for a return to a form of materiality that emphasizes the significance of the physical body and emotional life for individual subjectivity (Henriques et al., 1998). This has led to the adoption of a range of theoretical approaches which have been seen to provide a link between discourse and individual subjectivity, in particular, for critical discursive psychology. These include poststructuralist psychodynamic theory, in particular the writings of Lacan (Henriques et al., 1998; Parker, 1991), and Gibson's ecological theory of perception (Costall & Still, 1987; Gibson, 1979; Parker, 1991). Unfortunately, we do not have the space to consider these perspectives here, but see Hepburn (2003) for a good introduction to psychoanalytic approaches, and the first edition of this book (Augoustinos & Walker, 1995) for more details on Gibson's ecological account of human perception and behaviour.

A Post-Cognitive Psychology?

Does the advent of discursive psychology, and more generally the 'turn to language' generally associated with poststructural and discursive approaches, signal the beginning of the end of cognitivism in psychology and the emergence of a post-cognitive psychology (Potter, 2000)? If thought is no more and no less than language itself, then a substantial component of psychological inquiry and scholarship has been misplaced in its quest to identify, operationalize and measure underlying cognitive mechanisms and processes.

Whether we subscribe to the view that language is a medium for cognition, or that there is little outside language itself, the recent uptake of discursive psychology does force us to take discourse more seriously in our conceptual and empirical deliberations as social psychologists. Discursive psychology has attempted to establish an epistemology and ontology of social life that resists the inherent dualisms that have proliferated in psychology and the social sciences more generally – dualisms such as the individual versus the social, inside versus outside, cognition versus discourse, language versus practice (Wetherell, 1999). There remains, however, substantial resistance to collapsing these traditional dichotomies, even within critical psychology itself. It is clear, though, that the realist epistemological foundations of mainstream social cognition research, the quest for knowledge and truth through the application of positivist methods of science, will always be a bone of contention with the social constructionist and relativist notion of knowledge associated with the discursive approach (though a realist epistemology is not necessarily incompatible with some critical discursive work). Thus social cognitive approaches in social psychology remain largely unaffected by the 'postmodern' intellectual challenge to truth and certainty, and to discursive psychology more specifically.

Summary

Discursive psychology rejects the search for internal mental representations and the reliance on internal mechanisms to understand social life. Instead, discourse is seen as *constitutive* and *functional*, and hence is claimed to be the proper site of social psychological analysis. Discursive interaction is patterned and ordered, drawing on shared discursive resources such as interpretive repertoires to bring social reality into being and to manage interactants' identities.

Chapter Summary

Considered very broadly, 'social cognition' refers to theory and research which is aimed at describing and explaining how we, as human beings, experience and understand ourselves in the social world. In this chapter, we have presented four foundational theoretical orientations to this intellectual project: social cognitive, social identity, social representations, and discursive psychological approaches. The major theoretical premises of each orientation were considered, and form the basis of coverage of typical areas in each of the subsequent chapters in part two of this book.

Further Reading

Brown, R. J. (2000). Social identity theory: Past achievements, current problems and future challenges. *European Journal of Social Psychology*, 30, 745–778.

Edwards, D. (1997). *Discourse and cognition*. London: Sage.

Fiske, S. T., & Taylor, S. E. (1991). *Social cognition* (2nd ed.). New York: McGraw-Hill.

Hepburn, A. (2003). *An introduction to critical social psychology*. London: Sage.

Moscovici, S. (1998). The history and actuality of social representations. In U. Flick (Ed.) *The psychology of the social* (pp. 209–247). Cambridge: Cambridge University Press.

Potter, J., & Wetherell, M. (1987). *Discourse and social psychology: Beyond attitudes and behaviour*. London: Sage.

Tajfel, H. (1981a). *Human groups and social categories: Studies in social psychology*. Cambridge: Cambridge University Press.

Turner, J. C., Hogg, M. A., Oakes, P. J., Reicher, S. D., & Wetherell, M. S. (1987). *Rediscovering the social group: A self-categorization theory*. Oxford: Blackwell.

Part Two

3 Social Perception

How do we handle the enormous amount of sensory information that we receive in the course of our everyday lives? This has been a question that has long intrigued psychologists. Most of the time we respond to this constant flow of information almost instantaneously, apprehending and making sense of it in what appears to be an effortless and systematic way. Research in human perception and in cognitive psychology has traditionally concerned itself with the ways in which people perceive, understand, store and remember information about physical stimuli and objects. However, it was not until the 1980s that social psychologists began to systematically apply information processing models borrowed from the work in perception and cognition to isolate the mechanisms by which people come to understand the *social world* in which they live. Social psychologists began to enthusiastically embrace perceptual cognitive models to understand how people perceive and process social information, that is, information about people, groups and events. Given our limited cognitive capacities, how do we manage to cope with all this complex social information? By the late 1980s social cognition had become the dominant paradigm in social psychology and concepts such as schemas, categories, and stereotypes became commonplace. This chapter will deal primarily with these central concepts in social cognition and, as in other chapters, will discuss how alternative theoretical approaches such as social representations, social identity and discursive psychology have provided different understandings of these constructs.

Social Cognition and Social Perception

During the 1980s social cognition research began to posit that people apprehended and made sense of complex social information by simplifying and organizing this information into meaningful cognitive structures called schemas. The schema concept has appeared in various psychological writings, but the most influential tradition of research, which preceded the work on social schema theory, was Bartlett's book on *Remembering* (1932). Bartlett was an English psychologist whose research in the 1930s concerned human memory for pictures, figures and stories. He argued that people organize images and information into meaningful patterns and these patterns facilitate later memory recall. This view was different to the most dominant view at the time, which argued that people perceived and represented information as isolated elements. As with Bartlett's work, early research in social schema theory suggested that people are better able to remember information when it is organized around a theme compared to when it is not.

A schema is conceptualized as a cognitive structure, which contains general expectations and knowledge of the world. This may include general expectations about people, social roles, events and how to behave in certain situations. Schema theory suggests that we use such mental structures to select and process incoming information from the social environment. The best definition of a schema comes from the early work of Taylor and Crocker:

> [A] schema is a cognitive structure that consists in part of a representation of some defined stimulus domain. The schema contains general knowledge about that domain, including specification of the relationships among its attributes, as well as specific examples or instances of the stimulus domain. ... The schema provides hypotheses about incoming stimuli, which include plans for interpreting and gathering schema-related information. (1981, p. 91)

Schemas take the form of general expectations learned through experience or socialization, and thus give us some sense of prediction and control of the social world. It would be very difficult to function if we went about our everyday life without prior knowledge or expectations about the people and events around us. As such, schemas are theorized to be functional and essential for our well-being. As existing mental structures, they help us to understand the complexity of social life. Schemas help guide what we attend to, what we perceive, what we remember and what we infer. They are like mental short cuts we use to simplify reality. Early schema models posited that people are 'cognitive misers': many judgements and evaluations were said to be 'top of the head' phenomena (Taylor & Fiske, 1978), made with little thought or considered deliberation. This metaphor has been replaced however with one that views social thinking as more strategic and flexible: that people are more like 'motivated tacticians' (Fiske, 1992, 2004).

Thus, research on the schema concept aims to understand how people represent social information in memory and how new information is assimilated with existing knowledge; that is, how people are able to process, interpret and understand complex social information.

Schema types

The schema concept has been applied empirically to four main content areas: person schemas, self schemas, role schemas and event schemas (Fiske & Taylor, 1991; Taylor & Crocker, 1981). All schemas serve similar functions – they all influence the encoding (taking in and interpretation) of new information, memory for old information and inferences about missing information. We will briefly consider each of these four content areas in turn.

Person schemas Person schemas deal with abstracted conceptual structures of personality traits or person prototypes that enable a person to categorize and make inferences from the experience of interactions with other people (Cantor & Mischel, 1977). In most research these person schemas are actually referred to as trait prototypes, so we will use the terms interchangeably. One way in which we can facilitate our interactions with the many people in our lives is to categorize individuals in terms of their dominant personality traits. For example, we may categorize Woody Allen as a prototypical 'neurotic', and Robin Williams as a prototypical 'extrovert'. Trait or person schemas enable us to answer the question: 'what kind of person is he or she?' (Cantor & Mischel, 1979), and thus help us anticipate the nature of our interactions with specific individuals, giving us a sense of control and predictability in social interactions.

Self schemas How would you describe yourself? Self schemas refer to the conceptual structures people have of themselves. Markus defines them as 'cognitive generalizations about the self, derived from past experience, that organize and guide the processing of self-related information contained in the individual's social experiences' (1977, p. 64). Self schemas are thought to be well-elaborated structures which are linked to salient and largely stable individual traits and behaviour. They are components of the self-concept which are central to identity and self-definition. The self schema concept is therefore consistent with various psychological conceptions of the self which emphasize the static, enduring and self-protecting nature of the self-concept. We will discuss the research on self schemas and its relationship to other theories of the self in considerable detail in Chapter 5.

Event schemas Event schemas can be described as cognitive scripts that describe the sequential organization of events in everyday activities (Schank & Abelson, 1977). Thus, event schemas provide the basis for anticipating the future, setting goals and making plans. They enable the individual to set strategies to achieve such goals by specifying the appropriate behavioural sequences through which the individual must move to attain the desired state. So we know that the appropriate behavioural sequence for eating at a restaurant is to enter, wait to be seated by a waiter, order a drink, look at the menu, order the meal, eat, pay the bill and leave.

Schank and Abelson (1977) argue that our common-sense understanding of behaviour in particular situations is characterized by a large repertoire of unconscious knowledge and assumptions – a kind of behavioural pragmatics, which orients us in everyday life. This repertoire is stored in memory and activated unconsciously whenever it is needed. Indeed, Schank and Abelson argue that 'memory is organised around personal experiences or episodes rather than around abstract semantic categories' (1977, p. 17). This allows us to generalize from repeated experiences so that we do not need to process information from scratch every time we encounter a similar situation.

Role schemas Role schemas refer to the knowledge structures people have of the norms and expected behaviours of specific role positions in society. These can refer to achieved and ascribed roles. The former include roles which are acquired through effort and training, such as the doctor role or psychologist role, while the latter refer to roles which we have little control over such as age, gender and race. Achieved roles are usually occupationally related, and provide us with a set of normative expectations about the behaviour of individuals occupying certain positions.

Social cognition research on ascribed roles has been prolific, especially in the areas of gender and race stereotypes. Stereotypes are a type of schema which organize information and knowledge about people from different social categories. They are mental representations of social groups and their members that are widely shared (Hamilton & Sherman, 1994; Macrae, Stangor & Hewstone, 1996; Stangor & Lange, 1994). We will discuss this work in more detail later in this chapter and again in Chapter 7 when we consider the relationship between stereotypes and prejudice. It is important to emphasize at this point, though, that social cognition models suggest that categorizing people into their respective social group memberships is highly functional in that it simplifies social reality. Social categories such as man/woman, black/white, young/old are viewed as highly salient and prior to any other kind of person categorization. Fiske (1998) refers to age, gender and race as the 'top three' because they are the most central and visually accessible categories. On meeting someone for the first time, we are more likely to attend to obvious and salient cues such as gender, race, and age in guiding our interactions with the individual. With increased familiarity, these cues become less important and we may subsequently employ trait-based or person schemas in our interactions. The salience of social categories over trait schemas in person perception is attested to by Andersen and Klatzky (1987), who found social stereotypes to be associatively richer in structure and able to elicit more concrete and specific attributes than trait prototypes.

Categorization

Before we can apply a schema to a social object we need first to categorize the object. Historically, within the areas of philosophy and linguistics, categorization has long been considered a central and fundamental human cognitive tendency (Lakoff, 1987). The process of categorization is central to schema theory and to other theoretical approaches we will be discussing in this book. Borrowed from cognitive psychology and the pioneering work of Eleanor Rosch, the process of categorization refers to how we identify stimuli and group them as members of one category, similar to others in that category and different from members of other categories. Categorization is seen to be fundamental to perception, thought, language and action. Most of the time we employ categories automatically and with little conscious effort. Whenever we identify or label an object as something (a book, tree, animal) we are categorizing. Categories impose order on the complexity of the stimulus world, and by doing so allow us to communicate about the world effectively and efficiently.

Rosch's (1975) experimental work found that some members of a category act as cognitive reference points in that people consider them to be more representative of a category than other members. Rosch referred to these as prototypes. For example, people judged robins and sparrows to be better examples of the category 'bird' than were emus and penguins. Thus some instances contained within the category are considered more typical than others. Instances can therefore range from being quite typical to atypical. The most typical or prototypical instance would best represent the category. The prototype is the 'central tendency' or average of the category members.

Rosch found that participants identified stimuli which were judged to be more prototypical significantly faster as members of a category compared to stimuli judged as less prototypical. Essentially, when we categorize we compare the new instance or object to the category prototype. If it is relatively similar we would conclude that the instance fits the category. The more features an instance shares with other category members, the more quickly and confidently it is identified as a category member (Rosch, 1978).

Rosch found that some categories, like 'bird', have very clear boundaries, whereas other categories have 'fuzzy' boundaries. To classify an object as belonging to a particular category does not necessarily require that the object contain all the attributes of that category. However, the object must share some common features with other category members so that members of a category are related by 'family resemblance'. This is especially the case for social objects such as people and events where the boundaries for category inclusion are less clear. Social categorization is assumed to be a more complex process than object categorization in that social objects are variable, dynamic, interactive and therefore less predictable. As with non-social categories, members of a social category share common features, though some members are more prototypical than others. For example, consider our tendency to categorize or classify the people we know in terms of their dominant personality traits – John is 'neurotic', Sue is 'easy-going', Jane is 'shy'. Each of us has some representation of what it is to be 'neurotic', 'easy-going' and 'shy', though we may differ in what we consider to be a typical or representative instance of such behaviour. Similarly, social situations are categorized in terms of representative features so that certain behaviour is anticipated and expected in certain contexts. For example, one generally knows what range of behaviours and social interactions characterizes a party, which may be totally inappropriate in other social contexts. On the whole, however, category inclusion in the social world is a more variable process, which is shaped and influenced by a multitude of factors. Categorizing people and events allows us to simplify and structure the social world and thus anticipate future behaviour and experiences. Some predictability and coherence is thereby given to our everyday social interactions.

The prototype approach to category representation has been a very influential account of how social stimuli are stored and represented in memory. However, more recently it has been suggested that categories may not only be represented by some averaged abstraction, but by a number of specific and concrete instances or 'exemplars' of the category which have been encountered (Smith, 1998). The exemplar approach to category representation has considerable advantages over the prototypic view in that it is able to account

Table 3.1 *Summary of the characteristics of schemas/categories*

- Theory-driven structures
- Energy-saving devices
- Facilitate memory
- Evaluative and affective structures
- Hierarchically organized
- Social in origin
- Stable and resistant to change

for the variability and diversity of instances contained within a general category. For example, arriving at an abstracted average of two very different politicians such as Bill Clinton and Margaret Thatcher may be too cognitively demanding. These extreme instances may be better represented as concrete exemplars within an overall general category of 'politician'. As such, exemplars serve as more specific and concrete reference points. People probably rely on a combination of prototype and exemplar-based representations, depending on the social object in question and the conditions under which the information is processed (Hamilton & Sherman, 1994; Smith, 1998).

What are schemas and categories and how do they work?

Given our limited cognitive capacities and a challenging and overwhelming stimulus world, cognitive processes that simplify and structure incoming information are likely to be highly adaptive to everyday cognitive functioning (Macrae & Bodenhausen, 2000). As we have seen, one important way in which this is achieved is through the activation and implementation of categorical or schematic thinking. We want now to consider in more detail how schemas and categories function in information-processing terms: that is, how do they work as organizing structures which influence the encoding, storing and recall of complex social information. These characteristics and functions are summarized in Table 3.1.

Schemas/categories are theory-driven structures The most central function of schematic or categorical thinking is that it lends organization to experience. The internal cognitive mechanisms through which this is achieved are generally not well known, though hypothetical processes have been postulated. A category is matched against an incoming stimulus configuration so that the relationships between the elements of the category are compared to the incoming information. If the information is a good match to the category, then the constitutive elements of the category are imposed upon the information. Thus, a category guides identification of the elements of the incoming stimulus, thereby providing a context for its meaning, organization and internal representation. That is, categories provide us with expectancies that guide the processing of subsequent information (Macrae & Bodenhausen, 2000). Thus a significant proportion of our information processing is theory-driven rather than data-driven; that is, it relies on people's prior expectations, preconceptions and knowledge about the social world in order to make sense of new situations and encounters.

An inherent feature of theory-driven or categorical processing is that often it can lead to biased judgements. As existing cognitive structures, categories can 'fill in' data that are missing from incoming social information. In such ambiguous situations, categories can either direct a search for the relevant information to complete the stimulus more fully, or they can fill in the missing values with 'default options' or 'best guesses'. These are usually based on previous experiences with the particular stimulus. For example, consider an Australian university student who was about to meet someone for the first time, and the only information she had about this person was that he was a male college student from the United States, holidaying in Australia. If her previous experience with American college students was rather limited, then she may (erroneously) rely on limited assumptions and preconceptions about American college students to guide her. These preconceptions may have been drawn largely from popular films about American college students. With insufficient or ambiguous information she may 'fill in' the missing details with stereotypes drawn from such films. These film portrayals suggest that he is likely to be tall, blond, a good athlete, likes to drink and hang around with the boys, is preoccupied with sex, and drives a flash car paid for by his middle-class parents. However, if she learned that he was short, dull, clumsy and wore glasses, she may apply an entirely different stereotype – perhaps one borrowed from American college films once again – that of the college 'nerd'. However, if she then learned he was African-American, her expectations are likely to change again. So with ambiguous data the blanks are filled in with pre-existing assumptions and knowledge.

Categories can also provide short-cuts when processing information by the use of heuristics. For example, with limited information people may use the representativeness heuristic (Kahneman & Tversky, 1972, 1973) to determine to what degree a specific stimulus is representative of a more general category. Is Sue, who is shy and mild-mannered, more likely to be an accountant or a business executive? Another well-documented heuristic is known as the availability heuristic, which is the tendency to overestimate the frequency of an event or object due to its salience or the ease with which it can be brought to mind. For example, people may overestimate the incidence of crime in their community due to the salience and dramatic nature of such undesirable behaviour.

Schemas/categories are energy-saving devices Given the vast amount of information with which we are inundated continuously, categories can be likened to cognitive tools that we use to process information quickly and efficiently. As we detailed in Chapter 2, Macrae et al. (1994) have described categories and stereotypes as 'energy-saving' devices that free us from attending to every detail and piece of information. Macrae et al. suggest that the use of stereotypes and their probable unconscious activation (see also Devine, 1989a) frees up valuable cognitive resources which can be utilized elsewhere. In most day-to-day superficial interactions this kind of automatic category or stereotype-based processing is not only economical but also functional in some contexts.

The necessity to simplify information and to reduce cognitive effort through the use of 'energy-saving' devices such as stereotypes has often been lamented by social psychologists. Macrae et al. suggest that stereotype activation has perhaps been too maligned. Stereotype activation specifically, and inferential thinking more generally (Gilbert, 1989), may have evolved not because humans are cognitively lazy and slothful, but because we need to deploy our limited cognitive resources economically and functionally.

Schemas/categories facilitate memory Categories or schemas influence and guide what social information will be encoded and retrieved from memory. As mentioned previously, categories which are based on highly salient visual cues, such as gender, age and race, often have a determining influence on what is encoded and later remembered. Early memory research in this tradition generally found that categories facilitate the recall of information, so that a good stimulus match to a category facilitates overall recall and that category-consistent material is better remembered than category-inconsistent material. For example, Cohen (1981) presented participants with a videotape of a woman having dinner with her husband. Half the participants were told that she was a waitress; the other half were told she was a librarian. Those who were told she was a librarian were more likely to remember features and behaviour of the woman which previously had been judged by another group of participants to be prototypical of librarians (for example, wore glasses, drank wine). Likewise, participants who had been told she was a waitress were more likely to remember 'prototypical waitress behaviour' like drinking beer. Such studies tell us that we are more likely to notice, encode and subsequently remember information which is consistent with our initial expectations. Moreover, categories also influence processing time, with the research literature predominantly indicating faster processing times for category-relevant as opposed to category-irrelevant information. Thus people take less time to process, interpret and remember information which is consistent with their general expectations (Devine & Ostrom, 1988; Hastie & Park, 1986).

However, there is now considerable research contradicting this general rule. Several studies have found that inconsistent information or category-incongruent material, because it is novel and distinctive, may be better recalled than consistent information. Meta-analytic reviews of memory recall studies for category-consistent and inconsistent material have also produced contradictory findings. Rojahn and Pettigrew (1992), for example, concluded that memory is facilitated for category-inconsistent material. Stangor and McMillan (1992) in their review concluded otherwise: that memory was better for schema-consistent material. Recently, these inconsistent conclusions have been accommodated by proposing that human cognitive processing is flexible and sensitive to the situational and contextual demands with which perceivers are confronted (Quinn, Macrae & Bodenhausen, 2003). For example, in some situations and conditions categorical thinking is activated, whereas in others, perceivers rely on more piecemeal and individuated processing.

Theory-driven versus data-driven thinking To account for the apparent contradiction between data-driven and theory-driven (category) processing, Brewer (1988), among others, advanced a dual processing model of information processing. Categorical processing is used when the data are unambiguous and relatively unimportant to the person. However, if the data are less clear and are of considerable importance to the person, then a more individuating and piecemeal approach is used. Thus people use either of two strategies depending on the nature of the information to be processed.

In contrast to the dual processing model, Fiske and Neuberg (1990; Fiske, Lin & Neuberg, 1999) suggest that social information processing can be conceptualized as a continuum, moving from category-based processing to a more individuating data-based approach (see Figure 3.1). While processing can take place anywhere along the continuum, Fiske and Neuberg (1990) emphasize that most person impressions are primarily and initially category-based. In their words, category-based processing is always the 'default option'. Categorical and, as a consequence, stereotypical thinking, is more likely to occur when a perceiver lacks time, cognitive resources and the motivation to think carefully and accurately. While categorical thinking was typically thought to be motivated by people's cognitive 'slothfulness' or laziness, more

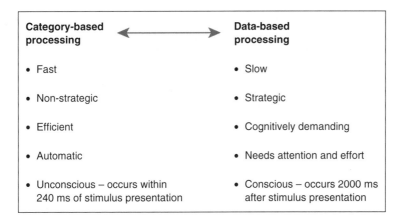

Category-based processing ⟷ Data-based processing	
• Fast	• Slow
• Non-strategic	• Strategic
• Efficient	• Cognitively demanding
• Automatic	• Needs attention and effort
• Unconscious – occurs within 240 ms of stimulus presentation	• Conscious – occurs 2000 ms after stimulus presentation

Figure 3.1   Continuum model of processing (based on Fiske & Neuberg, 1990)

recently it has been argued that categorical thinking is primarily the default option because it is the most cognitively efficient. Not only does categorical thinking facilitate the encoding of category-consistent information in a quick and effortless way, but it also sensitizes the perceiver to any category-inconsistent information. By processing category-consistent information quickly, any spare attentional and cognitive resources can be redirected to unexpected material that is more difficult and time-consuming to process (Macrae & Bodenhausen, 2000; Quinn et al., 2003; Sherman, Lee, Bessenoff & Frost, 1998).

Of course, there are many conditions and factors that determine whether perceivers deploy data-driven strategies as opposed to schema-driven strategies. When there is a strong motivation for accuracy and one is held personally accountable for decisions and outcomes, then people are less likely to rely on stereotypical impressions (Fiske, 1998). What is clear is that in-depth processing requires attention and effort whereas category-based processing is automatic and sometimes unconscious. For example, the time and effort we spend forming impressions of others depends very much on their relative importance to us, and our motivation in 'getting to know' them. Everyday superficial encounters often do not require us to go much further than to base our impressions of others around people's salient social group memberships, such as gender, race, age and occupation. Thus, social categorization is always the initial step in impression formation. Social categories access for the individual a range of preconceptions or stereotypes which are linked to the category. The individual may move beyond this stereotypic content if the target person's behaviour is in some respects ambiguous, incongruent with expectations, or there is a strong motivation for accuracy. This latter approach is argued to lead to a more detailed and individuated knowledge of the person (Fiske, Lin & Neuberg, 1999; Fiske & Neuberg, 1990).

Schemas/categories are evaluative and affective Since Zajonc (1980) argued for the distinctiveness of affect and cognition as separate systems, there has been increasing interest among social psychologists in the affective dimension in information-processing models. After all, one of the reasons why research on stereotypes is so prolific is because of the highly evaluative (prejudicial) consequences of stereotyping people, especially those from minority groups.

Conceptually, at least, schemas represent normative structures and thus provide a basis for evaluating one's experience. Importantly, this normative function can also access a rapid, almost automatic, affective or evaluative reaction to incoming information. Fiske's (1982) work on schema-triggered affect is central here. Fiske argues that some schemas or categories are characterized by an affective/evaluative component, and that when an instance is matched against a category, the affect/evaluation stored within the structure is cued. So, for example, we may experience automatic negative arousal at the sight of a prototypical politician, or fear and anxiety in the presence of a dentist. There is no doubt that many racial categories have a strong affective component, so that the mere sight of a person from a particular group may trigger emotions like fear and suspicion and evaluative judgements which are negative and derogatory.

Fiske argues that affect and evaluation may not be determined in a piece-meal online fashion, but may be accessed rapidly via their associative links to the category as a whole. Thus:

> affect is available immediately upon categorization, so evaluations and affect are cued by categorization, that is, by fitting an instance to a schema. In this view, a perceiver first comprehends an input, by assimilating it to an existing knowledge structure, and then evaluates the instance on the basis of the affect linked to the schema. (Fiske, 1982, p. 60)

This rapid affective response does not require an attribute-by-attribute analysis and hence saves time and processing. The category label is theorized to have an 'affective tag', which is the average or sum of the affective tags associated with the constituent attributes at the lower levels of the category. Thus an affective or evaluative response can be made without necessary reference to the lower-level attributes (Fiske & Pavelchak, 1986), provided, though, that the categorized instance is a good match to the category.

Schemas/categories are organized hierarchically Consistent with the work by Rosch and her colleagues on natural object categories, social schemas are theorized to be hierarchically structured with more abstract and general categories of information at the top of a pyramid structure and more specific categories at the bottom. This enables the person to move from the concrete instance to a more general level of inference. Thus information can be processed at different levels of abstraction as one moves through the category structure. Different schemas can also be linked to one another in a hierarchical manner where higher-order schemas subsume more concrete, lower-order ones. However, a strict hierarchical structure for organizing information is not the only way to structure social information. Structures which are simplistically linear or a complex web of associations also may be used. Social event schemas, for example, are comprised of action scenes which are organized in a temporal fashion. This temporal organization reflects the goal-directed nature of the behaviour contained within the event schema (Schank & Abelson, 1977). Many everyday events, such as seeing a doctor, attending a party, or cooking a meal, are highly consensual 'scripts' which organize behaviour in a temporal sequence. Inferences and predictions about future and intended behaviour are often predicated on the temporal actions contained within event schemas.

How a schema is organized structurally, therefore, depends upon its content and also on the degree of personal knowledge and relevance associated with the content. As with natural object categories, Cantor and Mischel (1979) found that middle-level categories in person taxonomies (for example, comic joker) are richer in information than are superordinate categories (extroverted person) and contain less overlap with objects in related categories (circus clown). In turn, schemas based on role stereotypes are much richer and more complexly organized than schemas based on trait prototypes (Andersen & Klatzky, 1987). The former are characterized by a more complex network of associative links. Social stereotypes are therefore better articulated and are more predictive knowledge structures than are trait prototypes. Information processing is also significantly faster for category-based structures than for trait-based structures (Andersen, Klatzky & Murray, 1990).

Like natural object categories, social stereotypes have been found to be differentiated into lower-order subcategories or subtypes. If you were asked to think of the 'typical' woman, and to list the characteristics and behaviours which come to mind, this would not be such an easy task. A superordinate category such as 'woman' may comprise a number of subtypes such as career woman, housewife, mother, feminist, etc. Listing the prototypical features of

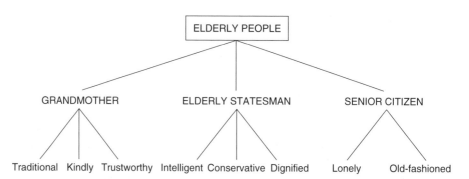

**Figure 3.2   The social category 'elderly people' differentiated hierarchically
into lower-order subtypes that are associated with distinctive personality traits
(adapted from Brewer, Dull & Lui, 1981)**

these subtypes is considerably easier than attributing characteristics to a much broader category. Brewer, Dull and Lui (1981) found this to be the case among young people's representations of the elderly. As Figure 3.2 demonstrates, the elderly category was differentiated further into three elderly subtypes, the 'senior citizen', the 'elderly statesman' and the 'grandmotherly' type. Each of these subtypes was associated with distinctive characteristics and traits. For example, at least half of the sample described the 'grandmotherly' type as helpful, cheerful and kindly, whereas the 'elder statesman' was described as intelligent, dignified and conservative.

The origins and development of schemas/categories: where do categories come from?
Schemas are learned or are acquired over time from direct and indirect experience of the social environment (Anderson & Lindsay, 1998). Through experience, we are said to build up a large repertoire of schemas (Rumelhart, 1984). Fiske and Dyer (1985) argue that schema development proceeds from an initial learning of a number of independent and unintegrated components to a single and integrated schematic unit with strong associative links between the components. These associative links become strengthened through experience and use, so that the entire structure is activated by triggering any of its components. So, for example, a young child's developing gender schema for 'female' in the first 18 months of life may begin with isolated and unintegrated bits and pieces of information and observations like girls play with dolls and are dressed in pink. Other features are added to this with experience and age, such as the genital characteristics of females, expected behaviour, preferred activities and interests and occupational preferences. Over time these different dimensions become integrated to such an extent that

when the 'female' gender category is used, all of the associated links in the structure are automatically activated.

As they develop, categories also become richer and more complex, containing more dimensions and detail. Well-developed and highly complex categories are also more likely to incorporate exceptions or contradictions. For example, it has been found that people who have highly expert political schemas are more likely to notice and tolerate ambiguities and information which is inconsistent with the schema (Fiske, Kinder & Larter, 1983). Similarly, children's gender schemas become less rigid during middle childhood when they realize that gender stereotypes are culturally relative (Huston, 1983). In short, with experience, categories become more organized and detailed, but also more flexible in accounting for contradictions. In other words, with experience schemas become more accurate and reflective of the complexity of social reality (Fiske & Taylor, 1991).

Schema/category stability and change Generally, it has been assumed that social schemas, once developed and strengthened through use, are stable and static structures. As a unified structure, a schema is activated as a unitary whole, even when only one of its components is accessed (Fiske & Dyer, 1985). In fact, research has indicated that well-developed schemas generally resist change and continue to exist even in the face of inconsistent and contradictory evidence. This is especially the case for strongly entrenched social stereotypes. A chauvinist's well-developed stereotype that women are inferior is rarely convinced otherwise even when confronted with evidence to the contrary.

There are conditions, however, when well-established schemas such as stereotypes are forced to change. If a person is confronted with many disconfirming instances of the stereotype, or if experience suggests that the schema is ceasing to be functional and adaptive, then changes and accommodations may be made. Weber and Crocker (1983) describe three possible models of schema change. The first is the bookkeeping model (Rumelhart & Norman, 1978), which suggests that people fine-tune the schema with each piece of information. Information contradicting the schema will lead to small gradual changes, but the experience of many contradictions and extreme deviations will lead to considerable change to the schema. The second is the conversion model, which argues that while minor inconsistencies are tolerated, schemas can undergo dramatic and sudden change in response to salient instances which clearly disconfirm the schema (Rothbart, 1981). Finally, the subtyping model suggests that disconfirming instances of the schema are relegated to subcategories. This model recognizes the hierarchical structure of schemas, characterized by the presence of more general and superordinate categories at the top, with more concrete and specific subcategories (types) at the bottom. Thus a schema can be differentiated hierarchically by the development of sub-types which accommodate exceptions to the schema, but by and large leave the overall schema intact. This model is therefore one which emphasizes the maintenance and perseverance of schemas rather than schema change (Weber & Crocker, 1983).

In a series of experiments Weber and Crocker (1983) attempted to differentiate the conditions under which stereotype change was most likely to occur. Their research provided most support for the subtyping model of schema change and some, though limited, evidence for the bookkeeping model. Little evidence was found for any dramatic change in the face of concentrated disconfirming instances, suggested by the conversion model.

In an interesting real-world study of stereotype change, Hewstone, Hopkins and Routh (1992) evaluated secondary-school students' representations of the police after a one-year implementation of a police–schools liaison programme. To improve relations and increase contact between young people and the police, a programme was introduced in which a police liaison officer was assigned to a particular school. Hewstone et al. (1992) found that the concentrated exposure and contact with the police liaison officers did little to change the students' stereotypes of the police. The liaison officers were, however, evaluated more favourably than the police in general but were also judged to be *atypical* of the group. Indeed, in a similarities rating task, students differentiated the school police officer from other police categories, such as a foot patrol officer and a mounted police officer. Furthermore, they tended to view the school police officer as sharing characteristics with other helping professionals such as teachers and social workers. In contrast, the other police categories tended to be perceived as relatively similar and to share characteristics with law and order professionals such as lawyers, shop security guards and traffic wardens. Again, what this real-world research suggests is that people who are exposed to and come into contact with individuals who disconfirm a group stereotype are less likely to change their stereotype of the group and are more likely to subtype the individual. Thus by isolating disconfirming instances, the stereotype remains intact.

Hewstone and his colleagues have found further support for the subtyping model (Hewstone, Johnston & Aird, 1992; Johnston & Hewstone, 1992), though importantly they have also found that the amount and kind of stereotype change which takes place depends on the variability of the social group in question. Concentrated salient instances which contradict a stereotype are more likely to bring about stereotype change for social groups which are perceived to be homogeneous rather than heterogeneous. Disconfirming instances in the latter are more likely to be absorbed or tolerated because variability is expected. In contrast, because homogeneous groups are perceived as less variable, any instances which disconfirm expectations are more likely to be noticed and given more weight. This suggests that stereotype change is more likely to occur for homogeneous groups under concentrated conditions. However, while Hewstone, Johnston and Aird (1992) found evidence suggesting that disconfirming evidence was more likely to be noticed in homogeneous compared to heterogeneous groups, this did not result in significant stereotype change. Thus there is a strong tendency to treat stereotype-inconsistent information, especially if extreme, as an isolated case. This may explain the oft-quoted lament by social psychologists that, despite interventions, social stereotypes are extraordinarily resilient and continue to persist (e.g., Lippmann, 1922).

Control and automaticity in social perception

Perhaps the most significant development in social cognition research over the last decade has been the study of control and automaticity in social perception (Wegner & Bargh, 1998). Indeed much of this research has been applied to the activation of categories and stereotypes in social perception, although as we will see in other chapters it has also been applied to concepts such as attitudes and causal attributions. Prominent researchers in this field have increasingly argued and sought to demonstrate empirically that perception and behaviour that is 'mindless' – that is, which occurs spontaneously beyond an individual's awareness, and is unintentional or uncontrollable – constitutes a significant part of our everyday functioning. Social psychological processes, which occur automatically and outside conscious awareness, do so through repetition and practice (Smith, 1998). Central to the automaticity literature is the guiding principle that humans will engage in conscious deliberate processing – processing that is effortful and intentional – only if they have to. The default option is to engage in categorical thinking that utilizes heuristic short cuts and stereotypic expectancies. Indeed, some researchers (e.g., Bargh, 1997) have argued that this kind of mindless and stereotypic thinking is inevitable and that perceivers have to work extremely hard to control the expression of categorical thinking. Bargh has coined phrases such as the 'cognitive monster of stereotyping' (Bargh, 1999) and the 'unbearable being of automaticity' (Bargh & Chartrand, 1999) to indicate the extent to which human thought and behaviour is dictated and governed by automatic processes. Indeed, Bargh (1997) claims that up to 99.44 per cent of our thoughts and actions are automatically driven! As we will see, though, there are other researchers who have challenged this view and have demonstrated that categorical and stereotypic thinking is far from inevitable.

Given the limits to what we can attend to among the complex array of social stimuli that we are confronted with in everyday life, Wegner and Bargh (1998) argue that there are four kinds of information that are 'most favoured' or have 'privileged access to our mind':

1. information about the self;
2. information that is frequently experienced or that we frequently think about such as attitudes and values that are important to us or define who we are;
3. negatively valued social behaviour; and
4. social category information.

The first three of these are dealt with in subsequent chapters on attitudes, self and identity, and prejudice. We deal with the last feature here.

Category activation   One of the enduring enigmas in social cognition research is that in everyday social perception people can be categorized in multiple ways; the same person can be categorized as a woman, as black, as a lawyer, as a mother, as a feminist, etc. What determines what category gets activated in the process of person perception and, indeed, whether the activation is unconditionally automatic? As we have already mentioned, Fiske (1999) suggests that age, gender and race are the three major categories that dominate person perception. Once a category is activated, knowledge and content stored in long-term memory associated with that category are also activated. It is this content of a category, and its accessibility, that has been used as an index of category activation in numerous social cognitive experiments. These experiments have borrowed the semantic priming methods from cognitive psychology (Neely, 1991) that demonstrated the increased accessibility of semantic associations following the prior presentation of a priming category. So, for example, prior presentation or exposure to the stimulus prime 'woman', should activate and make more accessible typical cognitive associations with the category such as 'feminine', 'soft', 'maternal', 'caring', etc.

Numerous priming studies of this kind have been conducted measuring the heightened accessibility of personality traits commonly associated with social categories. In one of the earliest studies of this kind, Dovidio, Evans & Tyler (1986) presented participants with a primary category label (black or white), followed by a series of personality characteristics that were either stereotypic or non-stereotypic of the priming category (e.g., musical, ambitious). Respondents were required to indicate as quickly as possible whether the trait could ever be descriptive or true of the primed category. Response times indicated that participants responded significantly faster when stereotypic, rather than non-stereotypic, items were preceded by the priming label. For example, participants responded significantly faster when the category 'white' was paired with 'ambitious', than when it preceded the word 'musical'. While this demonstrated the heightened accessibility of the categorical representation via the use of category primes, it did not demonstrate conclusively that category activation was automatic – that it was unconscious, unintentional and uncontrollable. Participants were made *explicitly aware* of the priming stimulus they were to judge. Automatic processing is usually evidenced in the absence of explicit attention being drawn to the primes by the requirements of the experimental task. Furthermore, the prime was presented for 2000 ms, followed by a blank screen for 500 ms before the target trait word appeared. This lengthy level of exposure would have easily allowed for controlled processes to kick-in.

More recent priming experiments have attempted to meet such requirements by obscuring the relationship between the category prime and target stimuli. This has been achieved either by presenting the priming stimuli below the threshold for conscious detection, usually for less than 200 ms, or by framing the task instructions in such a way as to conceal the association or relationship between the items. Many of these studies have indeed demonstrated that when the triggering stimulus is outside conscious awareness or appears irrelevant to the task at hand, perceivers are unable to avoid category activation – the associated cognitive representation in memory is inevitably triggered and activated. This has led to the rather pessimistic view that category-based processes such as stereotyping are cognitively inevitable, and that everyone is subject to the automatic activation of stereotypes.

Is stereotyping inevitable? As should be clear by now, social cognition models treat stereotyping as a cognitive process that is inextricably tied to categorization. Devine's (1989a) research was one of the first, and is among the best-known, studies to claim to demonstrate that all (American) people know the negative stereotype of African Americans, and automatically activate it when confronted with stereotype-related or group-related stimuli, even unconsciously. Knowledge and activation of the stereotype are the same for people high or low in prejudice. Devine argued that because stereotypes are learned early in life they become strongly ingrained and established in our memories. These consensual and well-learned knowledge structures are automatically activated in the mere presence of a member of the target group. During conscious processing, however, Devine found that low-prejudice people inhibit the negative stereotype of African Americans and replace these with their egalitarian beliefs and norms. In contrast, high-prejudice people do not inhibit the stereotype, because it is consistent with their beliefs about the group. Devine therefore argued that there was a *dissociation* between unconscious and conscious processing of stereotypes. At the unconscious level, the unintentional activation of the stereotype is equally strong for high- and low-prejudice people. In contrast, at the conscious and controlled level, low-prejudice people are able to inhibit the further activation of the stereotype as they replace this with their beliefs, thereby minimizing prejudicial or discriminatory judgement or behaviour toward the group.

Devine's research has become influential and widely cited. However, other research questioning the methodological adequacy of Devine's research found evidence contrary to Devine's dissociation model. For example, in an Australian study, Locke, MacLeod and Walker (1994) used more stringent methodological requirements for determining automatic and controlled processing, and found that only high-prejudice people automatically activated the stereotype, and that this stereotypic content also dominated their conscious processing. In contrast, low-prejudice people did not have the stereotype automatically activated, and thus did not need to inhibit it during conscious processing. Locke et al.'s research indicated that people's general attitudes (in this case, their prejudice levels) determined whether or not stereotyping was automatically activated. Similarly, in a study that primed the stereotype of African Carribean people living in Britain, Lepore and Brown (1997) found that only high-prejudice people activated the stereotype after having the category label 'Blacks' primed. These studies together suggest that high- and low-prejudice people are therefore distinguishable at the automatic level as well as at conscious levels of processing, and that 'bigots' and 'egalitarians' must hold different representations in memory about members of stigmatized groups. As Monteith, Sherman and Devine (1998) have suggested, years of practising the conscious inhibition of stereotypic beliefs by low-prejudice people may render these inhibitory processes automatic, so that stereotypic thinking is no longer activated.

Another factor that has been found to moderate or influence the automatic activation of categories and stereotypes is the perceiver's temporary processing of motivational goals. For example, in a series of experiments Blair and Banaji (1996) first found that gender stereotypes could be automatically activated when primes were presented below the level of conscious awareness. That is, participants responded faster to gender stereotypic than counter-stereotypic prime-trait pairings. Having established this baseline condition for automatically activating gender stereotypes, Blair and Banaji wanted to see whether this effect could be moderated or overcome by perceivers' intentional strategies. In a second study, half of their participants were instructed to expect stereotypic prime associations, whereas the other half was told to expect counter-stereotypic primes. Results indicated that at automatic levels of processing (i.e., under high cognitive constraints), participants with a counter-stereotype strategy produced significantly lower levels of priming than did participants with a stereotype strategy, indicating that the former were able to moderate their response under automatic conditions.

Similarly, Macrae, Bodenhausen, Milne, Thorn and Castelli (1997) found that automatic category activation and stereotyping do not occur under conditions in which the social meaning of a target is irrelevant to a perceiver's current information-processing concerns. Thus perceivers' intentions, motivations and goals appear to have important moderating effects on the automatic activation of stereotyping in everyday social judgement.

In summary, recent research has added important caveats to the thesis that stereotyping is inevitable and is in keeping with the shift away from the view that humans are cognitive misers, and towards a view that we behave more like motivated tacticians – engaging in automatic processing when there is little at stake, and controlled processing when the stakes are high (Chaiken & Trope, 1999). We return to this issue in Chapter 7 on prejudice.

Behavioural effects   While many studies have investigated the effects of stereotyping on social judgements, several studies have instead investigated the *behavioural* influences of stereotypes. In one experiment, Bargh, Chen and Burrows (1996) had participants complete a scrambled sentence task. Half of the participants unscrambled sentences that contained words related to the stereotype of the elderly (e.g., bingo, conservative). They found that the nonconscious activation of the elderly stereotype caused their participants to walk more slowly down the hall after finishing the experimental session compared to those who did not have the stereotype activated! That is, they behaved more in line with the stereotype of the elderly – slow and weak. Similarly, Dijksterhuis and van Knippenberg (1998) found that participants who were primed with the stereotype of a 'professor' performed significantly better in a game of Trivial Pursuit compared to participants who were primed with the stereotype of a 'soccer hooligan'. It is findings such as these, in experiments where participants are both unaware of the stereotype that is primed and have no idea that the two tasks are related in any way, that have led Bargh to conclude that stereotyping is inevitable and unavoidable in all of us – that we are all subject to *implicit* stereotyping in everyday life (Greenwald & Banaji,

1995). Moreover, such stereotypes not only influence our judgements and attitudes, but can also influence our behaviour. Chen and Bargh (1997) argue that perhaps the most insidious and pernicious consequences of such implicit stereotyping are in automatic behavioural confirmation effects (Snyder & Swann, 1978). Negative stereotypes may produce in the perceiver the very behaviour that is expected of a stigmatized outgroup member. If the outgroup member then reciprocates this behaviour (e.g., hostility, fear), the perceiver, having no explicit awareness of their own behaviour, attributes the negative behaviour to the outgroup member and not to themselves.

The limitations of automaticity research One of the most significant problems with the automaticity research is that it has relied almost exclusively on the use of verbal stimulus materials or category labels to study the activation of categorization and stereotyping. In everyday life and interaction, however, this is certainly not the case. Encounters with real people and real interactional contexts comprise a complex and dynamic display of visual and contextual cues. While categorization and stereotyping may be automatically primed through the use of verbal labels, there is no direct evidence to suggest that this is the case in 'real' encounters with people (Macrae & Bodenhausen 2000). Indeed, a recent study by Livingston and Brewer (2002) found that the 'black' stereotype was not automatically activated when black faces were used as experimental stimuli rather than a verbal label. Presumably more realistic and meaningful experimental stimuli should produce automatic stereotyping if this is a robust effect in the real world of everyday social perception and interaction. Even if we accepted automaticity effects produced in laboratory settings to be relatively reliable, there is still the important reservation that there is very little at stake for participants when participating in laboratory experiments utilizing these priming methods. In the real world of people and interpersonal encounters there is often very much at stake; motivational goals are likely to play a significant role in shaping our judgements, feelings and behaviours. We have already detailed above how such motivational goals are important in moderating automatic effects. In the laboratory there is very little at stake; there are no serious consequences for participants in activating stereotypes or making stereotypical judgements.

Of course, a perennial problem in such research is that in real encounters, and in the absence of verbal labels to dictate which category to activate, which category does the perceiver choose to activate among all the potential possibilities: race, age, gender, occupation, etc.? In one ingenious experiment, Sinclair and Kunda (1999) found that when participants received favourable feedback from a black doctor, trait words associated with the category 'black' were significantly less accessible than associations with the category 'doctor' compared to those who received negative feedback or no feedback at all. Thus when a black doctor had praised them, participants inhibited the category 'black' and activated the category 'doctor'. In contrast, participants who received negative feedback were more likely to activate the category 'black' than the category 'doctor'. Thus, once again, motivational goals feature as centrally important in this process, and strategically influence which categories get activated.

Social Identity Theory and Social Perception

As we have documented above, social cognitive models regard social categorization as emerging and developing from a fundamental cognitive need to simplify an overly complex social world. By categorizing individuals into their respective group memberships we are able to simplify reality and thus render it more intelligible. Moreover, this functional cognitive need to categorize is inextricably linked to stereotyping. As generalized descriptions of a group and its members, stereotypes are said to emerge inevitability and automatically from the categorization process. In sharp contrast to this perspective, social identity theory, and its corollary self-categorization theory, treats social categorization not as a process that simplifies perception, but as one that enriches and elaborates upon social perception. Stereotypes too are viewed as cognitive representations that enhance rather than simplify social perception.

Categorization enriches rather than simplifies perception

As with all things related to the social identity tradition, this view of categorization emerged from the seminal findings of the minimal group experiments (see Chapter 2 for details). While these experiments clearly showed that categorization into two groups is sufficient to produce intergroup competition, the experiments alone could not provide an adequate explanation of why group membership in and of itself can have this effect. To answer this question, Tajfel and Turner (1979) developed the concept of social identity. They argued that in such experiments participants identify with the minimal categories provided to them by the experimenter. Participants infuse these trivial and threadbare categories with *meaning*. That is, they use these categories to add meaning to the experimental context. Distinguishing themselves from the

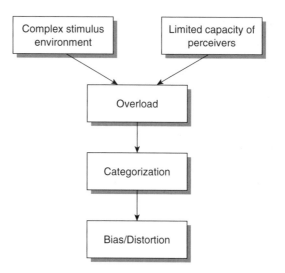

Figure 3.3   A graphic representation of the social cognitive approach to categorization (adapted from McGarty, 1999)

other group was one way in which participants could provide an identity for themselves and others. That is, participants cognitively redefined themselves as group members, perceiving a subjective sense of belonging to this particular group as opposed to the other group. And once a particular group membership becomes significant for self-definition or self-categorization as a group member, people will seek a positive social identity.

In this account of the minimal group findings, one of the central and most important functions of categorization then is to enrich and elaborate upon social perception rather than to reduce or simplify it. As McGarty (1999) makes clear in his systematic review of the categorization literature, there are fundamental differences between social cognition and SIT understandings of what categorization does and how it functions. On the one hand, social cognitive models view categorization as a necessary cognitive process by which information is reduced and simplified so that social perceivers are not overwhelmed with an oversupply of information (see Figure 3.3). In stark contrast, SIT sees categorization as a sense-making activity, which requires perceivers to bring to the fore their background knowledge and beliefs in order to infuse categories with meaning and relevance. This view of categorization as going beyond the information contained in a stimulus dates back to Bruner's (1957) approach to perception and cognition.

Earlier in this chapter we discussed the continuum model of perception and its central assumption that categorical perception compared to individuated perception is fast, requires few cognitive resources and is less cognitively demanding. Linked to this assumption, of course, is that categorical perception is less accurate and even distorting in comparison to a more individuated and piecemeal approach. This view that social categories *distort* or *bias* perception, and that perceiving people as individuals rather than group members is more accurate, is completely rejected by SIT and SCT (Oakes and Haslam, 2001). As we will detail below, stereotypes and stereotyping are given a whole new meaning from this intergroup perspective.

Stereotypes as psychologically valid representations

Despite the pragmatic concessions that social cognitive models make for categorical perception and stereotyping – that given our limited cognitive capacities and an overwhelming stimulus world, categorical perception is pragmatically useful and, in some contexts, even necessary – social cognitive researchers also lament some of the cognitive consequences associated with categorical perception. Stereotyping, for example, is assumed to be a bad thing because *ipso facto*, it entails *biased* perception. Oakes, Haslam and Turner (1994) provide a very different analysis of stereotyping based on self-categorization theory. This approach views stereotyping as a cognitive and psychological process that serves to orient people towards the 'actualities of group life' (Oakes et al., 1994, p. 155). Their central thesis is that group-based perception is just as cognitively and psychologically valid as individual-based perception. These authors argue that social-cognitive accounts are infused with an individualist assumption that person perception is more accurate, valid and meaningful than perception based on social group membership: that is, the 'psychological reality' of the group is absent from such accounts. Oakes et al. (1994) argue that *all* perception, including group-based, person-based and self-based perception, is relative, and involves the dual cognitive processes of categorization and stereotyping. The 'psychological reality' of group life, and the material and social intergroup relations existing within society at any particular point in time, are 'apprehended' through both categorization and stereotyping. In their own words:

> Categorization itself elaborates rather than reduces the information available in a stimulus. It is the crucial process which brings together our general understanding of and theories about the world on the one hand, and the material reality in which we live on the other. (Oakes et al., 1994, p. 113)

Stereotyping is associated with the perception, construction, and use of social categories, which can range in their degree of inclusivity from self, through interpersonal categories, to larger social aggregates. Given the social and material 'reality' of group life, it is argued that the process of stereotyping is psychologically valid and veridical. Effects such as the accentuation of ingroup similarity and the exaggeration of intergroup differences reflect the reality of intergroup relations. Rather than being prejudiced, stereotypic perception is therefore seen to be 'psychologically rational, valid and reasonable, that it provides veridical social perception (i.e., it reflects reality accurately)' (Oakes et al., 1994, p. 187). Social identity and self-categorization theorists question the robustness of cognitive phenomena which social cognitivists have linked to stereotyping, such as illusory correlations (Hamilton, 1979) and the outgroup homogeneity effect (Mullen & Hu, 1989), arguing that these effects are context bound and involve identification and motivational factors when intergroup social comparisons are made (see also McGarty, 1999).

Whereas social cognitive accounts conceptualize stereotypes as rigid, stored mental schemas with fixed and invariable content, waiting to be 'activated', self-categorization theory predicts that the process of stereotyping itself, and the content of stereotypes are fluid, dynamic, and context-dependent. The group is always defined in terms of a specific social relational context. This context will determine the nature of self–other comparisons that are made and will reflect the relative relations between a particular ingroup and outgroup. Specifically, the content and valence of a particular stereotype at a particular time is firmly related to the nature of the intergroup context in which that stereotype is embedded, and is thus always variable and flexible.

A series of studies by Haslam and his colleagues (Haslam & Turner, 1992, 1995; Haslam, Turner, Oakes, McGarty, & Hayes 1992) demonstrate this quite neatly. The study by Haslam et al. (1992) collected data at the start and end of the first Gulf War in 1991. Australian participants were asked to indicate what they thought 'Americans' are like, in a frame of reference that encouraged comparisons either with the Soviet Union or with Iraq. When compared with judgements made with no comparative framework, Americans were seen as aggressive in comparison to the Soviets, but less aggressive in comparison to Iraqis. Americans were seen as more arrogant than Iraqis at the start of the war, but less at the end of the war. These changes, which echo similar changes in the stereotypes of Japanese and Germans held by Americans before, during and after the Second World War (Gilbert, 1951), cannot be explained in a model of stereotypes which holds stereotypes to be fixed 'pictures in the head' of one group held by another. Instead, the content of stereotypes varies according to the intergroup context. SIT holds that the psychological reality of groups (of which stereotypes are part) reflects the intergroup reality of the context. Groups will manoeuvre their perceptions of themselves and of other groups to maximize the psychological contrast between the ingroup and relevant outgroups. This contrast must be on dimensions of importance to the groups themselves – that is, it must fit the normative relations between groups. In these ways, the stereotypes of groups continually vary depending on the material relations between groups, the fit between dimensions of differentiation and the intergroup context, and the comparative context surrounding each group. As such, stereotype change can occur only when there are objective social changes in intergroup relations.

In a similar vein, Leyens, Yzerbyt and Schadron (1994) argue for the psychological *utility* of stereotyping given the social realities of group life. They advance a social pragmatic view of perception, arguing for the interactional, motivational, and goal-oriented nature of thinking. These factors, together with cultural and naïve theories the social perceiver has about groups, influence and shape the stereotyping process. Like Oakes et al. (1994), these authors stress that social perception is flexible and context-dependent. Depending on the interactional and accuracy goals of the perceiver, people will rely on either categorical or more individuated information to make judgements about others. Categorical judgement is not always the rule, nor is it considered to be less accurate than individuated perception. Categories are 'reservoirs of meanings' (Leyens et al., 1994, p. 205), and stereotypes are 'naïve theories' about groups, which facilitate social perception and interaction. Stereotypes are useful reality-orienting resources that people use selectively when categorical judgement is considered appropriate and socially acceptable. Leyens et al. argue that 'people can't afford ... to do without stereotypes' (1994, p. 1) because they help to organize the social reality of the perceiver. Again, what this approach emphasizes is that, rather than simplifying and distorting perception, categories and their associated stereotypes elaborate and enrich social perception.

The approaches to stereotyping taken both by Oakes et al. (1994) and by Leyens et al. (1994) emphasize the need to distinguish between stereotypes and the process of stereotyping itself. A common theme is that while some stereotypes, as negative representations of particular groups, are 'bad' and should be condemned, stereotyping as a cognitive and psychological process does 'good' and *essential* cognitive work by locating individuals and groups within a society's social matrix. This social pragmatic approach to stereotyping is also shared by social cognitivists such as Susan Fiske, who has increasingly emphasized the pragmatic nature of social cognition – that 'thinking is for doing' (Fiske, 1992). However, even in this approach, thinking is construed primarily as a private activity that is located within the cognitive domain of the individual.

Social Representations and Social Perception

The relationship between the theory of social representations and research in mainstream social cognition has often been alluded to. Indeed, Moscovici's theory has gained some momentum outside Europe with the increasing realization that social representations can add a wider social dimension to social cognition approaches (Deaux & Philogène, 2001). Despite the qualitatively different 'feel' social representations theory and research has to social cognitive research, there are points of convergence and parallels between the two perspectives which are difficult to ignore. Both theories are 'knowledge structure' approaches to social thinking. Like social representations, schemas and categories have been construed as internalized social knowledge which guides and facilitates the processing of social information, and both are conceptualized as memory traces with an internal organizational structure (Fiske & Taylor, 1991; Moscovici, 1981, 1984). Schema research and social representations also emphasize the use of cognitive short cuts, or heuristics, in the processing of social information (Moscovici, 1981, 1984; Nisbett & Ross, 1980). Furthermore, both schemas and representations are conceptualized as affective structures with inherent normative and evaluative dimensions (Fiske, 1982; Moscovici, 1981, 1984). Thus social representations and social schemas as internalized social knowledge have similar processing functions; they are organized and stored in memory and guide the selection, meaning and evaluation of social knowledge.

Although the processing functions of social representations can be incorporated into the information-processing models typical in social cognition research, there are important divergences between the two theories (Semin, 1985). Schema theory, for example, is essentially an information-processing model predominantly studied within an individualistic perspective; the theory of social representations purports to be much more than this. It is a theory which attempts to understand individual social psychological functioning by making links with societal and collective processes The two theories are therefore articulated at different levels of explanation (Doise, 1986). Although there are similarities between social representations and social schema models, they remain at present distinct and different approaches (Moscovici, 1988). Schema theory, and research into categorical thinking in particular, is less inclined to take into account the social, interactive and cultural context within which human cognition takes place. Models central to this work have primarily focused on delineating the *processing* functions of categories and stereotypes, often without due consideration to context or content. For Moscovici, cognitive processes are viewed as being determined by content itself. Thus, social representations act as reference points for the selection, categorization and organization of social information (Semin, 1989).

We will now consider, in turn, a number of points on which the concepts of social schemas and social representations may be compared and contrasted, and show how social representations theory differs in its treatment of shared social knowledge. Given the many points of comparison which can be drawn between the two approaches, we devote more space in our discussion of the social representations perspective to social perception than to the social identity and discursive approaches.

Schemas and representations as theory-driven structures

Within social cognitive models, information processing is conceptualized predominantly as theory-driven. So, too, social representations have been conceptualized as 'theories' which individuals have about the nature of events, objects and situations within their social world. Both theoretical frameworks are concerned with the way in which existing knowledge structures are used to familiarize and contextualize social stimuli.

In social representations theory, anchoring is the process by which the novel or strange is rendered familiar, by comparisons with ordinary categories and classifications. As Billig (1988) points out, the process of anchoring bears strong similarities to information-processing mechanisms associated with schema models. The comparison and categorization of unfamiliar or novel social stimuli to similar categories is therefore an essential processing function of both schemas and representations. As with schemas, representations allow 'something unfamiliar and troubling, which incites our curiosity to be incorporated into our own network of categories and allows us to compare it with what we consider a *typical* member of this category' (Moscovici, 1981, p. 193, emphasis added). What is more, both theories regard the mechanisms of comparison, categorization and classification as universal processes; as inherent and central features of human cognition (Billig, 1988).

Both schema models and social representations theory emphasize how the activation and use of existing knowledge and preconceptions can bias social judgements. Schema models in particular stress how people use schemas to fill in missing information, direct a search for more information or provide the basis for applying short cuts for problem-solving. Similarly for Moscovici, the prototype, which is the basis upon which classifications are made, 'fosters ready-made opinions and usually leads to over-hasty decisions' (1984, p. 32).

Despite these similarities, there are important differences between the two approaches. First, as Billig (1988) has indicated, schema models have treated the processes of classification and categorization as elements of *individual* cognitive functioning. Social representations theory, on the other hand, regards anchoring as a *social* process: categories of comparison are seen as emerging from the social and cultural life of the individual, whose own experience is embedded in the traditions of a collectivity. In contrast, schema models have little to say about where these categories come from, treating them simply as cognitive structures originating and existing inside individuals' heads, not as structures which may reflect an historical and cultural reality.

The process of anchoring, as defined by Moscovici, implies something stronger than merely contextualizing social stimuli in a familiar categorical context. Moscovici seems to imply that objects and ideas are epistemologically located by the process of anchoring. Anchoring actually defines the nature of the stimulus by the process of allocating names and labels. Second, schema theory presupposes a rational view of people as information processors. The errors or biased judgements so typically found in such research are argued to be a result of people applying incorrect laws of judgement or making hasty decisions in the face of little data. Moscovici (1982) has argued that errors or bias are not purely a matter of bad information processing but reflect underlying preconceptions or social representations which lead to these distortions. For example, the so-called 'fundamental attribution error' (Ross, 1977), the tendency to attribute causality to the disposition of the person rather than to situational factors, may not simply be an error of judgement. As we will elaborate further in Chapter 5, its pervasiveness suggests that it is shaped by a strong individualist ideological tradition in western societies, or *social representation* which views the person as being the centre of all cognition, action and process. Thus, Moscovici does not view these errors in simple rationalist cognitivist terms, but as grounded in dominant preconceptions shared by collectivities.

Interesting points of convergence may also be drawn between the research on social representations and the automaticity literature. If social representations are pervasive, collective, and akin to 'common sense', then they are more likely to be activated automatically and to have an effect upon judgement of which the person is essentially unaware. In contrast, information with low cultural salience because of its novelty and distinctiveness is more likely to be data-driven. This tension between theory- and data-driven processing sits easily with Billig's (1988) proposal to look for countervailing cognitive mechanisms in human thought. In particular, the process of anchoring information should be juxtaposed with that of *particularizing* information, where data are treated as different and set apart because they fail to fit familiar categories of use. Billig emphasizes that, while particularization is not ignored by Moscovici (1982), he views it as a process which results from the initial anchoring or categorization of information, not as a process contradictory to anchoring. This is an interesting idea, for it leaves open the possibility of change in representations and may provide the mechanism by which to research the dynamic and changing nature of representations about which Moscovici speaks. The issue of change in representations will be discussed more fully later.

Schemas and representations as memory traces

Like schemas and categories, social representations have been conceptualized as memory traces which facilitate the structuring and recall of complex social information (Moscovici, 1981, 1984). However, little experimental research has been carried out in the representations literature on the recall and processing time of material related to representational structures. Indeed, Moscovici would probably eschew such efforts. While we share some of Moscovici's reservations about the usefulness of such information-processing approaches, research of this nature may none the less prove to be valuable. Experiments on the recognition and processing time of representations may be a useful means by which to identify the pervasiveness of certain representations. Images, values, ideas and categories that are easily recognized and quickly responded to by many people within a group may be a defining characteristic of a social representation. As we have already suggested, social representations are also more likely to be characterized by a certain degree of uncontrolled or automatic processing.

Indeed, it would not require much to reconceptualize cognitive scripts or event schemas as social representations in Moscovici's sense. Cognitive scripts are reliable knowledge structures from which to set goals and anticipate the future precisely because they are consensually based and socially prescriptive. The same could be said for social stereotypes. Social categories and the stereotypes they invoke are social representations, possessing all the features that Moscovici (1981, 1984, 1988) has attributed to representations: they are symbolic, affective and *ideological* representations of social groups within society which are extensively shared and which emerge and proliferate within the particular social and political milieu of a given historical moment. Categories do not simply exist in individuals' heads waiting to be activated. They are socially and discursively constructed in the course of everyday communication. Categories are flexible and dynamic representations that are constructed *in situ*, within a specific relational context at a particular point in time. Moreover, such group representations are viewed as emerging and developing from the social identities that are grounded in group life itself (Augoustinos & Walker, 1998). This point has also been emphasized by the social identity approach to categorization and stereotyping.

Social representations theory insists on the shared, symbolic and collective qualities of social categories. The shared, consensual and collective nature of stereotypes and the social categories upon which they are based were once central and defining features (e.g., Katz & Braly, 1933; Tajfel, 1981a). As Haslam (1997) has argued, this tradition is being eroded by recent cognitive accounts which define stereotypes as individual cognitive constructs residing 'in the minds of individuals' (Hamilton, Stroessner & Driscoll, 1994, p. 298), and 'which need not be consensually shared' (Judd & Park, 1993, p. 110).

Schemas and representations as evaluative and affective structures

We have defined schemas as evaluative and affective structures which, when activated, can access schema-associated feelings and judgements. Similarly, the process of classifying and naming (anchoring) in social representations theory is conceptualized as not only a cognitive process but also an evaluative one. Social categories for Moscovici are inherently value-laden.

> Neutrality is forbidden by the very logic of the system where each object and being must have a positive or negative value and assume a given place in a clearly graded hierarchy. When we classify a person among the neurotics, the Jews or the poor, we are obviously not simply stating a fact but assessing and labelling him [or her], and in so doing, we reveal our 'theory' of society and of human nature. (1984, p. 30)

An important issue is the degree to which affective reactions may be acquired and communicated to others so as to be shared reactions and not only idiosyncratic responses to social events. Nationalism and collective racism are cases in point.

Internal organization of schemas and representations

There are also similarities between schemas and social representations in their structure and function. As with schemas, representations have been theorized to be composed of interdependent and hierarchical elements (Abric, 1984). Whereas schemas are organized around a prototype or exemplar, representations are organized around a nucleus or core. A representation's core provides the affective and cognitive basis for understanding new information, for making the strange familiar. Surrounding the core is a host of peripheral elements. While the core is stable and situationally invariant, the periphery is flexible and adapts to varying situational forces. For example, Herzlich's (1973) work on health and illness in French society found the contents of the relevant representation to be structured around a dichotomy between the individual and society. In other work, Wagner, Valencia and Elejabarrieta (1996) showed that there is a 'hot, stable' core of elements defining the meaning of 'war', but that there is no such core for 'peace', arguably because representations arise in response to a threatening phenomenon. Moloney and Walker (2000, 2002) showed that the representation of organ donation has at its core the twin elements of 'gift of life' (which must be understood through its close relationship to 'death') and 'mechanistic removal of body parts'.

A significant difference however between the internal organization of schemas and representations, is the theorized role that contradictory elements play in the internal organization and structure of representations. In their work on organ donation, for example, Moloney and Walker (2000, 2002; Moloney, Hall & Walker, 2005) highlight how the tensions between the twin core elements in representations of organ donation generate change in the representation through time, and also generate orienting responses from people when confronted with challenging situations (e.g., imagining the brain death of a loved one). This contradiction fits neatly with Billig's (1988) suggestion that the major task of social representations research is to look for countervailing and dilemmatic themes. In contrast, schemas are theorized to be internally consistent, and thus lack the contradictory, dilemmatic, and dialectical properties of representations. Thus, schemas can change only in response to new information confronting or challenging their extant structure or content; representations can change for these reasons, or because internal contradictions produce a dynamism that must be resolved on its own terms.

The origins and development of representations and schemas

Social cognition models say very little about the social origins of schemas and categories. After all, where do such cognitive structures come from? As we have argued throughout, schemas and categories have been conceptualized within an individualistic perspective; that is, schemas are seen as cognitive structures which exist inside individuals' heads. Apart from research on prototypes and highly consensual and unambiguous event and role schemas, little theoretical or empirical work has been carried out to ascertain the degree to which various categories may be shared, or how they may arise from social interaction and communication. For example, Fiske and Dyer's (1985) non-monotonic schema learning model is a highly cognitive account of how schemas develop over time. Notwithstanding the importance of these processes in the acquisition and learning of schemas, they do not convey the social origins of such knowledge. Are any of these knowledge structures shared and, if so, by who? What is the nature of the social distribution of such structures; that is, are there group variations in their content and organization? Although we are told they are derived from experience, we are not told if particular schemas are more prevalent than others, because they are created and permeated by social institutions or widely shared cultural values.

Although the theory of social representations does not say very much about the processes involved in the acquisition and development of representations, it does contrast with social cognition models by categorically placing the study of cognitive structures within a societal and interactional context. The theory stresses that all knowledge is socially constructed by a given collectivity and that the attainment of knowledge is not an individual, internal process but a social interactional one. Developmental studies in the social representations tradition have argued that the child is born into a community which has generated its own ways of understanding and interpreting the world (Duveen & de Rosa, 1992; Duveen & Lloyd, 1990). In the process of socialization the child attains not only the content of this social knowledge, but also the dominant methods of thinking within the community. These are central features of a community's collective memory so that each child does not solely and individually have to solve each problem encountered: solutions and methods are already provided for the child by his or her cultural collectivity (Emler, Ohana & Dickinson, 1990). Thus, social representations originate from social interaction and construct the understanding of the social world, enabling interaction between groups sharing the representation (Duveen & de Rosa, 1992; Moscovici, 1985). The theory's clear imperative therefore is to look for group differences in the content and structure of social knowledge. This imperative is one that is also shared with social identity theory wherein attitudes, beliefs and attributions are treated as group-defining characteristics.

Notwithstanding diversity, social representations theory suggests that with increased social communication and interaction, representations of the social world become more consensual in nature. The extent to which representations are shared or consensual has attracted considerable critical debate within social representations theory (Moscovici, 1985; Potter & Litton, 1985).

There have been some attempts to measure consensus by some researchers but in ways that do not suppress individual variation. For example, several multidimensional scaling studies investigating the development of young people's representations of Australian society have demonstrated that, with increased age, individual variation in these representations decreased considerably (Augoustinos, 1991). Thus although there was not complete consensus, as socialization proceeded from adolescence to early adulthood, societal representations became more consensual and shared. In a similar vein, Hraba, Hagendoorn and Hagendoorn (1989) found that, while there was considerable agreement among respondents regarding the content of the ethnic hierarchy in the Netherlands, suggesting the existence of a shared representation, the form of the hierarchy varied across domains and different contexts of use. Together, these studies suggest that shared representations are not necessarily static structures, but are used in dynamic and flexible ways by different people across different contexts of use. Moreover, Doise, Clemence and Lorenzi-Cioldi (1993) have demonstrated that individuals orient themselves differently in relation to consensual meaning systems: whereas at the collective level social representations function as shared objectified structures, at an individual level there is variability as to how the elements of the representation are framed and articulated.

The stability of schemas and representations

Although some conditions may instigate and facilitate schema change, generally it has been assumed that social schemas, once developed and strengthened through use, are stable and static structures (Weber & Crocker, 1983). Moreover, as unified structures, schemas are activated in their entirety even when only one of their components is accessed (Fiske & Dyer, 1985). In contrast, representations are regarded by Moscovici to be dynamic and changing structures. He refers to the continual renegotiation of social representations during the course of social interaction and communication by individuals and groups. This suggests that such cognitive structures may be context-dependent – changing or being modified by situational constraints, disconfirming experiences, and changing historical representations over time.

Moscovici refers to representations as being imbued with a life force of their own: merging, repelling and interacting with other such structures and, indeed, with individuals and groups, suggesting a certain dynamism and changing quality that is absent from the social schema literature. However, once these structures are transformed into material and objective entities, they are said to become fossilized or static – their origins forgotten, coming to be regarded as common sense. This, of course, bears some similarity to the notion of schematic structures being unified and activated almost automatically through the associative links in the structure. Thus, while both theories suggest that, once developed, these cognitive structures may become resistant to change, they differ in the emphasis they place on the degree to which representations and schemas are flexible and dynamic during the course of their development and contextual use. Furthermore, the social representations literature suggests that, after a period of unquestioning acceptance or fossilization, subsequent sociological or historical forces may act to renegotiate and/or totally transform these structures. Abric (1984) has proposed that a representation may change if there is a radical threat to the central organizing structure of the representation – the nucleus. Change in the meaning and values attached to the peripheral elements will only lead to superficial change, but a transformation in the nucleus will change the whole nature and structure of the representation itself. The study of structure and the stabilizing core of representations may, therefore, be the vehicle by which to study the dynamic processes of evolution and change in representations.

Can social representations and schema models be integrated?

Notwithstanding the substantial epistemological differences between social representations theory and social cognition models, can they none the less be integrated to form a rich and comprehensive theoretical framework in social psychology? There have been conflicting positions regarding the conceptual utility and epistemological desirability of such integration. Allansdottir, Jovchelovitch and Stathopoulou (1993) refer to attempts to integrate social representations theory with traditional and mainstream approaches as 'gluing practices' which threaten to individualize and decontextualize the theory. They argue that many researchers have treated social representations as a 'convenient social package' which can be simply added to traditional notions. Of considerable concern to these authors is the 'statisticalization' of the concept by the use of traditional empirical methods to measure sharedness in representations and in the identification of a 'social representation' – methods such as multidimensional scaling and cluster analysis. As such, they argue: 'The theoretical integrity of the concept is compromised ... it is nominally there, but it cannot speak with its own voice' (Allansdottir et al., 1993, p. 9).

The concerns raised by Allansdottir and her colleagues are perhaps not overstated given the predominance of individualistic conceptual and methodological frameworks within social psychology. There is also little doubt that the use of quantitative techniques does run the risk of objectifying the concept of social representation so that a social representation is merely defined by its consensual nature or clustering structure. However, the notion of sharedness in social representations is central to the theory, and quantitative techniques to measure this, albeit limited, are nevertheless useful. Sharedness is not the sole defining feature of a social representation, but it is an *essential* feature which ought to be detectable using quantitative methods. Other important features need to be considered, such as the centrality of the phenomenon or object in social life, the extent to which it is objectified, and the social functions it serves. A social representation is not based on sharedness alone – not every social object is a social representation. This can be contrasted to schema theory, where a defining feature of a social schema is that it refers to a 'social' object, so that any social object can have its own organizational schema. Likewise, multidimensional and clustering techniques may be useful methodological tools but a social representation should not be equated with an identified cluster or structure alone (Augoustinos, 1993; see also Doise, Clemence & Lorenzi-Cioldi, 1993).

It is clear that quantitative methods are limited in their usefulness for studying the more interactive and dynamic aspects of social representations: how they emerge in the course of everyday conversation, and how they are constituted and transformed through discourse and socio-historical circumstances. As we will see below, such issues have been taken up by discursive psychologists in examining the discursive practices and resources that people use to describe objects and events in the world. Criticisms that social representations theory 'will drift towards cognitive reductionism' (Potter & Billig, 1992, p. 15) because of the cognitivist elements contained within it, have more challenging implications for the theory. Ridding social representations theory of inherent cognitivist traces necessitates denying the role of cognition in the construction of social reality, or, at the every least, remaining agnostic about this. This, of course, raises the spectre of reconceptualizing social representations in non-cognitive terms, such as interpretative repertoires or discursive practices. We now turn to examine how discursive psychology has approached the study of categorization and stereotyping from an explicitly non-cognitive framework.

Discursive Psychology and Social Perception

Thus far we have demonstrated how the use and application of social categories is assumed to be a pervasive cognitive tendency that serves either to simplify an overly complex world (as in the social cognition tradition), or to render it more intelligible (as in the social representations and social identity traditions). Despite some of the negative consequences associated with categorization and stereotyping – consequences such as objectification, distortion, bias, and prejudice (all of which have been lamented by social psychologists) – these dual processes are none the less seen to be cognitively and *pragmatically useful* because they help us to make sense of the world and our own place within it. Discursive psychology introduces yet another perspective to the study of categorization. Although discursive psychology does not deny that people use social categories to talk about the world (clearly they do, and in very interesting and strategic ways), it does challenge the view that social categories are rigid *a priori* cognitive entities. Categories are not treated as cognitive phenomena that are located in people's heads as preformed static structures that are organized around prototypical representations of the category. Rather, discursive psychology emphasizes that people constitute categories discursively in order to do certain things:

> Instead of seeing categorization as a natural phenomenon – something which just happens, automatically – it is regarded as a complex and subtle social accomplishment … this … emphasizes the action orientation of categorization in discourse. It asks how categories are flexibly articulated in the course of certain sorts of talk and writing to accomplish particular goals, such as blamings or justifications. (Potter & Wetherell, 1987, p. 116)

'Categories are for talking'

Although the theoretical approaches we have discussed thus far have a different view on the validity and 'reality-orienting' function of stereotypes, they none the less all share one central assumption – that the social categories upon which stereotypes are based reflect real and valid group entities in the social world. Categories such as man/woman, black/white, young/old, rich/poor, are treated as uncontested and non-problematic social objects, which are perceived directly through identifiable physical and social features. Although social representations and social identity theories are more inclined to emphasize the socially constructed nature of these categories, discursive psychology accuses them too of treating social categories 'as static features of a predefined macro-sociological landscape' (Wetherell & Potter, 1992, p. 74), or as *a priori* reified structures that can be switched on and off.

In contrast, discursive psychology is interested in 'how categories become constructed in different social contexts and how the method of construction creates a subjectivity for oneself and for those defined as Other' (Wetherell & Potter, 1992, p. 74). Categorization is not simply a cognitive, internal process based on direct and veridical perception, but a discursive practice which is 'actively constructed in discourse for rhetorical ends' (1992, p. 77). Edwards describes categorization as '*something we do, in talk,* in order to accomplish social actions (persuasions, blamings, denial, refutations, accusations, etc.)' (1991, p. 517, original emphasis). Some constructions are so familiar, pervasive, even banal, that they 'give an effect of realism' or 'fact'. People therefore come to regard category constructions not as versions of reality, but as direct representations of reality itself. Edwards argues that the experiential basis of categories is what makes them appear to be direct, perceptual and objective descriptions of reality. In this way, experiential realism operates as a rhetorical device in making claims about reality.

From a discursive perspective, the social categories used in talk are expected to be variable, flexible and shifting, depending on their varied functional and contextual uses. Categorization may be inevitable, but there is nothing inevitable about the particular categories, or the content of those categories, that are relied upon in any instance. As we have already emphasized, there are potentially many ways in which a particular person, group or event can be categorized. For example, a woman could be described as a 'girl', a 'lady', a 'female', a 'lawyer', a 'mother', etc. The aim of discursive psychology is to examine how categories are used in specific instances and what interactional or rhetorical work they perform in being used in this way, in this particular instance. Thus categories are treated as discursive resources used in talk to perform social actions. Similarly, categorization is treated as a kind of social practice rather than a cognitive process.

Discursive psychology's approach to categorization has been strongly influenced by Harvey Sacks's (1992) work in ethnomethodology and conversation analysis, which examines how categories are used in naturally occurring conversation and social interaction. This is in stark contrast to the experimental stimuli used in laboratory experiments that seek to understand the assumed perceptual and cognitive processes that underlie categorization and stereotyping. Inside the laboratory social categories are used unproblematically as verbal stimuli in experimental procedures designed to elicit either implicit or explicit evaluative responses, but outside the laboratory, in everyday talk and social interaction, social categories, even seemingly mundane categories, are used in flexible and context-specific ways. This conversation-analytic approach to examining how categories are deployed in everyday talk and what work they perform in social interaction has led to a significant tradition of research known as membership categorization analysis or MCA (Lepper, 2000; Watson, 1997) – a tradition in sociology which has developed largely in parallel to psychological theories of categorization.

So how are categories used in everyday talk? One study, for example, specifically focused on the social category 'Australian Aboriginal', and the contexts in which this category was deployed in discussions of race relations in Australia (Augoustinos, 2001). At face value, this social category hardly seems problematic: it refers to the indigenous peoples of Australia, who are largely regarded as a significant and salient social group within Australian society. Indeed, in most contexts, participants used this category unproblematically in their talk. More specifically, the category 'Aboriginal' was deployed without qualification when discussing the current social problems of Australia's indigenous people. However, when issues such as land rights, Aboriginal self-determination and identity came up, participants problematized the social category 'Aboriginal' by: (a) placing constraints on the definitional boundaries of the category, and (b) questioning the legitimacy of some who claim an Aboriginal identity. What this contextual selectivity demonstrates is the important rhetorical and ideological work that is being accomplished by the use of particular categorizations in different contexts.

One specific way in which participants placed limits on the legitimacy of the category 'Aboriginal' or, alternatively, on the legitimacy of an Aboriginal identity, was in the deployment of a unifying superordinate category and identity, 'Australian'. For example, in discussing race relations, some participants expressed the view that differences between people should be minimized and commonalities be highlighted. This is evidenced in the extract below.

M: [...] I don't know necessarily think that the way to resolve it is for what you were saying, 'you have your land, I'll have my land, let's live separately'. I don't think that's the way to really resolve it. I think I I tend to agree with you that we live in Australia, let's live together =

A: =Yep

M: And be Australians and umm work and work out a good way that we can all live together.

Repertoires of togetherness, the sharing of an Australian national identity, and the rhetoric of commonality, all feature in the above extract. The primacy afforded to a collective Australian national identity works to emphasize the commonality of people living in the same country, while also undermining the legitimacy of any differences that might disrupt this superordinate political goal. This suggestion also works to undermine the political and moral legitimacy of minority groups striving to have their varied social identities recognized and affirmed. In this way, existing differences in culture, socio-political history, and ethnicity can be subsumed (or even negated) by appealing to the nationalist moral imperative that all people living within the nation state adopt a superordinate national identity, that is, to be 'Australian'. Indeed, as Reicher and Hopkins (2001) have demonstrated, the use of national categories in this way is a central feature of nationalist rhetoric and a powerful means by which to mobilize public support for a variety of political projects (see also Reicher & Hopkins, 1996a, 1996b).

Another way in which participants placed definitional boundaries around the social category 'Aboriginal', was to question the legitimacy of categorizing individuals of mixed descent, who lead urban, non-traditional lifestyles, as 'Aboriginal' For example, one student said:

> B: Part of the problem is we don't really have any true Aboriginals any more, they're
>   all half-caste or quarter-caste … that's where you get problems because they've got
>   this conflict. I am Aboriginal but I have a white parent or I come from a slightly
>   white background and then you get this confli confusion.

What we see in this talk is the invocation of the category '*true Aboriginals*' to constrain and problematize the use of a more general category 'Aboriginals': a category that was used quite freely and unproblematically in other contexts by this particular speaker. Implicitly, what is also being problematized is the legitimacy of an Aboriginal identity for those of mixed descent: an issue that has received considerable political attention in Australia. Such discursive analyses therefore demonstrate that, rather than being routine, non-problematic, 'objective' group entities, social categories can be seen to be contingently shaped, strategic constructions serving local ideological and rhetorical ends (see Textbox 3.1).

Textbox 3.1

The politics of categorization: asylum seekers, refugees or illegal immigrants?

Australia's policies towards asylum seekers and their mandatory detention are issues that have generated considerable debate and controversy both within Australia and internationally. On August 26, 2001, this issue received increased international attention when a Norwegian container-shipping vessel called the *Tampa* rescued over 400 asylum seekers from a sinking vessel, but was refused entry into Australian waters by the Australian Government. This event became known as the 'Tampa Crisis' and signalled what was to become an increasingly entrenched position by the Australian Government of refusing entry to 'unauthorized boat arrivals' of people seeking asylum.

(Continued)

Textbox 3.1   (Continued)

Both the Australian Government and the media constructed this issue as a national 'crisis' that threatened Australia's 'border security' and sovereignty. The Government's policies, including the mandatory detention of asylum seekers (women and children included) in detention camps in remote areas of Australia, received majority support from the Australian public.

This issue has all the characteristics of what makes for classic social psychological research: social identity, intergroup relations, stereotyping, outgroup bias, prejudice, persuasion, and social influence are all implicated either directly or indirectly in the Australian public's response to asylum seekers. However, one social psychological construct that became most salient in the unfolding of events surrounding this issue was the nature of the social categories that came to be recurrently deployed to reference asylum seekers in both political rhetoric and media representations.

A variety of social categories were used to refer to asylum seekers, but the most frequently used category by the media and the Government was that of 'illegal immigrants', rather than 'asylum seekers' (to which they are legally entitled under international human rights law). To investigate the consequences that different social categories have for participants' subsequent attitudes and evaluations of the group, Augoustinos and Quinn (2003) designed a study informed by the social constructionist assumptions central to discursive psychology (and, to a lesser extent, social representations theory) but utilizing traditional questionnaire methods.

The study required three different groups of participants to read the same newspaper article that was either about 'asylum seekers', 'refugees', or 'illegal immigrants'. The only thing that varied in the three conditions was the category used to reference the group in question. Subsequent to reading the article, participants in each group were asked to provide their attitudes on several issues pertaining to the rights and treatment of 'asylum seekers/refugees/illegal immigrants' and to evaluate the specified group on a series of trait scales. Consistent with expectations, the study confirmed that different social categorizations elicited different attitudinal judgements. Specifically, participants in the 'illegal immigrant' condition produced the most negative attitudinal judgements. Thus, these results demonstrated that category labels do make a significant difference to people's subsequent evaluations of the group in question. Linguistic categories are therefore exceedingly powerful in constructing objects, people and issues in particular ways.

This study challenges traditional cognitive accounts of categorization that treat it as an innocuous, natural and routine ritual of cognitive life, and demonstrates how social categorization can be a political practice that serves ideological functions. But it does this by using traditional social psychological methods of research – an anathema to discursive psychology and social constructionism more generally.

What do you think? Is it possible to integrate such disparate traditions of research in this way so as to arrive at a better understanding of social perception and experience? Are experimental methods such as these useful in demonstrating how specific words and categories or *discourse* construct particular versions of the world?

Script formulations

We have seen how social cognition research views schemas as mental structures that are learned and generalized over time through direct and indirect experience with social objects. Within this framework, event schemas or scripts are viewed as sense-making templates that describe events, or mental rules that guide human behaviour in specific situations. Like categories, discursive psychology does not treat scripts as cognitive templates, but, rather, as a type of talk or discursive resource that is used to describe events in particular ways – as predictable, routine or as exceptional. Discursive psychology is interested in analysing the specific interactional contexts in which events are described in this way. What are people doing or attending to when they describe events as routine or, contrastively, when they are described as 'out of the ordinary' or departing from expectations? Edwards argues that:

> At stake in such descriptions are the normative basis of actions, and the accountability of the actors. That is to say, moral and normative issues of appropriateness, responsibility, and blame are at stake in how a person's actions or involvement is described. (1997, p. 144)

According to Edwards, one of the important functions of script formulations as descriptions is to project or 'build a picture of what kind of person the actor is – that is, his or her personality, disposition or mental state' (1997, p. 144). Thus script formulations are intricately tied up with dispositions. For example, when people's actions are described as normative and routine in a scripted situation such as eating at a restaurant, dispositional attributions about the actor are less likely to be inferred from the description. However, if someone's behaviour is described as 'abnormal' or highly irregular, then this makes the person's behaviour more morally accountable, providing a basis for making dispositional inferences. So instead of treating scripts as mental representations of actual events, they are seen as descriptions that do important work in everyday talk and conversation: they attend to matters concerning the normativity and moral accountability of the actor. As such, script formulations also perform important interactional and rhetorical work.

Chapter Summary

In this chapter we have examined concepts central to social cognition such as schemas, categories and stereotypes, and have considered how these have been used to understand how people make sense of the social world in organized and systematic ways. Schemas are cognitive structures which organize complex information in a meaningful way so that we can access the information readily when needed. Schemas help us to make sense of the world, they lend structure to our perceptions and experience, and they are stored in memory for later retrieval. These knowledge structures help guide a number of central cognitive processes such as perception, memory, inference and evaluation. Empirical research has primarily focused on person schemas (person prototypes), role schemas (stereotypes), self schemas, and event schemas (scripts). This research is embedded within a cognitive process model which borrows heavily from much of the work in cognitive science. More recent work in this tradition has moved away from the cognitive miser model of social perception to a more pragmatic approach that emphasizes the motivational and goal-oriented nature of thinking. Although the metaphor of the 'motivated tactician' has increasingly replaced that of the 'cognitive miser', the most significant development in this research during the past ten years has been in the area of automatic and unconscious processing, with some researchers claiming that much of our social perception occurs automatically outside conscious awareness.

In contrast to social cognition models that view categorization and stereotyping as 'energy-saving' processes that simplify perception, social identity and self-categorization theories claim that these two dual processes actually enrich and elaborate upon social perception by orienting us to the 'realities' of group life. Instead of viewing stereotypes as threadbare and impoverished representations of reality, this theoretical perspective sees stereotypes and the categories upon which they are based as rich and elaborate 'reservoirs of meaning' that define the social world and our place within it. Social representations theory extends this perspective by asking questions about the content and social origins of such representations. Schemas, categories, and stereotypes are not treated simply as internal cognitive templates, but as shared meaning systems that are shaped by cultural, historical and political factors. Thus, the theory of social representations attempts to understand how people make sense of the social world, but it does this by examining wider societal and social psychological processes. It is, therefore, much more than an information-processing model, articulated at the intrapersonal level of explanation. As we demonstrated in Chapter 2 with the research on social representations of biotechnology, this work does not limit itself to the study of simple cognitive structures, but is predominantly concerned with complex cognitive representations that emerge from the introduction of new ideas and scientific developments in society. As such, it is an ambitious theory which embraces multidisciplinary endeavours. Certainly, the theory of social representations can provide social cognitive processing models with a much needed societal context but, at the same time, 'social representations incontrovertibly partake of the nature of cognitive phenomena – even if certain of their characteristics partially escape being included within their framework' (Codol, 1984, p. 240).

Finally, discursive psychology does not treat social categories and scripts as features of the mind or cognitive states, but as 'topics of talk', as discursive resources that people use 'as part and parcel of talk's practical business' (Edwards, 1997, p. 20). This theme is reiterated in later chapters on attitudes and attributions. Again we see how discursive psychology inverts the traditional reality–cognition relation so that discourse or talk is viewed as primary, and reality and cognition are treated as talk's topics.

Further Reading

Deaux, K., & Philogène, G. (Eds.) (2001). *Representations of the social: Bridging theoretical traditions*. Oxford: Blackwell.

Edwards, D. (1997). *Discourse and cognition*. London: Sage.

Oakes, P. J., Haslam, S. A., & Turner, J. C. (1994). *Stereotyping and social reality*. Oxford: Blackwell.

Quinn, K., Macrae, N., & Bodenhausen, G. (2003). Stereotyping and impression formation: How categorical thinking shapes person perception. In M. Hogg and J. Cooper (Eds.), *The Sage handbook of social psychology* (pp. 87–109). London: Sage.

Wegner, D. M., & Bargh, J. A. (1998). Control and automaticity in social life. In D. T. Gilbert, S. T. Fiske & G. Lindzey (Eds.), *Handbook of social psychology* (Vol. 1, 4th ed., pp. 446–496). New York: McGraw-Hill.

4 Attitudes

Bill Clinton was; George W. Bush isn't. Paul Keating was; John Howard certainly isn't. Tony Blair wishes he were. *Cool* is a highly prized virtue. Indeed, it has replaced goodness, piety and servitude as *the* modern, secular virtue. *Cool* is an attitude of defiance to authority and Puritan traditions; it is a *'permanent* state of *private* rebellion'; it is an unashamed amalgam of 'narcissism, ironic detachment, and hedonism' (Pountain & Robins, 2000, pp. 19 and 26, emphasis in original). Far from being just a contemporary western combination of youthful exuberance and marketing savvy, *Cool* has a long and distinguished heritage over many centuries and continents. It has not, of course, always been known as *Cool*, but the *attitude* of *Cool* is identifiable in many places and in many times. Pountain and Robins' analysis of *Cool* highlights the analytic importance of *Cool* as an attitude. Their treatment of *Cool* is instructive for a social psychological understanding of all that *attitude* means. Pountain and Robins talk of the individual qualities of those labelled as *Cool*, which resemble contemporary social psychological understandings of *attitude*. But they also articulate *Cool's* long history, and its social and political significance. These aspects of *attitude* are often lost in social psychology. In this chapter we try to incorporate both these aspects of *attitude*, and argue for a broad, integrated understanding of what we mean by *attitude*.

What is an Attitude?

In the vernacular, we talk of people 'having' an attitude, sometimes of people 'having attitude', and sometimes even of people having an 'attitude problem'. We talk as though people have an attitude in the same way they have an ear, nose or toe. We confer upon 'attitude' the status of noun, denoting implicitly something real and tangible, something which influences the way the attitude-owner behaves. Indeed, so common is our usage of 'attitude' that the word 'has become almost invisible from familiarity' (Fleming, 1967,

p. 290). We don't stop to think what it is we mean when we so often invoke attitude. But it has not always been so. Fleming (1967) intriguingly traces the concept of attitude from its entry to the English language around 1710, through its use by the sociologist Herbert Spencer and the biologist Charles Darwin, and its use early in the 19th century to refer to a physiological state or physical orientation, to its current meaning. 'Attitude' has not always been a part of the common sense we take it to be now.

The everyday use of 'attitude' is loose. So too in social psychology. Definitions, models and theories of attitudes abound. Although attitudes have been the single most researched topic in social psychology, what is meant precisely by the term is more often than not left tacit, vague and inconsistent. It is useful, therefore, to be clear now about what social psychologists typically mean by 'attitude':

> ... attitudes are defined at least implicitly as responses that locate 'objects of thought' on 'dimensions of judgement'. (McGuire, 1985, p. 239)

and

> ... [an attitude is] a general and enduring positive or negative feeling about some person, object or issue. (Petty & Cacioppo, 1996, p. 7)

Attitudes are therefore first and foremost evaluations. They convey what we think and how we feel about some object, or attitude referent. All attitudes have a referent, an 'object of thought', a 'stimulus object'. Referents may be specific and tangible: George W. Bush, Brussels sprouts, and Jameson's whiskey may each be the object of an attitude. But so too may referents be esoteric, abstract and intangible; liberalism, equality and social psychology are the objects of attitudes as much and as often as are Bush, sprouts and Jameson's. By denoting the attitude-holder's 'orientation' to the referent, an attitude conveys that person's evaluation of the referent. Attitudes are expressed in the language of 'like/dislike', 'approach/avoid' and 'good/bad'; they are evaluative. When the object of the attitude is important to the person, the evaluation of the object produces an affective, or emotional, reaction in that person.

The two definitions above are essentially the same, but include different emphases. Several features are important here. The first is that attitudes have specific referents, and thus will only be relevant when a particular object, person or issue is categorized as being attitude-relevant. Thus the activation of an attitude refers 'to a process with at least some minimal cognitive activity' (Zanna & Rempel, 1988, p. 319). Although Zanna and Rempel take this to mean that attitudes are effortful, there is evidence that the required effort is minimal; so minimal, in fact, that attitudes can be activated and can function automatically. The view of Zanna and Rempel is similar to that of Pratkanis and Greenwald who, in their socio-cognitive model of attitudes, argue that 'an attitude is represented in memory by (1) an object label and rules for applying that label, (2) an evaluative summary of that object, and (3) a knowledge structure supporting that evaluation' (1989, p. 249). The second important feature of an attitude is that it is relatively enduring. Although attitudes can change, as a result of new experience or following some persuasive communication, an attitude is not usually considered to be a transitory evaluation, but rather an expression of a largely stable body of knowledge and experience with a particular object, person or issue.

The dimensions of judgement upon which attitudes fall may be universal or specific, socially shared or idiosyncratic. Some dimensions may apply, or in principle be applicable, to all referents. All referents – Bush, sprouts, Jameson's, liberalism, equality and social psychology – can be placed somewhere on a dimension ranging from bad to good, or from like to dislike. Not all referents, though, can be located on a dimension from stupid to smart, or 'cool' to 'lame'.

Social Cognition and Attitudes

'ABC models' of attitudes

The definition of attitude as evaluation is becoming increasingly common in social psychology, though still not universal. It replaces a previously widespread 'tripartite' definition of attitude: the so-called *'ABC model'* of *attitudes*. Stemming originally from the Yale Communication and Attitude Change Program at Yale University through the 1950s and 1960s, but sharing a fundamental viewpoint with many other philosophical traditions (Hilgard, 1980), the ABC model divides attitudes into three components: affect, behaviour and cognition. For this model, 'attitudes are predispositions to respond to some classes of stimuli with certain classes of responses' (Rosenberg & Hovland, 1960, p. 3). The three major classes of response are cognitive, affective and behavioural. As Figure 4.1 illustrates, cognitive responses to a particular stimulus are the knowledge and beliefs the person has about the stimulus object; affective responses are simply how the person feels about the object; and behavioural responses are simply overt behaviours. The model allows for these three responses to be inconsistent with one another, which is just as well because more often than not they are

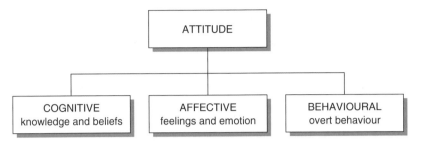

Figure 4.1 Tripartite (ABC) model of attitudes

(e.g., Breckler, 1984; Kothandapani, 1971; Ostrom, 1969). The degree of discrepancy between empirical measures of the three presumed components of the same attitude held by one person towards a single object is usually so large that the tricomponent model has largely been dismissed (e.g., Eagly & Chaiken, 1993; Pratkanis, 1989). And furthermore, by defining behaviour as a *component* of attitude, the problem of any putative relationship between attitude and behaviour is simply defined away. This is not a helpful resolution of one of social psychology's major perennial problems – do attitudes predict behaviour? We consider the problematic relationship between attitudes and behaviour later in this chapter.

How are attitudes organized?

Attitudes are conceptualized as having a definite structure. Eagly and Chaiken (1998) distinguish between the structure that derives from the relationships between the affective and cognitive (and perhaps behavioural) components of a particular attitude – the *intra-attitudinal structure* – and the structure that exists across attitudes and that organizes the associations between attitudes to a range of different attitude objects – the *inter-attitudinal structure*. Additionally, the concept of attitudes as knowledge structures (or schemas) gives rise to important properties of attitudes, including their accessibility and potential for automatic activation. In this section we consider the properties of attitudes that derive from their structure.

In many ways an attitude is like a schema (see Chapter 3), except that an attitude has the *evaluation* of that referent as its defining and central element. Three aspects of attitudes deriving from their structure as schemas have been considered particularly important: the *accessibility* of attitudes, the *activation* of attitudes, and the possibility of *ambivalent* attitudes.

Accessibility of attitudes   Some attitudes come to mind more easily than others. As it does with most cognitive constructs, social psychology distinguishes between the *availability* of an attitude and its *accessibility* (Higgins, 1996a). An attitude is said to be *available* if it exists within a person's cognitive structure; that is, if the person actually possesses that attitude. Attitude *accessibility* reflects the ease with which a particular attitude may be retrieved from memory (Fazio, 1989), and is usually operationalized as the speed with which the attitude can be accessed. The accessibility of an attitude at any given time is affected by structural properties of the attitude (attitude strength) and aspects of the context that serve to 'prime' particular attitudes as being relevant to that context. Accessibility is an important property of attitudes, because accessible attitudes govern behaviour more strongly than do less accessible attitudes (e.g., Fazio & Williams, 1986).

Most of the enduring differences between people in the accessibility of particular attitudes are considered to be due to the *strength* of their attitudes. An attitude is said to be strong if there is a consistent, well-rehearsed link between an attitude object and its evaluation. So if someone thinks about John Howard regularly, and each time evaluates John Howard in a moderately negative way, that person will be said to develop a strong attitude towards John Howard. Note that the strength of an attitude does not refer to its extremity (i.e., the degree of positivity or negativity in the evaluation), but rather to the frequency and consistency of its expression. To the extent that the association between an object and its evaluation is well developed through repetition in strong attitudes, strong attitudes are more accessible (more easily and more quickly activated) than weaker attitudes (Krosnick, 1989), and thus more influential on behaviour.

Not all our attitudes are active at any one time. It almost goes without saying that only a small set of our repository of attitudes is active at any given moment. Attitudes must be *activated,* or turned on, somehow. The process of *attitude activation* has received considerable research attention. Much of this work has drawn from principles of cognitive psychology. Attitudes are conceived of as nodes in memory, connected in an associative network. Nodes are activated when we categorize some experience in terms of them, and multiple nodes become connected through experiences of co-activation (such as 'kitten' and 'cute', or 'reality television' and 'dull'). The more frequently any connection is experienced the stronger that connection becomes. Drawing explicitly on this associative network model of attitudes, Fazio (1989) argues that an attitude is an association between a referent (object, person, issue) and its subjective evaluation. Thus, noticing an object in the environment and categorizing it as an instance of a particular type of object activates the node corresponding to that type of object in memory. Following this intial activation, activation will 'spread' from the object node to the evaluation node associated with it, in proportion to the strength of the association. When the association between the object and its evaluation is strong enough, simply noticing the object will cause the evaluation to become activated (Fazio, Sanbonmatsu, Powell & Kardes, 1986).

Automatic and implicit attitudes   Some connections become so well rehearsed that when one node is activated, the other is *automatically* activated. Automatic activation is said to occur if merely thinking about or noticing the attitude object produces the evaluation of that object even if evaluation of the object is not intended at that time (Bargh, 1997; Fazio et al., 1986). Several studies have found evidence for automatic activation of attitudes using a paradigm in which positive or negative attitude objects are used as primes for positive or negative adjectives (see Textbox 4.1). Results from these studies show clear evidence for automatic activation of the evaluation associated with an attitude object, although there is some disagreement about whether all attitudes are automatically activated, or if this effect holds only for strong attitudes (Bargh, Chaiken, Govender & Pratto, 1992; Chaiken & Bargh, 1993; Fazio, 1993). In a study designed to resolve various methodological difficulties in previous studies, Bargh, Chaiken, Raymond and Hymes (1996) found that strong and weak attitudes produced an automatic evaluation effect, as evidenced by the finding that positive attitude object primes facilitated reaction times for responses to positive adjectives and negative attitude object primes facilitated responses to negative adjectives.

Textbox 4.1

How can we tell whether attitudes are automatically activated?

In a study by Fazio et al. (1986), participants' attitudes to a range of different objects, groups and concepts were measured by asking them how good or bad each object was. The time taken to make each evaluation was also measured, and objects that were evaluated quickly were said to have strong attitudes, while those involving a longer response time were considered weak attitudes. Following this first task, participants were then asked to classify a number of different adjectives as either 'good' or 'bad'. The adjectives were presented to participants on a computer monitor and the time taken to make each evaluation ('good' or 'bad') was recorded. However, immediately prior to the presentation of each adjective, participants were primed with a label of one of the objects towards which their attitudes had previously been measured. Each prime was presented for 250 ms – too short a time for participants to think deliberately about how they would evaluate that object.

(Continued)

Textbox 4.1   (Continued)

The logic of this design is that, if attitudes are automatic, then the attitude object in each prime should automatically produce its corresponding evaluation. If the prime is followed by an evaluatively consistent adjective (i.e., a 'good' object followed by a 'good' adjective, or a 'bad' object followed by a 'bad' adjective), the evaluation of the adjective should be facilitated by the (automatic) evaluation of the prime, resulting in a quicker response time. In cases where the prime and the adjective are evaluatively inconsistent (i.e., a 'good' object followed by a 'bad' adjective, or a 'bad' object followed by a 'good' adjective), the evaluation of the adjective should be inhibited by the evaluation of the prime, resulting in a longer response time. On the other hand, if attitudes are not automatically evaluated, the responses to the adjectives should not be affected by whether the prime was a 'good' or 'bad' object.

Fazio et al. (1986) found evidence for facilitation and inhibition following primes that came from each participant's strong attitudes, but not when the primes were objects towards which the participants had weak attitudes. From this they concluded that the automatic activation of attitudes is moderated by the strength of the attitude, and that only strong attitudes are automatically activated.

Following the evidence that attitudes can be activated without deliberate intention or conscious awareness, in recent years social psychologists have begun to consider whether we may have attitudes that are outside of our conscious awareness (Fazio & Olsen, 2003; Greenwald & Banaji, 1995; Greenwald, Banaji, Rudman, Farnham, Nosek & Mellott, 2002; Greenwald, McGhee & Schwartz, 1998). If conscious processing is not required in order for attitudes to have (some of) their effects, perhaps we need not be consciously aware of all of the attitudes that we hold. Such *implicit attitudes* would be like conscious attitudes in that they consist of a relatively stable association between an object and its evaluation – the only (crucial) difference being that with implicit attitudes, the person holding the attitude may be unaware that they do so. According to Greenwald and Banaji's definition, implicit attitudes are: ' ... introspectively unidentified (or inaccurately identified) traces of past experience that mediate favorable or unfavorable feeling, thought, or action toward social objects' (1995, p. 8). In other words, implicit attitudes are evaluations of objects that people are unaware they hold.

Accepting the notion that we may hold attitudes that we are unaware of, or that our automatic attitudes may be different from those attitudes that we are willing to deliberately endorse, creates a new problem for attitude theorists: if our implicit and explicit attitudes are inconsistent or even contradictory, which should be considered our 'true' attitude? Wegner and Bargh

(1998) argue that people are inclined to see automatic responses as more genuine because they are not amenable to the kinds of self-presentational distortions that may affect the expression of more controlled responses. Wegner and Bargh also argue that automatically activated attitudes are more important in some respects than controlled attitudes, because they are more likely to predict behaviour. However, Dovidio, Kawakami, Johnson, Johnson and Howard (1997) have argued against a universal preference for automatic attitudes, proposing instead that implicit (automatic) attitudes may be important in predicting automatic behaviour while explicit (controlled) attitudes may be more likely to predict deliberate, considered behaviour.

Attitudinal ambivalence If attitudes have multiple cognitive and affective elements, it follows that these different elements may not always lead to the same evaluation. People are said to have *ambivalent attitudes* when they have both positive and negative evaluations of the same target. Ambivalent attitudes are perhaps particularly likely to be found for targets that are complex and differentiated and with which we have numerous encounters (such as groups of people) rather than for simple targets (such as Brussels prouts). The possibility of attitude ambivalence has long been acknowledged by psychologists (see Kaplan, 1972), and ambivalence has been associated with attitude instability and amplification (Eagly & Chaiken, 1993). Ambivalent attitudes are considered to be unstable because the evaluation that is expressed in a particular moment will depend on which elements of the attitude are most accessible at that time, and as there are large variations in the evaluations associated with different elements of ambivalent attitudes, the expressed evaluations of the target are likely to be correspondingly variable. Amplification refers to the tendency for people to make more extreme evaluations of targets towards which they hold ambivalent attitudes than of those about which their attitudes are more straightforward (Katz & Glass, 1979).

The realization that people often hold ambivalent attitudes has led to a rethinking of how attitudes should properly be measured. Traditional measurement of attitudes involved rating objects on bipolar evaluative dimensions, such as semantic differentials (good–bad; pleasant–unpleasant; warm–cold, etc.). However, these types of bipolar attitude measures give rise to 'the midpoint problem' (Kaplan, 1972): should neutral ratings on bipolar scales be interpreted as reflecting ambivalence or indifference towards the attitude object? A person who selects a midpoint rating on a bipolar scale that rates politicians from good to bad may: (a) believe that some politicians are very good and others very bad; (b) believe that politicians have some very good qualities (e.g., intelligence, public mindedness, enthusiasm) and other very negative qualities (e.g., vanity, dishonesty, ruthlessness); or (c) not have strong opinions about politicians.

Kaplan's solution to the problem of detecting ambivalence in people's attitudes was to separate traditional bipolar semantic differential scales into separate unipolar measures of positive and negative attributes. Although this method has been adopted by researchers in a number of areas, notably in the measurement of intergroup attitudes (e.g., Katz & Hass, 1988), the use of bipolar semantic differentials is still common in many areas of attitude assessment. We will return to the question of ambivalence when we consider what discursive psychology has to say about the traditional attitude construct.

Hierarchical structure of attitudes

Work on the spread of activation of attitudes largely assumes that each attitude exists as a discrete node in an associative network which has no structure other than horizontal associations formed through repeated co-exposure and rehearsal. However, in addition to these associative connections, we can also think of attitudes as existing in hierarchical relations to each other. In this view, some specific attitudes are understood as instantiations of broader, more generalized attitudes. One's attitude towards paid maternity leave, for example, may reflect and/or be derived from one's more general attitude towards working mothers, which may in turn reflect one's attitudes towards various aspects of feminism. Using different approaches, several researchers have examined the vertical, rather than horizontal, structure of attitudes. There is nothing necessarily conflicting or incompatible between these two approaches. It is quite plausible to imagine nodes (attitudes) having vertical structure, as well as associative or horizontal structure. We consider here Kerlinger's (1984) work on the structure of political attitudes as an example of the hierarchical structure of attitudes.

Kerlinger was concerned with how social and political attitudes are organized. Work prior to his had suggested that such attitudes could be arranged in a *bipolar* way, ranging from liberal to conservative (e.g., Eysenck, 1975; Eysenck & Wilson, 1978; Ferguson, 1973). In this view, liberalism is the *opposite* of conservatism, and someone who agrees strongly with a liberal item in an attitude scale is also presumed to disagree strongly with a conservative item in a scale. The bipolar assumption undergirds much work in the analysis of social and political attitudes (e.g., attitudes to women are usually assumed to range from 'traditional' to 'liberal', these two poles being opposed to one another – Smith & Walker, 1991; Spence & Helmreich, 1972). Kerlinger suggested that the two ideologies of liberalism and conservatism do not exist in opposition to one another, but, rather, are independent of one another.

Kerlinger's model starts with social referents – the objects of social and political attitudes, such as abortion, real estate, trade unions, money, racial equality and patriotism. Some of these referents are said to be *criterial* for liberals, and some are criterial for conservatives. A referent is said to be criterial for someone if it is significant, or salient, to that person. Whereas bipolar models would assume that referents criterial for liberals are also negatively criterial for conservatives, and vice versa, Kerlinger argues that liberals do not care about conservative referents and conservatives are indifferent about liberal referents. In other words, criteriality is generally positive or neutral, not negative. As an ideology, liberalism has one set of criterial referents and conservatism another, and the two are independent.

The evidence Kerlinger marshals in support of his theory relies on the factor analysis of criterial ratings (both liberal and conservative) of a large number of referents by a large number of people. That is, the structure Kerlinger talks about is identified *across,* not *within,* people, although it may be paralleled as a structure within one person. Factor analysis of criterial ratings typically produces about a dozen first-order factors, identifiable as things like religiosity, racial equality, civil rights, morality, and so on. When these first-order factors are themselves factor analysed, they produce two orthogonal second-order factors – liberalism and conservatism. These Kerlinger labels as ideologies, defined as a collection of shared beliefs, attitudes and values organized around some coherent core and often associated with a particular group in a social structure (Scarborough, 1990). Ideologies are *shared*: it is not possible for one person to 'have' an ideology. They do not 'exist' or 'reside' within any one person. Rather, they are bodies of thought themselves. They only have life to the extent they are shared, and hence can be said to be truly and only social – they are a product of social relations. We discuss the concept of ideology in detail in Chapter 8.

Considering the structure of social and political attitudes as being built upon ideologies returns us to issues raised at the start of this chapter. Most of the work in social psychology and sociology on attitudes has concerned the intraindividual structure of attitudes – their accessibility, whether they function automatically or can be controlled by conscious processes, how they are changed to maintain intrapsychic consistency, and so on – and how, if at all, attitudes are related to behaviours. Work on the ideological nature of attitudes is relatively scarce, but no less important. These two traditions of research are not incompatible with one another; instead, they are complementary. Work on the intraindividual, or micro-, level focuses on how attitudes work. Macro-level concerns place attitudes in a social context, and illustrate their fundamental *social* character. Attitudes are *social,* in origin, in function, and in consequence. They originate in social life, they communicate meaning, they are shared, and they have social consequence. We elaborate upon this issue further when we consider social identity, social representations, and discursive approaches to understanding attitudes.

Functions of attitudes

What are the functions of attitudes? Social psychology has furnished answers to this question in two different epochs, one in the 1950s and the other starting from the mid-1980s. In between, little was written about attitude function. Regardless of time, though, social psychology has focused on the functions attitudes serve for the individual attitude-holder, and has largely ignored the broad social functions.

The 1950s saw two separate, independent research programmes each focus on a functional analysis of attitudes, and each converge upon similar sorts of answers to the question of why we have attitudes (Katz, 1960; Smith, 1947; Smith, Bruner & White, 1956). The 1980s witnessed a return to functional analyses, and recast the earlier work into more contemporary forms. The newer work has been informed by, and has not departed radically from, the earlier work.

Katz (1960) articulated four functions of attitudes. The *knowledge function* is similar to the common understanding of what an attitude does. Attitudes help us explain and understand the world around us. In the Pratkanis and Greenwald (1989) definition, an attitude is a memorial representation of an object, and associated with that representation are rules about the labelling of the object, an evaluative summary of the object and a knowledge structure about the object. The knowledge function of attitudes helps us know the world.

Second, for Katz, attitudes serve a *utilitarian function*, by which is meant that they help us gain rewards and avoid punishments. Utilitarian functions underscore the social consequences that follow from the expression of certain attitudes. To be 'politically correct' is to hold and display attitudes for utilitarian reasons. The idea that attitudes can have utilitarian functions underlines the flexibility in people's expression of their attitudes. People are attitudinally labile, altering their 'attitude' to the same object according to the social context they are in. We will consider more closely some of the implications of this flexibility in people's expressions of their attitudes later in the chapter when we discuss discursive perspectives on 'attitudes'.

The third function is the *value-expressive* one. The expression of an attitude can sometimes be no more than a public statement of what a person believes or identifies with (probably strongly). Political statements painted on bus shelters (eat the rich, ban nuclear warships), stickers placed on car windows (Save the Planet), T-shirts adorned with slogans or group labels ('Just Stop It', Amnesty International), uniforms or sporting teams (Glasgow Celtic, LA Lakers, Fremantle Dockers), and clothing with manufacturers' labels displayed (Tommy Hilfiger, Levis, Lacoste); these are all public signs intended to convey a message about the owner. They signal to the world that you support Celtic and not Rangers, that you oppose the sweatshop labour practices of footwear manufacturers, that you can afford designer clothing and don't buy from the local K-Mart, and so on. There is no real point to such expressions, other than to tell the world something about who you are. You are what you wear, or at least what is adorned upon what you wear.

Finally, and less obviously, attitudes can serve an *ego-defensive function*. Such attitudes are usually deep-seated, difficult to change and hostile to the attitude object. The classic examples are homophobia and xenophobia. Each of these expresses strong hostility to some outgroup. According to Katz, at least some people who hold such attitudes do so because they are unconsciously denying some aspect of their own self. Homophobics, for example, are perhaps so hostile to homosexuals and homosexuality because they deny and do not wish to confront aspects of their own sexuality. Attitudes that serve this function thus project outward what are really internal, intrapsychic conflicts. In a dramatic illustration of this hypothesis, Adams, Wright and Lohr (1996) measured the sexual and physiological arousal of heterosexual men while they viewed sexually explicit videos of men engaged in homosexual activity. They found that the participants who had been previously identified as holding negative attitudes towards homosexuality and homosexual men showed *greater* sexual arousal while watching the videos than did the participants with more positive attitudes towards homosexuality. The researchers argued that the expression of negative attitudes towards homosexuality provides a defence against the assumed ego-threat experienced by straight men who experience some level of homosexual arousal.

Attitudes may simultaneously serve more than one function, and may be held or expressed for different reasons at different times. For example, a person's attitude to medically assisted reproduction may largely serve a knowledge function, being based upon what that person knows about IVF, donor insemination, and so on, and depending on how much that person needs to formulate an attitude to assisted reproduction. But the same attitude may also aid that person's relationship with an infertile relative, or it may also be the expression of more deeply held beliefs about God's will and the Church's position on procreation, or it may also reflect that person's own, perhaps unconscious, conflicted sense of their own sexuality and fecundity, or doubts about their genealogy.

The typology developed by Smith et al. (1956) closely resembles that of Katz, but describes only three functions: the *object-appraisal* function is the same as Katz's knowledge function, and the *externalization* function mirrors Katz's ego-defensive function. The value-expressive and utilitarian functions described by Katz are combined by Smith et al. into the single *social adjustment* function.

More recently, Herek (1986, 1987) and Shavitt (1989, 1990) have rejuvenated interest in the functions that attitudes serve by reinterpreting and recasting the earlier analyses. Shavitt's contribution combines the taxonomies of Katz and Smith et al. into a more parsimonious account. Thus, she describes attitudes as having a *utilitarian* function, which includes Katz's knowledge and utilitarian functions and Smith et al.'s object-appraisal function; a *social identity* function, which combines Katz's value-expressive function and Smith et al.'s social adjustment function; and a *self-esteem maintenance* function, which incorporates Katz's ego-defensive function and Smith et al.'s externalization function. Shavitt succeeds in making more stark the ties between attitudes and individual and social identities, and has also demonstrated how the success of attempts to change an attitude depends on the function that attitude serves for its owner.

Herek's reanalysis of attitude function breaks more with tradition, and leads him to propose two different kinds of attitudes: *evaluative* and *expressive*. The former are attitudes in which the attitude object is an end in itself, and the attitude functions to allow the individual access to the object itself. In contrast, expressive (or symbolic) attitudes are those in which the attitude object is a means to an end, by providing social support, increasing self-esteem or reducing anxiety. Evaluative attitudes may be *experiential and specific* (based on and restricted to a single object), *experiential and schematic* (based on experience with particular objects, but generalized to a class of objects) or *anticipatory* (based on expected, rather than direct, experience). Expressive attitudes may be social-expressive (based on the individual's need to be accepted by others), value-expressive (based on the individual's need to define self by expressing important values and aligning self with important reference groups) or defensive (based on the individual's need to reduce anxiety associated with intrapsychic conflicts). As with Shavitt's analysis, Herek suggests that strategies to change attitudes must consider whether attitudes are held for evaluative or expressive/symbolic reasons.

Herek's empirical work has focused on attitudes to homosexuality, but it has much wider relevance. For example, in the domain of racial prejudice (see Chapter 7), a distinction is commonly drawn between whites' anti-black prejudice which is based in self-interest and that which is based on symbolic beliefs. Further, attitudes formed for different functional reasons are likely to be more or less resilient. For example, few white Australians have much direct contact with Aboriginal people, but this does not prevent them from forming strong anti-Aboriginal sentiments. Because these sentiments are based on anticipatory rather than experiential factors, they are hard to disconfirm through direct experience, and hence are hard to change.

Note that in the above analyses of attitude function, the emphasis is very much on the functions for the individual attitude-holder. To be sure, some of the attitude functions do refer to social aspects (for example, the social adjustment function), but by and large the functions are theorized at an individual level. That is, the 'social' functions are conceptualized in terms of the social consequences *for an individual* of holding or expressing a particular attitude. Attitudes also serve *social* functions, though. There is relatively little research in the social cognitive tradition that directly investigates the social functions attitudes serve. We must turn to other theoretical perspectives later in this chapter in order to explore a more thoroughly social understanding of attitudes and their functions.

Attitudes and behaviour

One of the most enduring enigmas social psychologists have been concerned with is the relationship between attitudes and behaviours. The common-sense view of attitudes has it that attitudes directly cause a person to act in a particular way. If you know that someone feels strongly about practising safe sex, you can reliably predict that person's sexual practices across time and context, or so the story goes. Social psychology has known for a long time that the relationship between attitude and behaviour is not as simple as this, that as often as not behaviours appear to be quite unrelated to attitudes, and that behaviours can 'cause' attitudes as much as the other way around. Additionally, some researchers have argued for the need to distinguish between different types of attitudes, most notably between attitudes towards targets and attitudes towards behaviours (Eagly & Chaiken, 1998). Thus in attempting to predict people's sun-protection behaviour, for example, it is necessary to consider both their attitudes towards skin cancer *and* their attitudes towards applying sunscreen.

An early American sociologist, Richard LaPiere (1934), was perhaps the first to present evidence that the expressed attitudes of a set of people to a particular object do not particularly correspond to their behaviour towards the same object. In the early 1930s, LaPiere and a Chinese couple travelled the US west coast, staying at inns and campsites. This was a time of strong anti-Chinese feelings throughout the US, yet the trio was refused accommodation on only one occasion. After their trip, LaPiere wrote to all the managers of the establishments they had visited, and others they hadn't stayed at, asking if they would accept Chinese guests. More than 90 per cent claimed they would not. There is a disparity between the expressed attitudes of the managers of the inns and campsites and their overt behaviours.

This disparity has been noted in many studies over the years. Wicker (1969) summarized the results of 32 different studies, each of which contained a measure of individuals' attitudes to a particular object and a direct (not self-report) measure of behaviour towards the same object. The attitude–behaviour correlations reported in these studies rarely exceeded +.3, were often close to zero, and were even negative on some occasions. Thus, at best, attitudes appear to explain (in a statistical sense) up to, but rarely more than, 10 per cent of the variance in behaviour. So much for a simple, direct and strong link between attitudes and behaviour. Where does this leave the attitude construct? Of what use is such a construct if it doesn't help explain behaviour? The years after Wicker's widely cited review saw social psychology endeavour to refine attitude measurement techniques, on the assumption that perhaps the low correlations were a product of measurement error, and to specify more clearly under what conditions we do expect attitudes to be related to behaviour and under what conditions the two ought to be unrelated. Issues of attitude measurement are beyond the scope of this book, but a comprehensive review is provided by Himmelfarb (1993). We turn now to a brief consideration of the conditions under which attitudes and behaviours should be related, and to the processes by which behaviours can affect attitudes.

Social psychology produced two broad classes of response to the challenge laid down by Wicker: many have attempted to work with the relationship between a single attitude–behaviour couplet, attempting to find when the link is strong and when it is not; others have attempted to formulate and test a more elaborate model of the general link between attitudes and behaviour. We consider each in turn.

Strengthening the attitude–behaviour link   Many variables influencing the strength of the attitude–behaviour link have been identified. Some of the more important ones are listed here. First, attitudes about an object which have been formed through direct experience of that object appear to be more strongly associated with behaviour related to that object than are attitudes which do not rely on any direct experience (e.g., Regan & Fazio, 1977). It has been suggested that the link between behaviours and attitudes formed through direct experience is stronger because such attitudes are held with more clarity, confidence and certainty (e.g., Fazio & Zanna, 1978a, 1978b, 1981), because such attitudes are more accessible (able to be brought into consciousness easily) and stronger (Fazio, 1989), and because such attitudes are automatically activated upon presentation of the attitude object (e.g., Fazio et al., 1986).

Second, it has been suggested that attitudes which are more stable will show greater attitude–behaviour consistency than attitudes which are unstable (e.g., Ajzen & Fishbein, 1980). This proposal has two components. First, the greater the time between measuring the attitude and measuring the behaviour, the less strong will be the attitude–behaviour link (in LaPiere's case it was six months). This makes good sense, in that attitudes change, and the behaviour may be susceptible to the influence of many non-attitudinal factors. But second, even when the attitude and the behaviour are measured fairly well together, the link will still be stronger for stable – often more general rather than more specific – attitudes (e.g., Schwartz, 1978).

Finally, several individual differences have been found which affect the strength of the attitude–behaviour link. People who have been made self-aware (usually by placing a mirror next to them while they complete attitude scales) typically display much greater attitude–behaviour consistency than do people not made self-aware (e.g., Gibbons, 1978). People who are described as high self-monitors (that is, who monitor and regulate their own reactions through the reactions of others) typically show lower attitude–behaviour consistency than those people who are described as low self-monitors (who monitor internal reactions, rather than others' reactions – e.g., Zanna, Olson & Fazio, 1980), although the strength of the effect may also depend on variables such as attitude accessibility (e.g., Snyder & Kendzierski, 1982). Being asked to provide reasons for their attitudes may lower the consistency of people's attitudes and behaviours (e.g., Wilson, Kraft & Dunn, 1989). There is also growing evidence of cross-cultural differences in the tendency to believe that attitudes *should* correspond to behaviours (Kashima, Siegal, Tanaka & Kashima, 1992; Nisbett, 2003).

These lists of variables affecting the attitude–behaviour link are not intended to be exhaustive. They merely hint at a large literature pertaining to the problem. The point for present purposes is simply that the pessimism of Wicker (1969) may be allayed somewhat by a more detailed consideration of the many other factors which may be implicated in the relationship between attitudes and behaviour. Whereas the evidence demonstrating that attitudes lead to behaviour has often been weak, the evidence demonstrating that attitudes *follow* behaviours is much stronger.

Cognitive dissonance theory

Festinger's (1957) *theory of cognitive dissonance* is simple, but helps explain how it is that people change their attitudes in accord with their behaviour, rather than the other way around. The theory simply states that if a person holds two cognitions that are psychologically (not necessarily logically) discrepant, that discrepancy (dissonance) is uncomfortable, and the person is motivated to reduce the dissonance. Dissonance may be reduced by changing either or both of the cognitions, or by introducing a new cognition. For example, if I smoke and if I also know that smoking is bad for my health I ought to experience dissonance because these two cognitions are psychologically discrepant from one another. Note that there is nothing *logically* inconsistent between them; there is just a psycho-logical discrepancy. The dissonance I experience can be alleviated by changing one of the two cognitions or by introducing some new cognition. For example, I could give up smoking, but that's a difficult and unlikely thing to happen. Alternatively, I could alter my cognition that smoking is bad for my health. It is not unusual for smokers to argue that the evidence against smoking is not as strong as public health campaigns make out. Or, I could introduce some new cognition. I could, for example, accept that I smoke, and that smoking is bad for my health, but then get out of it by claiming that I smoke to relieve stress and gain pleasure, or that I am addicted to smoking and therefore unable to quit.

Applying the principles of cognitive dissonance theory to the relationship between attitudes and behaviour, we can see that if people engage in a particular behaviour, for whatever reason, they are likely to alter their attitudes to correspond to the just committed action. Suppose, for example, that a young child attending a mostly white primary school with a handful of Aboriginal children joins in with a group of older children to tease one particular Aboriginal child. The young child may not have had any attitude at all to Aborigines before teasing this one Aboriginal child, but it is unlikely that that child will remain agnostic regarding Aborigines, especially if the unpleasantness of the behaviour is pointed out by a teacher or parent or another child. Rather, the child will alter (or, in this case, invent) his or her attitude to correspond to the behaviour. Any dissonance will be displaced by another cognitive change – in this case, by developing a negative attitude to the Aboriginal child, and perhaps to Aborigines in general. To borrow the title of a chapter on a similar process, but one on a much grander scale – the dehumanization of the Viet Cong by American soldiers and the massacre of Vietnamese civilians at My Lai by American infantrymen – 'It never happened and besides they deserved it' (Opton, 1971). Attitudes follow behaviour, not the other way around. This principle applies, at least according to the proponents of cognitive dissonance theory (Aronson, 1968, 1989; Festinger, 1957), to any instance where a person engages in a behaviour which does not correspond with any pertinent attitude held before that behaviour. Cognitive dissonance is especially aroused when one of the cognitions in the syllogism is about *self*.

Cognitive dissonance theory is one of a family of *consistency* theories: it assumes that inconsistency is unpleasant, and that people are motivated to achieve consistency and balance. This assumption has been challenged by several critics (most notably, Billig, 1987), who argue that the desire to achieve and maintain consistency is a peculiar western cultural construction and that people are far more tolerant of cognitive and interpersonal inconsistencies than cognitive dissonance theory assumes. This is a theme central to discursive psychology which we will discuss later.

Self-perception theory

Cognitive dissonance theory has not gone unchallenged in its explanation of attitude change and the relationship between attitude and behaviour. In particular, *self-perception theory* was developed by Daryl Bem (1967, 1972) to explain precisely the same events as those cognitive dissonance theory purports to explain, but without recourse to elaborate, and in Bem's eyes unnecessary, psychological processes. Bem argued that we deduce our own attitudes to objects in the same way we deduce others' attitudes – by the processes of attribution, to be discussed in Chapter 5. Attribution theory suggests that observers attribute attitudes to an actor which corresponds with the actor's behaviour, and that this tendency is stronger when the action is chosen freely by the actor. Bem proposes a similar process in inferring our own attitudes. In Bem's words, the major hypothesis of self-perception theory is that 'in identifying his [or her] own internal states, an individual partially relies on the same external cues that others use when they infer his [or her] internal states' (1970, p. 50).

How is this theoretical stand-off resolved? Here we have two quite different theories, each purporting to explain precisely the same set of events. Which, if either, is right? It may appear to you, as it did to any number of researchers in the late 1960s and 1970s, that the thing to do is design and conduct an experiment which pits both theories against one another to see which one works. Unfortunately, it is impossible to design such a definitive, crucial experiment. Several tried, but each time there was always more than one possible explanation for the observed results. That's not how science – broadly defined to include social psychology and the other 'softer' social sciences – works. So it goes.

The picture painted by the accumulation of research on attitude change was neatly summarized by Fazio, Zanna and Cooper (1977). Self-perception processes seem to operate when behaviour falls within the 'latitude of acceptance'; but when the behaviour falls outside that latitude, cognitive dissonance processes appear to operate. 'Latitude of acceptance' and 'latitude of rejection' are terms from social judgement theory (Sherif, Sherif & Nebergall, 1965). Social judgement theory suggests that the dimension characterizing the range of possible attitudes to a particular object may be divided into these two latitudes. Any one person's latitude of acceptance comprises all those attitudes that person finds acceptable. All those attitudes the person finds unacceptable constitute the latitude of rejection. (A third, but usually ignored, area is called the 'latitude of non-commitment', and is made up of those attitudes the person does not care about either way.) Thus, according to social judgement theory, it is more fruitful to position a person within a range of possible attitudinal positions relative to some object than it is to argue that a precise single position represents that person's attitude.

The theory of reasoned action

The second reaction to Wicker's (1969) damning review attempted to theorize the attitude–behaviour relationship more fully than had been the case, rather than search for the conditions under which attitudes do and do not predict behaviour. The major representative of this work is Fishbein and Ajzen's *theory of reasoned action* (Ajzen & Fishbein, 1980; Fishbein & Ajzen, 1975). As the title of the theory implies, it is a theory about behaviour ('action'), and thus the attitudes that are relevant to this model are attitudes towards behaviour.

Fishbein and Ajzen argued that attitudes do not predict behaviours *per se*, but, rather, *behavioural intentions*. It is behavioural intentions which directly predict behaviour. Behavioural intentions themselves are a function of attitudes to the behaviour and what Fishbein and Ajzen called *subjective norms*. Subjective norms refer to what the individual actor believes his or her significant others believe he or she *should* do. The theory of reasoned action is really only applicable to behaviours under *volitional control*.

The theory of reasoned action has been used widely and has received considerable empirical support, in areas ranging from the decision to abort (Smetana & Adler, 1980) to the decision to breast- or bottle-feed a baby (Manstead, Proffitt & Smart, 1983), from smoking marijuana (Ajzen, Timko & White, 1982) to attending church (King, 1975). Meta-analytic summaries of the size of the association between attitudes and subjective norms, on the one hand, and behavioural intentions, on the other, show the average correlations ranging from .53 to .68, and between behavioural intentions and behaviour of just over .50 (Sheppard, Hartwick & Warshaw, 1988). These associations are considerably larger than the maximum of .30 reported by Wicker (1969).

Despite its empirical support, the model is not without its critics. It has been argued, for example, that personal norms (individual beliefs about the appropriateness of particular behaviours) and behavioural norms (what everyone else does, rather than what it is believed they expect to be done) are as important in the formation of behaviour as are subjective norms (e.g., Schwartz & Tessler, 1972).

Another criticism has been that even behaviour under volitional control does not necessarily conform to the model. Some behavioural routines are so scripted (Abelson, 1981) and rehearsed that they are adhered to mindlessly (Langer, 1989). Similarly, Bentler & Speckart (1979) have argued, and demonstrated empirically, that behaviours which have been performed in the past are more likely to happen again, simply because they have been performed and despite the actor's intentions to behave otherwise. New Year's resolutions are perhaps a good example of how difficult it is to cease certain behaviours despite all the best intentions to change.

The theory of planned behaviour

Finally, one of the authors of the original model, Icek Ajzen, has revised the model to become the *theory of planned behaviour* (Ajzen, 1988, 1989, 1991; Ajzen & Madden, 1986), to accommodate the fact that behaviours are often not under the volitional control assumed by the theory of reasoned action. The theory of planned behaviour retains behavioural intentions as central in the link between attitudes and behaviour, and still holds that behavioural intentions are the product of attitudes toward the behaviour and subjective norms. However, an important third factor is added – *perceived behavioural control* (see Figure 4.2). This factor refers to the actor's perception of the ease or difficulty of performing the behaviours. Some behaviours are easy to do once you decide to do them, others are harder. Some behaviours are easy not

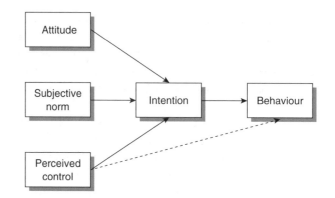

Figure 4.2   Theory of planned behaviour: perceived control affects the formation of behavioural intentions and the production of behaviour itself (independently of behavioural intentions). However, perceived control is not always consistent with actual control of behaviour – this is represented by the dashed line.

to do once that has been decided, other behaviours are much harder not to do. Perceived behavioural control affects the formation of behavioural intentions, and also, importantly, directly affects the production of behaviour itself, independently of behavioural intentions. Armitage and Connor (2001) conducted a meta-analytic review of 185 studies which used the theory of planned behaviour, and found that the model accounted for an average of 27 per cent and 39 per cent of the variance in people's behaviour and behavioural intentions, respectively. They also found that the variables in the theory of planned behaviour predicted behavioural intentions better than those of the theory of reasoned action – that is, that perceived behavioural control added to the prediction of behavioural intentions over and above the effects of attitudes to the behaviour and subjective norms.

Attitudes and Social Identities

So far we have been considering attitudes in terms of the functions they perform in 'locating "objects of thought" on "dimensions of judgment"' (McGuire, 1985). However there is another important sense in which attitudes are 'locating': expressing (and concealing) certain attitudes are a powerful means by which people can locate themselves relative to others in social space. That is, attitudes serve to locate an individual within the social matrix. When earlier theorists talked of the value-expressive function, it was from the point of view of the attitude-holder. But viewed from the other side, the expression of values through attitudes is required for social cohesion and evaluation (Dornbusch, 1987). A group member who is reticent about expressing an attitude on a matter of importance to the group will not usually be allowed by the group to remain silent on the issue. The group will enforce or extract an expression of attitude. This expression is an important marker of the individual's position relative to the group. It is important to the group that such positions are not far from the group's 'prototypical' position. Enforcing or extracting attitudes can be a potent form of social control, requiring a demonstration of group allegiance from the individual.

Indeed, attitudes have long been considered to be embedded in social relationships. In his influential balance theory, Heider (1958) argued that people were motivated to experience consistency between their attitudes towards specific other people, and their attitudes towards objects and issues. Specifically, Heider argued that we are motivated to hold attitudes that are similar to those of people we like, and different from those of people we dislike, but also that our liking or disliking of others can arise from our perception of the extent to which we share the same attitudes. Social identity theory (Tajfel, 1982) and self-categorization theory (Turner et al., 1987) have taken this idea further, arguing that similar attitudes can provide the basis for psychological group formation, or in other words, that shared attitudes can constitute a ground on which we divide the world into 'us' and 'them'. Prochoice and pro-life groups provide a clear example of psychological identification based on a shared attitude. Groups can also provide a context in which people can compare their attitudes to those held by similar others, to evaluate the appropriateness of their own attitudes. Festinger highlighted the fundamentally social nature of attitudes and the effect of social groups on the development of attitudes, claiming that 'an attitude is correct, valid, and proper to the extent that it is anchored in a group of people with similar beliefs, opinions, and attitudes' (1950, p. 272).

In thinking about how SIT and SCT can help us to understand people's attitudes it is helpful to distinguish between attitudes towards *social groups* and attitudes towards other kinds of social and non-social objects. While SIT and SCT are fundamentally concerned with the development and expression of attitudes towards one's own and other social groups (see Chapter 7), they have had much less to say about how membership in such groups might influence a person's attitudes towards *other* things. SCT can be read as providing a theoretical account of the influence of social identities on attitudes: to the extent that the expression of certain attitudes constitutes a group norm, SCT would predict that identification as a member of that group should lead to the expression of those normative attitudes. However, empirical research into this aspect of social identity and attitudes has been limited, and has tended to concentrate on the ways in which shared attitudes in a group tend to become more extreme (group polarization), and the role of social identity in making certain attitudes and norms salient in certain social contexts. We consider each of these in turn.

Group polarization

Social psychologists have long been aware that people's attitudes tend to become more extreme following discussion. The *group polarization effect* is the name given to the phenomenon in which attitudes become more extreme following contact with others who share the same initial tendency in their attitude (i.e., an initially positive or negative evaluation). Although not all group discussion of attitudes produces group polarization, it is a robust phenomenon that many theorists have attempted to explain. Most accounts of the group polarization effect rely on the notion that group discussion provides either (a) a new source of persuasive arguments in favour of the initial position (*informational influence*) or (b) information about others' views that provides a basis for social comparison (*normative influence*). According to the persuasive arguments account (e.g., Burnstein & Vinokur, 1977), discussion of attitudes with others provides exposure to arguments and information that may not have been considered in developing the initial attitude. Given a tendency for initial attitudes to be in a particular direction (which is required for group polarization to occur), it follows that these new arguments are likely to support the initial attitude, and lead to a more extreme position in the same direction as the initial attitude. The social comparison account of group polarization argues that people seek to enhance their positive differentiation from the group by enhancing their difference from other group members' attitudes in the direction favoured by the group. According to this view polarization occurs because people initially underestimate the extremity of others' attitudes, and so 'readjust' their own attitudes so as to maintain a more favourable (more extreme) position than other group members (Isenberg, 1986). For example, discussion of environmental conservation among people who initially express 'green' attitudes may see the attitudes expressed by people within the group become increasingly pro-green as they vie to position themselves as 'greener than thou'!

Both of these accounts have been challenged by self-categorization theorists (Turner et al., 1987). According to SCT, group polarization is produced by group processes, and cannot be reduced to either informational or social comparative processes. Group polarization will only occur to the extent that people psychologically identify with the group in which they are discussing their attitudes, and will occur as a result of the processes of group identification proposed by SCT. That is, on identifying themselves as members of a group, people apply the prototypical characteristics, in this case attitudes, of the group to themselves. Prototypical characteristics are those that follow the meta-contrast principle of maximizing between-group difference while minimizing ingroup difference. Thus, in cases where initial attitudes are already tending in a particular direction (positive or negative), the more extreme attitudes (rather than average group attitudes) will tend to be seen as prototypical, as these will serve to differentiate the group from outgroups taking an opposite view (Turner et al., 1987). The SCT explanation thus explicitly contradicts the social comparison explanation, by arguing that group polarization is produced by *conformity* to a polarized group norm (Hogg, Turner & Davidson, 1990), rather than by the need for positive *distinctiveness* postulated by the social comparison explanations. Evidence that group members perceive their ingroup norms as being more extreme than they are judged by non-group members (Mackie, 1986) supports this SCT account.

Attitude–behaviour relationships and social identities

As we have already seen, the relationship between attitudes and behaviour is a problematic one. Researchers working from the perspectives of SIT and SCT have argued that understanding relationships between attitudes and behaviour requires careful attention to the salience of social identities and the attitudes and behavioural norms associated with these identities. Different social identities are associated with different attitudinal and behavioural norms. Although the theories of reasoned action and planned behaviour have emphasized the role played by subjective norms in the attitude–behaviour link, Ajzen (1991) concluded in his review of 19 studies that the influence of such social factors is relatively weak compared to personal factors. Deborah Terry and her colleagues (e.g., Terry & Hogg, 1996; Terry, Hogg & McKimmie, 2000; Terry, Hogg & White, 1999), however, have challenged this conclusion, arguing that the concept of social norms in these models is problematic and is inconsistent with the way in which *social norms* are understood in SIT and SCT; that norms are tied to specific reference groups which are behaviourally relevant in particular contexts. As such, particular social norms would only be expected to influence behaviour when the social identities with which they are associated are salient in a particular instance. Terry et al. (2000) examined the role of group norms in moderating the attitude–behaviour link, in a study which manipulated normative information about the intended career choices of psychology students. Students were asked to nominate their preferred career in psychology from a list of three options (clinical psychology, organizational psychology and sports psychology), and were then provided with normative information which suggested that the career preferences of other psychology students were either similar (norm congruent) or different (norm incongruent) from their own. Students were subsequently provided with opportunities to attend an information session on one (only) of the three career paths, and were asked about their willingness to take a variety of steps to gain further information about their preferred career path. Although most students chose to attend a session about the career in which they had expressed interest, congruence between initial attitudes (preferred career) and subsequent behaviour (which career information session was chosen) was significantly stronger among participants who were exposed to attitudinally consistent group norms (i.e., who were led to believe that other psychology students shared their preferred career), than among participants who were exposed to attitudinally inconsistent group norms. In an earlier study, Terry et al. (1999) found that perceived group norms in favour of household recycling were predictive of intentions to recycle, but only among people who strongly identified with the group (in this case 'friends and peers'). Taken together, these findings provide some support for the argument that the role of attitudinal norms in guiding behaviour depends on the extent to which a person identifies with the reference group with which the norms are associated.

Attitudes and Social Representations

Throughout this chapter, it should be clear that social psychology has primarily treated the attitude construct as an *individual* phenomenon. Attitudes have primarily been conceptualized as individual and internal cognitive and affective states, or as behavioural intentions and predispositions. This belies how attitudes were originally formulated when the construct entered the social sciences.

Early social scientific approaches to attitudes (e.g., Thomas & Znaniecki, 1918–20; Wundt, 1897) argued that attitudes provide the links that tie individuals to their social groups, giving them a social position and social heritage, and allowing them to live socially. Attitudes were not, for these early theorists, mental structures. The sociological tradition of symbolic interactionism (Stryker & Statham, 1985) accepted this view and extended it to argue that attitudes, like all forms of meaning, arise through social interaction and communication. Mainstream social psychology has increasingly individualized the attitude construct (Jaspars & Fraser, 1984). Only recently have analyses emerged which reestablish the social nature of attitudes (Eiser, 1994; Fraser & Gaskell, 1990; Lalljee, Brown & Ginsburg, 1984). Consistent with the earlier work of Thomas and Znaniecki (which endeavored to understand the experiences of dislocation in Polish immigrants to the United States) and of the symbolic interactionists, an increasing number of theorists are again emphasizing that attitudes originate in and emerge from social life itself, through our everyday interactions and communications with others. Further, some attitudes are widely shared, providing cultural meaning and substance to everyday life. Shared attitudes are relied on to make sense of the social world and to orient ourselves to that world.

Historians of social psychology and its constructs have attributed the increasing individualization of the attitude construct to Gordon Allport's classic and influential contribution to this topic in the original edition of *A Handbook of Social Psychology* (1935). Allport defined an attitude as a global stimulus-response disposition for the purpose of explaining differences in behaviour in objectively similar situations. This view of attitudes resembled the behaviourist tenor of the times much more than it resembled the sociological origins of the construct. Allport's view, coupled with the important development of techniques to measure attitudes (Thurstone, 1928), signalled the beginning of the dominant positivist position, marked by a fetishistic desire to measure individuals' attitudes to just about any and every topic, and to search for individual differences in attitude which could predict differences in behaviour. Attitudes had become objectified, reified cognitive entities with a life of their own inside people's heads. As an individual cognitive and emotional predisposition, the attitude construct took on a methodological individualism which shaped the subsequent nature of attitude theories in social psychology. In Graumann's (1986) view, this led not only to the 'individualization of the social' but also to the 'desocialization of the individual'.

Contemporary theories of attitude can be contrasted with the more recent emergence of social representations theory. Social representations theory reinstates the collective and social nature of cognitive constructs like attitudes, beliefs and values. As we have previously defined them, social representations refer to the stock of *shared* common-sense knowledge and beliefs people within a collective use to orient themselves to the social world. Having a social constructionist emphasis, social representations are the building blocks used to construct and thereby understand social reality. Although some critics have suggested that the concept of social representations is closely allied to that of the traditional attitude construct (e.g., Jahoda, 1988), Moscovici warns that social representations are not simply 'attitudes' to social objects. The concept of social representations has been endowed with a different epistemological status to that of the traditional attitude construct, a status which recaptures a social, cultural and collective emphasis.

First, in contrast to the traditional attitude construct, social representations are theorized to be more complex cognitive structures akin to 'theories' or 'branches of knowledge' and beliefs. Social representations are therefore much more than just evaluations or judgements about specific objects or referents. They are frameworks of understanding that give rise to more specific evaluative judgements. For example, in our discussion of emerging representations of biotechnology in Europe in Chapter 2, we demonstrated how the Eurobarometer Survey, a quantitative questionnaire, was not on its own able to throw light on how favourable, negative, or ambivalent attitudes to biotechnology are generated. In order to understand how people came to understand and evaluate such technological advances it was necessary to examine underlying representations and understandings of complex notions such as 'nature', and 'life'. These, in turn, were shaped by religious, scientific and popular 'sci-fi' accounts and narratives that proliferate within the wider society. As such, 'attitudes' towards biotechnology are shaped and framed by pervasive cultural understandings and ways of making sense of the world (Gaskell, 2001). Indeed, hierarchical models of attitudes such as that developed by Kerlinger were developed precisely to take account of this complex organization and structure of attitudes. But, as we also explained, Kerlinger recognized that specific and discrete political attitudes were related to organizing ideological frameworks.

Although social representations cannot be simply equated with 'attitudes', social representations undoubtedly do have an evaluative dimension. As Moliner and Tafani (1997) have pointed out, the shared understandings encapsulated in social representations also provide a way of expressing evaluative judgements in ways that appear grounded in objective features of the target rather than subjective opinion. For example, to the extent that 'family values' are seen as positive, describing a political party as having policies that promote family values is a subtle way of expressing endorsement of that party.

Moliner and Tafani (1997) have examined whether aspects of the structure of social representations can usefully account for one of the problems that has plagued attempts to theorize attitudes as social representations: the question of consensus. In attempting to theorize the relationship between attitudes and social representations they write:

... the evaluative components of a representation can be regarded as pieces of information upon which individuals rely when manifesting their attitudes towards the represented object. In this view, the evaluative components of the representation form the underlying structure of the attitude. (Moliner & Tafani, 1997, p. 691)

Of particular interest here is the claim that social representations can have multiple evaluative components, so that, for example, representations of abortion can comprise evaluations of the rights of unborn foetuses, as well as evaluations of women's rights to control their bodies, to name just two. Moliner and Tafani argue that even when there is broad social consensus about the positiveness or negativeness of each component of a social representation, attitudes towards the object of that representation can none the less differ if those attitudes are based on different components of that representation. Thus in debates about abortion people do not usually focus on directly challenging the merits of their opponents' arguments (e.g., people who take a pro-life position in debates about abortion do not typically argue that women should *not* have control of their bodies), but instead work to promote the centrality of the component of the representation on which their attitude is based (e.g., that the abortion debate is fundamentally about the rights of the unborn, versus it being primarily about women's rights to reproductive choice).

An important and central function of representations and attitudes (as traditionally understood), is that they are a mechanism for the transmission and communication of social beliefs and knowledge. Communication and interaction are thoroughly social processes that functional approaches to attitudes have relatively neglected. The public expression of an attitude by an individual usually provokes some form of reaction from those around – attitudes are not usually expressed only to the gods, then to disappear in the social ether. The public reaction to an expressed attitude engages both the individual and the public in a rhetorical dialogue. Positions, views, beliefs, doubts, inconsistencies, related issues, and so on, are exchanged and debated upon. These processes force the individual, perhaps unwittingly, to resolve inconsistencies, to consider one attitude in relation to many, to figure out what he or she believes in and how strongly, to commit publicly to a position – in short, to think critically about his or her attitude and its object. While this communicative and *dialogical* function is a strong emphasis in social representations theory (and discursive psychology), it has received less attention in social cognitive models of attitudes. Indeed, the increasing interest and significance placed on the automatic activation of attitudes has relegated the interactive and dialogic features of attitude expression to the backseat.

Another social function of social beliefs and representations is that they play an explanatory, and hence justificatory, role in orienting the individual to the social world. An 'attitude' of dislike and disdain of the poor, of the unemployed, of people of a different class, of people of a different colour, serves not only to orient the individual to that particular social object, but also to position that social object, be it a person or a group, in social space. This helps to explain, as well as justify and reproduce, the social system which produced those social positions, and to defend the individual's own social position. This is an area in which social psychologists, especially those working within a social representations framework, have recently developed some interest. We will discuss these ideological functions in depth in Chapter 8.

To recap, then, a social representation is a collectively constructed and shared knowledge and understanding about a particular theme or issue or topic. It is almost atmospheric, and is certainly cultural. It is something which all members of a collective can access and use in understanding the events around them. It orients people to social objects, and is then, in this sense, a social 'attitude'. Importantly, it is the shared nature of attitudes as social representations that allows members of a collective to identify particular kinds of utterances and behaviours as evaluations. Without this sharedness, many of the sophisticated means by which we are able to communicate our attitudes would simply not work, because they could not be recognized by others.

Discursive Psychology and Attitudes

The traditional notion of an attitude and the assumption that it can be encapsulated by responses to items in a questionnaire scale assumes the existence of internal cognitive entities, which, as recent attitude research has shown, can be elicited automatically and often without regard to the context in which they are activated. In contrast, discursive social psychology argues social psychologists should look to natural talk or discourse to understand how evaluations are constructed and put together in everyday life. The anti-cognitivist epistemology underlying the discursive take on attitudes is best summarized by Potter and Wetherell (1987, p. 4, original emphasis):

> We do not intend to use the discourse as a pathway to entities or phenomena lying beyond the text. Discourse analysis does not take for granted that accounts reflect underlying attitudes or dispositions and therefore we do not expect that an individual's discourse will be consistent and coherent. Rather the focus is on the discourse *itself*: how it is organized and what it is doing. Orderliness in discourse will be viewed as a product of the orderly *functions* to which discourse is put.

The contextual variability of discourse: attitudes are situated evaluated practices

When discursive social psychologists have analysed the fine detail of what people actually say in everyday talk about their social world, they have found people's views to be fragmented, inconsistent and contradictory. That is, everyday talk is messy. This messiness is typically smoothed over by traditional quantitative and qualitative methods of research, which look for underlying consistency and coherence in people's attitudes. The use of aggregating quantitative methods, such as the reporting of mean results in questionnaire data and the use of gross categories to code qualitative data, homogenizes people's responses and thus suppresses this variability (Potter & Wetherell, 1987). These research methods then present an over-simplified picture of people's actual evaluative practices in everyday life. Discursive social psychology attempts to 'understand how everyday evaluations with all their contradictions and ambiguities are used' (Potter, 1998, p. 242).

This messiness is also glossed over by the cognitive epistemology underlying traditional social psychological theories, which have assumed an inherent human motivation for cognitive balance and consistency. This is clearly evident in the attitude theories we reviewed above, especially in Festinger's cognitive dissonance theory and in the enigma that has surrounded the attitude–behaviour relationship. Indeed, the search within traditional social psychology to measure and uncover stable and consistent attitudes, which can then predict people's actual behaviour, could be likened to the search for the 'holy grail'. Note how Fishbein and Ajzen shifted the focus away from the concept of 'attitudes' to 'behavioural intentions' in their attempts to predict people's actual behavioural practices. As Billig (1982; Billig, Condor, Edwards, Middleton & Radley, 1988) has argued, there has been little interest among social psychologists in theorizing the ambivalent and 'dilemmatic' nature of people's views and opinions, and that, far from producing discomfort, people probably tolerate considerable ambivalence in their lives. Discursive social psychology suggests that people's views and opinions depend on the particular discursive context in which evaluations are made and what these evaluations are designed to do:

> Evaluations are not treated as something that are carried around ready-made by participants but are worked up in a way that is suitable for what is being done. In discursive social psychology attitudes are *performed* rather than *preformed*. (Potter, 1998, p. 246, original emphasis)

From this perspective, then, people are expected to demonstrate variability in their views about the same issue or object in different contexts and settings. For example in a study analysing focus group discussions on race relations in Australia, Augoustinos, Tuffin and Rapley (1999) found that participants commonly deployed a historical narrative of Australia's colonial past to explain and account for existing social problems and inequities experienced by Indigenous-Australians. In this discursive context, participants emphasized the importance of history in understanding the contemporary plight of Indigenous people. Paradoxically, however, when the discussion shifted to whether Australians should acknowledge the historical injustices suffered by Indigenous people, the same participants also argued that a focus on history was not constructive and indeed was a constraint that prevented Australians from progressing to a better future. Such variability is predicted by discursive social psychology and is indicative of *rhetorical orientation and function*. In the former context, Australia's colonial past was used to justify and rationalize existing inequalities, in particular, to blame the imperialist British for the contemporary plight of Indigenous people. In the latter, the denial of history functioned to downplay the ongoing injustices experienced by Indigenous people and thus minimize the responsibility of present generations of Australians for these injustices. Thus evaluations are rhetorically organized to perform social actions such as blaming, excusing, justifying and rationalizing.

Attitudes are put together with discursive resources

In Chapter 2 we detailed how discursive social psychology has replaced the traditional attitude construct by identifying the discursive practices and resources that are drawn upon in everyday talk when people express opinions, argue and debate (Potter, 1998). These discursive resources include recurring patterns of talk such as interpretative repertoires (Potter & Wetherell, 1987) and rhetorical commonplaces (Billig, 1987) that participants mobilize in their talk. From this perspective, talk and discourse are viewed as *social practices*, and are analysed with the aim of showing how various linguistic resources and rhetorical devices constitute particular constructions of reality. Indeed there is now a large body of discursive research that analyses the interpretative repertoires and rhetorical commonplaces associated with a wide range of topics including race and prejudice (Augoustinos, et al., 1999; Nairn & McCreanor, 1991; Wetherell & Potter,

1992), gender and inequality (Riley, 2002; Wetherell, Stiven, & Potter, 1987), masculinities (Edley and Wetherell, 1995), and nationalism (Billig, 1995; Condor, 2000; Rapley, 1998).

Building on the study by Wetherell et al. (1987) discussed in Chapter 2, a more recent study by Riley (2002) on gender and inequality nicely demonstrates the points of difference between a discursive and a traditional approach to understanding attitudes on this particular social issue. Riley (2002) conducted open-ended interviews with professional men on their views about gender and inequality in the workplace. After analysing the interview transcripts in some detail, Riley found that equality was largely defined in terms of treating everyone the same, regardless of social category membership. In these accounts, social groups were stripped of their historical and social location in society and were positioned as equivalent and interchangeable. Discrimination was seen as transgressing this abstract ideal of equality and was constructed as any practice or principle that made one's social category membership salient. An 'individual abilities' repertoire that emphasized the importance of merit, regardless of social category membership, was also pervasively deployed to account for employment opportunities in the workplace. Riley demonstrated how these individualist and gender (social category) neutral repertoires functioned to legitimate the existing gender inequities in the workplace, and to undermine interventions that sought to improve women's opportunities. Moreover, she argued that such a neutral account of groups that masked differences in power and status relations negated the need for different or special treatment for historically disadvantaged groups such as women. Notably absent from the men's talk were alternative constructions of equality and discrimination that attended to the structural and social aspects of men's (privileged) and women's (disadvantaged) historical positions.

As we pointed out previously, an important feature of this discursive analysis is its ability to explicate how people manage to hold contradictory positions on gender and equality. On the one hand, these professional men were very supportive of gender equality in the workplace, but on the other, they were not prepared to support interventions such as affirmative action for women to facilitate this equality. Indeed, this was constructed as a discriminatory practice that transgressed abstract principles of treating everyone the same. As in Wetherell et al.'s (1987) study, these men could be described as 'unequal egalitarians'.

At this point it is important to be very clear about the claims of discursive social psychology. It does not claim, for example, that people cannot produce categorical responses of the kind that are typically formulated in

Textbox 4.2

Measuring ambivalent attitudes to women

Consider how a traditional cognitive approach involving a questionnaire scale measuring attitudes to gender equality might tap into this contradiction and ambivalence. It is quite likely, for example, that the participants in Riley's study might obtain quite high scores on egalitarianism when responding to questions such as: 'men and women should have the same opportunities in the workplace'; 'discrimination in the workplace is unacceptable'. No doubt, many of them would tick 'strongly agree' as their preferred response. As we have seen in Riley's discursive study, people can be quite adept at sidestepping such egalitarian commitments when it comes to the crunch.

Of course, it could be countered that a good questionnaire scale would be constructed with these matters in mind, and would include questions that measure more subtle forms of discrimination. Indeed, this solution has already been provided by the construction of scales that are designed to measure ambivalent sexism (Glick and Fiske, 1996), or subtle forms of racism (McConahay, 1986).

Below we have sampled some items from *The Ambivalent Sexism Inventory* (ASI) developed by Glick and Fiske (1996). Respondents are asked to indicate their agreement to 22 'statements concerning men and women and their relationship in contemporary society' on a six-point scale ranging from disagree strongly (0) to agree strongly (5). For example:

1. *No matter how accomplished he is, a man is not truly complete as a person unless he has the love of a woman.*
2. *Most women interpret innocent remarks or acts as being sexist.*
3. *Women should be cherished and protected by men.*
4. *Women seek to gain power by getting control over men.*
5. *When women lose to men in a fair competition, they typically complain about being discriminated against.*
6 *Women, compared to men, tend to have a superior moral sensibility.*

Items 1, 3 and 6 are taken to represent aspects of Benevolent Sexism, which is directed towards women who adhere to traditional gender roles, whereas items 2, 4 and 5 are representative of Hostile Sexism, which is primarily directed towards non-traditional women.

Think about these statements and how you and others might answer them.

- How well do these statements capture ambivalent attitudes towards women?
- What are some of the benefits in using such quantitative scales in measuring public attitudes?
- What are some of the disadvantages in measuring attitudes in this way?
- Is ambivalence a psychological state that can be located within the person?
- What benefits might there be in locating ambivalence in ideological discourses rather than in the individual? What are the disadvantages?

questionnaire response scales. Clearly, people can produce such 'free-standing' evaluations and individual opinions when they are asked to do so by researchers (Puchta & Potter, 2003). In ordinary talk and conversation, however, evaluations are rhetorically organized and occasioned by participants to perform social actions and functions such as justifying, explaining and defending. People may agree or disagree, but usually they do so with provisos, qualifications, explanations and justifications, etc. Within discursive psychology, the rhetorical organization and social functions of evaluations are 'grist to the mill' for the analyst.

Moreover, as we will discuss further in Chapter 7 on prejudice and racism, ambivalence is not seen as an internal cognitive or psychological state of individuals. Rather, as Billig (1996; Billig et al., 1988) argues, this ambivalence is located in broader ideological discourses within society that are organized around dilemmas linked to liberal individualist principles about justice, freedom, equality and individual rights. These liberal principles can be mobilized flexibly and in contradictory ways to do important rhetorical work: in some contexts they can be invoked to justify change in redressing disadvantage and improving a group's status, while in other contexts they can be used to justify and legitimate existing social relations. This flexible juxtaposition of liberal principles can produce a range of ideological dilemmas for members of any liberal democratic society as they argue and debate notions of fairness, equality and justice (Billig et al., 1988).

As Potter (1998) points out, this emphasis in discursive social psychology on contextualizing people's views and opinions in wider ideological discourses within society is similar to the social representations tradition which treats attitudes as emerging from widely shared representations. Where the two traditions depart, though, is that whereas social representations theory retains a cognitive epistemology, locating representations in the mind, as well as in the world, discursive social psychology refrains from positing an underlying cognitive machinery which drives what people say about the world.

The social cognitive approach to attitudes discussed presumes that attitudes are *things*, that they can be identified, measured, changed, and that they can exert causal influence on other things such as behaviours. All this isn't necessarily explicit; neither is it necessarily implied by McGuire's definition of attitudes as 'responses that locate objects of thought on dimensions of judgement'. But all this is explicitly, directly challenged by alternative, discursive approaches, which see 'attitudes' as having no ontological status, as being too variable across and within situations to uphold any inferences of consistency. Instead, 'attitudes' are seen as *evaluative practices* expressed in talk to perform social actions in specific interactional settings (see Textbox 4.3).

Textbox 4.3

The issue of 'attitude consistency'

A major limitation of individualistic, mentalistic, social cognitive approaches to attitudes is that they struggle to explain the *content* of attitudes and the *sharedness* of attitudes. By focusing on processes such as activation and accessibility, they ignore the origins and functions of the content of attitudes. This limitation is a general limitation of social cognitive analyses of *all* categorial processes, such as schemas, stereotypes, as well as attitudes. But what of the claim by discursive psychologists that stable and enduring cognitive structures such as 'attitudes' are difficult to locate in naturalistic data, such as everyday talk and conversation?

It is undoubtedly the case that individuals are not consistent in the way they express evaluations of objects in interaction. People who dislike Tony Blair, for example, do not always dislike him to the same degree, in the same way, or even at all, in different situations. What is apparently the same negative evaluation can *mean* different things in different situations. Even the category or object 'Tony Blair' changes depending on the situational context of that category. This poses problems for standard social cognitive accounts of attitude. However, does variability like this necessarily disallow consistency? Consider the many public speeches that Tony Blair has made during his time as Prime Minister of Britain. There would be, without a doubt, considerable variability and flexibility in his public utterances on a wide range of political, economic, and social issues. However, we would also see a fair degree of consistency. For example, consider Blair's expressed views on the war in Iraq. It is unimaginable to argue that Blair did not have an attitude to the war and a very strong attitude at that!

How then would discursive approaches explain and account for this cross-situational consistency? Discursive psychology invokes the concept of 'interpretive repertoires' to address this problem. If we go back to Tony Blair and his pro-war position on Iraq, we could, for example, identify two pervasive repertoires that Blair mobilized over time to justify his position on the war. First, there was the 'weapons of mass destruction or WMD repertoire'. Of course, when the WMDs didn't materialize, this justificatory repertoire was replaced with one that emphasized the need to remove the regime of Sadam Hussein and introduce 'freedom and democracy' in Iraq.

As described by Potter and Wetherell, the notion of interpretive repertoire is more descriptive than analytical or explanatory. The notion raises many issues about how such repertoires come to be generated as collective phenomena, how they can be contested or negotiated, and how they relate to individuals in interaction. Many would also argue that the notion also requires some concession to 'things beyond discourse'.

Chapter Summary

In this chapter we have examined one of the most frequently studied constructs in social psychology – attitudes. The traditional social cognitive approach to attitudes is that attitudes are enduring and stable cognitive structures that evaluate a specific object, person or issue. Some attitudes are more readily accessible than others and are thus more easily activated. In line with the recent move towards the study of automaticity in social cognition, studies have demonstrated that some attitudes are implicit and can be activated unintentionally, outside of our conscious awareness. Traditional approaches to the study of attitudes have addressed the enduring enigma concerning the problematic relationship between attitudes and behaviour. Systematic attempts have been made to develop theoretical models which can better predict this complex relationship, including the theory of reasoned action, and more recently, the theory of planned behaviour.

As the early functional approach to attitudes emphasized, attitudes are also important markers of social identity. Social identity and self-categorization theories suggest that shared attitudes are a basis for psychological group formation. Social groups have specific norms about particular attitudes so that the salience of particular social identities at any one time will influence the expression of normative attitudes and behaviour. In a similar vein, social representations theory emphasizes the group-defining and consensually shared nature of attitudes. Social representations theorists have been critical of the increasing individualization of the attitude construct within social cognition and insist on reinstating the interactive and dialogical features of attitudes.

Discursive psychology offers a radical theoretical respecification of the attitude construct. Instead of viewing attitudes as enduring and stable cognitive structures which organize people's views and feelings towards an issue, attitudes are understood as evaluative practices which have practical consequences in everyday social interaction (Potter, 1998). As such people's expressed evaluations are expected to be variable, inconsistent and even contradictory depending on the action orientation of their talk.

Further Reading

Eagly, A. H., & Chaiken, S. (1998). Attitude structure and function. In D. T. Gilbert, S. T. Fiske & G. Lindzey (Eds.), *Handbook of social psychology* (4th ed. pp. 269–322). New York: McGraw-Hill.

Fazio, R. H., & Olson, M. A. (2003). Attitudes: Foundations, functions, and consequences. In M. A. Hoff and J. Cooper (Eds.), *The Sage handbook of social psychology* (pp. 139–160). London: Sage.

Gaskell, G. (2001). Attitudes, social representations, and beyond. In K. Deaux and G. Philogène (Eds.), *Representations of the social: Bridging theoretical traditions* (pp. 228–241). Oxford: Blackwell.

Potter, J. (1998). Discursive social psychology: From attitudes to evaluations. In W. Stroebe & M. Hewstone (Eds.), *European review of social psychology* (Vol. 9, pp. 233–266). Chichester: John Wiley.

Terry, D. J., & Hogg, M. A. (Eds.). (1999). *Attitudes, behaviour, and social context: The role of norms and group membership*. Hillsdale, NJ: Erlbaum.

Attributions

Things happen. Cars break down, people fail exams, sports teams win and lose, people fall in love, marriages end in divorce, people lose their jobs, loved ones die, people fight in the streets, people kill others in war, ethnic groups try to eliminate other groups. Most people, most of the time, do not accept that the world in which they live is capricious, whimsical or random. For most people, most of the time, things happen for a reason. Events are caused. For life to be orderly and predictable, people attribute causes and explanations to events and try to understand why people behave the way they do. The ways in which people do this, the reasons why they attribute, how they attribute, the conditions under which they do and don't attribute, all constitute the subject matter of *attribution theory*.

Like the previous chapter on attitudes, we will review the study of attributions or causal explanations from four different theoretical frameworks: social cognition, social identity, social representations and discursive psychology. As with most social psychological topics, the study of attributions has largely been dominated by the social cognitive tradition, and indeed reflects the mainstream view of how people attribute causes to everyday events and behaviour. We will see, however, how other theoretical approaches have attempted to provide a more social and contextual account of attributing causality in everyday life.

Social Cognition and Attributions

Attribution theory dominated social psychology during the 1970s and 1980s and in that time a massive body of research was generated. Kelley and Michela (1980) reported that during the 1970s over 900 attribution studies had been published, and by 1994 Smith estimated that this number had quadrupled. More recently, research on causal attributions has waned, although much of this tradition has come to be subsumed under the field of 'ordinary personology'. Coined by Daniel Gilbert (1998), ordinary personology refers to the processes by which ordinary people come to understand others by inferring their temporary states and feelings and their stable and enduring traits and characteristics. As we will see below, this focus on understanding others shares many of the central concerns of attribution theory. Despite the enormous attention devoted to the study of attribution, social psychology has failed to develop a single, unifying, integrating theory of attribution (Gilbert, 1998). Rather, there are several 'mini-theories' of attributional processes. Historically, three of these are considered central – the contributions of Heider, Jones and Davis, and Kelley – and it is these that we consider here. These mini-theories are not in any real sense competing theories – they are not offered as rival abstract accounts of the same social phenomena. Rather, the discipline has treated these contributions as complementing one another. It is likely that they could be integrated into a single over-arching theory of attribution, though this has yet to be done.

Heider's (1958) naïve psychology

Fritz Heider was an Austrian Jew who fled the horrors of wartime Europe to the relative safety of the United States. Heider's most important work is his 1958 book *The Psychology of Interpersonal Relations,* in which he presages most of the work on attribution to follow. In this book, and in an earlier article (Heider & Simmel, 1944), Heider articulates a 'common sense psychology' or a 'naïve psychology of action'.

Heider's common-sense psychology views people as naïve scientists. People intuitively, or in a common-sense way, infer or deduce the causes of events around them. They naturally view the world as sets of cause and effect relations, even, as we saw at the beginning of Chapter 2, in an anthropomorphic way, when there is no causal relationship at all (Heider & Simmel, 1944; Michotte, 1963). The arrangement of objects and events into cause and effect relations constitutes a *causal system* in our cognitive architecture (Krech, Krutchfield & Ballachey, 1962). The question of which of the many available objects and events shall be taken as cause and which as effect is crucial; it almost defines the attributional process. Heider claimed that we tend to perceive a cause and its effect as a perceptual unit. Some objects and events combine more easily than others to form a causal unit, especially when the object or cause is a human actor and the event or effect is a social behaviour. Two prime determinants of 'unit perception' are similarity and proximity. In our intuitive causal systems, two events are more likely to be seen as causally related if they are proximal rather than distal. Temporal proximity is especially potent at influencing perceived causality. Likewise, greater similarity between two events makes them more likely to be perceived as a causal unit than is the case for dissimilar events.

Two further principles of causal inference are important. First, people tend to attribute behaviour to a single cause rather than to multiple coterminous causes; and second, causes of behaviour can be thought of as residing either within the actor or outside the actor somewhere in the situation. Causes within the actor are said to be *dispositional causes*, and include factors such as personality characteristics, motivation, ability, and effort. Causes outside the actor are *situational* and include factors such as the social context and role obligations. According to Heider, these two broad classes of cause are ipsative – the more one is favoured as an explanation of a particular behaviour the less likely the other will also be used. Heider noticed that people tend to emphasize dispositional or internal causes at the expense of situational causes when explaining behaviour. This tendency has become known as the 'fundamental attribution error', to which we will return later.

Jones and Davis's (1965) correspondent inference theory

The start of the ascendancy of attribution theory in North American social psychology is marked by the publication in 1965 of a paper by Edward Jones and Keith Davis, outlining their theory of correspondent inferences. This theory is the first systematization of some of Heider's earlier ideas. The basic premise of the theory is that, under certain conditions, people display a strong tendency to *infer* that people's actions *correspond* to their intentions and dispositions. That is, people like to infer that a person's behaviour matches an underlying stable quality in the person. For example, a *correspondent inference* would be to attribute someone's aggressive behaviour to an internal stable trait of the person, such as 'aggressiveness'. Jones and Davis argued that such inferences are motivated by our need to view people's behaviour as intentional and predictable, reflecting their underlying character. This in turn, enhances our sense of being able to predict and control other people's behaviour and thus our social interactions more generally.

In everyday life, however, making such correspondent inferences may not be straightforward. The information needed to make such inferences may be ambiguous, requiring us to draw upon cues that are maximally informative (reduce uncertainty about the causes of those behaviours). Jones and Davis (1965) outline three major factors affecting the process of making correspondent inferences: the social desirability of the behaviour, a person's choice in the behaviour, and the motivational variables of hedonic relevance and personalism.

Behaviours judged to be *socially desirable* are less informative than behaviours judged to be socially undesirable. When behaviour is socially desirable – desirable in the context in which it occurs, that is – it is normative or expected. Observing such behaviour is not informative to the perceiver because there are several alternative, equally probable, reasons why the behaviour occurred. The behaviour may have occurred because the actor is intrinsically a good person, chronically prone to commit such socially desirable behaviours (that is, a dispositional or internal attribution). But the behaviour may have occurred simply because it was expected; it was the right thing to do (a situational or external attribution). Either explanation is equally likely. The behaviour is uninformative because it does not help the perceiver adjudicate between the two competing explanations of the good, desirable, expected, normative behaviour.

This is not the case for socially undesirable behaviour. Such behaviours are counter-normative; they are not what is expected. Precisely for this reason they are more informative than socially desirable behaviours. In the latter case, dispositional and situational explanations for the behaviour are equally probable. For undesirable behaviours, the situational explanation has been eliminated; it is less probable than the dispositional explanation. Thus, the perceiver, the intuitive scientist, has data that reduce uncertainty, which help arbitrate between competing explanations. Undesirable behaviours are more informative than desirable behaviours, and allow the perceiver to make a dispositional attribution about the actor with confidence. The attribution about the actor's disposition is likely to be as negative as the observed behaviour.

A second important determinant of correspondent inferences is whether the actor freely chose the behaviour – *the principle of non-common effects*. The principle applies particularly when an actor has, or at least is perceived to have, free choice in action between several behavioural alternatives. Again, the principle works because under these conditions the behaviour is informative; it reduces uncertainty by implicitly favouring one explanation for the behaviour over other, competing explanations.

The desirability of outcomes and the principle of non-common effects are both cognitive factors influencing the attributional process. The final factor in the Jones and Davis theory of correspondent inferences is motivational, and includes two related constructs – *hedonic relevance* and *personalism*. An action is said to be hedonically relevant for a perceiver if the consequences of the action affect the perceiver; the welfare of the perceiver is either harmed or benefited by the action. Personalistic actions are a subset of hedonically relevant actions, and are characterized by the *intention* of an actor for the action to have hedonic relevance for the perceiver. Actions which are perceived to be hedonically relevant or personalistic are more likely to produce a correspondent inference about the actor than are other actions.

Kelley's (1967) covariation model

The analogy between the professional scientist and the everyday perceiver, first articulated by Heider, is brought to the fore in Harold Kelley's covariation model of attribution. The model rests on the *principle of covariation*, which asserts that before two events can be accepted as causally linked they must covary with one another. If two events do not covary, they cannot be causally connected.

The principle of covariation was used by Kelley as an analogy for the way in which people infer causation in their everyday lives. Kelley (1967) suggested that three factors are crucial in assessing covariation, and that different constellations of positions on these three factors lead to different types of causal conclusions regarding the specific behaviour in question. The three factors are *consistency, distinctiveness* and *consensus*. If they are thought of as independent of one another, the three dimensions constitute a cube – hence Kelley's model is often referred to as an attributional cube. The general context in which these three dimensions are applied is one where a perceiver attributes a cause to a person's response to a particular stimulus at a particular time. Consistency refers to whether that person responds in the same way to the same stimulus or similar stimuli at different times. Distinctiveness concerns whether the actor acts in the same way to other, different stimuli, or whether the actor's response distinguishes between different stimuli. Consensus is not a feature of the actor's behaviour, but of the behaviour of others: is there consensus across actors in response to the same stimulus, or do people vary in response? According to the covariation model, perceivers will decide, almost in a dichotomous way, that the actor acts either in the same way at different times (consistency is high) or in different ways (consistency is low), that the actor either shows similar responses to different stimuli (distinctiveness is low) or acts this way only in response to this particular stimulus (distinctiveness is high), and that the actor either acts in the same way as most other people (consensus is high) or acts differently (consensus is low).

Different constellations of positions on the three dimensions lead to different attributions about the causes of behaviour. An internal or dispositional attribution is most likely when consistency is high, distinctiveness is low and consensus is low. An external or situational attribution is most likely when consistency is high, distinctiveness is high and consensus is low. Other constellations lead to less clear attributions.

Two important factors were added to the covariation model by Kelley five years after his original formulation (Kelley, 1972) – *discounting* and *augmentation*. An event can have many causes. It sometimes happens that several plausible causes co-occur, but some would be expected to augment, or make more likely, the given effect, and some would be expected to inhibit, or make less likely, the given effect. If the effect occurs even in the presence of inhibitory causes, then the augmenting cause will be judged as stronger than if the augmenting cause and its effect had occurred without the inhibitory cause. Any single factor is discounted as a cause of an event if there are also other plausible causes present (Kelley, 1972).

Kelley's covariation model has one important requirement of perceivers, which is not included in either Heider's or Jones and Davis's models – namely, that perceivers utilize information from across times, situations and actors. Without such information it is impossible to make consistency, distinctiveness and consensus judgements. In contrast, the perceiver in the naïve scientist model or in the correspondent inference model makes causal attributions based on a single action performed by a single actor on a single instance. The point is an important one when attempting to evaluate how well the theory relates to every-day practice. People do not approach the problem of assigning cause to an action as though they are unaware or ignorant of the likelihood that other people would perform the same action in response to the same stimulus, or the same person would repeat the behaviour, or how that actor would perform in response to other stimuli. People do not consider each event as if it were new. On the other hand, people do not engage in the complex mental calculus described by Kelley's covariation model every time they assign a cause to an action. A resolution to this dilemma is offered by the concept of *causal schemas* (Kelley, 1972, 1973). Kelley's concept can be taken to refer to a set of stored knowledge about the relations between causes and effects. We each of us acquire through socialization an implicit causal theory of events. This implicit theory provides us with a ready-made attributional account of most events we encounter from one day to the next. It allows us to run on default most of the time, and we only have to devote attention to unusual, exceptional or important cases. We will return to this notion of causal schemas when we consider a cultural or social representations approach to everyday attributions.

The writings of Heider, Jones and Davis, and Kelley constitute the major theoretical foundations of attribution theory. Together, the three accounts provide a wide-ranging view of how people go about the business of making causal sense of their world. Each of these three theorists explicitly adopts the professional scientist systematically seeking the causes of events in Nature as an analogy of the layperson seeking causal understanding of the surrounding world. A consequence of this analogy is a view of the human perceiver as rational, as going about the attributional process in a fairly systematic, logical fashion. A moment's reflection is all that is needed to acknowledge that people typically do not act in this way – not even scientists. It is reasonable to think of attribution theory as being prescriptive – it describes how attributions perhaps should be made. Indeed, empirical research has found that people do not make attributions in such a systematic and calculated way. Rather, social perceivers demonstrate persistent biases when attributing causality to events and behaviour. We turn now to consider what these attributional biases are and possible reasons for their occurrence.

Attributional Biases

When an attribution deviates from the prescribed model, it is thought of as a biased attribution. Some attribution researchers refer to biases as *errors*. This implies that researchers know the *true* causes of behaviour. In all probability they don't. There are no validity benchmarks for assessing the veracity of an attribution. It is better, then, to refer simply to attributional biases, rather than errors.

The fundamental attribution error

[The *fundamental* attribution error] is the tendency for attributers to underestimate the impact of situational factors and to overestimate the role of dispositional factors in controlling behavior. (Ross, 1977, p. 183, original emphasis)

More recently, Gilbert (1995, 1998; Gilbert & Malone, 1995) has referred to this phenomenon as the 'correspondence bias'. The earliest empirical demonstration of the *fundamental attribution error (FAE)* was produced by Jones and Harris (1967), in which participants were shown to make correspondent inferences about an actor's attitudes based on the actor's statements about an issue. These inferences occurred even when the participants knew the actor had no choice in making the statement. In their first experiment, participants read a short essay on Castro's Cuba and then indicated what they thought was the true attitude of the essay writer to Castro's Cuba. Each subject read just one essay, but half of the essays were pro-Castro; the other half were anti-Castro. Given the time and the place of the study, the direction of the essay (pro- or anti-) constituted a manipulation of the prior probability of the behaviour – there simply weren't many Castro advocates

Table 5.1   *Mean attributed attitude scores (and variances in parentheses), according to essay direction and degree of choice*

Choice condition	Essay direction			
	Pro-Castro		Anti-Castro	
Choice	59.62	(13.59)	17.38	(8.92)
No choice	44.10	(147.65)	22.87	(17.55)

Source: Jones and Harris, 1967, p. 6

in North Carolina in the mid-1960s, making the pro-Castro essay an improbable, and hence more informative, behaviour. Layered over the manipulation of essay direction was the second manipulation, of choice. Participants were told that the essay they were to read was written as an answer in a political science exam. Half of the participants were also told that the essay writer was instructed to write an essay either defending or criticizing Castro's Cuba; the other half were told either that the essay writer was instructed to write a criticism of Castro's Cuba or that the writer was instructed to write a defence of Castro's Cuba. In other words, participants were led to believe that the essay's position had been either assigned (no choice, uninformative) or chosen by the writer (choice, informative). After reading the 200-word essay participants answered questions about what they thought the essay writer's *true* attitude was towards Castro's Cuba, and then indicated their own attitude towards Castro's Cuba.

If the informativeness of the behaviour was the most important factor determining whether or not a correspondent inference was made by the observer participants, then such an inference should be most evident among those who read a pro-Castro essay written by someone who could have chosen to write an essay criticizing or defending Castro's Cuba, and should be least evident among those participants who read the anti-Castro essay written by someone who was instructed what to write. The mean 'attributed attitude scores' – where scores can range from 10 (anti-Castro) to 70 (pro-Castro) – are reproduced in Table 5.1. There is indeed evidence here that participants made correspondent inferences – the inferred attitude matched the essay direction, and inferences are stronger in the choice conditions than in the no-choice conditions. But – and this is the important part for the FAE – correspondent inferences are still evident in the no-choice conditions. Even when participants were told that the essay writer was instructed to write either a pro- or an anti-Castro essay, they still infer that the essay writer has an attitude consonant with the views expressed in the essay. This is the

FAE: attributers (participants in the experiment) have apparently under-estimated the impact of situational factors and overestimated the role of dispositional factors in determining behaviour. Furthermore, experiment 2 in the Jones and Harris (1967) study demonstrated that emphasizing the choice manipulation did not diminish the attitude attribution effect, even under no-choice conditions participants were correctly aware of the essayist's choice or lack of choice, and that making the essay ambivalent did not much alter participants' attributions either.

Dispositional attributions are spontaneous and automatic Gilbert (1995, p. 106) concludes that attributing behaviour to dispositions rather than to situations is one of the 'most reliable and robust findings in the annals of research on human attribution'. Moreover, recent research has drawn upon the work on automaticity in social perception to suggest that making correspondent inferences is so pervasive that dispositional attributions are made spontaneously and without conscious awareness (Gilbert, 1995, 1998; Newman & Uleman, 1989, 1993; Uleman, 1999). In social cognition parlance, dispositional attributions are the 'default-option' – perceivers spontaneously attribute behaviour to people's traits because such attributions are 'quick and dirty' (Fiske, 2004). Quattrone (1982) was the first to propose a sequential model of attribution which suggests that once a behaviour is identified, dispositional attributions are always made first, spontaneously and without conscious deliberation, but these can be subsequently corrected by situational attributions if perceivers are motivated and have time to consider alternative explanations. Thus, whereas trait attributions are easy and effortless, situational attributions are corrections that require more effort and cognitive resources (Gilbert, Pelham & Krull, 1988). This sequential three-stage model of attribution is illustrated in Figure 5.1. A review by Trope and Gaunt (2003) concludes that situational attributions are more likely to be made if perceivers:

1. are made accountable for their inferences;
2. are not cognitively busy or distracted by pursuing other goals; or
3. when situational attributions are made salient, accessible and relevant.

But why should dispositional attributions be so effortless and less cognitively demanding than situational attributions? It is to this question that we now turn.

Explanations of the fundamental attribution error Several explanations of the FAE or correspondent bias have been suggested (Gilbert & Malone, 1995). These explanations tend to belong to one of two types: explanations based on

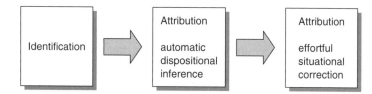

Figure 5.1 Quattrone's three-stage model of attribution (adapted from Gilbert, 1995)

psychological or cognitive processes, and explanations which seek the origins of the bias in social, cultural and ideological processes. Heider (1958, p. 54) himself was the first to advance a cognitive explanation, arguing that 'behaviour in particular has such salient properties it tends to engulf the total field'. Fiske and Taylor, in support of this cognitive explanation, describe how situational factors which give rise to behaviour, such as the social context, roles or situational pressures, are 'relatively pallid and dull and unlikely to be noticed when compared with the dynamic behavior of the actor' (1991, p. 67). The fundamental attribution error has therefore primarily been explained by the dominance of the actor in the perceptual field.

Another explanation is a motivational one that emphasizes the degree to which person attributions give us a sense of predictive control of other people's behaviour. Jones and Davis (1965) stressed this aspect of correspondent inferences: that such inferences are motivated by our need to view people's behaviour as intentional and reflecting their underlying personality traits. If we subscribed to a view that people's behaviour was unstable and fluctuated according to the situations in which they found themselves, then this makes predicting their behaviour and controlling our environment all the more difficult. Thus, dispositional attributions or correspondent inferences enhance our sense of prediction and control in everyday life and that is why we prefer them.

Others have suggested that this dispositionalist bias is not a universal law of cognitive functioning, but, rather, reflects the dominant ideology of individualism within European and American culture (Bond, 1983; Farr & Anderson, 1983; Moscovici & Hewstone, 1983). The tendency to favour personal over situational causation was first noted by Ichheiser (1949), but, instead of viewing this phenomenon as an individual 'error' or bias in cognitive judgement, he viewed it as an explanation grounded in American society's collective and cultural consciousness (Farr & Anderson, 1983). The dominant representation of the person in western liberal democracies is that of an important causative agent, over and above situational and contextual considerations. The FAE, then, may not be a cognitive or perceptual bias alone, but largely a product of western, industrialized constructions of the 'individual' as the source of behaviour. If, indeed, attributions and explanations are grounded in cultural representations of the person, then cross-cultural differences should be evident in the prevalence of person attributions. Indeed, as we will detail later, this has been largely confirmed by studies comparing the prevalence of dispositional attributions in individualist as compared to collectivist cultures (Miller, 1984). As we will see, the 'person' does not seem to enjoy the same degree of perceptual dominance among non-western people living in collectivist societies.

The actor–observer effect

> There is a pervasive tendency for actors to attribute their actions to situational requirements, whereas observers tend to attribute the same actions to stable personal dispositions. (Jones & Nisbett, 1972, p. 80)

Fritz Heider noted that actors and observers have different views of behaviour, of the situation, and of the causes of behaviours in situations. 'The person tends to attribute his own reactions to the object world, and those of another, when they differ from his own, to personal characteristics in [the other]' (Heider, 1958, p. 157). Think of the ease with which we explain our own socially undesirable behaviour (e.g., being rude or impolite) in terms of extenuating, stressful circumstances, but are less sympathetic when others behave in this way, attributing it instead to the person's character. Heider referred to this as a 'polar tendency in attribution'; Jones and Nisbett (1972) called it the *'actor–observer effect' (AOE)*.

A classic experiment demonstrating the AOE was one conducted by Ross, Amabile and Steinmetz (1977). This experiment adopted the format of a quiz game involving pairs of same-sex participants. One member of the pair was randomly allocated to the role of questioner, the other to the role of contestant. The randomness of the allocation was explicit to the participants. Twelve pairs of participants were in the experimental condition and six pairs were in the control condition. In the experimental condition, questioners were told to make up ten 'challenging but not impossible' general knowledge questions to ask of the contestant. While the questioner did this, the contestant was told to compose ten easy general knowledge questions, just to 'get into the spirit of the study'. In the control condition, questioner and contestant alike produced ten easy questions, after being told that during the quiz game itself the questioner would ask the contestant to answer ten questions compiled before the experiment by someone else.

Table 5.2   *Mean ratings of self and others' general knowledge by questioners and contestants in a quiz game experiment*

| | Ratings of | |
Ratings by	Self	Other
Experimental condition		
Questioner	53.5	50.6
Contestant	41.3	66.8
Control condition		
Questioner	54.1	52.5
Contestant	47.0	50.3

Source: Ross, Amabile and Steinmetz, 1977

After participants had composed their respective sets of questions, they took part in a quiz game. During the 'game', questioners in the experimental condition asked the contestants their ten difficult but not impossible questions; questioners in the control condition were given ten questions to ask of the contestants. The number of questions answered correctly was recorded by the experimenter. In testimony to the diligence of the questioners, the average number right was only four out of ten. After completing the quiz game, questioners and contestants rated self and partner on a number of dimensions, the most important of which for our discussion was 'general knowledge compared to the average Stanford student' (the experiment was conducted at Stanford University). Participants rated self and other on this dimension on a scale from 0 to 100, with 50 marked as 'the average Stanford student'. The mean ratings provided by participants are given in Table 5.2.

In the control condition, questioners and contestants did not really distinguish between self and other in terms of general knowledge relative to the average Stanford student – everyone rated self and other as about average. In the experimental condition, on the other hand, there are big differences in how each member of the pair sees self and other. The questioner does not really distinguish between self and other, rating both around average. The contestant, though, devalues self relative to average (presumably in response to getting only four out of ten right, on average) and increases the rating of the questioner relative to average (presumably acknowledging the difficulty of the general knowledge questions produced by the questioner).

What is startling about the results? Allocation to the role of questioner or contestant was random, and participants were aware it was random. So presumably, if the roles were reversed, the erstwhile contestant would have made up ten difficult questions and the former questioner would have got about four of them right. There is an asymmetry between the roles in terms of opportunity to express 'smart' behaviour. The questioner gets to call the tune; the contestant merely plays along. The role of the questioner confers an advantage on the questioner over the contestant. Questioners apparently recognize this, and neither elevate their own status nor lower the contestants'. But contestants appear to be unaware of, or to under-correct for, the advantage conferred upon the questioner.

In a second part of the experiment, Ross, Amabile and Steinmetz had confederates re-enact some of the questioner–contestant performances. Real participants witnessed these interactions under the apprehension that they were authentic. These participants then rated both questioner and contestant on general knowledge ability, relative to the average Stanford student. These participants, acting purely as observers, apparently saw the quiz game through the eyes of the contestant. The average rating given to the questioner was 82.08 and that for the contestant 48.92, thus mirroring the ratings provided earlier by the contestants themselves.

Explanations of the AOE   Competing explanations have been advanced for the AOE. Like the FAE, one explanation is perceptual and essentially argues that actors and observers quite literally have 'different points of view' (Storms, 1973). Actors cannot see themselves acting. From an actor's perspective, what is most salient and available are the situational influences on their behaviour – the objects, the people, the role requirements and the social setting. However, from an observer's point of view, the actor's behaviour is more perceptually salient than the situation or context. These different 'vantage points' for actors and observers lead to different attributional tendencies: situational attributions for actors and dispositional attributions for observers (Taylor & Fiske, 1975). A study by Taylor and Fiske (1975) attempted to test the perceptual salience hypothesis and is illustrated in Figure 5.2.

Two male confederates were seated opposite one another, and conversed for five minutes. Seated behind confederate A were two observers, each with confederate B, but not A, in their visual field. Two other observers were behind B watching A. And two further observers were seated at the side of the table in between A and B, and with both in sight. After witnessing A and B interact for five minutes, all observers were asked to rate each confederate on the dimensions of friendliness, talkativeness and nervousness, and the extent to which each confederate's behaviour was caused by dispositional qualities

Figure 5.2 **A schematic figure of a study that attempted to test the perceptual salience hypothesis. Two confederates sat facing each other and were engaged in conversation. They were observed from three different vantage points – from behind Confederate A, from behind Confederate B, and from midway between A and B. Consistent with the perceptual salience hypothesis, the results showed that observers sitting behind A, watching B, rated B as more causal, while those sitting behind B, watching A, saw A as more causal. The observers watching from midway between A and B perceived both as equally influential (based on Taylor & Fiske, 1975).**

and by situational factors. They also rated how much each confederate set the conversation's tone, determined the kind of information exchanged in the conversation and caused the other's behaviour. If Taylor and Fiske are right, the two observers behind A watching B should see B as more causal than A, the observers behind B watching A should see A as more causal than B, and the observers in between A and B should see A and B as about equally influential. This is exactly what they found. In a similar experiment, McArthur and Post (1977) manipulated actors' relative salience using strong lighting, and again attributions about an actor's behaviour were influenced by the actor's salience.

Other individualistic explanations of the same phenomenon have been suggested. For example, Jones and Nisbett (1972) originally suggested that actors and observers may possess different information about events and it is this that leads to the different attributions. Actors have access to their own feelings, desires and motivations, as well as to their own cross-situational behavioural history, of which observers are unaware. Evidence of informational differences between actors and observers has been provided by Idson and Mischel (2001), who found that observers are more likely to make situational inferences and fewer trait attributions about an actor's behaviour if that person is familiar and important to them. Presumably, then, the longer we know someone, the more knowledge we are likely to have about their behaviour across different situations.

Another individualistic (although more social and interactive) possibility hinges on the linguistic practices of actors and observers (Guerin, 1993; Semin & Fiedler, 1988, 1989; Slugoski, Lalljee, Lamb & Ginsburg, 1993). Different linguistic categories convey different information about an event. Semin and Fiedler (1988) suggest there are four linguistic categories referring to interpersonal relations: descriptive action verbs (e.g., A is talking to B); interpretative action verbs (e.g., A is helping B); state verbs (e.g., A likes B); and adjectives (e.g., A is an extroverted person). Adjectives convey more information about a person than do, say, descriptive action verbs, and hence lead to more dispositional inferences. It is hard to imagine making any sort of correspondent inference at all based on the statement 'A is talking to B', but it is hard to avoid doing so when presented with 'A is an extroverted person'. Indeed, the latter presumes a disposition. Semin and Fiedler (1989) showed, in a replication of the second experiment by Nisbett, Caputo, Legant and Maracek (1973), that actors tended to use the more concrete linguistic forms (descriptive and interpretative verbs) and observers tended to use the abstract forms (state verbs and adjectives) which permitted and conveyed dispositional assumptions. In contrast to purely cognitive models of attribution, this work emphasizes how language itself shapes attributions (but see discursive psychology's critique of this work below).

Both the actor–observer effect and the fundamental attribution error are two of the most vigorously investigated attributional biases. As we have seen, actors and observers diverge, sometimes quite markedly, in the inferences they draw from and the attributions they make about ostensibly the same event. However, the evidence reviewed in this section cannot support a strong form of either the AOE or the FAE. It appears that attributers do not make *either* a dispositional *or* a situational attribution. Rather, a weak form of the AOE and the FAE is more consistent with a wide variety of data. In this, attributers use *both* dispositional *and* situational factors in constructing causal sense of the events surrounding them, but tend to rely on one relatively more than the other depending on their perspective on events. While there is evidence that changing people's point of view alters their attributional accounts of events in that view, this does not imply any hard-wired, innate, psychologically or cognitively necessary attributional mechanisms. Developmental and cross-cultural evidence suggests that people must learn the attributional accounts favoured by their social milieu. This learning is likely to be so efficient that particular attributional accounts become automatic and unthinking. The AOE and the FAE can be considered biases in the sense that the same event is attributed differently depending upon the attributer's position relative to that event. We turn now to consider another class of attributional biases, the so-called 'self-serving biases'.

Self-serving biases

Theories of attribution tend to view the attributer as a dispassionate bystander of events, coldly processing information available to him or her. This is, of course, far removed from the heat of normal human interaction. People *are* involved, passionately or not, in the events around them. They, and their attributions, affect and are affected by others and by events. Often people make attributions which reflect *self-serving biases*, designed, consciously or not, to enhance their esteem in their own eyes and in the eyes of others.

Attributions for success and failure It is an all too common phenomenon that people accept credit for success and deny responsibility for failure. Students do it after passing or failing a course; athletes do it after winning or losing an event; even academics do it after having a manuscript accepted or rejected for publication (Wiley, Crittenden & Birg, 1979). Although the strength of the effect varies across cultures, the attributional asymmetry following success or failure has been noted from around the globe (Fletcher & Ward, 1988; Kashima & Triandis, 1986; Zuckerman, 1979).

Once again, both cognitive and motivational explanations have been promulgated to account for this attributional asymmetry. Weary (1981), for example, suggested that focus of attention towards self or away from self (Duval & Wicklund, 1973) and informational availability may be two cognitive mechanisms implicated in the phenomenon. However, most researchers advocate a motivational explanation in accord with an almost self-evident, common-sense explanation – people accept credit for success and deflect responsibility for failure because doing so makes them feel good and look good; it serves a self-enhancement motive. For example, Miller (1976) showed that the attributional asymmetry is accentuated when the task participants succeed or fail on is important to them. Schlenker and Miller

(1977) likewise showed that attributional egocentrism among majority and minority group members in groups that succeeded or failed could be explained by a self-enhancement explanation and not by information-processing biases.

Attributing egocentrically not only bolsters self-esteem, but also influences the impressions others have of the attributer. The evidence for the latter effect, though, is clearer than for the former. As but one example, Schlenker and Leary (1982) showed that audiences were generally most favourably impressed by actors who made 'accurate' attributional claims for their success; that actors who underclaim superior performance were liked more than actors who performed the same but who apparently boasted; and that audiences disliked actors who predicted that they would not do well, even when that prediction turned out to be accurate. It is clear that different attributional patterns following success or failure create different impressions on an audience: some kinds of attributions do seem to make the actor look good. Whether they also make the actor feel good is another matter.

Central to any self-enhancement explanation of attributional biases must be the predictions that self-esteem will increase following a self-serving attribution (an internal attribution following success or an external attribution following failure) and that self-esteem will decrease following a self-deprecating attribution (an external attribution following success or an internal attribution following failure). There is strong evidence (Maracek & Metee, 1972; Shrauger, 1975) that people chronically high in self-esteem make more self-serving attributions than do people chronically low in self-esteem, who tend to make more self-deprecating attributions. This is an important finding with clinical implications for the aetiology and treatment of depression, but it is not quite the same thing as evidence that changes in self-esteem follow particular attributions, which is the core of any self-enhancement explanation.

The absence of studies documenting attribution effects on self-esteem is curious, and perhaps due to two factors. First, many researchers appear to accept such effects as obvious and hence not needing empirical verification or falsification. Second, it is methodologically difficult to design an unconfounded experiment to test the hypothesis. A pure, experimental investigation would require the experimenter to allocate participants randomly to either an internal or an external attribution condition following either success or failure and to observe consequent effects on self-esteem. But participants make their own attributions; they cannot be allocated to an internal or an external attribution condition in the same way as they can to a success or failure condition. So direction of attribution cannot be experimentally controlled. It can only be investigated by allowing participants to make their own attributions. But allowing this automatically introduces a confound between participants' attributional direction and their prior self-esteem, since we know that people with chronic high self-esteem accept credit for success and deflect blame for failure and people with chronically low self-esteem tend to do the opposite. And who knows if these attributional styles cause or reflect differences in chronic self-esteem. There is thus no direct test of the central hypothesis of a self-enhancement explanation. None the less, the indirect evidence provided by tracking changes in self-esteem following particular types of attributions, perhaps separated by participants' prior chronic self-esteem, would be valuable.

Depression Implicit in the self-enhancement account of attributional biases is the notion that it is normal, functional and biologically adaptive to make such biased attributions because they help to create and maintain a positive self-esteem. Weiner's (1985, 1986) attributional theory of motivation and emotion argues that the kinds of attributions people make for success and failure elicit different emotional consequences and that these attributions are characterized by three underlying dimensions: locus, stability and control (see Table 5.3). The locus dimension refers to whether we attribute success and failure internally or externally; the stability dimension refers to whether the cause is perceived as something fixed and stable (like personality or ability) or something changing and unstable (such as motivation and effort); and the controllability dimension refers to whether we feel we have any control over the cause. Consistent with the self-enhancement bias, people who attribute their achievements to internal, stable and controllable factors are more likely to feel good about themselves. In contrast, attributing negative outcomes to internal, stable and uncontrollable factors is associated with negative emotions such as hopelessness and helplessness. Indeed, this attributional pattern for negative events and outcomes has been referred to as a 'depressive attributional style' and has been strongly linked with clinical depression (Abramson, Seligman & Teasdale, 1978; Kuiper, 1978; Lewinsohn, Mischel, Chaplin & Barton, 1980; Peterson & Seligman, 1984; Sweeney, Anderson & Bailey, 1986). While the learned helplessness model of depression (Abramson et al., 1978) views this attributional style as directly causing depression, others have argued this attributional tendency is merely a symptom of depression, reflecting the affective state of the depressed person. Whether cause or symptom, attributional retraining programmes, in which people are taught how to make more self-enhancing attributions, are being widely accepted as an important clinical intervention in the treatment of depression (Forsterling, 1985; Wilson and Linville, 1985).

Table 5.3 *Achievement attributions for success and failure*
(after Weiner, 1985, 1986)

	Locus	Stability	Control
Ability	internal	stable	uncontrollable
Effort	internal	unstable	controllable
Luck	external	unstable	uncontrollable
Task difficulty	external	unstable	uncontrollable

Do people attribute spontaneously?

Some psychologists have suggested that attribution theory exaggerates the extent to which people seek causal explanations for everyday occurrences and events: that the degree of attributional activity suggested by attribution research may simply be an artifact of the reactive methodologies used in such studies. Bear in mind that most attribution studies require, and indeed instruct, participants to indicate their agreement or disagreement with attributional statements provided by the researchers. So, do people spontaneously engage in causal thinking and, if so, under what conditions do they make causal attributions? Two studies address these questions directly.

Lau and Russell (1980) examined newspaper reports of 33 sporting events – the six baseball games in the 1977 World Series, and a number of college and professional football games. Although the primary intention of this study was to examine *kinds* of attributions for victory and defeat, the authors reported that more causal attributions were made after an unexpected outcome than an expected one. On a more serious matter, Taylor (1982) reported a study which found that 95 per cent of a sample of cancer victims spontaneously made attributions about the cause of their cancer, and 70 per cent of close family members of cancer victims made such attributions. These two studies suggest that people do in fact spontaneously make causal attributions about events around them, at least when those events are either unexpected or negative. Weiner (1985) concludes likewise in his review of spontaneous attributions, that people do indeed engage in spontaneous causal thinking, but mostly for unexpected events and especially when confronted with failure. This conclusion is consistent with that of others who have argued that people look actively for causal explanations for the unexpected or different (Forsterling, 2001; Hewstone, 1989b) and that in such situations the complexity of attributions increases (Lalljee, Watson & White, 1982). No doubt many events in social life are common, routine, everyday, and give no rise to the need for any sort of attributional analysis. For such events, people probably function *mindlessly* (Langer, 1989), or essentially run on automatic. However, people *do* make causal attributions under some conditions, and even when operating mindlessly people probably could generate causal attributions for the events passing them by if they were required to. Attribution theory, then, is not a well-formulated theory of an imaginary phenomenon.

Criticisms of classic attribution theories

Thus far in this chapter, attributing causes to behaviour and events has been presented primarily as an intraindividual cognitive phenomenon. In traditional attribution models individuals are construed as information processors who attend to and select information from the environment, process the information, and then arrive at a causal analysis of the behaviour or event in question. This is too simple. As we all know, social life in all its intricate complexity is a mass of individuals, couples, groups, sects, ethnicities, nations, all interacting and negotiating an ever-changing social reality which is reproduced, represented, and reconstructed. None of us interacts with any one other person as if that person were an abstracted, fixed and given *individual*. We all are social, contextualized, and cannot interact with or even perceive others as if we, or they, were otherwise. Yet attribution theory, as with so much of the rest of psychology, persists in theorizing the asocial, decontextualized fiction called the individual.

Drawing on Doise's (1986) 'levels of analysis' in social psychology, Hewstone (1988, 1989a) has argued that the bulk of attribution research has been articulated at the *intrapersonal* and the *interpersonal* levels. Kelley's (1967) covariation model of attribution is a good example of the former. In this, an individual perceives an event – usually behaviour enacted by another individual – and engages in a mental calculus estimating the consistency, consensus and distinctiveness of that event, before arriving at a conclusion regarding the cause of the event. The attributer turns only inward in this attributional search, without reference to interpersonal relations, dominant social representations, the language of causation, and their relative group memberships and identifications. Everything, apart from the event which triggered the attributional search, takes place internally within the calculating mind of the individual. The actor–observer effect and the fundamental attribution error are examples of attribution research which can be called interpersonal. Even here, though, the individuals in the interaction come to the interaction strictly as individuals: the individuals have no history, no power or status differentials, no social context. They are interchangeable, asocial, decontextualized, often disembodied individuals.

These models thus far have had little to say about the social, interactive, and cultural context within which causal attributions are made. Attribution theory has therefore been criticized for being predominantly an individualistic theory requiring a greater social perspective (Hewstone, 1983). Several social psychologists have attempted to develop a more social account of attributions and it is to these efforts that we now turn. In the remainder of this chapter we will document attributional approaches that are articulated at what Doise has referred to as the *intergroup* and *societal* levels of explanation. Finally, we consider work in the discursive tradition that provides a non-cognitive discursive psychological approach to understanding attributions and explanations.

Social Identity and Attributions

The extraordinary events of September 11, 2001 – the attacks on the World Trade Center in New York and the Pentagon in Washington – will undoubtedly be remembered as one of the most politically salient and defining events at the beginning of the 21st century. These attacks and their graphic portrayal on television (as they occurred in real time) stunned the world. The research on spontaneous attributions would suggest that such a negative and unexpected event is likely to generate considerable attributional activity. Indeed, as the enormity and significance of the attacks began to sink in, people tried to make sense of this event by looking for reasons as to why it occurred. Why would a group of individuals plan and execute such a brazen act of mass murder and suicide by flying planes into tall buildings? Here is how Tony Blair, the Prime Minister of Britain, attempted to make sense of this event in a speech he delivered the day following September 11:

> [T]he world now knows the full evil and capability of international terrorism which menaces the whole of the democratic world. The terrorists responsible have no sense of humanity, of mercy, or of justice. To commit acts of this nature requires a fanaticism and wickedness that is beyond our normal contemplation.

Over time, of course, we were provided with a range of explanatory accounts, by a variety of expert sources including other world leaders, politicians, the media, and social analysts. These explanations included accounts such as that of Tony Blair that attributed the cause(s) of September 11 primarily to the religious fanaticism and extremism of 'evil' terrorists, and accounts that attributed the cause(s) to geopolitical factors and the current state of international relations (Jellis & Gaitan, 2003). People's attributions for this significant event were not arrived at simply through a solitary cognitive process of information processing: people's social, cultural and political identifications significantly shaped their causal analysis and response to the events of September 11.

A social identity, or intergroup, approach to attributions examines how group memberships, social identifications, and intergroup relations affect what sorts of attributions people make. Although we will detail this work more comprehensively later in our discussions of stereotyping and prejudice (Chapter 7), we introduce here what Pettigrew (1979) has coined the 'ultimate attribution error'.

The 'ultimate attribution error'

Pettigrew integrated Ross's FAE into Allport's (1954) classical work on intergroup relations to formulate an analysis of how prejudice shapes intergroup 'misattributions'. Pettigrew (1979) noted how people typically make attributions that favour and protect the group to which they belong (ingroup) and attributions that derogate groups to which they do not belong (outgroup). In a joke about the rather grand title Ross gave to the FAE (it is unlikely that anything in the social sciences deserves the epithet 'fundamental'), Pettigrew (1979) named this ingroup serving and outgroup derogating attributional pattern, the *'ultimate attribution error'*. When a person is confronted with an unambiguously positive behaviour committed by a member of a disliked outgroup, that person will have trouble reconciling this with their negative stereotype of the group, and is unlikely to make a dispositional attribution. This positive outgroup behaviour is likely to be explained away or dismissed as either being due to external situational pressures or to the exceptional and thus unrepresentative nature of the ingroup member. In contrast, negative behaviour by an outgroup member will be attributed to stereotypic dispositions and traits that are associated with the outgroup. This pattern of attributions is completely reversed for ingroup behaviour: positive ingroup behaviour is attributed to dispositional traits and negative ingroup behaviour is attributed to external situational factors. Indeed, studies from around the world have demonstrated what may be a universal, certainly a pervasive, self-serving and ethnocentric pattern in the way we see and explain the events around us. These studies will be reviewed in some detail in Chapter 7, but to give you a sense of this attributional bias we present an interesting study emerging from the real world of intergroup conflict in Northern Ireland.

Hunter, Stringer and Watson (1991) published a simple study which illustrates the social psychological processes underlying the markedly different

Table 5.4   *Pattern of internal and external attributions made by Catholic and Protestant students for acts of violence committed by Catholics and Protestants*

	Catholic violence		Protestant violence	
	Catholic students	Protestant students	Catholic students	Protestant students
Attribution				
Internal	5	15	19	6
External	21	6	5	15

Source: Hunter et al., 1991, p. 263

perceptions of sectarian violence in Northern Ireland. In this study, Hunter et al. gathered newsreel footage of Catholic and Protestant violence in Northern Ireland. One scene showed a Protestant attack on a Catholic funeral, and the other showed two soldiers in a car being attacked by a group of Catholics. Both scenes had been rated as being comparable in their degree of violent content by a sample of Spanish and German foreign exchange students. Assured that the two clips were equally violent, Hunter et al. then showed them to Catholic and Protestant students at the University of Ulster. The clips were shown without sound so as to control for any possible effects of media bias. These students were then asked to 'explain in their own words what they thought was happening in the videos, and why they thought those involved had behaved as they had' (Hunter et al., 1991, p. 263). Students' reasons for the behaviour of the people shown in the video were coded as either an internal or an external attribution. The pattern of attributions was clear, and is shown in Table 5.4.

Clearly, Catholic students saw the causes of violent acts committed by Catholics as residing somewhere in the situation, but saw acts of violence committed by Protestants as being caused by dispositional factors. Protestant students behaved the same way, seeing Catholic violence as being due to the Catholic actors and explaining Protestant violence away to the situation. Yet the two groups of students were witnessing the same acts; acts which had previously been judged by presumably impartial Spanish and German students to be identically violent. It is little wonder that the search for a peaceful resolution to the troubles in Northern Ireland has taken so long.

The behaviour of the participants in the Hunter et al. experiment is not unusual. Studies such as that by Hunter et al. demonstrate that social perception, especially in situations involving partisanship, is rarely, if ever, neutral and dispassionate, and that the possibility of ever being able to apprehend a single 'true' account of social 'reality' is highly questionable. Such studies also suggest that differential attributions of this kind for ingroup and outgroup violence are probably linked to the maintenance and perpetuation of intergroup conflict. Ingroup serving external attributions for violence by both groups may serve to justify violence committed by one's own group and to view it as legitimate. Furthermore, internal attributions for the other group's violence may perpetuate hostilities and perhaps even lead to a self-fulfilling prophecy, whereby members of the outgroup come to act in ways the ingroup expects (Hunter et al., 1991).

Group differences in explanations for social issues

Not surprisingly, a considerable body of research has also indicated that social groups prefer different explanations for a range of social issues and problems such as poverty and unemployment. Explanations for these social issues, for example, are linked to political identifications and voting behaviour (Furnham, 1982a, 1982c). Thus, in Britain Conservatives rate individualistic explanations for poverty and unemployment as more important than Labour voters. In turn, Labour voters rate societal-structural factors as more important (see Table 5.5). Explanations are therefore not purely cognitive phenomena, but are collectively shared by those with similar political and social identities. We will return to this research in the section below on social representations and attributions.

Social Representations and Attributions

Doise's *societal* level of explanation (the fourth level in his nomenclature) is concerned with how social representations affect attribution processes and outcomes. If we accept that explanations for everyday events and experiences are social phenomena, which are negotiated and communicated during social interaction, then we require an approach which emphasizes the contents of social knowledge; an approach which is central to social representations theory. In this section we will draw upon social representations theory to articulate what a more social and cultural model of attribution might look like.

Like attribution theory, social representations theory also emphasizes the fundamental human need to understand and explain events in everyday life. Whereas the former seeks to identify the internal cognitive processes involved in making causal explanations, the latter locates these causal attributions not in individual minds, but in the cultural meaning systems embodied by social representations. While both theories emphasize the importance of explanation in social life, the two theories are articulated at different levels of

Table 5.5   *Comparisons between British Conservative and Labour voters'*
explanations for poverty

Explanations	Conservative	Labour
Individualistic		
1 Lack of thrift and proper money management by poor people	3.07	5.17*
2 Lack of effort and laziness by the poor themselves	3.57	5.02*
3 Loose morals and drunkenness among the poor	4.62	5.82*
4 No attempts at self-improvement among the poor	3.42	4.65*
Societal		
1 Low wages in some businesses and industry	3.27	1.95*
2 Failure of society to provide good schools	5.52	3.72*
3 Prejudice and discrimination against poor people	4.93	3.95*
4 Failure of industry to provide enough jobs for poor people	4.30	3.07*
5 Being taken advantage of by the rich	4.70	3.50*
6 Inefficient trade unions	5.21	4.10*
7 High taxes and no incentives in this country	4.93	3.95*
Fatalistic		
1 Lack of ability and talent among poor people	3.92	4.80
2 Sickness and physical handicap	3.82	3.20
3 Just bad luck	5.67	5.25
4 Lack of intelligence among poor people	4.25	4.67

*Significant at or below $p < 0.05$
Note: Numbers are means on a seven-point scale where a low mean indicates stronger agreement with the statement.
Source: Adapted from Furnham, 1982a, p. 315

analysis (Doise, 1986). Unlike the traditional tenets of attribution theory, social representations theory emphasizes the social and collective nature of explanations.

Moscovici and Hewstone have proposed that social representations should be viewed as the foundations upon which attributions are built (Moscovici, 1981, 1984; Moscovici & Hewstone, 1983).

A theory of social causality is a theory of our imputations and attributions, associated with a representation ... any causal explanation must be viewed within the context of social representations and is determined thereby. (Moscovici, 1981, p. 207)

Social representations form the foundations of people's expectations and normative prescriptions, and thus act as mediators in the attributional process (Hewstone, 1989a, 1989b). In a similar vein, Lalljee and Abelson (1983) advocate a 'knowledge structure' approach to attribution. Well-learned and consensual structures, such as highly organized event schemas or scripts (Schank & Abelson, 1977), do not usually evoke causal explanations because people come to expect the sequence of events that follows. People's prior expectations, beliefs, knowledge or schemas will determine for what incoming social information they will need to engage in causal attributions. Following the principles of schema functioning we detailed in Chapter 3, information which is consistent with a person's schema or representation will not require an in-depth search for causality, given that the information is expected and therefore automatically processed. However, information which is inconsistent with expectations or existing knowledge will require a more detailed search for an explanation.

> Thus social representations impose a kind of automatic explanation. Causes are singled out and proposed prior to a detailed search for and analysis of information. Without much active thinking, people's explanations are determined by their social representations. (Hewstone, 1989b, p. 261) (Please note, the original is in French; the above is Hewstone's translation into English)

The social foundation of such automatic explanations is that they are learned and thus socially communicated through language. Hewstone (1983, 1989a, 1989b) suggests that the use of cultural hypotheses to explain behaviour and events can be regarded as a kind of *'socialized processing'*. Culturally agreed upon explanations eventually come to be regarded as common-sense explanations. Each society has its own culturally and socially sanctioned explanation or range of explanations for phenomena such as illness, poverty, failure, success and violence. We will be looking at the range of explanations people make for such social issues within western industrialized societies later in this chapter. For now, the point we wish to emphasize is that people do not always need to engage in an active cognitive search for explanations for all forms of behaviour and events. Instead, people evoke their socialized processing or social representations.

The social origins of the fundamental attribution error

The study of perceived causation embodied in attribution theory concerns itself essentially with what passes as everyday social explanation. Central to the theory is that two main kinds of attributions are made by people to account for causality: dispositional or personal attributions, and situational or contextual attributions. These two modes of explanation correspond to what Billig (1982) refers to as the 'individual' and 'social' principles. Earlier we discussed one of the most consistent findings in attribution research – the fundamental attribution error, or the tendency to overattribute another person's behaviour to dispositional characteristics of the person, rather than to situational or contextual factors (Ross, 1977). We also indicated that whereas this bias has primarily been explained by cognitive and perceptual factors, namely the dominance of the actor in the perceptual field, others have suggested that this preference for person attributions may rather be grounded in an individualist culture.

The importance of individualism as an ideological doctrine specific to liberal democratic societies and, most particularly, within American social, cultural and political life, has been emphasized by political philosophers such as Lukes (1973) and Macpherson (1962). Lukes (1973), for example, documents how political, economic, religious, ethical, epistemological and methodological domains have been imbued with individualist tenets. Emerging as a philosophical doctrine in the nineteenth century with the advent of the capitalist mode of production, liberal individualism's central tenets emphasize the importance of the individual over and above society, and view the individual as the centre of all action and process. While this representation of the person may seem self-evident and not particularly controversial, the anthropologist Geertz points to its uniqueness:

> The western conceptions of the person as a bounded, unique, more or less integrated motivational and cognitive universe, a dynamic centre of awareness, emotion, judgement, and action organized into a distinctive whole and set contrastively both against a social and natural background is, however incorrigible it may seem to us, a rather peculiar idea within the context of the world's cultures. (1975, p. 48)

If, indeed, attributions and explanations are grounded in social knowledge, then cultural variations in the representation of the person should yield cross-cultural differences in the prevalence of person attributions. We now turn to a small number of studies which may help us to understand the impact of cultural representations on attributions.

Culture and attributions

Before any research was undertaken specifically to investigate the role of cultural influences on attributions, developmental research had documented a significant tendency for dispositional attributions to increase with age in western cultures. Whereas young western children predominantly make reference to contextual factors to explain social behaviour, western adults are more likely to stress dispositional characteristics of the agent (Peevers & Secord, 1973; Ruble, Feldman, Higgins & Karlovac, 1979). Anthropologists such as Shweder and Bourne (1982) have also noted that non-western adults place less emphasis on the dispositional characteristics of the agent and more emphasis on contextual or situational factors, compared to western adults. Of particular interest is that social psychologists in general are loath to explain these developmental and cross-cultural differences from within a social constructivist framework. Rather, these effects were initially explained within cognitive and experiential terms. For example, the relative infrequency of person attributions made by younger children was explained by reasoning that young children are limited in their cognitive capacity to make dispositional attributions because this requires the cognitive competence to generalize behavioural regularities over time. It was argued that children did not acquire the cognitive capacity to do this until they were older. Similarly, it was argued that non-western adults are less likely to make dispositional categorizations because the cognitive capacity to do so is more likely to be associated with the experiential conditions of complex modernized societies (Miller, 1984).

Joan Miller was among the first social psychologists to point out that such explanations disregard the possibility that developmental and cultural differences may 'result from divergent cultural conceptions of the person acquired over development in the two cultures rather than from cognitive or objective experiential differences between attributors' (1984, p. 961). Western notions of the person are essentially individualistic, emphasizing the centrality and autonomy of the individual actor in all action, whereas non-western notions of the person tend to be holistic, stressing the interdependence between the individual and her or his surroundings. The developmental or age differences in attribution merely reflect the enculturation process – the gradual process by which children adopt the dominant conception of the person within their culture.

Indeed, Miller's (1984) research confirms this cultural hypothesis. A cross-cultural study was undertaken to compare the attributions made for prosocial and deviant behaviours by a sample of Americans and Indian Hindus of three different age groups (8, 11 and 15 years), together with an adult group (mean age = 40.5 years). Miller found that at older ages Americans made significantly more references to general dispositions ($M = 40$ per cent) than did Hindus ($M < 20$ per cent), most of these dispositions referring to personality characteristics of the agent (see Figure 5.3). However, there were no significant differences which distinguished the responses of the 8- and

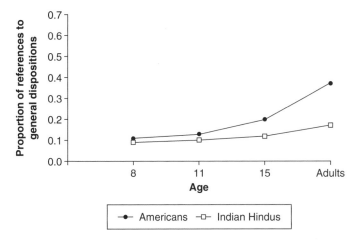

Figure 5.3 Cultural and developmental patterns of dispositional attribution (data from Miller, 1984)

11-year-old American children from those of their Hindu counterparts (the difference was an average of 2 per cent). While children displayed few cross-cultural differences in the number of contextual attributions they made, these were referred to frequently at younger ages in both Hindu and American children.

Within each culture, developmental trends indicated a significant linear age increase in reference to general dispositions among Americans and to the context among the Hindus, emphasizing social roles and patterns of inter-personal relationships. As Miller points out, 'such modes of attribution may be seen to be reflective of Indian cultural conceptions in their emphasis in locating a person, object, or event in relation to someone or something else' (1984, p. 968). For example, the following explanations were given by an American and Hindu participant in a story about an attorney who, after a motorcycle accident, left his injured pillion passenger in hospital without consulting with the doctor while he went on to work:

American: The driver is obviously irresponsible (agent-general disposition). The driver is aggressive in pursuing career success (agent-general disposition).

Hindu: It was the driver's duty to be in court for the client whom he's representing (context-social/spatial/temporal location). The passenger might not have looked as serious as he was (context-aspects of persons). (Miller, 1984, p. 972)

More recent cross-cultural studies have generally confirmed Miller's cultural hypothesis (Menon, Morris, Chiu & Hong, 1999; Morris, Menon & Ames, 2001; Morris & Peng, 1994). It appears, therefore, that the tendency to overrate personal/dispositional factors of the agent in western adults cannot be explained adequately by cognitive and experiential interpretations alone. The attribution 'bias' may not simply be a cognitive property or universal law of psychological functioning – it may be culture-specific. Though the agent of action tends to dominate the perceptual field for Anglo-Americans, the 'person' does not seem to enjoy the same degree of perceptual dominance among non-western people.

Lay explanations for social issues

It is clear that attributions or lay explanations for behaviour and events are not only the outcome of internal cognitive processes, but are, rather, social phenomena that are based on widely held and shared beliefs in the form of social and collective representations (Fraser & Gaskell, 1990). Just as Moscovici has referred to a 'thinking society', Hewstone (1989a) refers to an *'attributing society'* – our tendency to seek explanations within our predominant cultural framework. Our explanations for social phenomena are shaped not only by culture but also by scientific and expert knowledge. The diffusion and popularization of scientific concepts throughout society is occurring at a rapid rate through the mass media so that, increasingly, expert knowledge contributes to the stock of common sense which people draw upon to understand social reality. Thus, people can be regarded as 'amateur' scientists, 'amateur' economists, 'amateur' psychologists, etc., as they draw upon this information to explain a range of phenomena such as the causes of cancer, a depressed economy, or problems in their personal relationships. Some of this knowledge becomes an integral part of mass culture and, ultimately, what will come to be regarded as 'common sense' (Moscovici & Hewstone, 1983).

The attributions that people make for societal events and social issues provide us with rich insight into a society's prevailing explanations or meaning systems. Research on causal attributions for social issues has included everyday explanations for poverty (e.g., Feagin, 1972; Furnham, 1982a), unemployment (Feather, 1985; Furnham, 1982c), riots (Litton and Potter, 1985; Schmidt, 1972), and health and illness (Herzlich, 1973; Joffe, 1999; Pill & Stott, 1985). Previously we discussed social group differences in explanations for poverty and unemployment. This same research has found that people in western industrialized societies are more likely to attribute poverty to individualist-dispositional causes, such as lack of effort and laziness, than situational-societal causes (see Textbox 5.1). That is, people primarily hold the poor responsible for their plight. In contrast, notwithstanding social group differences, unemployment is predominantly attributed to societal and structural reasons such as economic recession and government policies.

Textbox 5.1

Lerner's (1980) just world hypothesis

When we consider the general tendency within western cultures to make dispositional attributions for other people's behaviour (the fundamental attribution error) and the preference among some social groups for individualistic explanations for a variety of social problems (e.g., poverty, unemployment, rioting and illness), we can see how such explanations emphasize and promote a belief that individuals determine their own 'fate'. This is linked to the phenomenon which Lerner (1980) has described as the *just world hypothesis:* the general belief that the world is a just place where good things happen to 'good' people and bad things happen to 'bad' people. 'Individuals have a need to believe that they live in a world where people generally get what they deserve. The belief that the world is just enables the individual to confront his physical and social environment as though they were stable and orderly' (Lerner & Miller, 1978, p. 1030). The belief in a just world is thus motivated by a functional and defensive need to view the misfortune of others as being, to some extent, 'deserved'. By viewing the world as stable and orderly and one in which we are not subject to random happenings, we protect ourselves from the possibility that misfortunes may strike us also at some time. Just world beliefs often lead to victim-blaming. The poor are blamed for being lazy and careless with money, the mentally ill for not having the strength of character to pull themselves together, women for being raped, etc. Thus such beliefs may provide the justification for the further and continual oppression of individual victims and marginalized groups in society.

It should, however, be made clear that victim-blaming is not only a feature of lay thought but also a pervasive feature of many theories within psychology. We have already emphasized the strong individualist elements and assumptions contained in many social psychological approaches, but what perhaps we have not made as clear are the victim-blaming tendencies which are often associated with such theoretical and conceptual approaches. To take just one notable social issue as an example. In reviewing all of the articles which appeared over a six-month period on the life experiences of African Americans, Caplan and Nelson (1973) noted that 82 per cent of these articles attributed African Americans' social problems to the personal shortcomings of this particular social group. Such person-centred explanations serve an important legitimating political function (Jost & Banaji, 1994; Jost & Major, 2001) in that the site of change and 'therapy' becomes that of the individual or group rather than the social, economic and political structures and institutions of society. It is politically more expedient to change individuals, than it is to change society.

Discursive Psychology and Attributions

An underlying assumption shared by the three theoretical approaches we have considered thus far is that attributing causality to everyday events and behaviour is primarily a perceptual cognitive process or activity. In stark contrast, discursive social psychology views explanations as things people do in everyday talk and discourse to accomplish social actions such as blaming, excusing, and assigning responsibility. This, of course, is in keeping with discursive social psychology's non-cognitivist epistemology and its emphasis on the action orientation of discourse or everyday talk. To date, the most comprehensive elaboration of a discursive approach to attribution is to be found in *Discursive Psychology* by Edwards and Potter (1992; see also Antaki, 1994; Edwards & Potter, 1993). Building on previous work in this tradition, Edwards and Potter (1992, p. 3) define attributions as:

> discursive topics, things people topicalise or orientate themselves to or imply in their discourse. These are not expressions of speakers' underlying cognitive states, they are viewed as situated and occasioned constructions that accomplish social actions. Within the model, remembering is understood as the situated production of versions of past events, while attributions are the inferences that these versions make available, and that participants treat as implied.

Like Heider, discursive social psychology regards the attributing of causality to events as central to everyday social life. However, unlike Heider and most attribution theorists who followed him, attributions are not understood as end products of a natural cognitive process of inference based on perceptual event information. Given the perceptual realism inherent in most social psychology, and in particular, social cognitive models, the issue of *what happened*, the event in question, is rarely if ever problematized. Within discursive social psychology, attributions are implied or presupposed by the actual description or reporting of events. Thus, attributional inferences are to be found in everyday naturally occurring talk as people describe and report on events around them.

Rather than studying naturally occurring attributions in everyday discourse, social psychologists have for the most part relied on artificial texts and invented scenarios or vignettes to study presupposed underlying cognitive processes that generate causal attributions. Previously we discussed how experimental stimuli (e.g., 'John laughs at the comedian') have been used to determine whether people make person or situation attributions, while factors such as the distinctiveness, consistency and consensus of the behaviour are experimentally manipulated. However, in the real world of naturally occurring discourse, an event or behaviour is rarely if ever described in such a decontextualized manner without reference to causal implications or to the speaker's own stake and interest in the matter. Discursive psychology argues that 'event description is not distinct from, nor accomplished prior to attributional work, but rather, attributional work is accomplished by descriptions' (Edwards & Potter, 1992, p. 91).

Description as attribution

Unlike traditional models of attribution such as Kelley's covariation model, which assume that causal attributions begin with the perception of a neutral event which is then cognitively processed, either automatically or in a complex computational manner, discursive social psychology insists that the description or reporting of an event is never neutral. Every description or account carries with it attributional inferences and implications. To illustrate this point, Edwards and Potter (1992, p. 97) provide a nice example of a newspaper article (originally cited by Brown, 1986), reporting on the death of 11 people at a rock concert.

> Eleven persons were trampled to death last night in a crowd of 8,000 concertgoers who waited for hours in near-freezing weather outside Riverfront Coliseum in Cincinnati then 'lost all sense of rationality' and stormed the doors. The concert, by the rock group, The Who, went on for three hours with most of the 18,000 fans inside oblivious to what one survivor called 'the nightmare' outside.

Edwards and Potter explain that, despite the relatively objective tone of the reporting, this account is none the less a particular *description* of the event, 'a discursive construction, already loaded with causal formulations and attributional concerns' (p. 98). The description itself offers possible explanations for the deaths, including 'the near-freezing weather' experienced by those waiting outside the concert venue and concertgoers who 'lost all sense of rationality'. Note that, despite the attributionally loaded description of the latter, its placement in quotation marks to indicate its status as reported speech and not the writer's own description, distances the writer from this attribution. This distanced footing adopted by the writer enhances the article's tone of neutrality while at the same time strongly inferring that the concertgoers themselves were responsible for the deaths (Edwards & Potter, 1992; Goffman, 1981).

The question of 'what happened', then, the actual description or account of an event, is always a discursively constructed version, which is rarely, if ever, neutral or independent. People produce versions of events in everyday text and talk that imply motives and attributions. Attribution theory, however, has never taken the issue of description seriously – it has left it untheorized and has not accounted for its rhetorical variability and flexibility. In discursive psychology, 'people do descriptions and thereby do attributions' (Edwards & Potter, 1992, p. 103). Attributions are not viewed as cognitive entities that are mentally calculated on the basis of perceived patterns and regularities in sensory information, but as socially situated practices that are oriented to accomplishing social actions such as assigning blame, motives and responsibility. Edwards and Potter's radical reorientation to the study of attributions is to study everyday discourse in its natural settings. In adopting such an approach they argue that:

> As soon as we start to study situated discourse, abstracted models of rational thought soon diminish in explanatory significance, as we discover how versions, explanations and inferences are constructed, implied and embedded in talk. It is in the accomplishment of social actions, rather than in the display of underlying cognitive representations, that we find orderliness in discourse. (1992, p. 103)

Internal versus external attributions: a problematic distinction

Another issue central to attribution theory that Edwards and Potter (1992) problematize is the distinction between internal (dispositional) and external (situational) attributions. Again, a discursive approach – the study of situated discourse – reveals that such a distinction is not easy to sustain when attributions are studied in their natural everyday use in text and talk. Going back to the newspaper article reporting on the concert deaths, a decontextualized reading might have us categorize the 'near-freezing weather' as a clear example of an external attribution for the concert deaths, and the concertgoers who had 'lost all sense of rationality' as a classic internal or dispositional cause. However, even if we were to accept that the crushing crowds were the direct cause of the event (a person attribution), their behaviour could be accounted for and explained by external situational factors such as the length of time they had to wait outside in the cold weather, or the poor handling of the crowd by authorities. Indeed, Brown's (1986) original analysis of attributions that were available for this event included person attributions such as the consumption of alcohol and drugs by concertgoers, strongly inferring that there was something about the concertgoers as a category of people that led to the tragic outcome. As Edwards and Potter (1992) make clear, however, these factors too can be recast as external ones 'depending on how they are discursively deployed' (p. 98). Within the legal system, where a discourse of blame and mitigation is most central, being under the influence of drugs and alcohol may serve as a powerful defence for one's actions. In such contexts, drugs and alcohol are constructed as external factors that are contrasted to the person's intentions and normative behaviour (internal factors). As Edwards and Potter explain:

> The point is that their status as internal or external causes is a function of their discursive deployment in action sequences such as blaming or mitigating, excusing or accusing. Intention rather than the cause's 'location' may become the operative criterion . . . The essential point is that internal and external causes do not figure as singular features of events, to be read off perceptually, or inferred automatically. They are propositional constructions, whose nature and operation are discursive and dependent for their sense upon the activity sequences (blaming, excusing, and so on) that they are a part of. (1992, p. 99)

Discursive psychology's focus on situated, naturally occurring discourse also contrasts with cognitive linguistic approaches to attributions such as the studies on verb semantics (e.g., Au, 1986; Brown & Fish, 1983; Semin & Fiedler, 1988) and those based on Grice's (1975) model of conversation (e.g., Hilton, 1990; Turnbull & Slugoski, 1988). Again, this work is criticized for its neglect of studying real discourse in natural contexts and its reliance on the use of decontextualized empirical materials in experimental settings. Although this tradition of research has taken the role of language in attributions seriously, it treats language as a system of linguistically fixed structures that impose meaning rather than a flexible and pragmatically occasioned tool or resource that allows people to accomplish a variety of things in different discursive contexts.

Constructing facts and the dilemma of stake and interest

Central also to discursive social psychology's constructivist epistemology is how descriptions are put together to appear factual or objective – as if they represent the true or real nature of an event. Potter (1996) refers to this as the 'out-there-ness' of a description or account. Given that at all levels of social life, from the interpersonal to the structural, competing interests and concerns are likely to produce different accounts or points of view, the dilemma of stake or interest is a pervasive concern for participants. Indeed, in everyday discourse, people's descriptions and constructions orient to concerns that their talk may be viewed as *interested*. Speakers can deploy a number of discursive devices to describe versions of events in ways that appear 'factual' and independent of their own interests, motives and desires (Potter,

1996). For example, to warrant the validity of a particular view or version of an event, speakers can emphasize their membership, or that of others, of a particular category, which entitles them to know and speak authoritatively about certain things. For example, doctors are expected to have special knowledge about health and illness, so citing such experts' works to establish the truth or factuality of a particular claim – 'Dr Brown says that two drinks a day is good for you'. This device is referred to as *'category entitlement'*. The factuality of a version can also be warranted by constructing it as consensual, as something upon which everyone agrees – 'everybody knows that men and women are different'. This device is referred to as a *'consensus warrant'*. Other warranting devices that speakers rely upon in everyday discourse include: the use of vivid description or reported speech, systematic vagueness, empiricist accounting, extreme case formulations, rhetoric of argument, stake inoculation, and lists and contrasts. For a comprehensive discussion of these devices see Edwards and Potter (1992) and Potter (1996).

Chapter Summary

In this chapter we reviewed how the major, classical attribution theorists proposed that people function in their day-to-day lives as though they were intuitive scientists, constructing implicit theories of everyday behaviour if they follow Heider's ideas; busily partitioning the variance of behaviour into main effects due to consistency, consensus and distinctiveness if they accept Kelley; or attempting to make the best dispositional inference they can from some actor's constrained or unconstrained behaviour if they are a Jonesian. Research on attributional biases shows just how bad we are as intuitive scientists, especially when it comes to discerning our own behaviour and its causes. We apparently bend and shape, distort and construe information from our ambient social environments so that, in the end, we look good both to ourselves and to others. For the most part, classic attribution theory attributes these biases to internal cognitive and perceptual mechanisms, though social motivations such as the need to understand everyday life, enhancing our sense of control and feeling good about ourselves are also central (Fiske, 2004).

Social identity theory extends a social motivational account of attributions by considering how group memberships, social identifications, and intergroup relations affect what sorts of attributions people make. Social groups based on class, ethnicity, gender, religion and sexuality perceive things differently and have different versions of the world that reflect their particular group's history, power and interests (see also Chapter 7). Social representations theory elaborates upon this social perspective by locating causal attributions not in the perceptual and cognitive workings of individual minds, but in the cultural meaning systems that are shared by collectivities and groups. Importantly, cross-cultural research has demonstrated how the fundamental attribution error or correspondence bias is not a universal cognitive phenomenon, but is specific to cultures and societies that are dominated by the ideology of individualism. Moscovici reminds us that explanations are also shaped increasingly by scientific and expert knowledge, which proliferates widely within society. Some of these explanations will eventually become accepted as common sense as people draw upon this knowledge to understand and explain aspects of their everyday life.

Lastly, we discussed discursive social psychology's take on attributions and explanations. Discursive social psychology is not interested in cognition – in underlying cognitive processes and entities – but, rather, in people's situated discursive practices. Attributions are seen as things that people do in their talk to accomplish social actions such as blaming, accusing, etc. Attributions are embedded in reports and accounts of events that occur in everyday talk, in descriptions of 'what happened', which in turn are situated in extended activity sequences in social interaction. Reports and descriptions of objects, events and behaviour are never neutral, but are discursively constructed in various ways that orient to participants' interests, stake and accountability. Discursive psychology thus emphasizes the need to study naturally occurring attributions in everyday discourse and social interaction.

Further Reading

Edwards, D., & Potter, J. (1992). *Discursive psychology*. London: Sage.

Forsterling, F. (2001). *Attribution: An introduction to theories, research and applications* London: Psychology Press.

Gilbert, D. T. (1998). Ordinary personology. In D. Gilbert, S. T. Fiske, & G. Lindzey (Eds.), *Handbook of social psychology* (Vol. 2, 4th ed., pp. 89–150). New York: McGraw-Hill.

Hewstone, M. (1989a). *Causal attribution: From cognitive processes to collective beliefs*. Oxford: Blackwell.

6

Self and Identity

Who are you? For many people, the first answer to this question is likely to be 'that depends'. Sometimes an answer to this question may rely on descriptions of our personalities: I'm kind, I'm determined, I'm sociable, I'm smart. Other times, role and relationship descriptions may seem most relevant to our sense of who we are: I'm a teacher, I'm a mother, I'm the coach, I'm single. Still other times, the question of 'who am I?' may be answered with reference to personal achievements (or lack thereof) or future ambitions, while other times, identification as a member of particular social categories may be of first importance: nationality when living or travelling abroad, or political affiliation during an election campaign. All of these types of self-description can be part of our self and identity. This chapter will consider various perspectives on the ways in which self and identity are formed, how they influence our behaviour and experience, and how these concepts are invoked in ordinary social life to perform certain kinds of social action.

Self and identity are concepts that we use in everyday life to refer to our own existence as entities in the world, and to locate ourselves relative to the other people and things in our environments. Although these terms are often lumped together and are sometimes used interchangeably, there are subtle differences in what social psychologists typically mean by these terms. *Self* is more often used to refer to people's beliefs about themselves, about their own ideas of who they are, and their personal characteristics, abilities, experiences, emotions and agendas. Our *identity* locates us in a world made up of different groups of people, and usually concerns the social groups and categories to which we do and do not belong. Our identity is affected by the importance of these groups to our sense of who we are and our attachment to these groups.

Defining what exactly is meant by the self and establishing the basis on which claims about self-knowledge can be made is a notoriously problematic task, which has been occupying philosophers (and, more recently, psychologists) at least since Descartes' famous attempt to resolve the problem: *I think, therefore I am*. Despite this, according to Gordon Allport, 'the existence of one's own self is the one fact of which every mortal – every psychologist included – is perfectly convinced' (1943, p. 451). Most contemporary psychological theorists of the self appear to agree with this view. As a consequence, the existence of the self as a knowable entity has been generally taken for granted, and both theoretical and empirical efforts have concentrated on specifying the structure (content and organization) of the self-concept and its functions. Or in other words, social psychological investigations of the self tend to be oriented towards one of two main questions: (1) what is the self *like*, and (2) what does the self *do*? As we will see, there have been a number of different approaches to addressing these questions, and correspondingly different answers. Furthermore, recent discursive investigations of the category of 'self' have introduced a third question: What kinds of social actions can be achieved by invoking the concept of 'self'?

In considering social psychological theorizing about self and identity, it is useful to think about how such theories are shaped by the dominant metaphors for the person within social psychology: the cognitive miser; the motivated tactician; the member of culture. We will argue that much of the renewed interest in the study of the self in the late 1980s and 1990s corresponded with the rise of the *motivated tactician* over the *cognitive miser*. In seriously considering the way in which people's experience and behaviour is shaped by their motivations and agendas, social psychology needed a way to think about differences between people in much more subtle terms than provided by traditional individual difference variables. Increased attention to and development of the idea of the self provided a conceptual source for specific motivations in the person, and thus was crucial in allowing a new kind of theorizing about social experience and behaviour. We argue that the shifts that are beginning to occur away from the idea of people as motivated individuals and towards the view of people as *members of culture* requires new ways of thinking about the self.

Textbox 6.1

Twenty statements test

On a blank piece of paper, write twenty answers to the question 'Who are you?' Sort each of your twenty answers into one of the following four categories.

Physical self statements – these identify the self solely in terms of physical attributes (e.g., 'I am male', 'I am dark-haired').

Social self statements – these locate the self in a social structure, identifying the self with a social position or status (e.g., 'I am a psychology student', 'I am a Radiohead fan').

(Continued)

Textbox 6.1   (Continued)

Reflexive self statements – these describe attributes which are not tied to a particular social position, but which only have meaning in a social sense (e.g., 'I am a happy person', 'I am tolerant of other people').

Oceanic self statements – these are global statements which do not differentiate one self from another (e.g., 'I am a human being', 'I am a child of God').

Was one or another category prevalent in your responses? What does this say about you and who you think you are? Would other people around you describe you in the same way? What does it mean about identity if your self-conception is different from how others describe you?

The Twenty Statements Test was developed by Manford Kuhn (1960; Kuhn & McPartland, 1954). Louis Zurcher (1977) proposed the categories described above as a simple way of considering the different ways in which people think about themselves. Zurcher noticed that through the 1950s, 1960s, and 1970s, increasingly more people provided reflexive self statements rather than physical or social self statements (in the United States, at least). He attributed this to accelerated social and cultural changes through those decades which made it increasingly difficult to define one's self in terms of social positions, since doing so requires a relatively stable social structure. Thus, even when one appears to think of one's self in very individual terms, thinking that way requires a particular pattern of social relationships and social structures – even thinking of ourselves individualistically is always conditioned by broader social forces.

Over the history of psychology, there have been many attempts to develop a comprehensive model of the self that incorporates people's past experiences and the effects that these have on their present understandings of and interactions with their world (e.g., Greenwald & Pratkanis, 1984; Markus, 1977; Mead, 1934/1962). We begin this chapter by discussing current cognitive models of the self, and evidence for ways in which the structure and content of the self is implicated in social behaviour and emotional experience. We then consider how social identity theory (Tajfel, 1981a; Tajfel & Turner, 1986) has emphasized the socially embedded nature of the self, and the extent to which our self is made social by the social groups and categories with which we identify, and which communicate our identity and position us in relation to other people. We end the chapter with a discussion of social constructionist and discursive perspectives, which have questioned the very notion of a stable, enduring self that is conceptually separable from the social contexts in which we live our lives, and which argue that our sense of self does not correspond to anything that 'really exists', but rather is constructed and reified in relationship with other people (e.g., Gergen, 1993, 1994).

Social-cognitive Approaches to Self and Identity

The self as a knowledge structure

In the cognitive models of the self, which now dominate the field, the self is generally considered to comprise all the knowledge that a person has about themselves (e.g., Cantor & Kihlstrom, 1987; Greenwald & Pratkanis, 1984; Higgins, 1987, 1995; Markus & Wurf, 1987). This includes memories of specific events and experiences, traits, attributes, habits, preferences, beliefs, values, plans, hopes and fears, as well as our knowledge of our social roles and relationships. In this view, everything that we know about ourselves *is* our self: our self-concept. This self-knowledge is usually considered as a set of symbolic representations that are stored in such a way that the interrelationships between specific representations are preserved (e.g., Bower & Gilligan, 1979; Greenwald & Pratkanis, 1984; Higgins, Van Hook, & Dorfman, 1988; Kihlstrom & Cantor, 1984; Kihlstrom & Klein, 1994), and aspects of this network are 'switched on' by our encounters with different situations and people.

Self schemas

In Chapter 3 we defined self schemas as the knowledge structures people have of themselves. Research on self schemas has primarily focused on the degree to which such structures affect the speed and efficiency with which information relevant to the self is processed (Higgins & Bargh, 1987; Markus, 1977; Markus & Wurf, 1987). Individuals are said to be 'schematic' on a particular dimension if they regard the dimension as a central and salient feature of their self-concept, and 'aschematic' if they do not regard the dimension as central to the self. For example, if you have a clear recognition and conception of how ambitious you are, then you would be classified as being self-schematic along this trait dimension. If you are unsure or ambivalent about how you would rate yourself along this dimension, then you would be classified as aschematic for ambition.

In one of the first studies to investigate the utility of the self schema concept and the implications it has for processing information about the self, Markus (1977) compared the self-descriptive, behavioural and predictive ratings of a sample of female students who were classified as either schematic or aschematic on the dimension of independence. She found that the schematic subjects (who rated themselves as high on either independence or dependence) were significantly more likely to endorse schema-related adjectives as self-descriptive and to respond to these significantly faster. Thus, schematic-independents were more likely to endorse independent-related adjectives and to endorse these significantly faster than the dependent words. Conversely, schematic-dependent subjects were more likely to endorse the dependent-related descriptions and to respond to these significantly faster than the independent words. While aschematic participants endorsed more of the dependent than independent words as self-descriptive, response latencies did not differ between these two sets of words, suggesting that they did not differentiate these as readily as did schematic-dependents. In further cognitive tasks which required participants to describe instances of past behaviour and make predictions about future behaviour, Markus found consistent response patterns which differentiated between independent, dependent and aschematic subjects. Together, these results were interpreted as providing empirical evidence for the operation of a generalized cognitive structure which organized, selected and interpreted information about the self along an independence–dependence dimension for schematic subjects.

The self schema concept emphasizes the stable, enduring and self-protecting nature of the self-concept (e.g., Greenwald & Pratkanis, 1984; Swann & Read, 1981) and is thus consistent with cognitive notions of the self that have been pervasive in social psychology.

Stability and malleability in the self-concept: the working self-concept

Cognitive models of the self are based on the assumption that people do in fact have a predictable way of relating to the word which is derived from their stable self-concepts. However, the existence of a stable self has been seen as something of a paradox, as, despite evidence suggesting that people actively resist information that is inconsistent with their views of themselves (e.g., Markus, 1977; Swann, 1985, 1987), many other studies have shown a large degree of variability in the self-concept across situations (e.g., Gergen, 1965; 1967; McGuire & McGuire, 1982; Mischel, 1968). Indeed awareness of the shifting nature of the self has a long history in psychology which can be traced at least as far as William James' famous assertion that 'A man [sic] has as many social selves as there are individuals who recognise him' (James, 1890/1952, p. 179). An integration of the seemingly inconsistent stable and malleable properties of the self was proposed by Markus and Kunda (1986) in their model of the working self-concept. They begin with a model of the self-concept as a cognitive structure comprised of a set of interrelated self schemas that are themselves related to the specific representations of the memories, beliefs and values that provide the body of self-knowledge from which those schema are derived. This structure, the *global self-concept*, is considered to be basically stable, although it can change gradually over time as a person acquires new information and experiences, or reinterprets existing information in the light of new experiences. From this basic position Markus and Kunda argue that, because the cognitive structure that represents knowledge about the self is so vast, limitations to human information-processing capacities allow only a subset of all potentially available self-knowledge to be accessible at any given time. The portion of the self-system that is accessible at a particular time is the *working self-concept*, and these accessible elements of the self-concept are the only aspects that influence the way in which one attends to, processes and recalls information at that time. Thus the working self-concept is the aspect of the global self-concept that affects behaviour and experience at a particular moment in time.

The content of the working self-concept at a particular time is considered to be influenced by a number of factors. Some self-representations that are interrelated with a wide variety of other representations, and that have been frequently accessed in the past, may be chronically accessible for some people (Bargh, 1989). These types of self-representations are similar to Markus' (1977) concept of self schemas. The accessibility of other self-representations may be influenced by more transitory factors, including situational cues, motivational factors, or mood (Kunda & Sanitioso, 1989). Some self-representations may become accessible through their associations with other accessible self-representations (e.g., Bower & Gilligan, 1979), or may be deliberately retrieved for various purposes, including the desire to counteract an undesirable representation of the self, or to regulate affect or behaviour (Markus & Nurius, 1986). This model can therefore account for both stability and malleability in the self: stability is provided by the relatively unchanging nature of the available self-knowledge and by the chronically high accessibility of some core self schemas in the global self-concept, while malleability is the result of the varying levels of accessibility of more peripheral self-representations in the working self-concept.

The working self-concept moves away from the models of self guided by the cognitive miser metaphor, in which self-knowledge is organized to maximize efficiency of retrieval of information about the self by giving a central role to motivation in determining the content of the working self-concept. In a study by Kunda and Sanitioso (1989), students were randomly allocated to conditions in which they were led to believe that either extraversion or introversion was associated with academic and professional success. Following this belief induction, in a supposedly unrelated study, participants completed a self-concept inventory. Participants who had been allocated to the extraversion-success condition rated themselves as significantly more extroverted than did participants in the introversion-success condition, who in turn rated themselves significantly more introverted than those in the extraversion-success condition. These findings show that the content of the working self-concept is influenced by what people are motivated to believe about themselves, and that, all other things being equal, people's working self-concepts tend to shift in the direction of situationally desirable attributes and away from undesirable attributes.

The working self-concept allows for the notion of the self as a multifaceted, dynamic structure, which can appear very different in different places and at different times. At face value, it seems to allow for the kinds of contradictory, inconsistent presentations of self that are invoked by some critics of cognitive models of the self to problematize the very notion of a coherent, stable self that somehow 'underlies' behaviour and experience (e.g., Gergen, 1967, 1993). However, although the working self-concept model is much more social than many other models of self, in that it allows for dramatic changes in the self as a function of social context, it still preserves an essential distinction between the individual, interior, cognitive self, and the external social contexts which the self encounters. In this view, social situations are seen as 'eliciting conditions' that influence the relative accessibility of various elements of a (still unproblematically separable) self. We will take up some criticisms of this view later in this chapter.

Possible selves

One of the most creative aspects of the self is its ability to imagine futures that have not yet occurred. The ability to picture oneself in a range of potential futures, to evaluate these futures and to aspire towards realizing or avoiding them is a powerful force guiding our behaviour in and experience of the present. Indeed, representations of the self in the future, or *possible selves*, have been considered a key aspect of motivation, providing a sense of contingency between one's present and future, and directing and organizing behaviour (Markus & Nurius, 1986). Possible selves can represent things that a person hopes for, expects or fears. As such, they provide a context within which present behavioural choices can be evaluated in terms of their likely future consequences, as different options may be considered in terms of whether they make valued or feared possible selves more or less likely to occur. Possible selves are not simply abstract wishes, expectancies or fears, but are grounded in one's current view of self, to provide an integrated representation of the self becoming the possible self. Markus and Nurius argue that these integrated representations of goals and the self are associated with representations of the behaviours needed to achieve them, providing a cognitive bridge between the actual self and future selves. In this way, possible selves represent the dynamic and temporally extended nature of the self-concept. Markus and Nurius argue that because possible selves are vivid and personalized representations of goals that have associated behavioural plans and strategies, they form stronger motivators of behaviour than more abstract, non self-referential representations of goals or values. The ability to generate positive possible selves, and general plans to achieve them, has been associated with positive affect and subjective motivation (e.g., Gonzales, Burgess & Mobilio, 2001; Oyserman & Markus, 1991; Ruvolo & Markus, 1992).

Several other researchers have developed future-related constructs that, although different from possible selves in some important ways, share the assumption that people's intentions and aspirations for the future are key to understanding their actions and self-concept in the present. These constructs include personal strivings (Emmons, 1986, 1996), personal projects (Little, 1983), and life tasks (Cantor, Norem, Langston, Zirkel, Fleeson & Cook-Flanagan, 1991; Cantor, Norem, Niedenthal, Langston & Brower, 1987). In all of these accounts, the present (or actual) self-concept is seen as deriving much of its meaning from its relationship to these future-based representations of the self. These future representations of self have an important role in the organization of everyday affective, cognitive and behavioural experience (Markus & Wurf, 1987), and researchers have found that the existence of representations of future selves towards which one strives are associated with high subjective well-being (e.g., Brunstein, Schultheiss & Grassmann, 1998; Emmons, 1986; Little, 1989) and motivation (Bandura, 1989a, 1989b; Gonzales, Burgess & Mobilio, 2001). Fundamentally, all of these views of the self-concept share the assumption that the self is a dynamic entity, capable of intentional change that is inspired by alternative representations of how the self could be (Markus & Wurf, 1987).

Self-discrepancy theory

Self-discrepancy theory was first put forward by Higgins (Higgins, 1987; Higgins, Klein, & Strauman, 1985) as a means of unifying some of the many theories on the emotional consequences of conflicting aspects of the self-concept. The work which Higgins endeavoured to integrate came mainly from the psychoanalytic tradition, and included such constructs as Horney's 'ideal self' (1950), Sullivan's 'good me' and 'bad me' (1953), and Freud's (1925) concept of the superego. Higgins sought to develop a classifying scheme that would integrate important aspects of these theories by specifying a systematic set of relations concerning the magnitude and quality of discrepancies between the actual self and various standards, and the affect associated with these self-discrepancies. Higgins and colleagues developed the argument that the self-system contains not only representations of one's actual self, but also idiosyncratic *ideal* and *ought self-guides* which form the internal standards against which the actual self is evaluated. The *ideal self* represents 'one's aspirations, hopes or goals', while the *ought self* represents 'rules, injunctions ... duties and obligations' concerning oneself (1985, p. 52). The crux of the theory is that the actual self is evaluated and regulated in relation to these internalized ideal and ought self-guides, and that the magnitude of discrepancies between the actual self and these self-guides is related to the intensity and quality of people's negative affective experience. Actual-ideal discrepancies are considered to make a person vulnerable to dejection-related affect, while actual–ought discrepancies are associated with agitation-related affect.

Support for the predictions of self-discrepancy theory has been found in a variety of contexts. The predicted relationships between actual–ideal discrepancies and dejection-related affect, and actual–ought discrepancies and agitation-related affect, have been found in several studies with college students (e.g., Higgins, Bond, Klein, and Strauman, 1986; Higgins et al., 1985; Strauman & Higgins, 1987) as well as in other populations, including pregnant women and new parents (Alexander & Higgins, 1993), and people with eating disorders (Strauman, Vookles, Berenstein, Chaiken & Higgins, 1991). For example, using statistical techniques to examine the unique relationships between each type of self-discrepancy and affect, Higgins et al. (1985) found that actual–ideal discrepancies were uniquely associated with the chronic experience of dejection-related affect and actual–ought discrepancies were uniquely associated with chronic agitation-related affect. However, other researchers have questioned the evidence of unique relationships between the specific types of discrepancies (ideal or ought) and distinct affective experiences (dejection or agitation), arguing instead for a general relationship between the magnitude of the people's self-discrepancies and their experience of negative affect (Tangney, Niedenthal, Covert & Hill-Barlow, 1998).

Both Markus & Nurius's (1986) possible selves approach and Higgins's (1987) self-discrepancy theory share the assumption that unrealized aspects of the self, in the form of the plans, goals or standards that a person has for themselves, provide an important context in which to understand the experience of the self at a given point in time. However, although these theorists agree on the importance of considering unrealized representations of the self, there is substantial disagreement concerning the primary functions of these representations. The possible selves approach is based on the thesis that unrealized representations of self serve a crucial role in providing motivation for the development of the self. Markus and Nurius argue that possible selves provide a cognitive link between the selves of the present and those of the future, and that they thus represent the dynamic nature of the self. Unrealized selves are seen from this perspective as serving an essentially positive function, providing motivation and direction for behaviour (without necessarily being motivated by the desire to avoid negative affect). In contrast, the central premise of self-discrepancy theory is that discrepancies between the actual self and the ideal or ought self-guides produce negative affect. Although self-discrepancy theory argues that certain (beneficial) self-regulatory processes may be engaged following the perception of self-discrepancies, in an effort to reduce the negative affect associated with the discrepancy it focuses on the idea that holding valued self-guides that are different from the actual self represents an inherently negative psychological situation. Recent work has attempted to reconcile these opposing views by proposing that the psychological consequences of unrealized self-representations depend on one's beliefs about the likelihood that one will become that self in the future (e.g., Boldero & Francis, 2002; Donaghue, 1999). That is, the consequences of *not being* one's alternative self in the present depend crucially on beliefs about one's potential to *become* the alternative self in the future.

Functions of the Self

One of the defining features of the self is that it is reflexive, in that it possesses the capacity for self-awareness. A major implication of this awareness of self-as-object is that it creates the potential for the *evaluation* of the self, and, based on this evaluation, the intentional *regulation* of the self.

Self-evaluation

How do we know what kind of person we are? Most judgements that people can make about themselves involve, at least implicitly, some form of comparison with others. Being tall, smart, tidy, neurotic or friendly are all relative rather than absolute conditions, which have little or no meaning without some sense of what other people are like in these respects. Comparison of the actual self with some standard for the self is thus the essence of self-evaluation. There is a wealth of evidence to indicate that self-evaluation is not a 'cold' cognitive process, involving objective compilation of the information available about the self, but, rather, that it is influenced to a substantial degree by the motivations that lead people to evaluate themselves in the first place (Taylor, Neter & Wayment, 1995). The motivation for self-evaluation can influence the ways in which people seek out, attend to, recall and attribute information about themselves (Swann, 1987; Taylor et al., 1995).

Traditionally, researchers have argued for one or more of three major self-evaluative motives: self-assessment, self-enhancement, and self-verification. The self-assessment motive is assumed to lead individuals to seek out information which is accurate and diagnostic, so that they can develop a view of themselves as they actually are (Festinger, 1954). Self-enhancement is argued to lead individuals to concentrate on sources of information that are as favourable to the self as possible (e.g., Kunda & Sanitioso, 1989), while self-verification is considered to encourage individuals to confirm their existing beliefs about themselves (e.g., Swann, 1987). More recently, Taylor et al. (1995) have argued that a fourth self-evaluative motive also needs to be considered, namely self-improvement. They argue that self-evaluation with the goal of improving the self is both conceptually and empirically distinct from each of the other three motives outlined above. In particular, the inclusion of a self-improvement motive allows for a future orientation to the process of self-evaluation, which captures the potential for change and aspiration within the self.

Self-esteem

Evaluations of ourselves give rise to another aspect of our experience of ourselves: our self-esteem. Self-esteem is 'the positivity of the person's evaluation of self ... it makes a value judgement based on self-knowledge' (Baumeister, 1998, p. 694). Although self-esteem is related to self-evaluation, it is not the same thing. Whereas self-evaluation represents one's judgement about one's relative performance or ability or possession of some attribute, self-esteem is the inferences drawn about the self from that evaluation, and can be mediated by, for example, the attributions made for one's performance, and the importance placed on particular aspects of the self. So, for example, seeing oneself as being unfit and overweight could have serious consequences for self-esteem ('I'm undisciplined, lazy and ugly, and no one will want to go out with me') or minor consequences ('Oh well, I have other priorities in life and I'll concentrate on becoming healthier once I've passed these exams'), depending on the attributions made and the importance of that aspect of self to the person's self-concept.

Self-esteem is an important explanatory construct in social psychology, as the desire to protect and enhance self-esteem is invoked in many theories as a basic motive underlying social behaviour. A review of the literature by Tesser (2000) found that self-esteem maintenance is implicated in a wide range of psychological processes, including social comparison (Taylor et al., 1995), attribution (Brewin, 1986), terror management (Greenberg et al., 1992), derogation-of-other (Brown, Collins, Schmidt & Brown, 1988), information processing (Tafarodi, 1998) and interpersonal violence (Bushman & Baumeister, 1998). However, even though the development of self-esteem is widely considered to be an important goal in western societies, Baumeister (1998) notes that it is unclear precisely why people are so invested in maintaining their self-esteem, as there is little evidence that having high self-esteem is reliably associated with other positive behaviours. While it is clear that having high self-esteem is associated with positive emotional experience, it appears that high self-esteem is better thought of as a valued end in itself, rather than as a means by which other socially desirable outcomes can be achieved.

Self-regulation

Most of the time there is a purpose underlying people's behaviour. Social psychologists have typically considered behaviour to result primarily from people's beliefs about the likely consequences of their actions (or inaction). The processes involved in instigating behaviour that is designed to bring about certain consequences fall under the general heading of self-regulation. That is, self-regulation involves deliberate engagement in and monitoring of behaviour with the intention of bringing about a desired outcome for the self, or avoiding an undesired outcome. Going to the library to begin research for an assignment, getting up early to exercise, braving a crowded shopping centre to buy a friend a birthday card, donating money to a charitable cause and going to the dentist for a check up are all examples of self-regulation because they all involve behaviours that are motivated by the consequences they will entail. Theories about self-regulation can be divided into two broad classes: those that focus on drives and those that focus on incentives.

According to drive-based theories of motivation and self-regulation, individuals engage in behaviour designed to reduce levels of arousal created by unmet needs. Such theories often seek to explain motivation in terms of differences in the extent to which individuals experience one or more of a set of common needs, such as the need for achievement, or the need for affiliation. Failure to fulfil these needs is considered to be associated with an unpleasant state of tension that individuals are motivated to act on in order to remove. A subset of the drive-based models of motivated behaviour is based on Festinger's (1957) theory of cognitive dissonance. The cognitive dissonance model is based on the idea that when people become aware that they possess inconsistent attitudes and/or behaviours, they experience a negative arousal state known as dissonance. The psychological discomfort associated with the experience of dissonance in turn motivates a change in either attitude or behaviour so that the dissonance is removed, and the discomfort alleviated.

In contrast to the dissonance-reduction models of self-regulation, which emphasize the negative consequence of goal non-achievement, incentive-based models emphasize the positive benefits of goal achievement. For example, Markus and Nurius (1986) argue that the integration of representations of goals with representations of the self, which is involved in the construction of possible selves, provides a means of assessing the desirability of the goal for the self, as well as assisting in the clarification of the behavioural strategies needed to reach the goal. The attractiveness (or unattractiveness) of the possible self in turn provides motivation for efforts to achieve (or avoid) it. Thus, according to this perspective, self-regulation can occur without necessarily being motivated by the experience of some form of psychological discomfort or tension.

Control-process models of self-regulation The approach motivation emphasized by incentive-based models and the avoidance motivation of dissonance-reduction models have been combined in Carver and Scheier's (1981, 1982) widely adopted control-process model of self-regulation. The model represents human self-regulatory systems as analogous to cybernetic feedback systems in which the state of a particular system is compared at regular intervals with a reference value that represents the goal-state of that system. The result of this comparison process depends on the valence of the reference point, which can be either positive or negative. A discrepancy between the current state and a positively valenced reference value produces approach behaviour that is designed to reduce the discrepancy, while a too-small discrepancy between the current state and a negatively valenced reference value produces discrepancy-increasing avoidance behaviour.

The reference values and associated feedback loops, which form the major metaphor for self-regulation in the control-process model, correspond to various levels of goal abstraction (Carver & Scheier, 1981). A reference value may represent any goal from an abstract principle (e.g., 'I want to be well-informed') through more specific examples (e.g., 'I will spend my free time reading rather than watching television'), to the muscle tension goals that represent physical enactments of the relevant behaviours (e.g., turning off the television, picking up the book). Carver and Scheier reflected these levels of abstraction in their distinction between principles and programmes. Principles represent specific end states that people want to achieve, whereas programmes represent strategies by which they plan (or hope) to get them. Principles and programmes may themselves be hierarchically nested, such that certain principles may reflect a 'higher' or more abstract principle (e.g., the principle of integrity might contain sub-principles of honesty and justice), and a range of increasingly specific programmes may all be related to the achievement of a particular principle. According to Carver and Scheier (1981), the reference values at different levels of abstraction are linked by the output function of the feedback loops that compare actual behaviour with the reference value. Thus, a system that returns a discrepancy between the reference value and actual behaviour would produce an output designed to reduce that discrepancy and that output would take the form of increased accessibility of the next most specific reference value and activation of the feedback processes with respect to it. This process continues until the reference value representing the physical enactment of the desired behaviour is reached or the enactment of a programme is frustrated.

The primary explanatory goal of the control-process model is to account for the initiation of self-regulatory behaviour that is expected to result from the perception of a discrepancy between the actual self and an alternative self. None the less, it is also possible to extend the model to predict that the extent to which the discrepancy-reducing system is working may have implications for how a person *feels* about themselves (i.e., for their *affect*). Carver and Scheier (1990) argued that affect is produced by a second-order self-monitoring system, which is responsible for monitoring the rate of progress of discrepancy reduction between the actual state of the self and its reference value. They argued that within this rate-monitoring system, the rate at which the discrepancy is reducing is compared with some standard for that rate. In this model, positive affect occurs when the actual rate of discrepancy reduction exceeds the standard, and negative affect occurs when the actual rate of reduction does not reach the standard. This aspect of Carver and Scheier's model has not been adopted by many theorists and discussion of its implications for alternative self theories will be returned to later in this chapter. However, it should be noted that, in this model, affect is conceptualized as a result of the relative success or failure of behavioural attempts to reduce a discrepancy, rather than simply an automatic consequence of the perception of a discrepancy. Thus, in their model, it is possible for a person to possess a self-discrepancy but not to experience negative affect provided the rate of discrepancy reduction is equal to or exceeds that person's standard. Carver and Scheier's model also provides a conceptual link between the perception of self-discrepancies and positive affect, as well as the negative affect that is the focus of self-discrepancy theory (e.g., Higgins, 1987).

Regulatory focus theory In recent years, self-discrepancy theory has shifted emphasis away from its focus on the relationships between the actual self and the ideal and ought self-guides, and towards the ways in which people regulate their behaviour in order to reach these desired states. In the reformulation and extension of self-discrepancy theory into regulatory focus theory (Higgins, 1997), Higgins emphasizes that pursuing an ideal self involves self-regulation that is designed to bring about positive, valued outcomes, while pursuing an ought self involves self-regulation that is designed to avoid negative or otherwise undesired outcomes. Higgins and Tykocinski (1992) tested this prediction by having participants with predominant actual–ideal or actual–ought discrepancies read an essay containing events framed in terms of the presence or absence of positive or negative outcomes. They found that participants with predominant actual–ideal discrepancies remembered more events framed in terms of the presence of positive outcomes (e.g., meeting a friend for lunch) and the absence of positive outcomes (e.g., going to see a film and finding that it was no longer showing), whereas participants with predominant actual–ought discrepancies remembered more events framed in terms of the presence of negative outcomes (e.g., getting up for an early class) and the absence of negative outcomes (e.g., having a test cancelled). This study thus provided evidence that people differentially attended to events framed in terms of negative or positive outcomes depending on their predominant self-discrepancy.

In an effort to combine these findings with those from studies based on self-discrepancy theory, Higgins (1995, 1996b, 1997) proposed a model in which predominant self-discrepancies and the corresponding tendency to frame situations in terms of either positive or negative outcomes are considered to be the manifestation of a person's underlying self-regulatory system. According to this model, two distinct systems are responsible for the regulation of pleasure and pain or, in the language of self-discrepancy theory, for the regulation of positive and negative outcomes.

Higgins (1995, 1997) argued that individuals develop systems to regulate both positive and negative outcomes, as adaptive functioning requires both. However, he proposed that a predominant self-regulatory system often develops during childhood as a generalization of the types of experience a child has with his or her caregivers. Drawing on the work of Bowlby (1973), Higgins argued that children have two basic needs, for nurturance and for security, which are often differentially valued by caregivers. Caregivers who are primarily oriented towards nurturance tend to focus on helping a child achieve things that they ideally want for them, and thus preferentially orient the child towards these types of self-guides. He further claimed that caregivers who have these types of ideal-based goals for children tend to direct the child's behaviour by providing nurturing, positive responses (presence of positive outcomes) towards desired behaviour and by withdrawing these responses (absence of positive outcomes) when the child behaves in an undesired way. Thus, over time, children exposed to this style of interaction would become oriented towards the presence or absence of positive outcomes. As their cognitive capacities increase and they are able to understand the likely responses of others to their behaviour, children who are focused on positive outcomes would be expected to self-regulate their behaviour in relation to maximizing the presence and minimizing the absence of these positive outcomes. This focus on positive outcomes would be reflected in the development of strong ideal self-guides. Higgins (1995) referred to this style of self-regulation as *promotion-focused*. This nurturance-focused style of interaction was contrasted with caregivers who are primarily concerned with security and who respond to children in terms of what they think the child ought or ought not to do. Carers with this orientation were considered more likely to respond to undesired behaviour from the child with direct punishments or reproaches (presence of negative outcomes). When a child behaves in the desired manner, these negative outcomes would not occur (absence of negative outcomes). Higgins argued that repeated exposure to this style of interaction would be expected to orient the child preferentially to the presence or absence of negative outcomes and, thus, towards strong ought self-guides. This style of self-regulation was labelled *prevention-focused*.

On the basis that promotion-focused people are oriented towards positive outcomes, Higgins predicted that they would tend to use self-regulatory strategies that would lead them to *approach* a state in which they would experience those positive outcomes. In contrast, the negative outcome orientation of prevention-focused people was expected to lead to the use of self-regulatory strategies that would allow them to *avoid* experiencing these negative outcomes. Some evidence has been found to support this prediction. A study by Higgins, Roney, Crowe and Hymes (1994) asked participants to choose the strategies that they would use to achieve a common goal ('to be a good friend'). They found a general preference for approach strategies (e.g., 'be open and willing to give of myself') over avoidance strategies (e.g., 'don't lose touch'). However, they also found that prevention-focused participants (those participants who had predominant actual–ought discrepancies) selected more avoidant strategies and fewer approach strategies than promotion-focused participants (those with predominant actual–ideal discrepancies). This and other studies (e.g., Higgins et al., 1994; Strauman, 1996) suggest that there is evidence for the idea that there are differences between people in their preferred strategies for self-regulation that correspond to the promotion- and prevention-focused systems proposed by Higgins, although there is as yet no direct evidence for the developmental explanation proposed by Higgins (1995).

Critiques of social-cognitive models of self

Although cognitive models of the self unquestionably dominate current conceptualizations of and research into the nature of the self, these approaches have been the target of sustained critique from a number of directions. Critics from the social constructionist and critical discursive perspectives question the assumption that the 'self' is located within the individual, and transported by him or her into various social situations in which various parts of the internal cognitive 'self-structure' become activated to influence experience and behaviour in that context. These critics argue that such an individualistic account of the self fails to capture the constitutive and creative nature of social life, in which selves emerge *from* the social structures, relationships and contexts in which people find themselves. In this view, selves do not go out into the world to display their pre-existing attributes and to impose their pre-existing agendas, but, rather, people encounter situations in which certain kinds of social actions are possible, and subjective selves emerge from (rather than create) these encounters. We will discuss these alternative accounts of the self in detail later in this chapter.

The other major critique of the models of self discussed so far comes from a cross-cultural perspective. Unlike the constructionist critics, scholars working from this perspective do not object to the cognitivism of the mainstream accounts, but, rather, to the individualistic, decontextualized nature of the self-representations that are usually considered to form the basis of the self-concept. The anthropologist Geertz's often-quoted observation (see Chapter 5) that western conceptions of an autonomous, demarcated self contrast markedly with those found in other cultures is again of theoretical significance. In their influential paper, Markus and Kitayama (1991) brought these debates into the mainstream of social psychological writings on the self with their argument that, for many of the world's cultures (although their work focuses particularly on Japanese and other East Asian cultures), notions of self are more fluid, and self-descriptions are more likely to be made in relational terms, rather than as the decontextualized trait descriptions common in the west (see also Nisbett, 2003). In their analysis Markus and Kitayama distinguish between an independent self-construal, which characterizes '... an individual whose behaviour is organised and made meaningful primarily by reference to one's own internal repertoire of thoughts, feelings and action, rather than by reference to the thoughts, feelings and actions of others' (1991, p. 226), and an interdependent self-construal, which involves '... seeing oneself as part of an encompassing social relationship and recognising that one's behaviour is determined, contingent on, and, to a large extent organised by what the actor perceives to be the thoughts, feelings and actions of *others* in the relationship' (p. 227, italics in original). However, although the distinction between these self-construals has been widely adopted by researchers making explicit cross-cultural comparison, much research into the self continues to be guided by highly individualistic notions of the self.

Social Identity Approaches to Self and Identity

Social identity theory (SIT) is explicitly a theory of intergroup behaviour, and as such has concentrated primarily on the consequences of social identities for the behaviour of people towards others who do not share the same social identities. We will discuss this work in depth in Chapter 7. In this chapter, we want to explore precisely what researchers working in the SIT tradition mean when they talk about 'social identity', and to consider the relationships between these perspectives on identity and other ways of conceptualizing the self.

SIT is based on the premise that the social groups and categories of which we are members form an important part of our sense of self and identity. According to Tajfel (1981a), social identity is '... that part of the individual's self-concept which derives from his [sic] knowledge of his [sic] membership of a social group (or groups) together with the value and emotional significance attached to that membership' (p. 251). Thus being an Australian, being a woman, being Aboriginal, supporting the Tigers, being an accountant, being vegetarian or belonging to Greenpeace are not neutral social facts about a person, but contribute importantly to how a person sees, understands and feels about themselves. Although the importance of these types of group memberships to identity is a central tenet of SIT, the concept of identity is somewhat under-theorized, and it is not always clear *why* group memberships are important to identity, and how this might vary with other aspects of self and identity.

SIT argues that people are motivated to think well of themselves (Tajfel, 1981a; Tajfel & Turner, 1986). Given that part of people's sense of self is bound up in their social identities (their social group and category memberships), the theory argues that people are motivated to seek positive distinctiveness for their ingroups. SIT has focused heavily on showing how the motivation to positively differentiate one's group from others tends to produce ingroup favouritism and (perhaps less reliably, see Brown, 2000) outgroup derogation. By seeing the groups that they belong to as being superior to others (at least in some aspects), people are able to bolster their social identity and enhance their self-esteem. This 'self-esteem hypothesis' has received support from some studies showing that increases in self-esteem follow from opportunities for positive differentiation, but has also been heavily contested (see Brown, 2000; Long & Spears, 1997; and Turner, 1999, for critical discussions of the role of self-esteem in SIT).

Identification

Although social identities are usually thought about in terms of memberships of particular social groups, Tajfel's emphasis in his original definition on '… the value and emotional significance attached to that membership' makes clear that membership alone is not sufficient for social identity. While a person's membership of a particular group or category may be more or less a social fact, SIT returns to the importance of individual psychology by emphasizing the importance of *identification* in moderating the consequences of social identity for the self. Thus social identity in SIT is comprised of both membership of and identification with particular groups. Most empirical work on SIT tends to treat a person's level of identification with their groups as a fixed attribute that will partly determine the psychological consequences of favourable or unfavourable intergroup comparison. However, it is possible to think of identification more flexibly, and to argue that shifting one's level of identification is a means of managing one's social identity by aligning or distancing oneself from a particular group depending on its favourability in a particular context. Indeed the strategic use of de-identification as a way of escaping the consequences of negative social identity was emphasized by Tajfel in early formulations of SIT (e.g., Tajfel, 1974, 1976, 1978), but more recent theoretical and empirical work from a social identity perspective has tended to consider identification as a stable characteristic of group members.

For example, Doosje and Ellemers (1997) report a series of studies investigating the responses of high and low identifiers to situations in which their social identity was threatened. SIT suggests that the usual response to threatened social identity would be to make ingroup-enhancing and/or outgroup-derogating judgements on dimensions relevant to the intergroup comparison. However, these biases in judgement are subject to social reality constraints, and in some circumstances a person may be unable to plausibly make favourable intergroup comparsions. Fans of a football team on a long losing streak will find it difficult to plausibly argue that their team is more talented than the reigning premiers, for example. Doosje and Ellemers (1997) argue that people who are high identifiers are more likely than low identifiers to respond to a threatened social identity by seeking alternative, 'socially creative', ways to achieve positive distinctiveness for their group as a whole. Low identifiers are more likely to maintain a positive identity through other 'individual mobility' strategies, such as distancing themselves from the group, or emphasizing the variability within their group.

Ascribed versus acquired social identities One dimension along which group or category memberships vary is the extent to which a person is able to choose whether or not to be a member. In SIT, group memberships over which we have little or no personal control (such as, for example, ethnicity or sex) are said to be *ascribed*, while memberships that we choose more or less freely (such as occupation, political affiliation, sporting team membership) are said to be *acquired*. It is important to note that this distinction does not rest on whether the membership is actually freely chosen or not, but, rather, on how it is perceived by others. Although both acquired and ascribed group memberships are routinely used as a basis for making judgements about people, the bases of these judgements differ in important ways. Acquired group memberships (i.e., those 'freely' chosen by a person) may be seen as an expression of personal attributes, preferences, beliefs and values. For example, a person's membership of the category 'vegetarians' may be seen as a reflection of their (implied) belief in animal rights or sustainable living, while another person's designation as a tour guide may imply that they are adventurous and enjoy meeting new people. Judgements made on the basis of ascribed group memberships are more likely to reflect assumptions about characteristics that are believed to be naturally associated with that group such as, for example, the assumption that a woman will be more emotional than a man. This assumption that certain groups have natural and inevitable differences between them is known as *essentialism*, and is an important basis for stereotyping of and prejudice against groups defined on the basis of ascribed characteristics (see Yzerbyt, Rocher & Schadron, 1997 for an extended discussion of essentialism in group perception).

Self-categorization theory

Most people have many potential social identities, only some of which are salient at any particular time. What makes our membership of some social groups and categories important and influential on our behaviour and experience at some times and not at others? Furthermore, why do we sometimes think about ourselves in terms of the characteristics that distinguish us from others and make us unique, while at other times we are more aware of those things we have in common with (some) others? Self-categorization theory or SCT (Turner, Hogg, Oakes, Reicher & Wetherell, 1987) is an extension of social identity theory that has developed to address this question. Its central premise is that social identities are not fixed, and that they shift in our awareness in response to our assessments of the relevant dimensions of the social context in which we encounter members of our own and other groups. SCT argues that our social identities reflect our position in a world where important issues are at stake, where the interests and agendas of particular groups are often in conflict. The social identities most likely to be salient in particular situations are those which make the most sense of the interests of those involved in the interaction.

As we emphasized in Chapter 2, SCT claims that at any given point in time our identity can be experienced on one of three qualitatively distinct levels: personal, social or human (see Figure 6.1). The distinctions between these levels of identity rest on the extent to which we are aware of similarities and differences between ourselves and others. At the human level of identity it is our similarities with others, those things that we have in common with all humanity, that form the focus of our identity. At the personal level, it is our unique, individuating characteristics around which our identity is focused. At the social level, which is the main concern of SCT, identity is centred on the simultaneous awareness of similarities and differences; similarities between ourselves and members of our ingroups are contrasted with differences between ourselves and members of outgroups.

Self-categorization at one level or another follows the principle of meta-contrast. Categorization always occurs within a social context; it can never be acontextual. Within any one context there always exist several classificatory possibilities. The choice of one possibility over another is determined by the

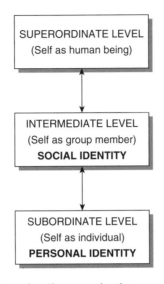

Figure 6.1   Different levels of self-categorization

meta-contrast ratio. The meta-contrast ratio is the ratio of the perceived inter-category differences and the perceived intracategory differences. When the social categories in a situation have meaning for the individuals in that situation, then personal self-categorizations become more salient when the meta-contrast ratio is small (that is, perceived intercategory differences do not greatly exceed perceived intracategory differences), and social self-categorizations become more salient when the meta-contrast ratio is large (that is, perceived intercategory differences greatly exceed perceived intracategory similarities).

Individual ingroup members are more or less *prototypical* of the ingroup, but prototypicality is relative, shifting with differing comparative contexts. An individual's ***prototypicality*** is defined by the ratio of the perceived differ-ence between that individual and the other individual members of the ingroup, and the perceived difference between that individual and outgroup members. The more an individual resembles other ingroup members (that is, the distance between that individual and the other ingroup members is small) and the more that individual is unlike outgroup members, the more that person is prototypical of the ingroup. The popularity and social attractive-ness of specific individual ingroup members is a direct function of individual prototypicality (e.g., Hogg, 2001).

Identity, either personal or social, is thus a fluid and contextualized phe-nomenon. The same relations between people can be perceived either as

glossary

glossary

differences forcing them into different social categories or as similarities binding them within the same social category, depending on the comparative context. For example, a social psychologist at a meeting of the psychology department in which he or she works will likely perceive few commonalities with others in the room, unless it is a department fortunate enough to be blessed with several social psychologists. However, the same social psychologist attending a meeting of a university-wide committee is now likely to perceive more commonalities between self and the other psychologists, because of the presence of others providing a greater array of differences. On the other hand, when that social psychologist attends a meeting of social psychologists, differences among all these social psychologists are likely to loom large on the psychological horizon. How one self-categorizes depends entirely on the social context; what is a difference in one context becomes a commonality in other.

Depersonalization and self-stereotyping

In SCT, the process of shifting one's identity away from the personal level towards a particular social identity is called *depersonalization*:

> Depersonalisation refers to the process of 'self-stereotyping' whereby people come to perceive themselves more as the interchangeable exemplars of a social category than as unique personalities defined by their individual differences from others. (Turner et al., 1987, p. 50)

Thus, according to SCT, identifying as a member of a particular social group involves applying the social stereotype of that group to oneself. Hogg and Turner (1987) demonstrated this effect in a study in which university students completed a range of self-descriptive measures following an activity designed to manipulate the salience of their gender identity. Gender salience was manipulated by having participants debate a controversial issue (such as euthanasia, or video censorship) in one of two conditions: with a member of their own sex against two opposite sex members (gender-salient condition), or with a single member of their own sex (gender non-salient condition). Following these debates, participants in the gender-salient condition described themselves in more gender-stereotypical terms than did those in the gender non-salient condition. However, closer examination of the stereotype items endorsed showed that, although men applied both positive and negative aspects of the gender stereotypes to themselves when gender was salient, among women only the positive aspects of the stereotype were endorsed more strongly in this condition. In fact, women were *less* likely to apply negative stereotypes of women to themselves when gender was salient than when it was not. As Hogg and Turner noted, this differential acceptance of positive and negative aspects of a stereotype shows that the application of stereotypes to the self does not proceed in an automatic or inevitable way from the salience of a self-categorization, and suggests that members of marginalized or low-status groups (such as women) may be particularly sensitive to the implication that they possess negative stereotypical characteristics of their groups.

We can see, therefore, that people differentially apply the positive and negative aspects of their groups' stereotypes to themselves depending on the context in which that self-stereotyping occurs. Other researchers have shown even greater flexibility in the content of stereotypes as they are deployed by members of the same group for different purposes. In their study of Scottish identity in the context of debates about the devolution of the Scottish Parliament, Reicher, Hopkins and Condor (1997) found that their Scottish participants drew on many highly contrasting 'stereotypes' of what it means to be Scottish, and that the content of their stereotypes was strategically aligned with their political arguments. For example, Scots described their fellow nationals as variously headstrong or cautious, fiercely independent or warmly communal, depending on the political position for which they were arguing.

Furthermore, there is no reason to assume that the relationship between salient self-categorization and self-stereotyping is unidirectional. SCT theorists argue that one important factor influencing the salience of a social identity at a given moment is the fit between the self and the relevant social group (Oakes, Turner & Haslam, 1991). Seeing oneself (i.e., one's 'personal' identity) as having characteristics that are stereotypical of a particular group increases the fit between the self and the group, thereby increasing the likelihood that one will experience oneself in terms of that social identity. For example, in a study of relationship satisfaction among couples in long-term heterosexual relationships, Donaghue and Fallon (2003) found that men and women who described themselves in traditional sex-stereotypical terms were more likely to judge their relationships with their opposite sex partners on the basis of group norms for their sex (that is, by comparison with other men or women) than by comparison with their partners. In contrast, men and women who were low in sex-stereotypical characteristics were more likely to compare themselves with their partner than with same-sex others. These findings suggest that the extent to which men and women see themselves in sex-stereotypical terms influences the extent to which they understand their intimate relationships as an intergroup (involving a man and a woman), rather than an interpersonal (involving two people) context.

Social identities and structural models of the self

Deaux and her colleagues have argued that social identities can be best understood as important organizing concepts within the cognitive self (Deaux, 1993; Deaux, Reid, Mizrahi, & Ethier, 1995; Reid & Deaux, 1996). In their model, cognitive representations of self-attributes are stored in the self-system in terms of the social identities with which they are associated. Thus, they argue for a self-system comprised of a hierarchically structured self of cognitive representations in which the self-attributes associated with individuals' particular group or category memberships, or their social roles, are represented within the same cognitive structure. In this way, when a particular social identity becomes accessible, the set of personal attributes associated with that identity also becomes accessible. This model of the relationship between personal and social identities thus explicitly resists the depersonalization that SCT argues occurs when people operate in terms of their social identities. Whereas in SCT people are considered to shift between personal and social identities, Deaux's model argues for a more integrated self-concept, which, to paraphrase the title of Deaux's (1992) paper, personalizes identity (by the idiosyncratic personal characteristics associated with various identities) and socializes self (by conceptualizing self-attributes as being attached to particular social identities).

Deaux's model of the structure of the self-concept suggests that, rather than distinguishing between (social) identities and (personal) selves, it may be useful to think about the self-concept in terms of identity-specific self-representations (e.g., Deaux, 1993; Marsh, 1993). Deaux et al. (1995) argue that specific domains of life are likely to be associated with particular social identities and, therefore, with particular personal attributes, and that self-representations that are similar to each other are likely to shift in accessibility in a related manner as the probability that they share many of the same situational and motivational cues is high. Thus, it may be that the potentially infinite number of possible working self-concepts that could be constructed from combinations of self-representations contained within the self-system may, in practice, largely be able to be reduced to a smaller set of identity-specific self-concepts that reflect the identities made salient by the particular configuration of situations and motivations in which one generally finds oneself.

Identity politics

Claiming and rejecting certain social identities is not a socially or politically neutral act. As we have seen in our discussion of self-categorization theories, identities do not simply report certain social facts about ourselves and others, they also serve to define allegiances and hostilities, and to draw the lines along which social judgements are made and social rewards distributed. Although the use of identity-related terms to identify people and groups of people is ubiquitous, both in social psychology and in everyday social life, identity categories are often highly problematic. Consider the example of 'race' (see Hall, 1992, Hirschfeld, 1997, and Sampson, 1993 for further discussions of this issue). Job applications, census forms, psychological surveys, and many other ordinary events frequently require people to indicate their race by ticking a box or giving a short answer. Clearly implied in this instruction is the notion that racial categories 'exist', that is that they correspond to something that is 'out there' in the world, and that to state one's race is simply to report an uncontested fact. But racial categories are by no means clear: what is required for someone to be 'Aboriginal' or 'Caucasian' or 'African'? There are no clearly defined criteria for these classifications, and even if there were the increasing numbers of people with mixed-'racial' heritage make the boundaries of these categories extremely unclear. Yet, despite these fundamental problems, race continues to be a highly important social category. Why?

The example of race highlights a crucial issue in the politics of identity. The dilemma can be simplified as follows. On the one hand, imposing the category of 'race' as a social identity misrepresents and reduces the multiple and complex ethnicities of many people, and encourages the homogenization of members of 'racial' groups. It can also serve to essentialize and rationalize differences between groups. The acceptance of racial categories as real and natural is required for stereotyping of, and prejudice and discrimination against, people on this basis. In this view, constructive social interaction and harmonious interpersonal relations would be better served by encouraging the abandonment of racial categories. However, this decategorization (or de-identification) approach ignores the fact that, although 'race' may be a biological fiction, it is a social reality, and members of the same 'racial' group are likely to have many experiences in common and their interests are likely to be aligned in many ways. The issues become particularly important when one's group is disadvantaged. Effective political action for social change requires the recognition of the 'reality' of these groups, and requires identification with other members of the group if social change is to take any form other than individual mobility. Hence the dilemma: effective action for change often requires the adoption of an identity which does not provide a good fit to many of the members of the groups so identified, and which reinforces what is a highly dubious categorization in the first place. Is reductionism and sometimes serious distortion of people's lived experience the price that must be paid for effective social action?

Textbox 6.2

Identity politics and affirmative action

Identity politics begins from the position that, as members of society, people are not all the same. Differences in surface characteristics (such as skin colour or sex) are associated with differences in political access so that, as Alcoff (2003) explains, categories based on 'race', ethnicity, gender, sexuality, disability, religion, class and age, to name a few, are also markers of status and opportunity within society. She writes:

> ' ... one's placement in [these] social categories of identity has an enormous impact on one's life, determining the job prospects, career possibilities, available places to live, potential friends and lovers, reactions from police, credence from jurors, and the amount of presumptive credibility one is accorded by one's teachers, students, neighbours, and co-workers.' (2003, p. 3)

Identity politics is at its core an attempt both to make visible and to remedy systematic identity-based injustice.

One of the most widely practised remedies for identity-based oppression is affirmative action. Affirmative action policies are most commonly found in educational institutions and workplaces, and they are designed to compensate for some of the disadvantages which members of low-status or otherwise marginalized groups experience within these institutions. Typically, affirmative action policies take the form of quotas (i.e., a certain percentage of people employed at a particular level or admitted to a particular course in a university must be from group X) or different selection criteria for members of the targeted minority group(s). Affirmative action policies are designed to partly redress the inequality of opportunity experienced by members of different identity groups both at the individual level (by making it easier for some members of marginalized groups to gain access to education and jobs) and at the group level (by the changes in stereotypes of these groups that will (perhaps) follow from the success of individual group members).

However, affirmative action policies, and identity politics more generally, do not sit easily in liberal democracies which hold the idea that all citizens are equal. Because affirmative action policies explicitly treat people differently on the basis of their group membership, critics argue that these policies are themselves discriminatory and unfair (to members of high-status groups), and that the only way to ensure a just society for all members is for all policy to be 'colour-blind' (or gender-blind, etc.); that is, for people to succeed or fail in gaining access to opportunities solely on their individual merits. This position is rejected by 'colour-conscious' policy advocates, who argue that identity-based oppression is so deeply ingrained in the institutions and other social practices of a society that it will not be redressed without explicit recognition and active efforts that acknowledge the differences in experience and opportunity afforded to members of

> **Textbox 6.2   (Continued)**
>
> different identity groups. Colour-blind policies attempt to present group differences as superficial and inconsequential: a veneer that can be easily lifted to remove the effects of prejudice and discrimination. Colour-conscious policies argue that 'surface' differences will never be able to be ignored, and that attempts to do so really amount to a requirement for marginalized groups to attempt to assimilate to dominant groups. Identity politics is a politics that embraces differences: people are to be treated with justice in all their differences, not in spite of such differences (Kruks, 2001).

Social Representations Approaches to Self and Identity

Even though the solipsistic values of contemporary western life may tempt us to believe ourselves to be each our own, unique, original creation, no self comes to being in a vacuum. In previous chapters we have discussed how the shared social representations of objects and ideas that exist in a culture provide us with ways of seeing those objects and things. Now, our discussion turns to how the very notion of 'self' is itself the subject of shared social understandings, and how ideas about what it is to have a self, and what kinds of properties a 'self' might be conceived of as having, depend on these social representations and discourses of self.

We have already discussed some critiques of dominant socio-cognitive models of the self which assume an individualistic view of the person. These cultural critiques have emphasized that the taken-for-granted individualism of dominant models of self fails to capture important features of the selves of people living in more collectivist cultures. We have already discussed the empirical evidence (see Chapter 5) that the ways in which we think about 'the person' are strongly culture-bound (e.g., Geertz, 1975; Lukes, 1973; Markus & Kitayama, 1991; Triandis, 1995). Shared social beliefs about what people fundamentally *are* defines the task of 'self making': developing a 'self' in an individualist culture involves identifying one's stable traits and talents, and forming a robust sense of mastery and autonomy, whereas creating a self within a collectivist culture requires an understanding of one's roles and responsibilities in relation to others. Ironically, although social cognition researchers have become more sensitive to cultural differences in the self-concept in the last decade or so, this sensitivity has not really loosened the grip of individualist meta-theory; in cross-cultural studies of self, individualist/collectivist self-construal is routinely included as an individual difference variable. Thus the importance of culture to the formation of self-concept, where it is even acknowledged, is reduced to the level of 'individual psychological culture' (Ratzlaff, Matsumoto, Kouznetsova, Raroque & Ray, 2000; see also Kwan, Bond & Singelis, 1997). But social representations do not just provide the 'building blocks' which an individual may or may not use in the construction of self; social representations also form the context in which that self exists and encounters others, and therefore the effects of these representations cannot be reduced from the social level of analysis (see Donaghue & Ho, 2005, for further discussion of this point).

How should we conceptualize the relationships between the social representations that surround the development of self in a given society and the particular selves of individuals within that society? Breakwell and Millward (1997) argue that the shared constructions of reality captured in social representations form '… the backdrop for individual identity development' (p. 30). In this view, although social representations do not directly control the development of one's sense of self in an inevitable or proscriptive way, the social representations associated with one's group memberships constitute a kind of social expectation that needs to be addressed in one's self-concept. Thus, being a woman, for example, does not necessarily entail that one will have particularly stereotypically feminine behaviours, but it does mean that one must 'take a position' on one's femininity. Social representations can be seen as constituting 'social facts' that must be negotiated in developing one's identity in the world.

Psy-disciplines and discourses of the self

So far in this book, when we have talked about discourse we have primarily concentrated on the analysis of how the specific ways in which particular accounts are constructed in everyday communication (conversation, newspapers, entertainment media, etc.) can be seen as achieving particular forms of social action. This kind of analysis tends to focus on the fine detail of the way in which things are said and versions of events are 'worked up' in particular instances, rather than more generally on the typical content of such communications. Foucauldian analyses of discourse (see Chapter 2), on the other hand, are concerned with the ways in which various institutional practices (such as the practice of 'science', or the regulation and government of people) produce a range of social discourses, also known as 'regimes of truth', that form the subjectivity of those they 'describe' and regulate. Subjectivity, in this sense, refers to people's private experience of themselves; our deep and particular sense of who we are. At the heart of Foucauldian analyses is the contention that *systems produce subjects*; that is, that social discourses subjectivize people, producing in them a subjectivity that more or less matches the requirements of the power/knowledge regime in which those discourses are created. The social discourses that Foucault analyses weave together lay experience, expert knowledge, institutional practice, and symbolic representations into a powerful edifice that simultaneously proscribes what is correct, moral or beneficial, and provides the means through which deviations from these proscriptions are exposed and regulated (Foucault, 1970, 1972, 1986). The multifaceted, socially shared, and culturally pervasive nature of these discourses makes them similar (in some important ways, at least) to Moscovici's social representations.

It can be argued that in its study of the self, psychology has also become a dominant force in *producing* our contemporary experience of our selves. According to Foucault, we become objects of the discourses that 'know' us, and are produced in terms of the characteristics and capacities that those discourses make meaningful. For example, as members of contemporary western societies, we think of ourselves as having a sexual orientation (usually heterosexual, homosexual, or bisexual) not because underlying sexual orientation is the inevitable source of our sexual preferences and behaviours, but because psychology has come to think of sexual behaviour in this way, and has developed powerful discourses and regulatory practices *that produce us* as people with particular sexual orientations. Not knowing (i.e., 'being confused' or 'in denial') one's sexual orientation is produced as a psychological problem in contemporary life by the discourses that produce sexual orientation as a stable feature of people. This is not to say that sexual orientation, like any aspect of our subjectivity, isn't 'real', but, rather, that *all* of the terms in which we think about ourselves, and the corresponding characteristics, beliefs, emotions and desires that we see ourselves as having, are given to us by the social (and in this case, psychological) discourses in which we are constituted.

In addition to creating the terms in which we think about ourselves, Foucault (1970, 1980) argues that the power/knowledge regimes (and particularly the 'psy' disciplines; primarily psychology, psychiatry and psychoanalysis) concerning the self provide us with the means to engage in the monitoring, or *surveillance*, of our selves. Foucault adopts as a metaphor Bentham's model of the panopticon – a hypothetical prison in which individual prisoners' cells surround a central observation tower, backlit so that every move of each prisoner is visible to the central guard. The panoptican allows the control of large numbers of prisoners by few guards because the design of the prison involves the prisoners in policing their own behaviour. Prisoners' behaviour will be controlled by very few overtly powerful guards, because prisoners will not know whether they are observed at any given moment.

The constant *possibility* of observation resulting from relentless visibility means that prisoners become self-monitoring and (theoretically) no coercive control is required. Foucault argues that the 'regimes of truth' that are brought into being by those conferred with expertise in particular domains are internalized by individuals and make visible (and therefore subject to surveillance) certain ways of being. Individuals then actively monitor themselves, and thus compliant behaviour is produced without the need for external enforcement. Discourses of the self provide a corresponding range of:

> technologies of the self, which permit individuals to affect by their own means or with the help of others a certain number of operations on their own bodies and souls, thoughts, conduct, and way of being, so as to transform themselves in order to attain a certain state of happiness, purity, wisdom, perfection, or immortality. (Foucault, 1988, p. 2)

Following Foucault, Nikolas Rose has written extensively about how the rise of the psy-disciplines in particular has produced certain ideas about what it is to be human which powerfully shape the way that members of contemporary western societies come to experience themselves. He writes:

> ... in these societies, human beings have come to understand and relate to themselves as 'psychological beings', to interrogate and narrate themselves in terms of a psychological 'inner life' that holds the secrets of their identity, which they are to discover and fulfil, which is the standard against which the living of an 'authentic' life is to be judged. (Rose, 1996, p. 22)

Rose argues that, rather than simply discovering and investigating aspects of people that are 'already (in) there', psychological discourse *creates* an idea of selves, which have certain characteristics capacities and propensities for certain kinds of dysfunction. It also creates the expertise by which such problems can be managed. Psychological discourse thus produces people with a set of recognizable and predictable predilections, passions and problems, and, if they pay attention to the advice of 'psy' professionals, a more or less matching set of technologies to enable them to manage and regulate themselves. In contemporary life, virtue is achieved by conscientiously applying these techniques to oneself; by the willingness to constantly take part in a quest for perfection:

> Contemporary individuals are incited to live as if making a *project* of themselves: they are to *work* on their emotional world, their domestic and conjugal arrangements, their relations with employment and their techniques of sexual pleasure, to develop a 'style' of living that will maximise the worth of their existence to themselves. (Rose, 1996, p. 157, italics in original)

Textbox 6.3

Identity projects: what does your toilet cleaner say about you?

Nikolas Rose (1996) argues that as 'psy-discourses' become more ubiquitous in social life and the creation of perfected, authentic 'selves' become the central achievements of our lives, communicating those selves takes on great significance. Much of our mundane, everyday activity takes on the responsibility of showing the world who we are: consumer decisions are recast as *identity projects*.

> Consumers are constituted as actors ... assembling a 'life-style' through acts of choice in a world of goods. Each commodity is imbued with a 'personal' meaning, a glow cast back upon those who purchase it, illuminating the kind of person they are, or want to come to be. (Rose, 1996, p.162)

Find three or four examples of the different ways in which discourses of self and identity are used in marketing. What is each product (implicitly or explicitly) promising to say about the person who purchases it? Can you detect differences between the identity-messages promised by products in these contemporary advertisements and examples from 10 or 20 years ago?

Although there are many differences between 'typical' social representations research and Foucauldian approaches to understanding the forms of shared understanding that shape social life, they each none the less emphasize the ways in which socially shared ideas about the world (including the 'selves' that inhabit it) provide the forms in which objects in the world (including 'selves') are constituted. These forms influence what is 'thinkable' about the self, and the kinds of qualities and capacities we consider ourselves and others as having, and the dimensions on which we look for variability between ourselves and others. Although subjectivity feels private, consideration of the social representations and social discourses surrounding the experience of self draws attention to the ways in which our sense of who we are is fundamentally a product of social life.

Discursive Approaches to Self and Identity

The socially constructed self

Social constructionist and discursive theorists of the self tend to approach the idea of the self with quite different explanatory aims to social cognitive theorists. Rather than seeking to account for the *effects* of the self on behaviour, social constructionists are usually more concerned with understanding the way in which people experience a sense of self; their *subjectivity*. As we have discussed above, subjectivity refers to one's interior experience of being, or one's own subjectively private experience of self. Psychologists working from a constructionist perspective are concerned with how such an apparently private aspect of experience as our subjectivity is produced by the social environments we inhabit. Furthermore, theoretical accounts of self and identity produced from a constructionist perspective do not seek to find consistency and continuity across times and places, but instead emphasize the ways in which various accounts of self are *situated* (occurring in specific physical and social contexts) and *occasioned* (produced in response to some specific social requirement).

Self-presentation People often behave in dramatically different ways in different contexts. One of our skills as competent members of our culture is the ability to make reasonable predictions about how other people are likely to interpret and react to things we might do or say to them. On the basis of these predictions, we can modify our behaviour to try and elicit the kinds of responses we desire from others. This manipulation of the self is known as self-presentation.

Self-presentation is not a new phenomenon. Symbolic interactionists, including George Herbert Mead and Erving Goffman, began writing about self-presentation in the first half of the last century, and Goffman's (1963) famous metaphor of social life as a performance in which actors seek to create particular impressions on audiences within specific contexts has been highly influential in social psychology. Symbolic interactionism is based on the idea that people represent the world symbolically, and then interact with the world on the basis of their symbolic representations. So, if you and I are having a conversation, I am not interacting with you, but, rather, with my symbolic representation of you, just as you are interacting with your symbolic representation of me. Additionally, symbolic interactionism emphasizes that the representations that we develop of things in the world, including ourselves and other people, develop in the interactions that we have with those people and things. The representations that we develop of the world are *social*, because they are all developed in social contexts, and so reflect those aspects which the particular social context makes meaningful.

How is this relevant to self and identity? Symbolic interactionists argue that we develop symbolic representations of ourselves as a result of our interactions with others. Cooley's (1902) widely adopted metaphor of the *looking glass self* argues that we develop a sense of ourselves and of the attributes and qualities that we possess through the reflected appraisals of others. How others see us becomes how we see ourselves. I come to know myself as smart, or funny, or serious, or selfish through having others interact with me in ways that suggest these things. Just as we form a sense of our physical selves through seeing ourselves reflected in polished pieces of glass, we develop a sense of our psychological selves through seeing ourselves reflected in the social mirrors of the people around us. However, just as we might strike a pose in front of a physical mirror in order to produce our most attractive reflection, symbolic interactionists argue that we also 'pose' in front of our social mirrors, by presenting ourselves in ways that we believe will elicit desirable reflections of ourselves from those we encounter in our social lives. It is this behaviour that is referred to as self-presentation, and symbolic inter-actionists are concerned with studying how we manipulate our presentations of self to suit (our understandings of) the requirements of different social situations.

The symbolic interactionist tradition forms the basis for more recently developed social constructionist and discursive theories of self and identity, albeit with some crucial differences. Kenneth Gergen (1991, 1994), in his writings about the socially constructed self, argues that the conditions of con-temporary (western) life, with its increasingly sophisticated technologies for communication, has fundamentally changed the subjective experience of the self. Briefly, he argues that the work and social practices of contemporary life have dramatically increased the number and variety of people with whom most of us interact, resulting in increasingly frequent and sophisticated shifts in self-presentation, as we attempt to present ourselves to best advantage in a wide range of different social contexts. As we engage in this *strategic manipulation* of our presentations of self, Gergen argues that it becomes more and more difficult for us to retain the idea of a coherent, underlying, 'authentic' self (see Rose, 1996). Despite this, however, the ideal of an inte-grated, authentic self is so entrenched in western culture that the initial response to the awareness of the strategic presentations of the self in differ-ent contexts is guilt and dissatisfaction at what is experienced as disconnec-tion from one's 'true' self, the existence of which is still unquestioned. According to Gergen, many people remain mired in this guilt, but others resolve the guilt by abandoning the belief that there is an integrated, 'real' self somewhere inside, and instead begin enjoying the opportunities to construct and play with identities in different situations. Gergen refers to this experi-ence of self as the *pastiche personality*. The pastiche personality revels in the play of identities, ' ... avoids looking back to locate a true and enduring self, and simply acts to full potential in the moment at hand' (1991, p. 150). However, throughout this shifting play of identities there is still an overriding sense of coherence intrinsic to the self, an inner 'self of selves' (James, 1892) that is directing the superficial play of identities. In the pastiche personality, the notion of personal, internal agency is still present.

Gergen argues that experience of the self as this kind of pastiche is quickly becoming normative in contemporary western life, and that this shift will also tend to erode the lingering commitments to the notion of the authentic inner self. This erosion will itself have further consequences. Gergen writes:

> As self-constructions cease to have an object (a real self) to which they refer, and one comes to see these constructions as a means of getting on in the social world, one's hold on them is slowly relinquished. They slowly cease to be one's private possessions. The invitation for one construction as opposed to another is, after all, issued from the social surrounds; and the fate of this construction is also determined by other persons. One's own role thus becomes that of participant in a social process that eclipses one's personal being. One's potentials are only realised because there are others to support and sustain them; one has an identity only because it is permitted by the social rituals of which one is part; one is allowed to be a certain kind of person because this sort of person is essential to the broader games of society (1991, p. 157).

This changing consciousness marks the transition to what Gergen calls the *relational self*. Selves are no longer considered the site of some essential, individual characters, but are, rather, the 'manifestations of relationship' (1991, p. 146). The modernist view of social life is turned on its head: rather than individuals meeting and interacting and 'having' relationships, in this view relationships are primary and create the selves of those who participate in them. However, Gergen is quick to acknowledge that this view of the self is by no means widespread. Indeed, the nature of our language and particularly of the available forms that we have for accounting for experience and action, require and reinforce the notion of individual subjects whose intentions, beliefs, emotions and other inner states are responsible for producing the everyday actions that constitute the social world. As Gergen points out, while we can easily speak of the feelings, wishes or intentions of the 'individuals' participating in relationships, we have no language to ask about what the relationships want, or hope for, or intend. As numerous scholars have argued, the limits of our language strongly shape what it is possible for us to think, and so a language in which agency resides within individual actors produces a subjectivity in which individuals act. None the less, there are indications of a gradual reorientation away from this autonomous view of 'self', with increasing emphasis on the ambiguity of action, on the possibility of multiple readings of actions, and on the role of culture and context in the production of 'individual' actions.

It is in moving beyond the pastiche personality that the 'strong' social constructionists break seriously with the symbolic interactionist tradition. Whereas the symbolic interactionists implicitly rely on a kind of 'self of selves' which oversees our shifting self-presentations, strong social constructionist theorists explicitly reject such an idea, or at least the notion that this self of selves is somehow outside of and prior to social life.

Textbox 6.4

The 'authentic' self

Nikolas Rose (1989, 1996) has argued that there are strong normative pressures in contemporary western life for people to have an integrated and authentic sense of self.

Can you identify examples from popular culture (TV shows, books, movies, etc.) that illustrate this claim? What kinds of moral connotations are associated with the notion of finding and/or expressing one's 'authentic self'?

Can you find counter examples that show evidence of people displaying Gergen's idea of the 'pastiche personality'? What are the moral connotations here?

Talking about the self

One doesn't have to go very far to find examples of people talking about themselves. The making of statements that purportedly report on some aspect of one's personal characteristics, motives, intentions, feelings, desires, thoughts, beliefs, values, memories or experiences is ubiquitous in contemporary social life. As with other topics, discursive psychologists are interested in statements about the self not for what they reveal about the inner life of the speaker, but for the social actions that these kinds of statements can perform. Statements in which people make claims about their own personal traits (e.g., 'I'm such a perfectionist'), feelings (e.g., 'I'm really upset about this'), and capacities (e.g., 'I've never been much good at maths') are considered not as reflections of more or less stable inner states, but in terms of the particular interactional functions they serve in the specific circumstances in which they are uttered (Antaki, Condor & Levine, 1996; Antaki & Widdicombe, 1998). Depending on the context, a statement such as 'I'm really upset with you' could be used to elicit sympathy, to accomplish blaming, to account for poor performance, to excuse cruelty, and no doubt many other social actions.

Other theorists working in the broad discursive tradition have placed a somewhat different emphasis on the role of language in producing our notions of self and identity (and, consequently, our *experiences* of self and identity), focusing on the kinds of things that language *allows* people to say about themselves. Like Gergen, these theorists begin from the premise that '... we cannot approach an investigation of the self by assuming that there is an entity corresponding with the word – that there is a natural class of thing denoted by "self" that is separable from its context' (Lewis, 2003, p. 228). Indeed Rom Harré argues that concepts of self are bound with the terms available to refer to ourselves and others in language, and that self is a 'theory' that allows concepts of choice and agency, and thereby morality, into accounts of our own and others' behaviour. Rather than corresponding to some existing entity, the term 'I' marks 'a mere point in psychological space' (Harré & Van Langenhove, 1999, p. 7) which provides the reflexivity needed to produce an account of action in which one decides, chooses, intends, wills, etc. to perform certain social actions. As Harré points out, 'I' allows a person a certain distance on their actions and experiences (or the activities of 'me'), from which it is possible to reflect on, judge, and, crucially, to position oneself as choosing from among multiple possible actions. As Lewis writes, 'without the presumption of choice, agency is an empty notion – and choice requires that the person is capable of adopting a superordinate perspective (is capable of reflexive awareness). The reflexive possibilities provided by the iterative use of personal pronouns allow just such a self to emerge' (2003, p. 232). Such accounts allow people to be considered responsible for their actions, and so allow a discourse of social responsibility and morality.

Morality and the social constructed self   One of the recurring criticisms of the constructionist notion of self is that it is morally relativist – that it allows no basis on which certain actions or accounts of the world can be preferred over others and, correspondingly, no basis for establishing certain actions as moral or immoral. If there can be no appeal to any principle or observation or value as being ultimately or universally true, then according to some realist critics (e.g., Parker, 2002) we are left in a morally chaotic world in which 'anything goes'. This analysis assumes, however, that without universal truths there can be no social truths or values around which social life and private subjectivity are organized. But concepts of 'truth' and 'value' and 'right' and 'wrong' are not excluded from socially constructed accounts of subjectivity and social action. Indeed, the socially negotiated grounds for establishing things as 'true' or 'factual' or 'objective', and the ways in which people use these concepts and orient their accounts of their own and others' behaviour around them, are of great interest to many discursive theorists. The critical difference in the relativist perspective (as compared with the realist) is that truths are seen as being local, negotiated understandings that are produced in social life, rather than immutable, objective principles that order and direct the way in which social life develops (Edwards, Ashmore & Potter, 1995).

Chapter Summary

Starting with the wide range of different ways in which people characterize themselves, in this chapter we have examined how the everyday concept of self has been theorized in social psychology. Social-cognitive models consider self as 'self-knowledge', and produce models that emphasize the organization of self-knowledge, and how particular kinds of self-representation are accessed in different situations. In addition to considering the kinds of attributes that people see themselves as actually having, researchers have also become interested in people's ideas about possible alternatives to the way they are now. These possible, ideal, and ought selves are seen as providing much of the context for people's current experiences of self. The plans that people have for achieving these alternative selves in the future, as well as the current discrepancies from them, are considered to be important contributors to people's experience of themselves in the present. We have also discussed how the reflexive nature of the self allows (and perhaps forces) people to engage in processes of self-evaluation and self-regulation, the assessment of how one is doing compared to others, and intentional efforts to modify aspects of one's self. All of these social-cognitive models of the self are concerned with the ways in which the knowledge that people have about themselves becomes relevant in particular circumstances, and how this self-knowledge guides behaviour and affect.

Social identity perspectives on the self consider how the social groups of which we are members impact on our sense of self. This perspective sees all experiences in social life as occurring on a continuum from interpersonal to intergroup interaction. The further we move towards the intergroup pole, the more depersonalized our sense of self becomes, as we think of ourselves more and more in terms of those characteristics that we share with other group members. Although SIT stresses the importance of social group memberships to one's sense of self, it returns to the individual level of analysis by emphasizing the role of identification with the group in affecting one's experience of social identity.

Social representations research considers the ways in which socially shared representations of 'the self' and of the social groups that contribute to one's sense of identity shape the context within which people develop their self-concepts. Although individuals can differ in the extent to which elements of particular social representations are incorporated into their self-concepts, the importance of social representations in forming the social environment surrounding these selves means that social representations cannot be reduced to individual difference variables. In providing the atmospheric conditions in which selves encounter each other and go about the business of their lives, social representations are irreducibly social phenomena. We discussed the work of Rose, who has extended Foucauldian analyses of the role of discourse in producing subjectivity, arguing that dominant psychological ideas about the nature of self are working to produce a contemporary subjectivity that is sharply focused on the identification and fulfilment of one's 'authentic' inner capacities and desires.

Finally, we turned to the influential social constructionist work on the development of self and identity. Following from the symbolic interactionist tradition, scholars such as Kenneth Gergen have analysed ways in which the conditions of contemporary life are undermining the notion of an integrated and stable self. Instead, he argues, the constructed nature of the self is being revealed in the ordinary experiences of everyday life, and is provoking a crisis as the ontological basis of self apparently unravels. Gergen argues that the challenge for people in a postmodern world is to construct a sense of identity which does not require the 'self' to be a faithful reflection of inner capacities and qualities but which, rather, sees the self as a constructed achievement of relational social life.

Further Reading

Antaki, C., & Widdicombe, S. (Eds.) (1998). *Identities in talk*. London: Sage.

Baumeister, R. F. (1998). The self. In D. Gilbert, S. T. Fiske & G. Lindzey (Eds.), *Handbook of social psychology* (Vol. 1, 4th ed., pp. 680–740). New York: McGraw-Hill.

Gergen, K. J. (1991). *The saturated self*. New York: Basic Books.

Markus, H., & Wurf, E. (1987). The dynamic self-concept: A social psychological perspective. *Annual Review of Psychology, 38*, 299–337.

Onorato, R. S., & Turner, J. C., (2004). Fluidity in the self-concept: The shift from personal to social identity. *European Journal of Social Psychology, 34*, 257–278.

Rose, N. (1996). *Inventing ourselves: Psychology, power and personhood*. Cambridge: Cambridge University Press.

Prejudice

Prejudice is a pernicious, pervasive and persistent social problem. Although its deleterious effects are experienced most acutely by its targets, everyone is diminished by prejudice. The study of prejudice has been a central focus of social psychology for most of the last century, and social psychological attention to prejudice has only increased in recent times. In many ways, social psychology has, in a *de facto* kind of way, accepted understanding prejudice as the litmus test of its own value as a perspective on the social world and of its value to the world. This is perhaps fair enough. The horrors of the most extreme forms of intergroup violence, exemplified most clearly by the genocides of the Holocaust, of Cambodia, of Rwanda, and among the states of the former Yugoslavia challenge any theory of humanity. To the extent that social psychology does not, or cannot, provide an adequate account of such atrocities, it falls short of the mark of an adequate understanding of human experience.

In common parlance, prejudice is often said to mean 'to pre-judge' someone or something. That is, it refers to the practice of forming an opinion or value of someone or something in the absence of direct experience of that person or thing. This meaning stems from the word's Latin roots (*pre + judicium*). Social psychology has provided many different definitions and conceptualizations of prejudice over the years (e.g., Duckitt, 1992; Milner, 1981). Despite this variety, contemporary social psychology largely follows, directly or indirectly, Gordon Allport's classic definition of prejudice from his 1954 book *The Nature of Prejudice*: 'Ethnic prejudice is an antipathy based upon a faulty and inflexible generalization. It may be felt or expressed. It may be directed toward a group as a whole, or toward an individual because he [sic] is a member of that group' (p. 9).

As Milner (1981) notes, this definition succinctly captures the five main features of almost all the different definitions of prejudice in mainstream social psychology.

1. Prejudice is an attitude.
2. It is based upon a faulty and inflexible generalization.

3. It is a preconception.
4. It is rigid and resilient.
5. Prejudice is bad.

As with the other topics we have examined in this book, this chapter examines perspectives on prejudice from social cognitive, social identity, social representations, and discursive approaches.

Social Cognition and Prejudice

Social cognitive approaches to the understanding of prejudice focus on aspects of individual psychological functioning. Mostly these are aspects of how individuals process information about themselves and others. Analyses of cognition are closely related to analyses of personality, and stable individual differences in personality have often been tied to similar differences in cognitive processes. Indeed, conceptually it is difficult to disentangle 'personality' from 'cognition'. For this reason, we first consider in this section two influential approaches to the study of prejudice that are commonly classified as personality approaches – focusing on authoritarianism and social dominance respectively. This is followed by coverage of socio-cognitive research that examines the complex relationship between stereotyping and prejudice, bringing to the fore again some of the material we discussed in Chapter 3.

The prejudiced personality

Prejudice is often thought to be the manifestation of a particular kind of personality. We are all familiar with the bigot – the person who rejects any and all outgroups, who believes in the prime importance of his or her own group, who is intolerant, who is hostile to individual members of outgroups, who often is servile to his or her superiors, and who, depending on our own stereotypes, is male, blue-collar or unemployed, poorly educated, and has not traveled. The bigot is a clearly identifiable personality type, or so we tend to believe. But if you were to ask for all the bigots in a crowd to raise their hand, no one would. We all know bigots, but no one identifies him- or herself as a bigot.

The idea of a bigoted or prejudiced personality has widespread intuitive appeal, and social psychology has searched for more than half a century to uncover the bigot and how the bigoted personality is predisposed to prejudice (e.g., Adorno, Frenkel-Brunswik, Levinson & Sanford, 1950; Altemeyer, 1981, 1988, 1996, 1998; Stone, Lederer & Christie, 1993). Two approaches are discussed here: the authoritarian personality, and social dominance orientation. Neither approach neatly fits the usual understanding of 'personality', as both incorporate broader social and ideological processes. Neither are these approaches strictly 'social cognitive', although both are related to consistent individual differences across individuals in their cognitive processes.

The authoritarian personality   The rise of fascism in Germany provided the impetus for a group of workers at the University of California at Berkeley to examine the psychological factors which allow fascist regimes to operate. Through extensive survey and interview research, and being guided by a psychodynamic theoretical approach, these researchers developed a portrait of the 'authoritarian personality' (Adorno et al., 1950).

Adorno et al. identified nine different dimensions which together define authoritarianism (1950, p. 228).

1. *Conventionalism*: Rigid adherence to conventional, middle-class values.
2. *Authoritarian submission*: Submissive, uncritical attitude toward idealized moral authorities of the ingroup.
3. *Authoritarian aggression*: Tendency to be on the lookout for, and to condemn, reject, and punish people who violate conventional values.
4. *Anti-intraception*: Opposition to the subjective, the imaginative, the tender-minded.
5. *Superstition and stereotypy*: The belief in mystical determinants of the individual's fate; the disposition to think in rigid categories.
6. *Power and 'toughness'*: Preoccupation with the dominance–submission, strong–weak, leader–follower dimension; identification with power-figures; over-emphasis upon the conventionalized attributes of the ego; exaggerated assertion of strength and toughness.
7. *Destructiveness and cynicism*: Generalized hostility, vilification of the human.
8. *Projectivity*: The disposition to believe that wild and dangerous things go on in the world; the projection outwards of unconscious emotional impulses.
9. *Sex*: Exaggerated concern with sexual 'goings-on'.

Of these dimensions, three are particularly important: *conventionalism* (rigid adherence to conventional social values and mores), *authoritarian submission* (an unquestioning subservience to one's moral and social superiors) and *authoritarian aggression* (a vigilance for, and hostile rejection of, those who violate conventional social values and mores). Authoritarian personality types become that way, according to Adorno et al., because of particular patterns of family structure and child-rearing. Authoritarian families are hierarchically organized around a stern, strict father who uses physical punishment capriciously. Authoritarianism is regarded as a personality dimension, and those high on the dimension (authoritarians) are more prone to prejudices of all kinds.

The authoritarian personality work has been extensively critiqued on both theoretical and methodological grounds (see Billig, 1976; Brown, 1965; Christie & Jahoda, 1954, for examples). One particularly telling critique came from research that established that regions and social settings notorious for prejudice and discrimination (e.g., the southern United States, South Africa) were no more afflicted with authoritarianism than were other regions (e.g., Minard, 1952; Pettigrew, 1958, 1959).

After a long period of relative neglect, the construct was revived and revamped by Altemeyer (1981, 1988, 1996, 1998), and this is described in the next section. Adorno et al.'s work on the authoritarian personality is often criticized for explaining prejudice as *just* a personality disorder. This is unfair. The Adorno et al. work is impressive partly because it is *not* just a personality theory. Rather, it builds an analysis of the intertwined relationship between personality structure and function, on the one hand, and social structure and function, on the other. This latter analysis is particularly informed by Marx. The work is also impressive in its scope and its range of methods, both of which are much grander than any contemporary research. None the less, it is fair to depict the work as essentially a personality-based approach to understanding prejudice. Its conceptualization of 'personality', though, is more social than is normally granted.

Adorno et al. explicitly set out to understand the psychology of fascism, in direct response to the horrors of fascist regimes in Germany and elsewhere prior to, and during, the Second World War. They argued that fascist ideologies can always be found, in all societies. The question, though, is what makes fascism appeal broadly at some times, in some places, and not others? They sought the answer in personality dispositions. However, they were well aware that personality does not arise *in vacuo*. Personality is a function of patterns of family structure and authority, of the organization of the state, and of other social structural factors. For fascism to become a dominant political force, as it did in Germany during the 1930s, they claimed that there must be an ideological receptivity and a personal susceptibility to the anti-democratic characteristics of fascism. By ideology, they meant the broad organization of opinions, beliefs, attitudes and values. Ideology 'exists' both within individuals, and, more importantly, independently of individuals as a feature of a particular social organization at a particular time (see Chapter 8 for a fuller treatment of ideology).

Adorno et al. were not the first ever to describe the set of characteristics that they label the authoritarian personality. Brown (1965, pp. 477–478) points out that in 1938 E. R. Jaensch, a German psychologist (and also a Nazi), described two personality types: the S-Type and the J-Type. We would describe the former type today as a liberal; one who favours nurture over nature as an explanation of behaviour, one who is tolerant, one who does not favour capital or corporal punishment. The latter, the J-Type, is almost identical to Adorno et al.'s authoritarian personality type: rigid in outlook, definite in judgement, firm and stable. The behaviours described by Adorno et al. and by Jaensch are the same; the values placed upon those behaviours are opposite. What for Adorno et al., and probably for most in modern western countries, is rigid and inflexible is reliable and stable for Jaensch; what is tolerant and understanding is flaccid and weak. Duckitt (1992) cites a similar example of work done in South Africa by MacCrone, describing a 'frontier' personality type which closely resembles the authoritarian personality type. Brown's (1965) example highlights the ease with which cultural values are transmitted into 'objective' social scientific research, and the dangers of failing to recognize this.

Right-wing authoritarianism   Altemeyer (1981, 1988, 1996, 1998) reasoned that there was little in the way of face validity, and even less empirical support, for the classification by Adorno et al. of authoritarian responses into their nine different dimensions. Instead, he suggested that there are only three reliably identifiable dimensions, and he has spent many years and a great amount of research endeavour demonstrating these three dimensions (among other things, too). Altemeyer's three dimensions of authoritarianism are:

1. *authoritarian submission*: a high degree of submission to the authorities who are perceived to be established and legitimate in the society in which one lives;
2. *authoritarian aggression*: a general aggressiveness, directed against various persons, that is perceived to be sanctioned by established authorities;
3. *conventionalism*: a high degree of adherence to the social conventions that are perceived to be endorsed by society and its established authorities. (1996, p. 133)

Altemeyer based his account on social learning theory rather than Freudian psychodynamics. He argues that most children are fairly authoritarian. This may simply reflect the fairly powerless position they occupy in the family and in society, the fact that they heavily depend on those in authority, particularly their parents and other caregivers, the fact that there are strong sanctions imposed upon them for violating estabished patterns of authority, and the fact that they are eagerly learning a social grammar that will allow them to become autonomous functioning members of society. This general point also fits the literature on the development of prejudice – majority group children start off fairly ethnocentric, and only around the age of ten do they (or some of them) become less ethnocentric (Aboud, 1988; Nesdale, 2001).

This general reasoning of Altemeyer's is the opposite of that of Adorno et al., and different from that of most social psychological research on prejudice and intolerance. It assumes that the problem to be described, explained and understood is how we come to be tolerant. Adorno et al., on the other hand, assumed tolerance and were trying to explain bigotry.

Children 'lose' their authoritarianism, according to Altemeyer, by experience. Having contact with minorities, gays, drug users, radicals and so on (all the people who are 'different' and who become the targets of items in scales to measure authoritarianism), as well as being treated unfairly by authorities, and especially so during adolescence, the developing young adult becomes less authoritarian. Those who move in 'tight circles' and who do not have such experiences remain highly authoritarian.

Altemeyer constructed over a period of years a scale to measure authoritarianism which has all the hallmarks of psychometric merit that were lacking in Adorno et al.'s F-scale. Scores on Altemeyer's scale correlate consistently, strongly and positively with scores on a variety of measures of prejudice – correlations are often in the order of .5 or .6. These correlations are of the same order as those typically found between the F-scale and various measures of prejudice. Notably, Altemeyer has been unable to find evidence of authoritarianism on the left wing of politics. His scale is thus known as a right-wing authoritarianism (RWA) scale, and his theory is a theory of right-wing authoritarianism. This does not necessarily mean that it is irrelevant to situations outside of western democracies. The meaning of 'right-wing' and 'left-wing' varies across societies, historical epochs, and political systems and ideologies. In Russia, for example, hard-line Stalinist communists are often referred to as 'right-wing', in relation to newly established patterns of political authority. The same hard-line Stalinists could be nothing but 'left-wing' in Washington. An important point here is implied by Altemeyer's definition of authoritarian submission. To recap, authoritarian submission refers to 'a high degree of submission *to the authorities who are perceived to be established and legitimate in the society in which one lives*' (Altemeyer, 1996, p. 133, our emphasis). Obviously, which authorities are 'perceived to be established and legitimate in the society in which one lives' depends on historical and geographical accident. The established and legitimate authorities in the Soviet Union before Gorbachev are not the same as the established and legitimate authorities in the USA under Reagan.

Altemeyer appears, then, to have salvaged the authoritarianism construct. He has embedded it within a different, and, for many, a more palatable, theory; he has developed a psychometrically valid scale, he has established that authoritarianism is only a feature of the political right-wing, and, most importantly for our present purpose, he has established consistent, large and positive correlations between authoritarianism and prejudice.

Altemeyer has also managed to divorce the construct of authoritarianism from the political analysis of fascism developed by Adorno et al., which, for some, may be a bonus. It is a portable theory of how individuals become shaped by their social experiences to come to have one orientation or another to established patterns of authority, applicable to understanding support for the death penalty, views on migration, and a myriad other contemporary social issues. What we also have is a theory that cannot explain what Adorno et al. set out to explain – the rise to dominance of a particular form of political organization. By separating authoritarianism from fascism, we can't explain phenomena broader than patterns of individuals' views on a host of social issues. We can't explain how it is that a nation can come to embrace a totalitarian form of political and social organization.

Another concern about Altemeyer's theory of right-wing authoritarianism was first raised by Duckitt (1992). Duckitt contends that a single underlying construct can explain all three of Altemeyer's dimensions of RWA. For Duckitt:

> each [of Altemeyer's three dimensions] can be seen as an expression of an intense (and insecure) identification with one or more important social groups (usually national, ethnic, tribal, or societal) and a consequent emphasis on and demand for group cohesion. Authoritarianism can therefore be defined as a set of beliefs organized around the normative expectation that the purely personal needs, inclinations, and values of group members should be subordinated as completely as possible to the cohesion of the group and its requirements. (1992, pp. 209–210)

This is a fascinating, and so far under-researched, contention. It provides a number of significant advantages over Altemeyer's approach, and over the original Adorno et al. approach.

First, and like Altemeyer's approach, it removes authoritarianism and ethnocentrism from the realm of the psychologically twisted, and makes them (possible) 'normal' features of the social environment. Second, and unlike Altemeyer, it explains *why* Altemeyer's three dimensions covary. Third, and unlike Altemeyer, it returns the link between authoritarianism and fascism. As Duckitt suggests, 'conceptualizing authoritarianism in terms of intense group identification that creates a demand for the subordination of individual group members to the cohesion of the group helps clarify why fascist ideology is such a pure expression of authoritarianism' (1992, pp. 210–211). And finally according to Duckitt, and unlike Altemeyer, it helps explain *why* authoritarianism is related to prejudice: authoritarianism and prejudice are joined through the mediating influence of social identity.

One aspect of Duckitt's reconceptualization of Altemeyer's reconceptualization of Adorno et al.'s conceptualization of authoritarianism is deficient, though, and leads us to the next and final section dealing with personality approaches to prejudice. Duckitt talks of an intense and insecure identification with one or more important social groups as being the foundation of authoritarianism which leads to a norm of individual subordination to the group. He is silent on the nature of 'group'. It is obvious that not all groups are equal, either psychologically to the individual, or in terms of social power and prestige. Fascism requires identification (intense and insecure) with *particular* groups – especially with the nation, but also with 'racial' groups. Intense and insecure identification with groups such as the American Psychological Association is irrelevant to political movements such as fascism (as far as we know, anyway). It is only intense and insecure identification with *some* groups that matters. Perhaps also the identification with some groups *within a social hierarchy* matters. This orientation to patterns of social hierarchy among groups leads us to consider recent work on *social dominance theory*.

Social dominance theory   Social dominance theory (SDT) has been developed recently by Sidanius and Pratto (1999; Pratto, 1999; Pratto, Sidanius, Stallworth & Malle, 1994; Pratto, Stallworth & Sidanius, 1997; Sidanius, 1993; Sidanius, Devereux & Pratto, 1992; Sidanius, Pratto & Bobo, 1996). Sidanius and Pratto claim that SDT is a general theory of intergroup conflict, incorporating aspects of work on the authoritarian personality, social identity theory, and other sources.

Sidanius and Pratto start with the observation that *all* human societies are structured into group-based social hierarchies. This stratification is due to evolutionary reasons. Groups at the top of the hierarchy possess disproportionately more positive social value than other groups (all the good things in life, both material and symbolic, and including wealth, status and power). Groups at the bottom of the hierarchy have disproportionately more negative social value, including poverty, ill-health, limited access to good education and jobs, and greater arrest and imprisonment rates. The focus of SDT is on the social psychological mechanisms that reproduce this social inequality.

Social stratification in all societies is organized along three dimensions: age, gender, and what Sidanius and Pratto call *arbitrary-set* dimensions. The first two dimensions are invariable and inevitable features of *all* human societies. However, it is the last dimension that is of particular importance here. Arbitrary-set hierarchies arise only in societies that produce economic surplus – that is, they are not to be found in hunter-gatherer societies. Arbitrary-set hierarchies can be based on almost any criterion that can be used to establish group differentiation. The criteria can be large and general, such as 'race', ethnicity, religion, class, nationality, or they can be small and more local, such as particular street gangs, families, or the graduates of particular schools. Age and gender stratifications rarely produce extreme forms of violent social control. The most extreme form of intergroup violence – genocide – is a feature *only* of arbitrary-set hierarchies. Sidanius and Pratto claim that genocide and *all* other forms of intergroup conflict are manifestations of the same human tendency to create and to perpetuate group-based social hierarchies.

This generic human tendency to create and to perpetuate group-based social hierarchies exists in societies along with a countervailing tendency to attenuate group-based hierarchies. This latter tendency leads to less hierarchy and greater equality across groups. Although Sidanius and Pratto attribute hierarchy-enhancing motives to evolutionary forces, they do not specify the origins of hierarchy-attenuating motives. They do note, though, that hierarchy-attenuating motives are a feature of many ideologies, from Christianity to Marxism. Perhaps it is no accident that such ideologies of equality arise as revolutionary ideologies, opposed to the *status quo* of the time and place (see also Chapter 8 for a discussion of ideologies of dominance and resistance).

A notable feature of many societies is that they often maintain inequality with a minimum of intergroup friction. This is not to say that societies do not sometimes have to resort to state-sanctioned force to maintain an inegalitarian *status quo*. But often there is no need for such violence. This can only be achieved, according to Sidanius and Pratto, through the essential functioning of *legitimizing myths*. These are sets of attitudes, beliefs, values, prejudices, stereotypes and ideologies '... that provide moral and intellectual justification for the social practices that distribute social value within the social system' (Sidanius & Pratto, 1999, p. 45). Legitimizing myths can also serve to undermine group-based hierarchy, and serve instead to promote group equality. Whether a legitimizing myth enhances or attenuates group-based hierarchy is referred to as myth's *functional type*.

Legitimizing myths have another important feature too – their *potency*. This refers to the extent to which the myth helps to 'promote, maintain, or overthrow a given group-based hierarchy' (Sidanius & Pratto, 1999, p. 46). A myth's potency depends on its consensuality, embeddedness, certainty, and mediational strength. *Consensuality* refers to the extent to which the myth is shared throughout a society (see the later section on social representations). An important issue here is the extent to which the myth is shared by members of groups in different positions within the group-based hierarchy (i.e., whether those at the 'bottom' accept the myth as much as those at the 'top'). When subordinate groups accept the legitimizing myth, then society has less need of coercion to maintain the group-based hierarchy.

Embeddedness refers to the extent to which the legitimizing myth is a part of other ideological aspects of the society. Notions of racism are deeply embedded within many contemporary western societies because of their strong links to such cultural imperatives as individualism and belief in the secular Protestant work ethic. The *certainty* of a legitimizing myth is the extent to which there is doubt about it within the society, and whether the 'certainty' of the myth is supported or challenged by prevailing cultural institutions such as science or religion. Finally, the *mediational strength* of a legitimizing myth refers to the extent to which the myth is linked to social policy outcomes.

Some people consistently support group-based hierarchies; others consistently are opposed to group-based hierarchies. This stable individual difference is known as *social dominance orientation* (SDO), and is measured by the SDO scale (Pratto et al., 1994). Higher scores on the scale indicate a greater tendency to support group-based hierarchies. SDO scores vary with gender (males score higher), personality and temperament, education, religion, and, not surprisingly, whether one is a member of a dominant or subordinate group.

SDO is *not* conceptualized by Sidanius and Pratto as a legitimizing myth itself. Instead, it is a stable predisposition to accept legitimizing myths. SDO is '... a ubiquitous motive driving most group-relevant social attitudes and allocative decisions' (Sidanius & Pratto, 1999, p. 57). This feature of SDT resembles the notion of the authoritarian personality.

Men consistently score higher than women on SDO, and high-SDO people are more often found in jobs that enhance existing social hierarchies, such as in business, the police, and the armed forces (Sidanius & Pratto, 1999; Sidanius et al., 1996). High-SDO people perform better than low-SDO people in hierarchy-enhancing jobs, and the converse is the case for hierarchy-attenuating jobs (Pratto, Stallworth, Sidanius & Siers, 1997). SDO scores are about as strongly positively correlated with prejudice as are RWA scores, but SDO and RWA scores are only weakly related to each other, if at all. Duckitt (2001) has proposed a dual-process theory of ideology and prejudice, in which authoritarians focus on perceived threat to ingroup values in a dangerous world, and people high on SDO focus on perceived threat to ingroup status in a competitive world. Thus, although there are surface similarities between SDO and RWA, the two constructs focus on different facets of group status (and hence are only slightly correlated with one another) and lead to prejudice (and other outcomes) through different paths.

While both SDO and RWA appear to be personality-based theories of prejudice, SDO in fact has stronger links with social identity approaches (see below). Indeed, SIT provided the primary theoretical basis for the development of SDO theory (Sidanius & Pratto, 2003). Recently, there have been strong debates about the commonalities and differences between SDO theory and SIT (Sidanius & Pratto, 2003; Turner & Reynolds, 2003). SIT theorists claim there are fundamental incompatibilities between SDO theory and SIT; SDO theorists counter that SIT critics misunderstand and distort the nature of SDO. Much of these debates focus on the degree to which SDO is situationally invariant and on the extent to which low-status and high-status groups share the same system-justificatory ideologies. It would seem that these debates have focused almost exclusively on SDO as an individual-difference (i.e., personality) variable, and have ignored some of the theoretical elaboration of constructs such as the potency, embeddedness, and mediational strength of legitimizing myths. It also seems unlikely that such debates can be resolved empirically, but, rather, require hard theoretical work (see Textbox 7.1).

Textbox 7.1

The social dominance orientation scale

Below you will find seven items from the original SDO scale developed by Pratto et al. (1994). Respondents are typically asked to indicate their responses to each question on a seven-point scale ranging from (1) strongly agree to (7) strongly disagree.

- Some groups of people are simply not the equals of others.
- This country would be better off if we cared less about how equal all people were.
- Some people are just more deserving than others.
- It is not a problem if some people have more of a chance in life than others.
- To get ahead in life, it is sometimes necessary to step on others.
- All humans should be treated equally (reverse scored)
- In an ideal world, all nations would be equal (reverse scored).

(Continued)

Textbox 7.1 (Continued)

Do you think social dominance should be treated as a personality predisposition or trait variable as Sidanius and his colleagues suggest?

What difficulties do you see in conceptualizing social dominance in this way?

Do you think that hierarchical social systems in which dominant groups oppress subordinate groups are inevitable because they are adaptive in evolutionary terms?

What of claims that such group-based hierarchies are maintained by the tendency for low-status groups to support the *status quo* and to endorse legitimizing myths?

For an interesting and stimulating debate on these issues see the following articles which appeared in the *British Journal of Social Psychology*: Schmitt & Branscombe (2003); Schmitt, Branscombe & Kappen (2003); Sidanius & Pratto (2003); Turner & Reynolds (2003); Wilson & Liu (2003a, 2003b).

Prejudice as an attitude

We started this chapter with Allport's (1954) classic definition of prejudice as an antipathy towards a group and its members. This sits easily with a view of prejudice as an attitude. In Chapter 4, we saw that attitudes are typically understood as evaluations of objects. Prejudice is, then, a special kind of attitude in which the object being evaluated is a group and/or its members. Most contemporary social cognitive work on prejudice accepts this notion of prejudice as an attitude.

Racism is a kind of prejudice. Prejudice is an antipathy towards a group and its members; racism is a kind of prejudice that arises when groups are defined on the basis of 'race'. Although 'race' is entrenched in both popular usage and scientific discourse as a taken-for-granted, essentialist category, geneticists and biologists discredited the validity of 'race' as a scientific category as long ago as the 1930s (Richards, 1997). Despite this, the concept of 'race' continues to be used unproblematically in psychology as a 'natural' kind of variable in ways that reinforce the commonplace view that it is a biological and genetic reality (Tate & Audette, 2001). As Hopkins, Levine and Reicher (1997) argue, this is especially the case in social cognition research, which treats racial categories and racial categorization as based on 'the empirical reality of observable or imagined biological differences' (p. 70), rather than social and ideological constructions. This is not to say that racial categories are not real in their consequences or that people do not treat them as 'real'.

Much of the social psychological work on prejudice has focused on racism, but has rested on a tacit assumption that our knowledge of racism can apply equally to other forms of prejudice, such as antipathies based on gender, class, religion or social class. This is a doubtful assumption that needs to be explored much more fully by social psychology. Much of the material we present in this section is based on research on racism, and almost all of that is based on research on racism in the United States. Whether it applies to other forms of prejudice, or even to racism in other countries, is an open question.

Racism used to be simple. It used to involve a straightforward rejection of, and hostility towards, a minority group. This kind of racism, sometimes called 'old-fashioned racism' (Sears, 1988), was segregationist, and overtly accepted and advocated white supremacy. It was once the dominant, acceptable and normative view of race. In most western countries, the normative view of prejudice and racism has changed markedly in recent times. It is now no longer as socially acceptable to believe in racial superiority, or to express prejudice. The norm of egalitarianism is now much stronger. This is not to say that racism has disappeared. Rather, the form of racism has changed. Old-fashioned racism has been replaced with a more subtle variant.

Surveys of public opinion on 'race' issues in most western countries have shown considerable change in the decades since the Second World War (Schuman, Steeh, Bobo & Krysan, 1997). It was once common and acceptable for majority group members (and even minority group members) to support segregation, oppose miscegenation, and believe in the innate superiority of white people. Now such views are cast with opprobrium. Public attitudes have changed on these matters, to be apparently more open, accepting and tolerant. This shift was picked up on by social psychology and other disciplines in the early 1970s (although perhaps the earliest social psychological work to address this issue was almost a decade earlier – Pettigrew, 1964). A distinction became commonly accepted between *old-fashioned* and *modern* racism. There is a variety of different analyses of 'modern' racism, each with a different name for the phenomenon, and each with a different analysis of how and why 'modern' racism works the way it does. Common, though, across these approaches is the view that racism has not simply disappeared but, rather, is just more subtle, and that racism (and hence prejudice) is an attitude. In this section we will consider some of the major social psychological approaches to the modern forms of racism.

Symbolic and modern racism   The first social psychological conceptualization of the 'new' racism was termed *symbolic racism* (Sears & Kinder, 1971; Sears & McConahay, 1973). The construct of *modern racism* was developed by

McConahay out of the symbolic racism notion (McConahay, 1982, 1986). The two approaches are very similar, although there are some differences.

In the context of US race relations, symbolic racism, like old-fashioned racism, involves a rejection of African Americans and their recent gains. However, this is based on values and ideology rather than a straightforward dislike. Kinder and Sears define symbolic racism as:

> a blend of antiblack affect and the kind of traditional American moral values embodied in the Protestant Ethic. Symbolic racism represents a form of resistance to change in the racial status quo based on moral feelings that blacks violate such traditional American values as individualism and self-reliance, the work ethic, obedience, and discipline. Whites may feel that people should be rewarded on their merits, which in turn should be based on hard work and diligent service. Hence symbolic racism [would express itself in opposition to] political issues that involve 'unfair' government assistance to blacks; welfare ('welfare cheats could find work if they tried'); reverse discrimination and racial quotas ('blacks should not be given a status they have not earned'); forced busing ('whites have worked hard for their neighborhoods, and for their neighborhood schools'). (1981, p. 416)

Thus, symbolic racism emphasizes a resentment of African Americans which is embedded within wider moralistic American values such as the Protestant work ethic. Kinder and Sears found that political behaviour such as voting preferences for mayoral candidates in elections involving African American candidates were better predicted by measures of symbolic racism than by perceived 'realistic' threats by African Americans. This was true for people for whom direct threats to 'the good life' were tangible (in terms of jobs and schools) *and* for people who stood to lose little from African American gains. Kinder and Sears conclude that racial prejudice is motivated more by symbolic resentments than by tangible threats.

Symbolic racism thus has two distinctive features. The first is an outright rejection of the principles of old-fashioned racism. Symbolic racism rejects segregationism and supremacy, and endorses egalitarianism. But, second and somewhat paradoxically, it also rejects African Americans (and other outgroups). Rejection is a function of anti-black affect and a strong adherence to traditional values of individualism. This often leads to opposition to social programmes designed to address social inequalities. Within the symbolic racism framework, this antagonism is not from a desire to maintain segregation in employment or education. Rather, it is because social programmes such as affirmative action violate deep-seated, cherished, traditional values. The most important of these values are '... individualism and self-reliance, the work-ethic, obedience, and discipline' (Kinder & Sears, 1981, p. 416). A symbolic racist reaction to affirmative action and busing stems from the belief that African Americans are benefiting unfairly from social programmes that violate individualism, self-reliance, the work ethic, obedience, and discipline – all the things that, in a sense, make up the 'American character'. Such programmes are 'unAmerican'.

Although many, perhaps even most, European Americans endorse egalitarianism, they retain cultural vestiges of anti-black affect. Whereas once that affect may have been plain dislike or even disgust, it is now more likely to be anxiety, distrust, fear, hostility, or perhaps just arousal (Stephan & Stephan, 1985, 1993). These affects may not be as strong as earlier forms, but they are, none the less, still negative. This negative affect colours behaviour.

The concept of *modern racism* is close to that of symbolic racism. People who are modern racists deny that they are racist, and also deny that racism is still a problem. That does not mean that they are not prejudiced, though. They still object to African Americans. They believe that African Americans are no longer confronted by racism and can now compete fairly in the marketplace on an equal footing with all other people. They believe that African Americans are 'pushing too hard, too fast and into places where they are not wanted' (McConahay, 1986, p. 93), that this is unfair, and that African Americans are gaining an undeserved share of social resources. Modern racists do not see their beliefs as constituting racism. Racism, for them, is comprised of beliefs in biological inferiority. Rather, they see their beliefs as being empirical 'facts'. People vary in the strength with which they accept the different tenets of modern racism, hence modern racism can be measured as an individual difference variable.

Most of the research and theoretical work on modern and symbolic racism has focused on relations between European Americans and African Americans. However, the concept has been applied to 'race' relations in South Africa (Duckitt, 1991), the UK (Brown, 1995), and Australia (Pedersen & Walker, 1997), and in other intergroup contexts – for example, gender and the work on modern and benevolent sexism (Glick & Fiske, 1996; Swim, Aikin, Hall & Hunter, 1995; Tougas, Brown, Beaton & Joly, 1995).

Ambivalent racism   The modern racism perspective assumes unidimensionality in racist attitudes. This has been challenged both empirically, using re-analyses of the data used by modern racism theorists (e.g., Bobo, 1983), and conceptually (Katz & Hass, 1988; Katz, Wackenhut & Hass, 1986). Katz and Hass (1988) argue that the racial attitudes of whites toward blacks have become complex and multidimensional. They suggest that ambivalence is a pervasive feature of racial attitudes – pro-and anti-black attitudes often exist side by side within the one (white) individual. Further, they argue that these sentiments are rooted in two core independent American values. Pro-black attitudes reflect humanitarian and egalitarian values which emphasize the ideals of equality and social justice. On the other hand, anti-black attitudes reflect values embodied within the Protestant ethic, such as hard work, individual achievement and discipline. Katz and Hass (1988) report a study demonstrating that both pro- and anti-black attitudes coexisted in their white student samples: anti-black attitudes were positively correlated with values embodied within the Protestant ethic and pro-black attitudes were positively correlated with values within an egalitarian-humanitarian perspective; but anti-black attitudes were unrelated to egalitarianism and pro-black attitudes were unrelated to belief in the Protestant ethic. These results have important social and theoretical implications. They suggest that the enduring nature of racism and anti-black prejudice may be due to the link to core, central values, embedded deeply within American culture. They also suggest that attempts to strengthen pro-black attitudes in the community may succeed without having any effect on anti-black attitudes. Theoretically, the results highlight the inadequacy of unidimensional, bipolar conceptions of attitudes – in this case, racial attitudes.

Aversive racism The ambivalent racism perspective develops a multidimensional, dynamic model of how individual European Americans express attitudes towards African Americans. Developed more or less contemporaneously, the aversive racism perspective provides an alternative, but similar, account of the same phenomena. Building on the psychoanalytic position of Kovel (1970), Gaertner and Dovidio (1977, 1986) distinguish between aversive and dominative racism. *Dominative* racism resembles what the modern racism perspective calls old-fashioned racism: it is blatant, 'red-necked', and overtly discriminatory. In contrast, people who are described as *aversive* racists:

> ... sympathize with the victims of past injustice; support public policies that, in principle, promote racial equality and ameliorate the consequences of racism; identify with a more liberal political agenda; regard themselves as non-prejudiced and non-discriminatory; but, almost unavoidably, possess negative feelings and beliefs about blacks (Gaertner & Dovidio, 1986, p. 62)

Aversive racism refers to a contradictory combination of generally positive beliefs about African Americans and a generally negative affect towards African Americans. This contradictory combination creates persistent ambivalence within aversive racists. Unlike the modern racism perspective, though, Gaertner and Dovidio posit that aversive racists are motivated to exclude their negative affect from awareness, and strive to maintain an image to self and to others of being liberal and unprejudiced. This ambivalence is strongly susceptible to situational influence, and the way it is resolved at any one time depends on a variety of situational factors. How it is resolved at one time is not necessarily the same as the way it is resolved at others, and indeed, unless the situation makes the ambivalence salient, it is not necessarily resolved at all.

According to Gaertner and Dovidio, the aversive racist's desire to maintain an egalitarian self-image is always dominant. In situations where that self-image may be challenged, aversive racists will act in ways to avoid such challenges. However, where that self-image can remain untarnished, the negative affect of aversive racists will tend to drive their behaviour. Aversive racism is thus not construed as an individual difference variable, and is not amenable to measurement in the way that modern racism is claimed to be. Instead, the theoretical position requires that the phenomenon be investigated experimentally.

The description of aversive racism resembles that of ambivalent racism. Both aversive and ambivalent racists strive to maintain an image, to themselves and to others, of being non-prejudiced. Both accounts are built upon the notion of intraindividual conflict, and both accounts imply that the resolution of the conflict is largely non-conscious. There are differences between the accounts, though. The site of the contradictions is different. For the ambivalent racism perspective, the conflict is between pro- and anti-black attitude structures and their underlying value systems; for the aversive racism perspective, it is between an openly endorsed egalitarian attitude and value system and negative feelings of 'discomfort, uneasiness, disgust, and sometimes fear, which tend to motivate avoidance rather than intentionally destructive behaviors' (Gaertner & Dovidio, 1986, p. 63). Gaertner and Dovidio also are not as generous or optimistic as Katz and Hass about the prevalence of genuinely pro-black attitudes.

Subtle racism Building on Allport's (1954) classic analysis of prejudice, Pettigrew and Meertens (1995; Pettigrew, Jackson, Ben Brika, Lemaine, Meertens, Wagner & Zick, 1998) distinguish between *blatant* and *subtle* prejudice. Derived from theoretical analysis, rather than deduced empirically, Pettigrew and Meertens posit a multidimensional model of both blatant and subtle prejudice. Blatant prejudice, which is 'hot, close, and direct' (Pettigrew & Meertens, 1995, p. 58), has two components: threat and rejection, and opposition to intimate contact with the outgroup. Subtle prejudice, which is 'cool, distant, and indirect', has three components: the defence of traditional values, the exaggeration of cultural differences, and the denial of positive emotions. Using survey data from almost 4,000 respondents in 7 independent probability samples from 4 western European countries, Pettigrew and Meertens demonstrate that blatant and subtle prejudice are 'separate but related' constructs, and report evidence from structural equation modelling supporting the proposed multidimensional structure. They also cross-categorize respondents using their scores on blatant and subtle measures, forming distinct categories of *bigots* (high on both), *subtles* (high on subtle, low on blatant), and *equalitarians* (low on both). The category constituted by low scores on subtle and high scores on blatant is assumed to be an error category. Pettigrew and Meertens report large differences across bigots, subtles and equalitarians in their responses to several different public policy questions dealing with immigration.

Stereotyping

In the social cognitive approach to understanding prejudice, stereotypes are given a prominent role. We saw earlier in Chapter 3 that stereotypes are an example of a schema. In this section, we develop the notion of stereotypes as schemas, and look at research demonstrating the cognitive consequences of thinking about groups schematically. Finally, we look at evidence linking stereotype activation to prejudice.

What is a stereotype?   A stereotype is a mental representation of a social group and its members (Fiske, 1998; Hamilton & Sherman, 1994; Nelson, 2002); it is a 'picture in the head' (Lippmann, 1922). But, more than just a picture in the head, a stereotype is a cognitive structure with mental life. A stereotype is a schema, with all the properties of schemas as discussed in Chapter 3 – it organizes and integrates incoming information; it directs attention to particular events and away from others; and it colours the retrieval of information. But if that's all stereotypes were, social psychologists would not have accorded them special status and attention. Stereotypes differ from most other schemas because of their social consequences. Stereotypes derive their form and content from the social context surrounding the individual, and their operation leads to social injustice.

The term 'stereotype' was introduced to the social sciences by Walter Lippmann (1922), who, as a journalist, borrowed the phrase from the world of printing. In printing, a stereotype is the metal cast that is used to make repeated and identical images of a character on paper. Lippmann used the term by analogy to refer to the ways in which people apply the same character to their impression of a group and its members. When someone, say a white Anglo-Saxon Protestant, views all blacks as stupid, or all Jews as venal, or all women as emotional, they are applying the same cast to their impression of all members of the particular group.

Stereotyping refers to the process of activating and using a stereotype. Stereotypes and stereotyping are inherently social. They cannot be anything but social, since they are of a social category, and they are shared. The social or cultural representation of a group is a social stereotype. Since the early work by Katz and Braly in the 1930s, social stereotypes are known to be shared and, more or less, universally identifiable by all the members of a culture. Thus, most people in Australia can easily describe the stereotype of Aborigines, precisely because the social stereotype of Aborigines has a social life, existing in the culture beyond the individuals and groups who expound it. For the same reason, most Australians are unable to identify the stereotype of Aberdonians or Mauritians or Zulus. These groups do not have social life in Australia. But, as Devine (1989a) pointed out, being able to identify and reproduce a social stereotype does not necessarily mean that one believes that stereotype (see below). The stereotype that any one person has of a social category is known as an individual stereotype. Undoubtedly, there are strong associations between social and individual stereotypes, but it is too simple to assume they are identical.

'Whether favorable or unfavorable, a stereotype is an exaggerated belief associated with a category. Its function is to justify (rationalize) our conduct in relation to that category' (Allport, 1954, p. 191, original emphasis). Allport was talking, of course, about individual stereotypes. His view was extremely influential for two or more decades: social psychology thought of stereotypes as wrong, or inadequate, or exaggerated, mental depictions of a social group. They were more than just Lippmann's 'pictures in our heads'; they were *inaccurate* pictures. Allport emphasized, though, that stereotypes sometimes do bear some resemblance to the world as it is; that is, that stereotypes sometimes contain a 'kernel of truth'. We will discuss the thorny debate over the 'kernel of truth' hypothesis in the next chapter on ideology.

As we detailed in Chapter 3, stereotypes are usually studied using the techniques of cognitive psychology, on the basis that stereotypes are schemas. Recent research in this tradition is not usually concerned with describing the particular details of the content of a stereotype, but, rather, focuses on what stimulates stereotypes into activation, and on how stereotype activation affects subsequent information-processing, person perception, and interpersonal judgements – that is, this work is primarily about process, not content; about stereotyping, not stereotypes. Stereotypes themselves are not measured.

Instead, response latencies, priming effects and other assorted tricks of the cognitive psychology trade are used to examine the online processing of stereotypic information.

As outlined in Chapter 3, stereotypes, as schemas, direct mental resources, guide encoding and retrieval of information, and save cognitive energy – in short, they make perception of people and groups more efficient (Quinn et al., 2003). Stereotypes only demonstrate these properties once they are activated. If a stereotype, or any schema, is not activated, it is of no consequence. The consequences may follow automatically and unconsciously. Stereotypes become activated usually by having stereotype-related information presented to the stereotype holder. Information can be relevant to a stereotype by being either stereotype-consistent or stereotype-inconsistent. Either way, once such information is presented the stereotype is activated.

Stereotype activation As we have seen, recent research suggests that stereotypical thinking can be prompted unconsciously and automatically. Automaticity has a particular and narrow meaning in cognitive psychology and is used to refer to both cognitive processes and cognitive effects. The former refer, for example, to how the subliminal presentation of group labels affects our encoding of information in ways that are consistent with these labels. The Macrae et al. (1994) study described in Chapter 2 is a good example of automatic and unconscious encoding. Participants were not aware of how they were encoding information or of how their encoding was affected by a group label presented to them subliminally. Indeed, most people are usually unaware of the processes their cognitive systems are engaged in. An example of an automatic effect is provided by the initial reaction of a person to a member of a disliked outgroup. Typically, the store of information a person has about a particular social group – that is, the social stereotype of that group – is activated automatically when the person is confronted by a member of that group or by a symbol of that group. Research examples of the automatic activation of stereotypes are described below.

A cognitive process or effect is considered to be automatic if it satisfies one of several criteria (Bargh, 1984, 1989; Hasher & Zacks, 1979; Schneider & Shiffrin, 1977): it must not require conscious intention, attention or effort; or it must be resistant to intentional manipulation; or it must happen beyond any awareness. Automatic processes and effects happen rapidly, and do not use cognitive processing capacity. If a process or effect fails to satisfy these criteria, it is considered to be controlled. Controlled processes are susceptible to conscious intervention, require cognitive effort, and are amenable to consciousness.

There is now ample evidence that stereotypical trait information about a group can be automatically activated by exposure to a group-related stimulus (Augoustinos, Ahrens & Innes, 1994; Bargh, 1999; Devine, 1989a; Dovidio, Evans & Tyler, 1986; Fiske, 1998; Gaertner & McLaughlin, 1983; Kawakami, Dion & Dovidio, 1998; Kawakami & Dovidio, 2001; Locke & Johnston, 2001; Locke et al., 1994; Locke & Walker, 1999; Macrae & Bodenhausen, 2000; Perdue, Dovidio, Gurtman & Tyler, 1990; Quinn et al., 2003). Since most stereotypes of real groups are predominantly negative, the automatic activation of such stereotypes does not augur well for attempts to lessen any pernicious effects of those stereotypes. The activation and schematic operation of stereotypes would matter little if they were unrelated to prejudice, and perhaps hence also unrelated to discrimination. We now turn to consider the possible relationship between the activation of negative stereotypes and prejudice.

Stereotypes and prejudice The model implicit in much of the social cognitive research is simple – stereotypes are activated by group-related stimuli, this leads to prejudice, which in turn leads to discriminatory behaviour. However, the evidence linking stereotypes to prejudice is surprisingly scant. Of course, one influential model of the stereotype-prejudice link is Devine's dissociation model (Devine, 1989a) which we touched on in Chapter 3.

Devine's model starts with the premise that there is a social stereotype attached to most, if not all, of the major groups in our society. As members of our society, we are all exposed to these social stereotypes so often through the course of our socialization that we acquire an internal, mental representation of the social stereotype. This knowledge of the social stereotype is possessed equally by all members of society, and is rehearsed so often that it becomes *automatically* associated with the group it represents. This is not to say that all members of society will equally endorse the social stereotype. Individuals differ in their level of prejudice against the target group: some people are high and some are low in prejudice. Whereas previous models, and 'common sense', suggest that individual differences in stereotyping are associated with individual differences in level of prejudice, Devine's model suggests that all members of society have equal access to the social stereotype of well-known groups, and consequently the mental representation of that stereotype will be automatically activated upon presentation of any group-related symbol. This activation will occur equally for individuals high and low in prejudice. Only once the stereotype's content has been activated for long enough to become amenable to conscious intervention will differences between high- and low-prejudice individuals emerge. High-prejudice individuals will allow the automatically activated stereotype content to persist, but low-prejudice individuals will intervene in the online processing of this information, deliberately inhibiting that automatically activated material and deliberately activating other, more positive material. Thus, Devine's model provides cause both for optimism and pessimism: the former because she removes the earlier assumption that stereotypes inevitably lead to prejudice; and the latter because everyone, regardless of their beliefs and level of prejudice, has a store of stereotypic negative information which is automatically activated by a group-related stimulus.

Although Devine's model has some intuitive appeal and has been widely influential, methodological and conceptual criticisms limit the model's validity. Incorporating these criticisms leads to a more complex, conditional, socio-cognitive model of the links between stereotypes and prejudice. This revised model posits that any group-related stimulus will still trigger an automatic activation of information (although a study by Lepore and Brown (1997) suggests it is a stereotype-related stimulus, not a group-related stimulus, which will trigger this effect). However, the information activated is not the same for all people. High-prejudice people with a detailed cognitive representation of the target group will activate a store of predominantly negative, stereotypic information. Low-prejudice people will activate both positive and negative information. In other words, the mental representations the two groups of people possess are different. Underlying this difference, high-prejudice people lacking a detailed cognitive representation of the target group will still automatically activate a set of negative information, but that set is a generic set, defined by, and activated because of, its negativity, not because of any fundamental relationship with the target group. This is a kind of neuronal ethnocentrism, in which the cognitive system of a high-prejudice person automatically rejects and derogates *any* outgroup. Once the activated information proceeds online until it is amenable to conscious manipulation, high-prejudice people perceive no need to modify it, because it does not conflict with any personal belief systems they hold or with any sense of social identity they possess. For low-prejudice subjects, though, the negative parts of the set of positive and negative information which was automatically activated do contradict their personal beliefs and their social identity as a tolerant, prejudice-free person. Although they will not always inhibit this negative information, they will be motivated to do so when they become aware of it.

The suggestion that personal belief systems, personal identity, and social identity all play a role in the mental life of stereotypic information indicates that stereotype activation is more conditional, more strategic, and more amenable to change than is allowed for by a gloomy, simple, model in which a cognitive miser automatically, unthinkingly activates stereotypic information whenever he or she is confronted by a symbol of a group. Indeed, it now seems to make little sense to think of 'automatic' activation as being 'automatic' in the sense that it is inevitable and immutable (e.g., Dasgupta & Greenwald, 2001; Rudman, Ashmore & Gary, 2001; Wittenbrink, Judd & Park, 2001). There is now reasonable evidence that, even in the presence of a group symbol, stereotypes may not be activated when people are too cognitively busy (Gilbert & Hixon, 1991); or when they are motivated by interactional goals to think of the person in individuated terms (Pendry & Macrae, 1996); or when the context does not require people to *judge* others (Locke & Walker, 1999). An important lesson from these studies demonstrating the conditional automaticity of stereotype activation is that cognitive processes always occur in, and depend on, a human interactional context.

The tacit model in social cognition research of a simple, direct, unmediated pathway from stereotypes to prejudice is, thus, too simple. The pathway is conditional and bi-directional. Group-related stimuli only activate stereotypes when those stereotypes are contextually relevant. The content of the activated stereotype is different for different people, even though most people in any culture can readily identify the content of the social stereotypes pertaining to the major groups in that society. And finally, people are differentially prepared to suppress, modify, or leave alone stereotypic material once it is activated, depending on their beliefs and values about *stereotyping* itself.

These conclusions about the complexity of the relationships between stereotypes and prejudice are echoed in a meta-analysis reported by Dovidio, Brigham, Johnson and Gaertner (1996). Dovidio et al. report that, in the context of research examining the linkages between stereotypes of African Americans, racial prejudice and discrimination, individual stereotyping is modestly related to prejudice and independently modestly related to discrimination. These relationships were moderated, though, by issues such as whether the measures used by researchers focused on affective or cognitive aspects of stereotyping and by whether the measures allowed for deliberated or spontaneous responses.

Social Identity and Prejudice

In this section, we develop some of the general principles of SIT and SCT and apply them to the analysis of prejudice. Some authors have interpreted SIT bleakly to imply that theoretically prejudice, stereotyping and other forms of negative intergroup relations, are inevitable from the SIT perspective. Indeed, that the minimal group experiments are fundamental in establishing that the mere categorization of people into ingroups and outgroups is the first step towards intergroup discrimination and prejudice. Many researchers have used the findings of the minimal group experiments to argue this case and to claim that intergoup discrimination and prejudice is an unfortunate but inevitable by-product of the cognitive need to categorize people into their respective group memberships (Hamilton & Trolier, 1986; Messick & Mackie, 1989; Stephan, 1985; Wilder, 1981). This is too simple, and is a misreading of SIT. In this section, we will consider how SIT and SCT challenge this view of prejudice.

Does categorization incite intergroup hatred?

In a provocative chapter entitled, 'Distortion v. meaning: Categorization on trial for inciting intergroup hatred', Oakes and Haslam (2001) explicitly challenge the pervasive view within social psychology that categorization is the cognitive mechanism at the heart of prejudice. In Chapter 3 we detailed the social cognitive position that social categorization, dividing the social world into 'us' and 'them', is driven by our cognitive need to simplify the 'blooming, buzzing confusion' in the social environment. At the same time, however, group-based or category-based perception is seen as distorting because people are not viewed as individuals in their own right but, rather, as prototypical group members. As Oakes and Haslam (2001, p. 184) put it, social cognition claims that, 'when we perceive through the medium of social categories we do not see what is really there'. This, of course leads to stereotyping, which much of the social cognition research suggests can occur automatically and outside conscious awareness. And stereotyping of course is just one step away from producing discrimination and prejudice. This linear relationship between categorization, stereotyping and prejudice is illustrated in Figure 7.1. Notwithstanding some of the qualifications that social cognitivists have placed on this directional, and by implication, causative link between these three processes (e.g. Devine, 1989), it is none the less the case that categorization in and of itself is seen as the cognitive basis for prejudice, driven primarily by our limited processing capacities.

To 'unpack' this assumption from a SIT and SCT perspective we need to return to some of the material we covered in Chapter 3 concerning categorization and stereotyping. Clearly SIT and SCT propose a different view of these psychological processes. Indeed, within SCT there is no such thing as non-categorical perception. All perception is categorical, even individual-based perception. When we perceive our self, even when we think of our self

Figure 7.1 The proposed linear relationship between categorization, stereotyping and prejudice

in the most personal terms, we are categorizing. Thinking of people (including self) in personal terms rather than group terms is simply moving the level of categorization from a higher order to a lower order (see Figure 6.1, Chapter 6). It is no less categorical for that. Nor is higher-order categorical perception any better or worse, or more or less accurate, than lower-order categorical perception. According to SCT, categorization is always oriented to the goals of the perceiver, and the function of categorization is always to elaborate and enrich perception (see, for example, McGarty, Yzerbyt & Spears, 2002; Oakes, Haslam & Turner, 1994; Reynolds & Turner, 2001). This sees stereotyping as applying to one's self and ingroup as much as to others and outgroups, and the process of stereotyping as the product of the social and psychological relationship between groups in a particular context. Thus stereotyping (and indeed all categorization) is not just a by-product of the miserly way people engage cognitively with the world, but, rather, is a full and active engagement with the *social* reality of that world – a world made up of social and status group hierarchies.

Moreover, as Oakes and Haslam (2001) argue, categorization should not be maligned because it is also the crucial process through which cooperative, harmonious and interdependent relationships are made possible through superordinate categorizations and identifications. Going back to Figure 6.1 (Chapter 6), people can categorize self along a continuum ranging from the subordinate level (personal identity) to the superordinate level (self as human being). This superordinate level of categorization makes possible empathy, cooperation and collective mobilization between nation states for example. The United Nations is a concrete example of an institution that mobilizes around this level of superordinate categorization, requiring nation states to subvert their own specific and particular national interests (social identity) for the sake of universal global interests and concerns. Human rights legislation is another instance where categorization and identification at a superordinate level makes possible the sharing of universal principles of justice and human decency. As such, categorization *per se* cannot be held responsible for all the ills of the world, such as intergroup hatred and hostility, war, genocide, etc.

Categorizing self and identifying at the level of the nation as opposed to a superordinate category such as 'human being' will shift and change depending on particular social and political contexts and how people make sense of these contexts. Such categorizations and identifications are not fixed and static. For example, it makes perfect sense to self-categorize and identify as an 'Australian' during an Olympics swimming event, but to self–categorize and identify first and foremost as a member of the global community during the Olympics opening ceremony. While the former is likely to invoke intergroup competition, the latter functions to emphasize intergroup cooperation and harmony. Nor is it the case that national identity *always* functions to differentiate self from others. National identity can also be invoked as a superordinate category that unifies and integrates different social and ethnic groups within the nation state. Thus the category of 'nation' can be used flexibly and for a range of political projects (Reicher and Hopkins, 2001): on the one hand national identity and notions of 'who belongs' can be mobilized to incite intergroup hostility and conflict, but national identity can also be used in ways that promote an inclusive and culturally diverse society. This again reinforces the point that social categories and identities are not merely routine and mundane entities; they are inherently political in nature and can be used as political weapons for mobilizing support for both discriminatory and inclusive social policies (see Textbox 3.1 in Chapter 3).

Prejudice is a group phenomenon emerging from intergroup perceptions of the social structure

Three core principles underlie SIT: intergroup categorization, identity, and comparison. The conjoint operation of these principles has also led to the view that prejudice is an inevitable outcome of any interaction structured along group lines, because in any such interaction people will be motivated to enhance their social identification with one group and not another through making intergroup comparisons along dimensions valued by the group. Even if the self-esteem motive is removed from this analysis and replaced by a motive to achieve optimal distinctiveness (as has been suggested by Brewer, 1991) or to reduce subjective uncertainty (as posited by Mullin & Hogg, 1998), prejudice and other forms of intergroup tension are often still seen to be an inevitable outcome. Again, SIT is not so bleak though.

Tajfel was careful to insist that the operation of the self-esteem enhancement motive does not necessarily lead to ingroup enhancement and/or outgroup derogation (i.e., to prejudice). Rather, SIT posits that what people strive to achieve is *positive intergroup differentiation*. This is not the same as ingroup enhancement or outgroup derogation, though those are all too frequent examples of positive intergroup differentiation. Rather, groups and their members strive to achieve some sort of differentiation from other, related, groups in ways that are shaped by the nature of the intergroup context. Groups and group members strive to achieve positive intergroup differentiation from other groups *on dimensions of importance to their groups*. Sometimes those dimensions of importance emphasize tolerance, generosity and beneficence. Intergroup differentiation can be positive in many different ways, depending on what the group accepts normatively as its self-defining characteristics and on the nature of the intergroup context. People who strongly identify with their nation are, in contemporary times, perhaps likely to seek confirmation of their national superiority relative to other nations and to derogate 'foreigners'. People who strongly identify with their local community recycling centre are not. People who strongly identify with their Aryan heritage and who wish to keep that heritage 'pure' are likely not to be keen on other sorts of people. People who identify strongly with the ideals of the Esperanto movement are.

It is important to note in these examples that neither SIT nor SCT would claim that identification with a nation, or with a recycling group, or with an ethnic group, or with a universal language movement is a stable, persistent characteristic of a person. Neither are these identifications 'pictures in the head' that light up whenever a relevant stimulus in the environment turns them on. Instead, these identifications are social categories that make psychological and social sense in a particular context, which become important to people in that particular context, and the meaning of which depends on the complex and shared reality of that context.

SIT suggests that achieving positive intergroup differentiation is especially important when social identity is threatened (Tajfel & Turner, 1986). Threats to social identity generally come about when perceived intergroup relativities suggest that one's ingroup is socially devalued, though they can also derive from intragroup pressures to ensure ingroup cohesion and uniformity. How people respond to threats to social identity depends critically on whether the ingroup has high or low status in the intergroup context.

The social identity of low-status group members is often threatened by the low status of their group. It would be wrong to claim that all members of all low-status groups feel threatened in this way even some of the time, let alone carry it around as a never-ending burden. Group status is, after all, context dependent, and ever variable. And social identity depends on one's status within the group as much as, or perhaps more than, the status of the ingroup relative to some outgroup. None the less, SIT predicts that people respond to threats to social identity by striving for positive differentiation from relevant outgroups. How they do so depends on the perceived *legitimacy* of the status difference, the perceived *stability* of the intergroup hierarchy, and the perceived *permeability* of group boundaries. Combinations of these critical variables, which together can be thought of as subjective belief structures (Hogg & Abrams, 1988), lead to different behavioural consequences.

Members of low-status groups who believe that the intergroup structure is stable, but the boundaries between groups are permeable, are likely to attempt to leave the ingroup for another. This is likely whether the status difference is seen to be legitimate or not. 'Passing' is an example of such a strategy, but more common examples are attempts at upward social mobility through hard work or by gaining further education or qualifications. These behaviours are individual, rather than group, strategies brought about mostly by the perception of group permeability.

Attempts to challenge the intergroup *status quo* are more likely when the intergroup structure is believed to be unstable and illegitimate, and especially so when group boundaries are seen to be impermeable. Under these conditions, members of low-status groups have little choice but to either accept their unfortunate and unjustified lot in life, or challenge the intergroup hierarchy. These are the conditions likely to produce *intergroup* behaviours designed to challenge the privilege enjoyed by the high-status group. There are two primary forms of these *social change* behaviours. The first, called *social creativity* within SIT, endeavours to redefine the important dimensions of difference between groups. The 'Black is beautiful' political movement in the United States during the civil rights era of the 1960s is often cited as an example of the revalorization of a previously stigmatized identity. The second, called *social competition* within SIT, refers to direct confrontation between low-status and high-status groups, with a clear aim of politically redefining the status hierarchy. Such concerted intergroup efforts require political coordination. They are often categorized as either *legitimate* or *illegitimate*, depending on whether they exploit generally accepted political processes to achieve social change or step outside normal politics. A famous example of the former, in which social psychology played a role, was the decision in 1954 by the US Supreme Court in the case of Brown v. the Board of Education of Topeka, Kansas. That decision followed a legal case brought by the NAACP directly challenging the segregation of state schools. The decision ruled that such segregation was unconstitutional, and ordered that all school districts desegregate 'with all due haste'. Examples of 'illegitimate' attempts to produce political change are provided by just about all examples of civil unrest and civil war.

High-status groups naturally have a different set of responses to perceived status differences. High-status groups generally show more ingroup bias than do other groups (Bettencourt, Dorr, Charlton & Hume, 2001). They are also more likely to believe that the status differential is less than members of lower-status groups believe (Exline & Lobel, 1999), that their higher status is legitimate, and that intergroup boundaries are stable. Leach and his colleagues have recently developed a model of responses likely when high-status group members do recognize their advantage (e.g., Leach, Snider & Iyer, 2002). In this model, when high-status group members focus on the low-status group they are likely to experience indignation, disdain or pity when the status difference is seen as legitimate, but moral outrage or sympathy when the difference is illegitimate. However, when focused on themselves, they are likely to experience pride if the group difference is legitimate, or fear, guilt or gloating if the difference is illegitimate. Of most relevance to our understanding of prejudice are the responses of disdain, which is essentially a dislike and rejection of others (easily manifest as prejudice), and moral outrage, which is essentially required for high-status group members to take political action aimed at diminishing their own advantage and working towards greater equality between groups.

Social identities and prejudiced attributions

In this section we return to the research on intergroup attributions which we touched on in Chapter 5; in particular, the research in Northern Ireland by Hunter et al. (1991). The results of this study, and of other similar studies (see below), demonstrate that explanations for behaviour and events are shaped by intergroup relations. Essentially, the same violent behaviour in the Hunter et al. study was explained entirely differently depending on the social positions of the attributer and the perpetrator (Catholic or Protestant). It is not just a simple case of the attributer overestimating the role of dispositional factors in controlling behaviour, as the FAE would have it. Several implications can be drawn from this research. First, social perception, especially in situations involving partisanship, is rarely, if ever, neutral and dispassionate. Second, the possibility of ever being able to apprehend a single 'true' account of social 'reality' is questioned. And third, the patterns of interpretations and attributions produced by subjects in such experiments highlight the inadequacy of attribution theories as they are normally constructed.

In his account of this intergroup phenomenon – ironically referred to as the 'ultimate attribution error' (UAE) – Pettigrew (1979) suggested that these attributional patterns will be stronger when group memberships are salient; when the perceiver believes he or she is a target of the behaviour in question or is otherwise highly involved in the behaviour; when the groups involved have histories of intense conflict and have strong stereotypes of each other; and when group memberships coincide with national and socio-economic status differences. All of these preconditions are factors that SIT and SCT see as central to prejudice.

Perhaps the earliest direct demonstration of group effects on attributions was a study carried out by Taylor and Jaggi (1974), who presented Hindu office workers in India with a series of vignettes describing several behavioural episodes. Half of the episodes described a positive behaviour – stopping to help someone, for example – and the other half described a negative behaviour – going past someone who needed help. Crossed with the positivity or negativity of behaviour was the religion of the actor – half the actors described were Hindu, and half were Muslim. When the Hindu subjects were asked to make attributions about the cause of the behaviour described in the vignette they read, they behaved in just the way Pettigrew's UAE predicts they ought to. Positive behaviours performed by a Hindu (ingroup) actor were attributed to the actor's disposition, whereas negative behaviours performed by a Hindu actor were attributed externally. The opposite pattern was observed when the actor was described as a Muslim.

Thus, a number of studies together now show that attributing a positive or negative, successful or unsuccessful, behaviour to something about the actor or something about the actor's situation is not simply an individual process (Greenberg & Rosenfield, 1979; Mann & Taylor, 1974; Stephan, 1977). The group memberships of both the attributer and the actor are important in formulating attributions about the causes of behaviour. The studies do not provide unequivocal support for Pettigrew's notion that attributions will always favour the ingroup, though. Two studies by Hewstone and Ward (1985) highlight how broader societal factors, as well as group-level factors, are important in determining patterns of attributions.

Hewstone and Ward's first study attempted to replicate the findings of Taylor and Jaggi (1974), using Chinese and Malay subjects in Malaysia. Using the standard method, subjects were presented with a vignette description of a positive or negative behaviour performed by either a Chinese or a Malay actor, and attributions of the cause of the behaviour were gathered. Examining the proportion of all attributions which were internal reveals that the Malay subjects made the typical ingroup-favouring set of attributions, but the Chinese subjects did not produce attributions favouring the ingroup. Instead, their attributions tended to resemble those of the Malay subjects. The results of Hewstone and Ward's first study are presented in Table 7.1.

Hewstone and Ward then replicated their study with Chinese and Malay subjects in Singapore. Once again, the Malay subjects produced attributions

Table 7.1   *Proportion of all attributions which were internal in Hewstone and Ward's (1985) two studies*

	Chinese subjects		Malay subjects	
	Positive behaviour	Negative behaviour	Positive behaviour	Negative behaviour
Malaysian samples				
Chinese actor	0.39	0.54	0.27	0.46
Malay actor	0.57	0.24	0.66	0.18
Singaporean samples				
Chinese actor	0.40	0.49	0.39	0.44
Malay actor	0.48	0.37	0.70	0.27

Source: Hewstone & Ward, 1985, p. 617 and p. 619, Tables 1 and 3

favouring the ingroup, and the Chinese subjects showed only a slight tendency to favour the outgroup. Clearly, then, group effects on attributions are not consistently in favour of the ingroup at the expense of the outgroup. Hewstone and Ward argue that the different effects of group membership on attributions demonstrated by the Malay and Chinese subjects in their Singaporean and Malaysian samples reflect the actual social positions of the two groups in the two societies. The Chinese in Malaysia have a devalued minority group status, occupying a 'middleman' position in the economy. This position is strengthened by the Malaysian government's policies. In Singapore, even though the Chinese also occupy a 'middleman' position, the society is much more openly plural, and there is no government policy promoting any one particular ethnic group.

All the studies described above have relied on ethnicity, 'race' or religion to demonstrate group effects on attributions. Such effects are also apparent in studies using other social groups. A large body of research on intergroup achievement attributions has found a significant tendency for perceivers to make more favourable attributions for males than for females when explaining success and failure. Deaux and Emswiller's (1974) study is one of the most well known of these. These authors found that on a stereotypically masculine task (identifying mechanical tools) a male actor's success was more likely to be attributed to ability than the same success by a female actor. However, on a stereotypically female task (identifying household utensils) no differences were found in attributions for male and female success. As with studies using 'race', ethnicity or religion, a large number of studies have now documented the prevalence of an attributional pattern of male enhancement and female derogation on tasks leading to success and failure, and that this pattern is found in women as well as men (e.g., Etaugh & Brown, 1975; Feather, 1978; Feather & Simon, 1975; Feldman-Summers & Kiesler, 1974, experiment 2; Garland & Price, 1977; Nicholls, 1975; and Sousa & Leyens, 1987). Not all studies have found the effect, and more recently Swim and Sanna (1996) have queried its magnitude and robustness.

There is, thus, a considerable body of evidence demonstrating that attributions depend on the relative group memberships of the person making the attribution and the target of the attribution, whether the group be based on 'race', ethnicity, gender or even social class (Augoustinos, 1991; Hewstone, Jaspars & Lalljee, 1982). However, as Hewstone (1990) concludes after reviewing 19 published studies examining the UAE, the effect is not consistent in a simple way. The UAE is formulated in terms of ingroups and outgroups, and posits that attributions will be group-serving. The 'error' appears to operate in more subtle and complicated ways than a simple reliance on an ingroup–outgroup classification. All the studies cited above which include as subjects members of both majority and minority groups in the society in which the study takes place, find that minority group members do not attribute in a way which favours the ingroup. The kinds of attributions majority and minority group members make, then, appear to reflect not only an underlying motive to favour the ingroup, but also the broader social stereotype and social status of the groups in question.

The fact that attributions vary depending on the social group memberships of the attributer and the target is one thing, but the importance of this lies not in the fact that it happens but rather in its *social* consequences. Intergroup attributions rely on stereotypes or cultural representations of groups, and, once made, they lend a pernicious bite to intergroup interactions. In an important early paper, Tajfel (1981b) emphasized this social function of stereotypes, which reinforces the point that stereotypes are about people and groups, and hence are not equivalent to schemata about other non-social categories. Tajfel argued that stereotypes help people maintain and defend their systems of values and identity; they help to explain and justify patterns of intergroup hierarchies prevalent at any particular time; and they help to differentiate the ingroup from relevant outgroups positively. Some of these ideas have only recently been developed more fully: the explanatory function of stereotypes has been elaborated by Yzerbyt and his colleagues (Yzerbyt & Rocher, 2002; Yzerbyt, Rocher & Schadron, 1997); and the system-justificatory function of stereotypes has been developed into system-justification theory by Jost and others (Jost & Banaji, 1984; Jost &

Kramer, 2002; Jost & Major, 2001). The system-justificatory function of stereotypes raises issues of ideology, which will be returned to in Chapter 8.

Social Representations and Prejudice

So far in this chapter we have examined approaches to prejudice which emphasize the tendency, stronger in some people than others, to make hasty judgements about others based on their group memberships (the social cognitive perspective), and which emphasize identity, relatedness and separateness based on group criteria (the social identity perspective). Moscovici and Perez (1997) suggest that there are two different conceptualizations of prejudice, which we suggest map on to the social cognitive and social identity perspectives respectively. One conceptualization is based on 'categorical prejudices', the other on 'ideological prejudices'. In the former, features of others are simplified through group categorizations, and accomplish the denigration of others by the creation of distance between ourselves and others through this categorization process. In the latter, widely shared conceptions of society and the groups comprising society (i.e., ideologies) are used to simplify and to give order to criteria for group membership which otherwise are arbitrary. These two notions of prejudice permeate the social representations approach to prejudice too. Categorical prejudices serve to index the distance between self and other (and especially groups of others); ideological prejudices serve to create the distance in the first place. The social distances between groups reflected in common stereotypes do not exist outside of, or separate from, cognitive and ideological understandings of those groups. Rather, the distances are created by those very cognitive and ideological processes. Very often, Moscovici and Perez (1997) argue, groups establish social distances in order to make similar others dissimilar. In other words, prejudice does not arise from the categorical perception of others at some social distance, but instead social distance is produced from prejudice as a means of differentiating self and the ingroup and others. This can be achieved indirectly too. For example, Hraba, Hagendoorn and Hagendoorn (1989) demonstrated that Dutch students maintain a social hierarchy *among* ethnic groups rather than *against* those groups, but indirectly that hierarchy among ethnic groups also establishes a hierarchy against them.

The social representations approach to prejudice is thus not completely discrete from the social cognitive and social identity perspectives that we have already examined in this chapter. It is differentiated more by its relative emphasis on particular aspects of prejudice than by a totally different methodology or conceptual understanding.

Stereotypes *are* social representations

The earlier section on social cognitive approaches described the information-processing functions of stereotypes. From this perspective, stereotypes can be easily viewed as social schemas: they are theory-driven, stable knowledge structures in memory; they have internal organizational properties; and they are learned by individuals, usually during their early years. This has been the dominant conceptualization of stereotypes within the social cognition literature. Relatively scant attention has been paid to the symbolic, political, and ideological nature and functions of stereotypes. But stereotypes are more than just cognitive schemas. Stereotypes are social representations: they are objectified cognitive and affective structures about social groups within society which are extensively shared and which emerge and proliferate within the particular social and political milieu of a given historical moment. Stereotypes do not simply exist in individuals' heads. They are socially and discursively constructed in the course of everyday communication, and, once objectified, assume an independent and sometimes prescriptive reality. It is naïve to argue that stereotypes are simply the by-product of the cognitive need to simplify reality. For what gives stereotypes their specific form and content? Why are stereotypes group-serving and, in many cases, system-serving? Why do members of minority groups often internalize negative social stereotypes of their ingroup? A schematic or cognitive account of stereotypes and stereotyping has enormous difficulty answering such questions. It is only when stereotypes are conceptualized more as social representations or as ideological representations that the inherently social and political nature and function of stereotypes can be understood. We have more to say about this in Chapter 8.

Without a doubt, the stereotypes of commonly known groups in any society are shared by members of that society. Indeed, the early empirical research by Katz and Braly (1933) used the degree of consensus across people about whether a particular trait (e.g., 'musical') did or did not describe a particular group (e.g., African Americans) as the criterion for whether the trait was stereotypical or not. The same principle underlies much of contemporary social cognitive research on stereotypes – consensus is used as the defining criterion of trait stereotypicality. It is hard to imagine how social cognitive research on stereotypes could proceed otherwise. Social cognitive research distinguishes between 'individual stereotypes' (the 'pictures' held by any one person about a group and its members) and 'social stereotypes' (the social 'picture' of a group, which everyone knows whether they believe it or not). Devine's (1989a) dissociation model rests on this distinction too. All this notwithstanding, social cognitive research has little – in fact, almost nothing – to say about stereotype sharedness. In contrast, social representations research focuses almost exclusively on sharedness.

Stereotypes are shared through language, through the communication of ideas in the various mass media, and through social roles and norms (Stangor & Schaller, 1996). Shared stereotypes do more than reflect the world 'out there'. They are, in fact, the product of group interaction, negotiation, of political struggle, of ideological positioning. They are also a function of the representation of society itself. Stereotypes express the real, material relations between groups, consistent with SIT, but those relations between groups are themselves conditioned by the broader pattern of social life in society as a whole. Groups do not exist in relationship with one another alone, in some abstracted acontextual vacuum. Thus, social representations research insists that stereotypes are always a part of, and cannot be considered separately from, the broader pattern of social, political and ideological relationships within society.

All this is not to say that stereotypes, as social representations, are uniformly shared, monolithic and hegemonic. The theory certainly allows for intergroup differentiation in knowledge of, and endorsement of, stereotypes, and for the continual transformation of stereotypes through the ebb and flow of intergroup relations. We consider one particularly novel research programme in the social representations tradition by Gina Philogène, which documents the political struggle to change the stereotypes associated with black Americans in the Unites States through the introduction of a new social representation – 'African American'. This research broadly demonstrates the social representations approach to the study of stereotypes and prejudice, especially stereotypical differentiation between groups, and the fundamental role shared representations play in establishing group identities.

'African American': the emergence of a new social representation

The name or denomination that has been used to identify and refer to Americans of African descent has changed markedly throughout that country's history. This has included categories such as 'Slaves', 'Coloreds', 'Negros', 'Blacks', 'People of Color', 'Afro-Americans' and 'African Americans'. As Philogène (1994, 1999) argues, the evolutionary trajectory of these category names reflects the changing historical and political dynamics of intergroup relations in the US. Significantly, African Americans themselves have been at the forefront of these changes in their continuous political struggle to define and represent themselves in ways that have challenged stereotypical and primarily negative constructions held by the dominant white majority. In December 1988, at a meeting of African American leaders, a decision was made to change the official denomination of this group from 'Black' to 'African American'. As Philogène explains, this represented a significant shift away from the use of what had been, up to that time, 'racial' markers such as skin colour for self-categorization and social identity. The category 'African American' in contrast emphasized culture and ethnicity rather than race, and was in keeping with the naming practices of other ethnic groups in the US such as 'Japanese American' and 'Mexican American'.

This new category quickly became widely adopted, not only by African Americans, but also by white Americans, as the preferred and most socially acceptable term for use in public discourse. By 1990 a quarter of the African American community were using this name, and by 1991 a third (Smith, 1992, cited by Philogène, 1994). Philogène's research explains the ways in which this new representation became anchored to existing representations of black Americans and in the process became objectified and naturalized in American public consciousness. As Moscovici himself emphasizes, the process of naming – in assigning names to classify people and social objects in specific ways – is not only of symbolic significance, it also provides a structure and organization within which people can elaborate meanings, identities and explanations. This new label – African American – not only represented a symbolic break with past practices of emphasizing race and colour, but also allowed for a new space within which African Americans could define and position themselves in relation to other groups, in particular, the dominant white majority. It also allowed for the development of alternative perceptions, attitudes and opinions about black Americans by the white majority.

As Philogène (1999) explains, however, this new representation did not completely replace existing representations and practices. After all, there was a long and proud history of identifying as 'black' within the US that was associated with the civil rights movement and with explicit political mobilizations around this category which were specifically aimed at celebrating one's racial identity. None the less, the introduction and solidification of African American as a preferable alternative enabled a move away from static and essentialist racial categories that were associated with division and conflict. It also enabled African Americans to be represented as a cultural and ethnic group like other groups within a multi-ethnic pluralistic society. The adoption and internalization of this new category was particularly prolific among young, urban and college-educated African Americans. Philogène (1994, 1999) argues that this new social representation became anchored to this specific demographic group, and in the process projected an image of African Americans that countered and replaced previous negative stereotypes associated with black Americans. This demographic group was associated with social mobility, professional advancement and political engagement. These characteristics served to emphasize class distinctions within the African American community and thus accentuated the group's heterogeneity. African Americans were no longer seen as an undifferentiated homogeneous social category in US political and social life.

Philogène's (1994) empirical research found that by 1994, a majority of 'black' and 'white' participants indicated that the term 'African American' projected the most positive image of this social group. In a relatively short period of time this new category had taken on widely shared meanings. Moreover its increasingly pervasive use in communication and social interaction transformed this symbolic category into a 'material reality'. 'African American' ultimately became a normative and naturalized 'taken-for-granted' category that came to represent the group as a whole in ways that challenged previous representations and stereotypes. As Philogène argues:

> [the] prototypical representation of [African Americans] is clearly much closer to the mainstream of America than those shown and referred to as Blacks. The images associated with 'African American', reinforced by the term's nearly exclusive use in the ideological context of a multicultural society, accentuate common interests and shared values. (1994, p. 106)

Discursive Psychology and Prejudice

Discursive psychology views racism as interactive and communicative, and as located within the language practices and discourses of a society. It is through everyday language practices, in both formal and informal talk, that relations of power, dominance and exploitation become reproduced and legitimated. The analytic site for discursive psychology is how discursive resources and rhetorical arguments are put together to construct different social and 'racial' identities, and to provide accounts that legitimate these differences and identities as 'real' and 'natural'. It has also examined in some detail how linguistic resources are combined in flexible and contradictory ways to reproduce and justify racial and social inequalities in western societies. We will return to these themes later, but before doing so, we detail what this research tradition has had to say about the nature of contemporary racist discourse.

Racist discourse: the language of prejudice

Most western countries have witnessed a resurgence of debates and controversies concerning issues of race, racism, multiculturalism, nationalism and immigration. Discursive psychology focuses on the detail of what is actually said, argued and discussed in such debates about 'race', ethnicity and intergroup relations more generally. This involves analysing not only everyday talk and conversation, but also formal institutional talk found in political speeches, parliamentary debates and newspaper articles. Discursive studies in the Netherlands (Essed, 1991a, 1991b; Van Dijk, 1991, 1993; Verkuyten, 1997, 1998), Belgium (Blommaert & Verschueren, 1993, 1998), France (Taguieff, 1998), Britain (Gilroy, 1987; Reeves, 1983), the USA (Goldberg, 1996, 1999), New Zealand (Nairn & McCreanor, 1990, 1991; Wetherell & Potter, 1992), and Australia (Augoustinos, Tuffin & Rapley, 1999; Rapley, 1998) have found that the language of contemporary racism (or racist discourse) is flexible, contradictory and ambivalent. These studies have identified common and recurring tropes and rhetorical devices that are combined in flexible and contradictory ways by majority group members, and which function primarily to deny attributions of racism, construct minorities negatively, and justify and legitimate existing social inequalities.

The denial of racism   As Van Dijk (1993) has argued, one of the most ubiquitous features of contemporary racist discourse is its denial. In everyday talk, such denials are usually found in formulaic disclaimers such as '*I have nothing against migrants, but …*', or the most familiar disclaimer of all, '*I'm not racist but …*'. A prejudiced or racist identity is no longer a valued identity, and majority group members display and attend to this social opprobrium in their talk (Condor, 2000). Typical discursive strategies that people use in their talk to deny or downplay racism include mitigation, justification, reversal and victim blaming (Van Dijk, 1992).

For example, in their analysis of student talk on contemporary race relations in Australia, Augoustinos et al. (1999) found that, although participants acknowledged the existence and undesirability of racism in Australian society, they also distanced themselves from accusations of overt racism by employing 'neutral' accounting, a distanced footing and by attributing (culturally understandable) racism primarily to older generations. Several rhetorical strategies were identified that worked to diminish the legitimacy of the view that Aboriginal people can be seen as victims of racism. These included arguments that Aboriginal people were perpetrators of racism themselves, oversensitive to racial prejudice, and used claims of discrimination as excuses whenever things did not go their way. These arguments were deployed in combination with discursive moves and rhetorical strategies that enhanced the self-presentation of speakers as balanced, neutral and fair. For example:

> A: I think that is another point about discrimination umm whenever something doesn't go the group's way they cry discrimination *(Mmm)*. Umm with the Aborigines if they don't get something its discrimination for females it's the same, with other minority groups its all the same *(umm)*. And I think that discrimination is now an excuse people are using to or a crutch that if something doesn't go their way it's sort like a child throwing a tantrum, they cry discrimination. I know it *does* exist and it *shouldn't* but I think that it's been taken vastly advantaged of *(Mmm)*.

In this extract, the speaker, A, argues that minority group (Aborigines, females) self-interest determines when claims of discrimination will be mobilized. This suggestion works to undermine the genuineness of discrimination claims. In this account such claims are constructed as 'excuses', used to bolster a selfish, political agenda. The developmental metaphor of the child 'throwing a tantrum' positions Aboriginal responses to discrimination as an overreaction, lacking in maturity and emotional balance. By implication, of course, other (white, male, majority group) members are balanced, mature and realistic. Note how the speaker heads off any imputations that her or his views are biased or unreasonable by acknowledging the existence and undesirability of discrimination ('I know it does exist and it shouldn't'). What we see here is evidence that participants are clearly attending to the necessity of managing their self-presentation in interactive contexts by presenting themselves as neutral and balanced (Antaki, Condor & Levine, 1996).

Positive self and negative other presentation In the above extract we see how speakers are able to present themselves positively while at the same time constructing problematic identities for minority group members. Drawing again from the same study by Augoustinos et al. (1999), one of the most pervasive features of participants' talk was the negative construction and problematization of Aboriginal people. This negativity did not manifest itself in what most would regard as traditional prejudiced talk (i.e., old-fashioned racism), but rather as a delicate, flexibly managed, and locally contingent discussion of the contemporary 'plight' of Aboriginal people. Given the overrepresentation of Aboriginal people among the poor, the unemployed, the ill and the imprisoned in Australian society, it is not surprising that discussions focused on such 'problems'. What is surprising, however, is the degree to which these problems and social inequities were accounted for by the use of discursive resources which legitimated and rationalized the current 'plight' of Aboriginal people. One such discursive repertoire drawn upon by participants to account for the contemporary social problems faced by Indigenous people was an imperialist narrative of Australia's colonial past. Aboriginal problems were represented largely in social-Darwinist terms as problems of 'fit' and of 'adaptation' to a superior culture that was introduced by the British in the course of 'settlement'. Aboriginal people's failure to fit into, or 'gel' with, the dominant culture was viewed as preventing them from improving their status through upward social mobility. In this way, Aboriginal people were constructed as culturally inferior, as failing to survive in a superior culture, and, thus, as being accountable for their own social and economic disadvantage. The extract below is one example that demonstrates how indigenous people were constructed as 'primitive' and technologically inferior in contrast to the invading British.

> B: I think too and also when you look at history you look back at the fact that the Aborigines were very very primitive *(Mmm)* and they confronted our culture that was superiorly [*sic*] more advanced, the wheel had been invented and whatnot but the Aborigines hadn't seemed to to advance past that very primitive stage and whatnot *(Mmm)*. Umm, they had sort of had no modern technologies as such as the British had. Like the British had gun powder and alcohol and these things, ahh, I think that was another big problem.

In this extract we can see how the categories of 'race' and 'culture' are constructed or put together rhetorically to rationalize the existing social order of inequality between Indigenous and non-Indigenous Australians. It is therefore in the dynamic process of discursive interaction itself that particular social objects, categories, and subjectivities are defined and constructed. Likewise, in their study of the language of racism in New Zealand, Wetherell and Potter (1992) found the categories of 'race' and 'culture' were used by the Pakeha (white majority) respondents as contrastive categories to define the Maori people as a distinct biological group of people who shared similar physical characteristics, values and personality characteristics. These categories were used predominantly to contrast Maoris with the Pakeha majority who were represented as the 'norm' of New Zealand society. While Pakeha society represented civilization, progress and modernism, Maori were the repository of 'culture'. In this way, the Maori people were always constructed as the 'Other': exotic, steeped in culture and separate. While many of the respondents spoke favourably of a Maori cultural identity, ultimately this identity was viewed as secondary to a homogeneous and unifying 'national' identity. The category of 'nation' was used in Pakeha talk to limit and constrain the aspirations of a Maori identity, which was seen to undermine and threaten national unity. Indeed, nationalist discourse of this kind is also a ubiquitous feature of contemporary 'race' talk (Rapley, 1998).

Justifying and legitimating the status quo Wetherell and Potter's (1992) detailed discursive analysis of racial 'prejudice' in New Zealand also emphasizes how talk is organized rhetorically around the proficient use of a range of liberal and egalitarian arguments that draw on principles of freedom, fairness, individual rights, and equal opportunity. These also functioned to deny attributions of racism and, further, to legitimate and justify existing inequitable social relations. Specifically, Wetherell and Potter identified ten common, 'rhetorically self-sufficient' or 'clinching' arguments that were routinely used by respondents to this effect. These arguments, which they described as having similar status to socially acceptable clichés, provide a basic accountability; they represent familiar cultural verities; they are beyond question. In Wetherell and Potter's words, 'having constructed a version in these terms no more need be said, no further warrant need be given' (p. 92). The following list characterizes the general forms of these rhetorically self-sufficient arguments (Wetherell & Potter, 1992, p.177):

1. Resources should be used productively and in a cost-effective manner.
2. Nobody should be compelled.
3. Everybody should be treated equally.
4. You cannot turn the clock backwards.
5. Present generations cannot be blamed for the mistakes of past generations.
6. Injustices should be righted.
7. Everybody can succeed if they try hard enough.
8. Minority opinion should not carry more weight than majority opinion.
9. We have to live in the twentieth century (or twenty-first century).
10. You have to be practical.

These stock devices are described as 'rhetorically self-sufficient' or 'clinching' because they reflect common-sense maxims that are central to liberal-egalitarian discourses of rationality, justice, freedom and individual rights. These same 'self-sufficient' arguments have also been found in other research on racist discourse in New Zealand (McCreanor, 1993; Nairn & McCreanor 1990, 1991) and in the analysis of the public debate in Australia on Reconciliation, and whether to apologize to Indigenous Australians for historical injustices (Augoustinos, LeCouteur & Soyland, 2002; LeCouteur & Augoustinos, 2001) (see Textbox 7.2). It is important to emphasize that these common-sense maxims are used in flexible and often contradictory ways, and should not be viewed as cognitive templates or schemas that underlie racist discourse. Rather, Wetherell and Potter (1992) define them as 'tools' or 'resources' which are combined in variable ways by speakers to do certain things, most notable of which is to avoid a 'racist' identity and to justify existing social relations. Like Billig et al. (1988), Wetherell and Potter argue for the fragmentary, dilemmatic and contradictory nature of people's views, an approach which is considerably different from the social psychological concept of attitude as an enduring, stable and consistent cognitive response. Indeed, as we will argue in the next chapter, these common rhetorical arguments about practicality, equality, individual rights and majority opinion are cornerstones of a liberal-individualist ideology.

Textbox 7.2

Self-sufficient arguments in political rhetoric

The extract below comes from a speech that the Prime Minister of Australia, John Howard, made to the Reconciliation Convention in May 1997. In this speech Howard justifies his refusal to offer a national apology on behalf of the nation for past injustices against Indigenous people, specifically, for past government practices of the forced removal of Indigenous children from their families and communities – who came to be called the 'Stolen Generations'. Also in this speech, Howard attempts to draws definitional boundaries around what the nebulous concept of 'Reconciliation' should mean to Australians.

Analyse the extract below by paying particular attention to how he mobilizes a number of rhetorically self-sufficient arguments. Which of these can you identify from Wetherell and Potter's list? How are they invoked? What functions do these arguments serve? How might counter-arguments be framed? (see Augoustinos et al., 2002 for a detailed analysis of this speech)

But this optimism, my friends, about the reconciliation process cannot be blind. We must be realistic in acknowledging some of the threats to reconciliation.

Reconciliation will not work if it puts a higher value on symbolic gestures and overblown promises rather than practical needs of Aboriginal and Torres Strait Islander people in areas like health, housing, education and employment.

It will not work if it is premised solely on a sense of national guilt and shame. Rather we should acknowledge past injustices and focus our energies on addressing the root causes of current and future disadvantage among our indigenous people.

Textbox 7.2 (Continued)

Nor will the reconciliation process work effectively if one of its central purposes becomes the establishment of different systems of accountability and lawful conduct among Australians on the basis of their race or any other factor.

The reconciliation process will only work effectively if it involves and inspires all Australians.

Reconciliation is not helped if its critics are able to claim that resources directed towards Aboriginal and Torres Strait Islander people who are disadvantaged have not been well or wisely used.

However much some may wish to believe otherwise, there is evidence that some programmes designed to address indigenous disadvantage have, in fact, encouraged dependency rather than individual initiative and personal responsibility.

Locating prejudice: in the mind or in society? The 'appropriation' and use of liberal and egalitarian principles to argue for 'racist' and discriminatory practices is, of course, a central feature of contemporary theories of modern racism which we described earlier in this chapter. These theories argue that, unlike 'old-fashioned' racism, which is predominantly characterized by white supremacist beliefs, contemporary racism is more subtle and insidious (Pettigrew & Meertens, 1995). Although extreme negative affect towards minority groups has been tempered by egalitarian values, this negative affect (conscious or unconscious) has not been entirely eradicated and persists in the psyche of majority group members. The contradiction between negative affect and liberal values is argued to produce considerable psychological ambivalence so that individuals struggle between their emotions and their beliefs (Gaertner & Dovidio, 1986). Moreover, the modern racist denies that he or she is prejudiced; any conscious and obvious negative feelings and attitudes are justified by 'matter-of-fact' observations that minority groups transgress central values such as hard work, thrift and self-reliance.

Although theories of modern racism bear similarities to the findings of discursive work on the conflicted and contradictory nature of contemporary race discourse, there are, nevertheless, important differences between traditional and discursive approaches. Theories of modern racism do make reference to wider social, historical and ideological factors that have influenced and shaped the content and form of racism and prejudice over the years. However, these theories, and the questionnaire research methods that have been used to investigate variants of racism, primarily position racism as an individual and psychological 'problem'. The ambivalence and contradictions that are manifest both in questionnaire responses and in people's talk are located 'within the emotional and cognitive domain of the individual' (Wetherell & Potter, 1992, p. 197). In contrast, discursive psychology:

> locates the conflicts and dilemmas within the argumentative and rhetorical resources available in a 'liberal' and 'egalitarian' society ... The conflict is not between a feeling and a value, between psychological drives and socially acceptable expressions or between emotions and politics, but between competing frameworks for articulating social, political and ethical questions. These conflicts and dilemmas could be said to be realized in a 'psychological' form when the members of society begin to discuss, debate, explain, justify and develop accounts in the course of social interaction and everyday life. (Wetherell & Potter, 1992, p. 197)

From this perspective, racism or prejudice ceases to be an individual or psychological state and becomes, rather, a structural feature of a society which is 'organized around the oppression of one group and the dominance of another group' (Wetherell & Potter, 1992, p. 198). Individuals utilize whatever ideological resources a society makes available in order to justify and legitimate racist outcomes, but this is always viewed primarily within the context of oppressive structural arrangements which need continually to be justified and legitimated for their maintenance and reproduction.

By locating prejudice primarily within the individual rather than in broader social/cultural domains, social psychological theories have colluded in conceptualizing prejudice as an individual pathology. In doing so, the categories of the 'prejudiced individual' and the 'tolerant individual' have been constructed and reified as entities with clear definitional boundaries. In the words of Wetherell and Potter, 'Prejudice remains a personal pathology, a failure of inner-directed empathy and intellect, rather than a social pathology, shaped by power relations and the conflicting vested interests of groups' (1992, p. 208). Prejudiced individuals are seen to be irrational and illogical, requiring some kind of attitudinal and moral 'rehabilitation'. Prejudice is viewed primarily as a 'state of mind' which requires change through education and training. Politically, this has the effect of deflecting attention from the political necessity of societal and structural change.

Chapter Summary

We began this chapter by detailing traditional personality approaches to prejudice such as the authoritarian personality and the more recent, social dominance orientation. Although these perspectives are strictly speaking not social cognitive, they none the less share some important similarities in that they locate prejudice primarily within the psychological and cognitive domain of the individual. Prejudice, authoritarianism, or social dominance orientation, are all constructed as personality or attitudinal predispositions that are determined by either psychodynamic factors, socialization, or receptiveness to legitimizing myths about the social order. Social cognition models of prejudice have largely emphasized cognitive and perceptual processes that are seen as being the foundational basis for prejudice. Our limited cognitive capacities and our need to simplify social reality through the dual processes of categorization and stereotyping are seen as *predisposing* us to prejudice and discrimination. Social cognitive research on categorization and stereotyping therefore suggests either explicitly or implicitly, that prejudice is cognitively inevitable and in some instances very difficult to suppress. As various critics have argued, such approaches tend to 'naturalize' prejudice and intergroup discrimination so that they come to be seen as normal human responses – and in some cases merely by-products of our cognitive hardwiring. 'Everyone is prejudiced' is a common catchphrase of the 'new' modern racism that is often used to rationalize and legitimate prejudice. Of equal concern is the assumption in social dominance theory that humans have evolved with a natural biological drive for systems of social organization that are characterized by group-based hierarchies.

Despite claims that SIT (and, in particular, the minimal group experiments) also provides further evidence for the inevitability of intergroup prejudice and bias, SIT and SCT researchers have strongly challenged this interpretation. SCT argues that the dual processes of categorization and stereotyping are not automatic and rigid processes that simplify perception. Rather, they are flexible and context-specific psychological processes that enrich social perception and orient us to the social hierarchies and relations that exist between groups in society. In order to understand prejudice and social conflict we need to understand the nature of relationships between groups and how these various groups perceive the stability and legitimacy of the existing social structure. Prejudice is therefore not an individual psychological phenomenon but an intergroup one.

Like SIT, social representations theory emphasizes the centrality of group identities and shared symbolic meaning systems in understanding prejudice and intergroup relations. Stereotypes are not viewed simply as internal cognitive schemas that simplify reality, but as objectified shared meaning systems that serve ideological functions. Moreover, this approach seeks to understand the social processes that are implicated in political movements that seek to change and transform dominant representations of marginalized social identities (such as African Americans). In this way, social representations theory is as much about understanding social change and transformation as it is about understanding social stability.

Finally we reviewed the discursive approach to studying prejudice and everyday racism. Discursive psychology locates prejudice and racism not within the psychology or cognitive processes of the individual, but within the language practices and discourses of a society. Discursive psychology has analysed the ways in which discursive resources and rhetorical arguments are put together to construct 'racial' differences, and to represent marginalized groups as the 'other'. This tradition locates these language practices or 'ways of talking' at a societal level, as products of a racist society rather than as individual psychological and/or cognitive products. The analytic site therefore is not the 'prejudiced' or 'racist' individual, but the discursive and linguistic resources that are available within an inequitable society. While this approach has been able to identify how linguistic resources are combined in flexible and contradictory ways to reproduce and justify racial and social inequalities, it says very little about the possible underlying psychological processes that are linked to the deployment of specific language practices in specific contexts. That is, it makes no claims regarding 'what is going on inside the person' when using racist discourse.

Further Reading

Allport, G. W. (1954). *The nature of prejudice*. Reading, MA: Addison-Wesley.

Oakes, P. J., & Haslam, S. A. (2001). Distortion v. meaning: Categorization on trial for inciting intergroup hatred. In M. Augoustinos & K. J. Reynolds (Eds.), *Understanding the psychology of prejudice, racism and social conflict* (pp. 179–194). London: Sage.

Philogène, G. (1999). *From Black to African American: A new social representation*. Westport, CT: Greenwood-Praeger.

Quinn, K., Macrae, N., & Bodenhausen, G. (2003). Stereotyping and impression formation: How categorical thinking shapes person perception. In M. Hogg & J. Cooper (Eds.). *The Sage handbook of social psychology* (pp. 87–109). London: Sage.

Wetherell, M., & Potter, J. (1992). *Mapping the language of racism: Discourse and the legitimation of exploitation*. Hemel Hempstead: Harvester Wheatsheaf.

8 Ideology

In the preceding chapters we have attempted to bring together research and scholarship in social psychology that has considered how people perceive and understand their social world and how the forms of social life within which we live create opportunities and constraints on the performance of various kinds of social actions. In attempting to broaden social psychology's predominantly narrow view of social life as emerging from the interaction of sovereign individuals, we have sought to emphasize the role of those aspects of social and cultural life that are not reducible to the individual – such as social representations and discourse. In doing so, we have emphasized that there are important aspects of social life that cannot be accounted for solely by reference to the thoughts, feelings and actions of individual members of a society, but, rather, that certain systems of belief and ways of approaching the world have a life of their own. These forms of shared social beliefs are not, however, independent of or prior to the kinds of phenomena for which they seek to account, and differences between groups in their ability to shape the form and content of these representations means that we must pay attention to the way in which such representations serve the interests of particular groups within society at the expense of others. Consideration of the ways in which the ability to promote certain forms of social understanding of social life is bound up with the economic, social and institutional power of some groups over others brings us squarely into the territory of ideology.

In considering the wide range of conceptual and empirical work on the perception and understanding of the social world, we have thus far said little about the role ideology plays in constructing social reality for individuals and groups. We have, however, talked extensively about the constitutive nature of social representations and discourse. It may be helpful, therefore, to briefly distinguish between these constructs and the related concept of ideology.

Van Dijk argues for ideology as '... the interface between social structure and social cognition ... ideologies may be very succinctly defined as the *basis of the social representations shared by members of a group*' (1998, p. 8, original emphasis). This definition draws attention to the cognitive and social aspects of ideology, and presents ideology as the socially shared (but individually held) beliefs that are manifest in social representations and social discourse. In a similar vein, Stuart Hall (1996) locates ideology as being grounded in social cognition, while emphasizing the social function of ideology as a means by which different social groups account for their and others' positions in social structures: '[B]y ideology I mean the mental frameworks – the languages, the concepts, categories, imagery of thought, and the systems of representation – which different classes and social groups deploy in order to make sense of, figure out and render intelligible the way society works' (1996, p. 26). Although questions about what ideology 'is' and how we should conceive of it are contested between different approaches to its study, we can none the less begin our discussion from the position that when we talk about ideology we are referring to the beliefs, opinions and social practices that support certain representations and constructions of the world, which, in turn, serve to rationalize, legitimate, maintain and (re)produce particular institutional arrangements, and economic, social and power relations within a society.

It should not be surprising to hear that ideology has been described by many as the most contested and elusive concept within the social sciences. Both McLellan (1986) and Larrain (1979) provide thorough historical accounts of this concept. Indeed, McLellan warns that all attempts to define ideology are ideological in themselves: something which will become apparent throughout this chapter as we consider various ways in which ideology has been conceptualized, theorized and empirically investigated. It is important to point out that some of the research we will be reviewing, particularly of the social psychological variety, has rarely been viewed as research into ideology. Indeed, we will argue that research in certain areas of social psychology has 'unwittingly' uncovered ideological elements in everyday thinking.

Social Cognition and Ideology

The role of ideology in social life has been long debated and argued within political and social theory, but has largely been ignored by social psychologists. There have been rare exceptions like Michael Billig, who has not only delineated the relationship between ideology and social psychological theory (1982), but also written extensively about the role of ideology in the everyday life of the ordinary person. More recently, John Jost and colleagues have written explicitly about the role of ideology in system-justifying social beliefs and practices (Jost & Banaji, 1994; Jost & Major, 2001), although this perspective has yet to be widely taken up by other researchers. However, even while staying clear of the debates about the nature and function of ideology in other disciplines, social psychologists have studied a range of phenomena closely associated with ideology, albeit under a range of different labels: political belief systems; values; and stereotypes.

Ideology as political belief systems

The dominant approach to ideology in the social sciences has been to view ideology as a coherent set of political beliefs and values, such as those embraced by formal political parties. The empirical tradition linked with this conceptualization of ideology has involved large-scale surveys aimed at examining the political, economic and social attitudes of the mass public. The primary aim has been to determine the underlying structure of these beliefs in terms of a liberal-conservative (or sometimes left-wing/right-wing) political framework. This tradition of research culminated in Converse's (1964) work, which concluded that the American public displayed little internal consistency in their political attitudes. People's views on a specific issue do not always predict their views on other related issues. Similarly, McClosky (1964) found that although the American public generally endorsed the principles of freedom and democracy in their abstract form, they were inconsistent in their application of these principles to specific instances. Thus, it was argued that there existed little ideological coherence amongst the American electorate, whose knowledge and understanding of politics was, at best, rudimentary.

Instead of an over-arching belief system that organized large amounts of information, the public was found to have clusters of simple, concrete and personally relevant ideas which displayed little consistency. It was argued, therefore, that the public, unlike the political elite, did not think 'ideologically'. The public displayed confusion over the meaning of conservative as opposed to liberal ideological dimensions, and did not share with political elites a conservative versus liberal conceptual frame of reference by which to structure and organize their political knowledge. Indeed, some surveys found that a substantial number of people were unable to place themselves along a liberal–conservative attitudinal continuum because they had not given the matter much thought (Erikson, Luttbeg & Tedin, 1980). Thus, Kinder and Sears (1985) concluded that the American public was largely 'innocent' of ideology.

The notion that the public is politically uninformed and ideologically inconsistent has formed the paradigmatic core of American political science over the last three decades. Critics of this research, however, have argued that simply because the public does not structure political beliefs in the same manner as do the political elite, it does not necessarily follow that the content of these beliefs is devoid of ideology. The presence or absence of a logical cognitive structure, it was argued, is not necessarily synonymous with the presence or absence of ideology (e.g., Bennett, 1977; Marcus, Tabb & Sullivan, 1974). In an effort to salvage the notion that people's political orientations do possess some degree of organization and coherence, Sniderman and Tetlock (1986b) proposed that people organize and structure their attitudes according to a likeability heuristic – that is, by their pattern of likes and dislikes. They argue:

> Affective processes … play an especially crucial role in giving mass beliefs what structure they do possess. The building blocks of political coherence, we shall propose, are personal likes and dislikes of politically strategic small groups. Even citizens who know little about political ideas or the political process can put together a consistent political outlook, provided they at least know whom they like and, perhaps more important, whom they dislike. (1986b, p. 79)

The use of a 'rule of thumb', a determining affective principle, is consistent with the cognitive miser view dominant in social cognition research. Here we are reminded yet again that in understanding the social world people in general are unmotivated to think too deeply about issues. As Sniderman and Tetlock put it, 'the resultant ideological understanding of mass publics may be a crude and simplified one; but so are most effective ways of understanding a complex world' (1986b, p. 89). We will contrast this view of the person as a limited thinker with Michael Billig's portrayal of the person as an 'ideological dilemmatician' later in this chapter.

A more substantial criticism of this research concerns the manner in which the concept of ideology has been defined. Equating ideology with political identifications such as 'liberal' or 'conservative' in North America, 'Labour' or 'Tory' in Britain, and 'Labor' or 'Liberal' in Australia restricts the concept of ideology to formal political belief systems. We believe that this particular conception neglects the link between ideology and everyday life – the role which ideology plays in representing everyday social reality outside the domain of formal political issues and debates. Moreover, simply equating ideology with political identifications also strips the concept of its critical component (McLellan, 1986; Thompson, 1984). From within this perspective, ideology is primarily used as a descriptive and neutral concept which refers to any formal belief system. This also has been the predominant use of the concept of ideology by psychologists (e.g., Eysenck & Wilson, 1978), and particularly by political psychologists (Kinder & Sears, 1985; Sniderman & Tetlock, 1986b; Stone & Schaffner, 1988). While there is nothing inherently wrong with defining ideology in this way, restricting the definition of ideology to a coherent system of political beliefs as embodied within the rhetoric of western democratic political parties, focuses only upon party political issues and the formal processes of political decision-making.

Another common usage of the concept of ideology is to equate ideology with political extremism and rigidity. It is common, for example, for political commentators to distinguish between politicians and policy makers who are 'ideological' as opposed to those who are 'pragmatic'. The decline of Nazism and Stalinism after the Second World War led to many American political scientists declaring the 'end of ideology' (e.g., Bell, 1960; Lipset, 1960). Indeed, the recent decline of Soviet and east European communism has led to proclamations that capitalism has been vindicated as a rational, value-free and objective way of organizing society – a social and economic system free of ideology. This view has been argued by Fukuyama (1992), who has declared liberal democracy to be 'the end of history'. The cessation of the Cold War has also been characterized as ending one of the most significant ideological battles in history. It is arguable, however, that this recent historical event signals the end of ideology in the way in which people construct and understand their everyday lives. To argue this is to ignore or downplay the inherent ideological currents within liberal democratic societies themselves and within everyday life outside formal politics.

Ideology as consciousness

Traditionally, ideology has been treated as a cognitive construct which permeates human consciousness. From within this perspective ideology is to be found in the values, beliefs, attitudes and opinions which people hold. As Gaskell and Fraser (1990) suggest, one of the functions of widespread beliefs and values is that they may provide legitimacy to the socio-political structure of a society. We would argue that, to the extent to which they do so, such cognitions can be considered to be ideological in nature. For example, individualist values of achievement and competition contribute significantly to the support of a capitalist socio-cultural system. Studies have found that as children grow older they are more likely to regard inequalities of wealth and income as inevitable and legitimate (Lewis, 1990; Stacey, 1982). They are also more likely to embrace equity principles of economic distribution rather than principles of equality (Bond, Leung & Wan, 1982; Sampson, 1975). That is, children learn to accept over time that resources within society are (and should be) distributed according to individual inputs (effort, abilities and skills). As Sampson (1975) argues, equity values encourage and legitimate individual competition and personal advancement at the expense of cooperation, communion and equality. Indeed, Sampson suggests that the forms of relations which dominate in the economic sphere tend to be adopted in other areas of human conduct.

Perhaps a classic example of ideological thinking that social psychology unwittingly discovered is the fundamental attribution 'error' or 'bias'. In contrast to the cognitive explanation which mainstream psychology has advanced for this bias, we have argued throughout this book that this bias demonstrates the dominance of dispositional explanations over situational explanations in western culture. Increasingly, it has been recognized that this attributional phenomenon is not a universal cognitive bias, but is culture-specific, reflecting an underlying ideological representation of the person as the centre of all action and process (Bond, 1983; Hewstone & Augoustinos, 1995; Ichheiser, 1949; Miller, 1984; Nisbett, 2003).

False consciousness and system-justification

So far we have described the dominant ways in which ideology has been defined by mainstream social science. In the past decade, however, social psychologists have increasingly adopted an approach which is informed by conceptualizations of ideology that view ideology as the means by which relations of power, control and dominance are maintained and preserved within any society (see Jost & Banaji, 1994; Nosek, 2004). In this view, ideology is a tool of the powerful that is used to preserve and promote their own interests by supporting existing social relations. These ideological tools are viewed as the means by which power and control within western liberal democracies have come to be wielded increasingly by covert and subtle means and less by the use of overt force. Specifically, social psychologists have begun to consider the ways in which certain attitudes and beliefs (such as social stereotypes and beliefs in meritocracy) can be understood in terms of the 'system-justifying' functions that they serve. Jost (1995), for example, has suggested that much of what passes as social cognition – the errors, biases and distortions found in human thinking – is essentially the social-psychological study of false consciousness. Such views have emerged largely from Marxist accounts of ideology and it is to these we now turn.

Marx and ideology   Marxist-influenced accounts of ideology are particularly relevant because they have systematically attempted to explain the role of ideology in contemporary liberal democracies. Marx's early writings emphasized the illusory role which ideology plays in portraying society as cohesive and harmonious, whereas his later writings emphasized the role ideology plays in making sense of people's everyday social interactions within a capitalist society. According to Marx, ideology functions to conceal social conflicts by embodying ideas, values and language which justify existing social and economic inequalities. The ideology of freedom and equality within capitalist society is reinforced by the individual's apparent experience of free exchange in the market-place. Marx viewed ideology as concealing the 'real relations' of dominance and inequality that exist in capitalist societies (Larrain, 1983; McLellan, 1986).

Central to an analysis of the ways in which ideologies produce system-justifying effects is the Marxist notion of 'false consciousness'. When people in general come to view the existing social and power relations as natural and inevitable, when stereotypes mystify and obfuscate the 'real' relations of dominance and exploitation within a society, then we have what Marx referred to as false consciousness. False consciousness is often represented as a cognitive or psychological state of mind. Such psychological accounts of false consciousness locate distortions, false beliefs, biases, etc. within the perceptual and cognitive domain of the individual subject. The individual is seen as failing to perceive reality accurately and thus to recognize his or her true self and group-based interests.

Although the notion of false consciousness has been central to understanding many of the system-serving practices of people whose own personal and social interests are clearly *not* served by the system, labelling this as 'false' consciousness is, however, epistemologically problematic. The Marxist concept of false consciousness is often paired with the assumption that it is possible to arrive at a true or veridical version of reality. As we have seen, this assumption is considered highly problematic from a social constructionist and discursive perspective. We will return to this thorny issue later but for now concur with others who have argued that it is conceptually unnecessary to endow beliefs and opinions which are system serving with the status of falsehood (Eagleton, 1991; Hall, 1996). There is little to be gained and little hope of resolution of claims and counter-claims about the 'falseness' or otherwise of the beliefs held by individual members of particular social groups, by treating some people and groups as having privileged access to an unmediated reality. It is for such reasons that ideology is no longer equated with false consciousness, with mystifying, distorting or false beliefs. Rather, ideology refers to any beliefs, representations, discourses and practices which serve to legitimate and sustain existing social and power relations, irrespective of their truth status. We will elaborate on these issues later when we consider group-based approaches to the study of ideology, in particular when we discuss the system-serving functions of stereotypes and stereotyping.

Social dominance theory and system justification

One theory which explicitly addresses beliefs that justify the social system is social dominance theory (see Chapter 7). Social dominance theory centres on the claim that 'all social systems will converge toward the establishment of stable, group-based social hierarchies' (Sidanius & Pratto, 1993, p. 177). According to Sidanius and Pratto, ideologies provide various 'legitimizing myths' which serve as resources to support these social hierarchies. However, in addition to the 'hierarchy-enhancing legitimizing myths' that reinforce existing relations of power and dominance, competing ideologies can provide 'hierarchy-attentuating legitimizing myths' which promote egalitarian, rather than dominating, relations between groups. The use of hierarchy-enhancing versus hierarchy-attenuating ideologies is considered to result from individual differences in levels of social dominance orientation (SDO), as well as from aspects of the intergroup context. In this view, therefore, the extent to which ideology is implicated in social relations is a matter of individual differences (in SDO): the effects of the dominant social ideology are ultimately filtered through the 'personal ideology' of each individual. What is perhaps the most problematic aspect of SDO is the claim that system justification is biologically driven through the operation of distant evolutionary forces, an assumption that has been strenuously critiqued by SIT and SCT theorists. It is to these approaches to ideology that we now turn.

Social Identity and Ideology

Marx argued that the economic relations of a society, its dominant mode of production and constituent social relations, form the base for a society's ideological superstructure. Not only were the superstructural elements of a society the expression of the dominant material relations, but they were also an outgrowth of class domination. Ideology was inextricably linked with intergroup (specifically interclass) relations. In *The German Ideology*, Marx argued that:

> The ideas of the ruling class are, in every age, the ruling ideas: i.e., the class which is the dominant material force in society is at the same time its dominant intellectual force ... The dominant ideas are nothing more than the ideal expression of the dominant material relationships. (Marx & Engels, 1846/1947, p. 39)

This dictum is perhaps one of the most well-known and most criticized notions within Marxist social theory. Criticized for being too economically determinist and reductionist, Marxist theory has subsequently emphasized the need to articulate more complex interrelations between economic and non-economic influences, which together shape a society's ideological form. The work of Foucault, for example, has emphasized that modern power is not always economic in nature, nor is it simply embodied and exercised by the economically dominant classes and the institutions of the capitalist state. For Foucault, modern power is diffused and dispersed throughout all layers of society and is largely exercised through discursive and behavioural rituals which become internalized norms by which people live out their everyday lives. We will return to some of Foucault's ideas on power later, but for now we will discuss how social psychology has incorporated the fundamental notion that ideologies are about managing the relations between social groups differing in status and (economic and other forms of) power.

Several social psychological theories offer accounts of intergroup relations that draw more or less heavily on notions of ideology to explain certain features of intergroup behaviour. System-justification theory (Jost & Banaji, 1994) and social identity/self-categorization theory are the most prominent of these. The ways in which ideology is used in these theories to account for the actions and experiences of group members provides an insight into how ideology is conceptualized in each of these theories.

System-justification theory: stereotypes as ideological representations

While the pervasive and resilient nature of social stereotypes was lamented earlier this century by social psychologists who viewed them largely as cognitive constructs used to justify prejudicial attitudes and discriminatory behaviour, increasingly stereotypes and the process of stereotyping have taken on a more benign status (Condor, 1988). Consistent with the dominant information-processing approach to cognition, stereotypes are now seen to be an inevitable product of the need to categorize and simplify a complex social world. In this way, stereotyping is losing its negative connotations and is being viewed as servicing the cognitive needs of individuals. As we argued in the previous chapter, stereotypes can be seen to be first and foremost *ideological* representations which serve to justify and legitimize existing social and power relations within a society (Jost & Banaji, 1994; Jost, Banaji & Nosek, 2004; Jost & Hunyady, 2002). Indeed, it could be argued that much of the research on stereotypes and stereotyping is largely a social psychological study of the role of ideology and power in everyday human thinking.

Jost and Banaji (1994) have argued that, while social psychological theories have emphasized the ego- and group-justification functions of stereotypes, very little has been written about the role of stereotypes in system-justification. They define system-justification as 'the psychological process by which existing social arrangements are legitimised, even at the expense of personal and group interests' (1994, p. 2). These authors draw on a number of empirical findings in the stereotype literature that an ego- and group-justification approach has significant difficulties in explaining. Foremost is the oft-found tendency for members of marginalized groups to apply and internalize negative stereotypes to themselves and to their group as a whole. Negative self-stereotyping is certainly not self-serving, nor does it accord very well with social identity theory's maxim that groups will strive to maintain a positive ingroup identity or at least some degree of positive distinctiveness from outgroups. The favouritism towards dominant outgroups that is sometimes associated with low-status groups is difficult to reconcile with the group-protecting and enhancing principles of SIT. It is for these reasons that Jost and Banaji (1994) advance the view that stereotypes serve important ideological functions: that they, in effect, support, rationalize and legitimate the *status quo*. In their words:

> Stereotypes serve ideological functions, in particular that they justify the exploitation of certain groups over others, and that they explain the poverty or powerlessness of some groups and the success of others in ways that make these differences seem legitimate and even natural ... Based on theories of and data on self-perception, attribution, cognitive conservatism, the division of social roles, behavioural confirmation, and the belief in a just world, we stipulate a process whereby stereotypes are used to explain the existing social system and the positions and actions of self and others. (1994, p. 10)

Contrary to the view that stereotyping is fundamentally a product of individual motivational requirements (and, we would add, cognitive requirements), Jost and Banaji argue that the process of stereotyping is linked to the information-processing needs of an 'ideological environment'. Thus the process of stereotyping is not simply an individual or intergroup cognitive process. Stereotyping becomes a collective and ideological process linked to the power and social relations of a particular society within a particular historical context. Drawing from research on the 'automatic' activation of stereotypes, Jost and Banaji suggest that the ideological environment is pervasive and insidious, so much so that stereotypes can emerge spontaneously and unconsciously, even among people who consciously embrace egalitarian values and beliefs (Devine, 1989a).

However, Jost and Banaji go further than to argue for the ideological, legitimating functions of stereotypes. They also argue that stereotypes reflect 'false consciousness'. As discussed earlier, labelling certain beliefs as 'false' necessarily invites arguments about what is 'true' or 'real'. Substantiating the truth or falsity of the content of stereotypes, however, is far from being simply an empirical issue. Indeed, in accounting for why stereotypes are so pervasive and resistant to change, several social psychologists have put forward the insidious 'kernel of truth' proposition regarding stereotypes (e.g. Judd & Park, 1993; Levine & Campbell, 1972; McCauley & Stitt, 1978). Because of their commitment to a realist epistemology, Jost and Banaji are forced to consider the relationship between stereotypes and social reality. Given Jost and Banaji's critical Marxist approach, and their commitment to an objective scientific 'truth' about stereotypes, it is not surprising that they argue against the notion that stereotypes are based on veridical perception. Implicitly, this invites others to empirically confirm or challenge their views of stereotypes as false representations. Social psychologists who have attempted to empirically evaluate the truth or falsity of stereotypes have faced considerable conceptual problems in doing so (see Textbox 8.1). For how does one establish in an 'objective', disinterested way whether African Americans are essentially more aggressive than white Americans, or whether women are 'really' more nurturing than men? Such empirical concerns seem futile and simply lead to 'scientific' claims and counter-claims. Addressing the kernel of truth argument at this level of analysis – whether the content of stereotypes reflects the actual characteristics of members of a particular group – is pointless for there is no disinterested and objective way of measuring the accuracy of stereotype content (see Oakes & Reynolds, 1997). The most cautious realist argument that has been advanced is that by Oakes and her colleagues (e.g., Oakes et al., 1994; Oakes & Reynolds, 1997, 2001), who argue that stereotypes are veridical to the extent that they reflect the nature of social intergroup relations within a society at a particular point in time, emphasizing the relative and self-interested nature of social perception which necessarily produces different world-views and perspectives. All perception is influenced and shaped by the needs, goals, interests and motivations of the perceiver. Self-interested perception or 'perceiver-readiness' ensures that perception is psychologically veridical, practical and helps orient people to their social-relational position in society. Thus according to this view, stereotypes do not reflect the internal characteristics of individual members of a group, but the 'emergent properties of the social category as a whole' (Oakes et al., 1994, p. 193).

Textbox 8.1

Measuring stereotype accuracy

McCauley and Stitt (1978) attempted to evaluate the kernel of truth argument by using the diagnostic ratio (DR) method of measuring stereotypes. McCauley and Stitt collected DR estimates for seven different characteristics as they applied to African Americans when the study was done, and then compared these DRs with actual DRs obtained from official government documents. The two sets of DRs are presented in the table below. The actual and the estimated DRs correlate .62 with one another. McCauley and Stitt point out that the stereotypes being expressed by their subjects would seem to contain more than just a kernel of truth: the subjects seem well able to predict the actual DRs. Further, the estimated DRs fail to exaggerate the criterion information, being either reasonably accurate or an underestimation. On the basis of these results, McCauley and Stitt claim that stereotypes can be, and in this case are, veridical.

Actual and estimated diagnostic ratios (percentage of African Americans/ percentage of all Americans)

Characteristic	Actual DR	Mean estimated DR
Completed high school	0.65	0.69
Illegitimate	3.1	1.96
Unemployed last month	1.9	1.98
Victims of crimes	1.5	1.77
Welfare	4.6	1.82
Four or more children	1.9	1.43
Female head of family	2.8	1.77

Source: Adapted from McCauley and Stitt, 1978, p. 937, Table 2

McCauley and Stitt's (1978) study seems to provide strong evidence that stereotypes help orient the perceiver to a set of objective conditions in the real world; that is, that stereotypes have a basis in the objective nature of social groups, and therefore are, in a sense, justified. Several reasons mitigate against interpreting the data in this way, though.

McCauley and Stitt's position is that the characteristics they measured are purely descriptive, yet one of the features of stereotype function is that they are *explanatory*. To believe that African Americans do not complete high school at the same rate as other Americans, or that African Americans are more likely to be illegitimate, is, psychologically, as bland as believing that African Americans have darker skin than other Americans. These statements all only serve to mark the target group. Yet the invidious part of stereotypes is that they *attribute* fixed and essentialist qualities to the target group and its members; that is, that they function

---

Textbox 8.1 (Continued)

as *explanations* as well as descriptions. A stereotype contains not only the phenotypic, descriptive characteristic that African Americans do not complete high school at the same rate, but also the essentialist ascription of laziness and stupidity as an explanation of why they fail to complete high school at the same rate. In one large American study, Apostle, Glock, Piazza and Suelze (1983) show that it is *how* whites explain perceived differences between blacks and whites, and not the recognition of differences *per se*, that serves to determine how those whites evaluate blacks and evaluate government programmes designed to aid them.

Overall, then, system-justification theory takes a (neo) Marxist view of ideology as the beliefs, values and social practices that rationalize, legitimate and naturalize the privileged position enjoyed by high-status groups over low-status groups. 'Ideological' beliefs are simply those that serve to reproduce extant economic and social relations between groups. Crucially, in this view, system-justifying actions are produced because the ideology of dominant groups (the ideology that supports 'the system') is accepted by members of lower-status groups. This brings us to a consideration of what social identity theory has had to say about group-specific interests and ideology.

Social identity theory and ideology

In his social-cognitive-discursive theory of ideology, Van Dijk (1998) explicitly rejects the conceptualization of ideology as singular and (solely) reflective of the interests of dominant social groups. He argues instead that intergroup relations within a society are typically characterized by *competing* ideologies: ideologies of dominance and ideologies of resistance.

> … [I]deologies positively serve to empower dominated groups, to create solidarity, to organise struggle and to sustain opposition … ideologies serve to protect interests and resources, whether these are unjust privileges, or minimal conditions of existence. More neutrally and more generally, then, ideologies simply serve groups and their members in the organisation and management of their goals, social practices and their whole daily social life. (1998, p. 138)

Rather than ideologies being properties of societies and serving to order and reify intergroup relations within that society, this view presents ideologies as properties of groups which serve to organize (potentially) contested relations, conflicts and power struggles between those groups.

Social identity theory and self-categorization theories also consider ideologies to be fundamentally rooted in intergroup relations (Hogg & Abrams, 1988). However, the relationship between group boundaries and ideological positions is not simple or obvious, and indeed achieving ideological hegemony (see below) is a major ground on which intergroup contests are played out. SIT stresses the important role of the perceived legitimacy and stability of status differences between groups to the way in which group identity is experienced (see Chapter 7). Ideological domination is one of the means by which status relations between groups are legitimized and preserved, but the achievement of ideological supremacy is never final.

Issues concerning ideology come most sharply into focus in SIT when considering the phenomenon of outgroup bias. Although the theory is better known for highlighting the ways in which people are usually biased in favour of their ingroups, there are also circumstances in which people (usually members of low-status groups) show biases *against* their own groups in favour of (usually higher-status) outgroups. SIT argues that this apparently paradoxical outgroup bias is most likely to occur when the higher status of the outgroup is considered to be legitimate (Turner & Reynolds, 2003). Furthermore several social identity researchers have argued that members of high-status groups are also motivated to see their status advantage as legitimate in order to avoid feelings of guilt (e.g., Branscombe, Ellemers, Spears & Doosje, 1999; Leach, Snider & Iyer, 2002). Legitimacy is thus a core dimension of intergroup relations, and as we have already seen, establishing the legitimacy of status relations between groups is the core business of ideology. In the words of Spears, Jetten & Doosje:

> legitimacy arguably forms a crucial link between the 'social' and the 'psychological' wings of the theory, forming a bridge between social structure and 'social reality' on the one hand, and the motivational impetus to seek or maintain a positive social identity on the other … People have to identify with the categories but they also have to feel that the social structure or social reality warrants the social claims implied in discrimination, ingroup bias, and other attempts to assert group identity. (2002, p. 338)

Although there are clearly circumstances in which outgroup favouritism occurs, Spears et al. (2002) warn that we should not always take apparent displays of outgroup favouritism at face value. They argue that sometimes displays of outgroup favouritism may be more the product of strategic considerations than internalized inferiority. Furthermore, the things that one can say, and the actions that one can take, about one's own or other groups are limited by the 'social realities' of the context in which they take place. Spears et al. argue that there are more 'social reality constraints' on the expression of positive attributes of low-status groups than high-status groups, which limit the ability of low-status group members to credibly engage in ingroup favouritism. For example, it is hard to make an argument that one's own group is more intelligent than an outgroup if educational and employment outcomes clearly favour the outgroup. However, ingroup favouritism may be more likely to occur in intragroup contexts, and may form an important basis for the development of the 'ideologies of resistance' emphasized by Van Dijk (1998).

Social identity theory thus holds out the hope that dominated and lowstatus groups can develop ideologies that will contest their domination and that may motivate efforts towards social change. However, it is strongly alert to the ways in which the ability of groups to develop and express such ideologies is constrained by the 'social reality' in which they exist.

Social Representations and Ideology

Given the breadth and scope of Moscovici's theory of social representations, a theoretical approach highly conducive to the study of ideology, it is somewhat surprising that few social representations researchers have concerned themselves with the contents and functions of ideological representations. This is surprising given the European origins of the theory: European social psychologists have not been as reluctant to move into explicitly political territory as their North American counterparts.

Ideological hegemony

Thus far we have adopted a definition of ideology that focuses on individual and group-based cognitions (such as values, beliefs and representations) that serve to maintain and legitimate the *status quo*. But system-serving beliefs and representations can have this effect only if they are widely shared and accepted within and between different groups in society. This brings us to consider Antonio Gramsci's writings on ideological hegemony and their application to contemporary discussions about the social cohesiveness of western liberal democracies. Gramsci's concept of hegemony has been used to understand the widespread perceived legitimacy and support western societies receive from the majority of their citizens. Hegemony refers to the ways in which:

> A certain way of life and thought is dominant, in which one concept of reality is diffused throughout society in all its institutional and private manifestations, informing with its spirit all taste, morality, customs, religious and political principles, and all social relations, particularly in their intellectual and moral connotation. (Williams, 1960, p. 587)

Although Gramsci's notion of hegemony is linked to that of ideology, Gramsci himself did not use the term ideology to refer to a hegemonic outlook.

Consistent with the Marxist definition of ideology at the time, ideology referred to distorted perceptions, mystification or false beliefs. However, if we define ideology as beliefs, representations, discourse, etc. which function to legitimate the existing social, political and economic relations of dominance within a society, irrespective of their 'truth' status (the definition we have preferred to give ideology), then Gramsci's notion of hegemony can be viewed as referring to a dominant and pervasive ideological outlook within a society. Indeed, many cultural analysts have used the Gramscian notion of hegemony in this way to understand the continual system support which characterizes contemporary western societies, and we shall do the same for the arguments that are to follow.

Within any society at any given time various conceptions of the world exist which are not structurally or culturally unified. The hegemonic process can be described as the way in which a particular 'world-view' or moral philosophical outlook diffuses throughout society, forming the basis of what is described as common-sense knowledge or 'objective truth'. Many factors influence what world-view becomes widely shared and dominant, one important factor being the ability of a philosophical outlook to 'make sense' of the structural organization of the society: the dominant social, political and economic relations.

Gramsci, however, was highly critical of simple economistic accounts of the development of a society's moral, political and cultural outlook. He emphasized the need to analyse all levels of society, in particular civil society where religious, moral and social patterns of perception emerged and proliferated. It is important to make clear, however, that Gramsci did not view hegemony as being imposed by force by the dominant classes. For Gramsci, hegemony is not achieved through coercion, but, rather, is freely consented to by the people. It is a philosophical and moral outlook that has won the 'hearts and minds of the people' (Bocock, 1986). Gramsci emphasized the common-sense nature of a hegemonic world-view, endowing it with an almost 'folklore' quality. Such an outlook becomes powerful and pervasive, Gramsci argued, because it is able to make sense of people's everyday lived experience and is intimately linked to the practices of everyday life. For Gramsci, common sense, the primary resource of human thought, is imbued with philosophy – all people are philosophers:

> It is essential to destroy the widespread prejudice that philosophy is a strange and difficult thing just because it is the specific intellectual activity of a particular category of specialists or of professional and systematic philosophers. It must first be shown that all men [and women] are philosophers, by defining the limits and characteristics of the 'spontaneous philosophy' which is proper to everybody. This philosophy is contained in: 1. language itself, which is a totality of determined notions and concepts and not just of words grammatically devoid of content; 2. 'Common sense' and 'good sense';

3. Popular religion and, therefore, also in the entire system of beliefs, superstition, opinions, ways of seeing things and acting, which are collectively bundled together under the name of 'folklore'. (1971, p. 323)

There are certain elements in Gramsci's writings on hegemony which have interesting parallels to Moscovici's theory of social representations. Both Gramsci and Moscovici emphasize the centrality of common sense in everyday thinking and in the understanding of social reality. Unlike theories within social cognition which stress the distortions, biases and errors in lay thinking, common sense is not viewed as an impoverished source of knowledge and ideas. It is imbued with moral, philosophical, cultural and political traces. Common sense in both theories is socially and historically contingent, subject to change given political and historical transformations. Furthermore, both Gramsci and Moscovici write about the dissemination of ideas and knowledge from the intellectual realm to the rest of society. There are strong similarities between Gramsci's interest in the way in which philosophical ideas articulated by intellectuals trickle their way down into the consciousness of the people, and Moscovici's descriptions of how scientific concepts which originate in the reified universe of science diffuse throughout the rest of society, contributing to the stock of common-sense knowledge which people draw upon to make sense of their social world. Gramsci referred to intellectual ideas and scientific knowledge, which becomes a part of everyday common sense as 'organic'. According to Gramsci, ideas and beliefs are organic in so far as they inform the practical consciousness of everyday life. As Billig and Sabucedo (1994) suggest, in many respects Gramsci seems a more suitable intellectual ancestor than Durkheim for social representations theory. This would give social representations theory a political emphasis by linking it to the study of hegemony more generally and ideology more specifically.

Discussions of ideological hegemony are also related to debates over the existence of a cohesive and totalizing 'dominant ideology' (Abercrombie, Hill & Turner, 1990). A crude version of hegemony has been used to explain almost anything, from the failure of Marxist predictions about the inevitable demise of capitalism, to the acceptance by the masses of capitalist relations of production. The working classes were seen to have failed to recognize their true economic and political interests; worse still, they had internalized the bourgeois values of their oppressors. Indeed, the German critical theorists such as Adorno, Horkheimer and Marcuse described the acquiescence of the working classes to capitalism as false consciousness (Agger, 1991). More recently, cultural and social theorists emphasize the extent to which contemporary western life is characterized by the conspicuous consumption of goods bought for their symbolic value (Baudrillard, 1983), a preoccupation which some argue undermines the development of critical political awareness (Lash & Urry, 1987).

There is little doubt that some analyses of ideological hegemony are overly simplistic and deterministic. Human agency and autonomy disappear and consciousness is determined and directed by powerful structural forces (Thompson, 1984). While Moscovici (1988) has referred to hegemonic representations, he rejects the view that everyone is always under the sway of a dominant ideology. This crude version fails to acknowledge the constructionist and reflexive capacities of people. Billig (1991; Billig et al., 1988) has also argued against this version of ideological domination which treats people as passive and gullible pawns, duped by an array of ideological managers and institutions which serve the interests of the dominant classes.

Indeed, Abercrombie et al. (1990) argue that there is little empirical evidence to suggest the existence of an uncritical acceptance of dominant ideas, values and representations among dominated groups. Rather, it is the ideological cohesion within dominant high-status groups and ideological disunity and fragmentation within subordinate groups which helps maintain the stability within liberal democracies. The cohesiveness of liberal democracy is due not to the internalization of legitimating societal values and beliefs among dominated groups, but to the everyday economic need of these groups to participate in the wage labour system central to capitalist economies. It is this behavioural compliance to the 'reality' of capitalism – to what Marx referred to as 'the dull compulsion of the economic' – which sustains and preserves the system (Abercrombie et al., 1990).

Notions of singular 'dominant ideologies' are also criticized on the grounds that they grossly oversimplify the complexity and multidimensionality of status relations between the myriad groups (which are themselves fluid and contextual) which comprise any society (e.g., Hall, 1989, 1996). While rejecting a complete reduction of social processes to economic factors, Hall retains a Marxist emphasis on the crucial role of economic relations in the production of social relations, arguing that changing economic practices and conditions (such as the decreasing demand for traditional blue-collar workers; the rise of the 'information economy'; the increasing casualization of labour), have produced new social and sub-cultural allegiances. As a consequence, traditional ideas about the relations within and between traditional class-based or ethnicity-based groups no longer hold.

Hall's discussion of the failure of traditional accounts of ideology to deal with the 'New Times' produced by the changing socio-economic conditions in western liberal democracies, echoes one of the central themes emphasized by postmodernist commentators in the last two decades: the increasing fragmentation and diversification of modern societies (Lyotard, 1984). The pluralism embodied in postmodernism renders the notion of a unified and coherent dominant ideology as unrepresentative of contemporary culture.

Similarly, Moscovici (1988) has argued that hegemonic representations are more difficult to locate in modern capitalist societies, and are more characteristic of small traditional societies.

Although postmodern accounts of western society have provided interesting and stimulating commentaries, emphasizing the increasing diversity and plurality of contemporary life, like Hall, we would argue that many of these analyses underestimate the unifying and legitimating features of certain representations and discourses. While ideology may be less important in contributing to the cohesiveness of liberal democracy than some have assumed, is it the case that it has no role to play at all?

Individualism and liberalism as social representations

While few empirical studies have found evidence of a dominant ideology in modern democracies, there is considerable evidence of the recurring prevalence of certain ways of making sense of the world. The liberal individualist conception of the person as the centre of cognition, action and process is one of these sense-making practices. Indeed, as we discussed in detail in Chapters 5 and 6, this conception of the person has been described as a pervasively shared representation which permeates all aspects of social life within western liberal democracies (Lukes, 1973). Linked to this conception of the person are individualist values of achievement and the preference for personal and individualistic explanations for achievement and social mobility over situational and contextual explanations. The development of a cultural emphasis upon individual achievement, the causes of which are primarily located within the individual, has been referred to by some theorists as 'possessive individualism' (Macpherson, 1962). Indeed, individualism has been described as the most pervasive ethos characterizing liberal democracies because it has the ability to make sense of the social conditions of a capitalist society. Individual merit and success are largely rewarded in such societies, and competition, which forms the cornerstone of economic relations, is heralded as the most effective and efficient means by which to motivate people in most spheres of social life.

As a dominant value orientation, individualism is an inherent feature of liberalism, the political creed around which most western capitalist democracies are structured. Stuart Hall (1986b) documents the historically dynamic development of liberalism within England since the 17th century. So responsive was liberalism to the changing historical and social circumstances in England that a number of variants of liberalism developed, ranging from the conservative to more progressive and reformist versions. Throughout the 20th century recurring experiences of economic crises seriously challenged the classic liberalist emphasis on *laissez-faire* capitalism. Liberalism embraced the necessity for social change by attempting to 'humanize' capitalism. This culminated in increased state intervention in the market economy and the development of the modern capitalist welfare state. Hall argues that liberalism managed to maintain its hegemony because of its ability to accommodate a range of political inflections. While social democratic parties have embraced the more reformist and progressive versions of liberalism which emphasize the need to redistribute wealth and protect the casualties of the system, conservative liberalism has continued to stress the importance of free competition and market economics in combination with the rhetoric of tradition and authority. Liberalism's remarkable flexibility has enabled it to become adopted by different political positions and to serve the interests of different social groups.

Despite the differences and contradictions between social democratic and conservative variants of liberalism, the two strands share a number of core concepts which are fundamental in identifying them as part of a particular ideological discourse. The liberalist conception of the world is premised on the 'sovereign individual'. Liberalism abstracts the individual from society. All individuals possess certain inalienable rights which are viewed to be consonant with the essential character of human nature. The freedom of individuals to maximize self-interest and to take part in social, political and religious activities of their own choosing is regarded as most important. The competition and struggle for material resources is viewed as an expression of a natural human drive. An open meritocracy in which individuals are free to compete and maximize self-interest is regarded as a 'natural' society. A market economy which allows all individuals to compete, sell and buy, accumulate wealth and improve their position in society is regarded as a 'natural' economy. Society and economy organized around market principles are seen to be consistent with the fundamentals of human nature. Indeed, as Fredric Jameson (1991) has argued, the proposition that 'the market is in human nature' has solidified and reified the market economy as an essentialist category.

Liberalism has been able to maintain its hegemony not only because it forms the basis of philosophical reasoning for many of the major political parties in liberal democracies, but also because it forms the basis of spontaneous everyday thinking by ordinary people. Hall documents the way in which components of philosophical liberalism have become widely diffused throughout English society, 'informing practical consciousness' and becoming an important component of English common sense:

> So much so that, to many of those who constantly think within its limits, it does not appear to be an ideology at all, but simply an obvious way of making sense of things – 'what everybody knows'. However, this 'obviousness' is itself a sign that the ideas do belong to a particular ideological configuration – they are obvious only because their

historical and philosophical roots and conditions have somehow been forgotten or suppressed. (1986b, p. 35)

While many social theories emphasize the way in which individuals are primarily social beings, and in some way constituted by society, liberalism abstracts and separates the individual from society. 'Liberalism thus played a role in constructing our prevailing common sense or "spontaneous awareness" of ourselves today as separate, isolable and self-sufficient beings' (Hall, 1986b, p. 41). This is best captured by Margaret Thatcher's infamous claim in the 1980s that 'there is no such thing as society', only individuals.

Thus far in this section, we have attempted to demonstrate the ways in which liberalism and individualism, as particular constructions of reality, have become diffused throughout society and contributed to the stock of common-sense knowledge and truth which people draw upon to make sense of the world. We are not suggesting that liberalism as an ideological outlook is embraced and articulated as a coherent belief system, but that salient and central components become expressed in fragmentary ways. Indeed, we suggest that many of the system-justifying and legitimating social psychological constructs that Jost and Banaji identify, such as stereotypes and just world beliefs, are underpinned by this moral-philosophical outlook. Such cognitive constructs and their system-rationalizing effects emerge from historically specific ideological currents – currents which make sense of and justify the existing patterns of social relations. Ideology is not a system of falsehoods and illusions promulgated by dominant groups, but as Mepham (1972, p. 17) suggests, is 'firmly grounded in the forms of our social life' and thus has a material reality.

Billig (1982, 1991) has argued that it is an oversimplification to characterize modern liberal democracies as individualistic, pointing out that both individualist and collectivist values coexist within contemporary capitalism. Hall also makes this clear in his historical account of variants of liberalism. Likewise, in the previous chapter we noted the research of Katz and Hass (1988) in the United States, which has demonstrated the coexistence of two largely independent value systems among the American public: humanitarianism-egalitarianism and the Protestant work ethic. While the former emphasizes the importance of political equality and social justice between individuals and groups, the latter stresses the importance of hard work, individual achievement, self-reliance and discipline. In practice, these two core values often lead to feelings of ambivalence towards marginalized groups such as African Americans and the poor. Concern for the welfare and justice of these groups is tempered by beliefs that individuals in such groups transgress cherished values such as hard work and self-reliance. This is based on the assumption that another person's lower social status within a society is a result of their own personal shortcomings and failures.

Despite the fragmentation rhetoric of postmodernism, we suggest that liberal individualism continues to exercise ideological constraints on the way people think, live and behave in contemporary societies. Indeed, as Johnson (1992a) argues, postmodernists may have exaggerated the decline of liberalism as a grand narrative within contemporary western society. For example, Lyotard's focus on the increasing plurality of discourses and fragmentation of consciousness fails to acknowledge the resurgent influence of New Right liberalism, or neo-liberalism as it is sometimes called. Neo-liberalism has been endorsed not only by the conservative Liberal-Coalition government in Australia since it came into power in 1996, but also by Tony Blair's 'New Labour' government in Britain. Johnson (1992b) argues that economic debates and policies within western democracies are still largely being shaped within the liberal continuum that Hall describes.

Grand meta-narratives like liberalism continue to have influence not only in political economy, but also in other domains. Patriarchy, positivist science and the domination of nature by technological progress are ideological discourses which also have a contemporary relevance. There is no doubt that perspectives that challenge and undermine these do exist. The feminist critique of contemporary society has clearly had a discernible impact at all levels of society, from the structural to the personal. Nevertheless, despite changes, women are still underrepresented at the highest levels of employment; and are still doing the bulk of the housework and parenting despite working full time. Although patriarchy has been significantly challenged, it remains largely intact. Moreover, while liberal feminism has successfully managed to gain a voice within some contemporary political debates, more radical feminist perspectives have been largely ignored and/or marginalized.

Discursive Psychology and Ideology

There is little doubt that contemporary social theorists who have concerned themselves with the study of ideology have come increasingly to regard language and discourse as *the* location of ideology. The traditional arena for ideology, consciousness, has been replaced by the study of everyday discourse, ranging from the mundane or everyday talk to more formal and institutional discourse. As we have shown throughout this book, the study of everyday discourse is being adopted enthusiastically by an increasing number of social psychologists. Potter and Wetherell's (1987) book *Discourse and Social Psychology* reflects the wider paradigmatic shift from the study of 'consciousness' or cognition, to the study of discourse. Thompson describes the emerging fascination with language thus:

> ... increasingly it has been realised that 'ideas' do not drift through the social world like clouds in a summer sky, occasionally divulging their contents with a clap of thunder

and a flash of light. Rather, ideas circulate in the social world as utterances, as expressions, as words which are spoken or inscribed. Hence to study ideology is, in some part and in some way, to study language in the social world. (1984, p. 2)

As with social representations theory, everyday communication (the 'unceasing babble' to which Moscovici refers) is viewed as fundamental in producing and transmitting meaning in social life. Language is the medium by which relations of power are communicated and relations of domination are created and sustained. From this perspective, ideology is no longer an idealized set of cognitive objects, but a range of socially situated discursive practices which have material effects and consequences (Eagleton, 1991).

Discourse and ideology

Within discursive psychology, ideology is linked to the ways in which discourse (text and talk) is used in specific contexts to produce specific meanings and versions of reality. The discursive study of ideology examines the processes by which particular versions of reality are constructed, rationalized, legitimated and endowed with the status of 'truth', and the means by which some versions come to dominate, while others are undermined and disempowered. It is primarily interested in the discursive practices or interpretative repertoires that people use to argue, debate, convince and justify their versions or accounts of the social world. Analytic inquiry focuses specifically on how particular representations of reality are put together, detailing the discursive resources (both linguistic and rhetorical) that are relied upon in any instance to build such representations. Moreover, critical discursive psychology links the analysis of text and talk to patterns of power and group interests in society at large, and asks questions about whose interests particular versions of the world serve, and what political and social consequences they have. While this approach to ideology has been seminal in poststructural and critical inquiry, it has attracted only a small number of researchers within social psychology itself.

Throughout this book we have presented examples of discursive research, which have primarily focused on social issues relating to 'race', gender and culture, demonstrating the ways in which discourse is used and put together by members of a language community to construct specific representations of such issues. Our primary emphasis has been to illustrate the *constitutive* nature of discourse (see Textbox 8.2). In our discussion of discursive approaches to social categorization, for example, we argued that traditional approaches to categorization (including both social cognition and social identity/self-categorization theory), rarely problematized social categories – treating them as reflecting social reality as it really is. In contrast we presented discursive work which demonstrates how categories in themselves are able to define and construct particular representations of reality. The categories that people deploy and mobilize in specific contexts are important because they communicate something of the 'taken-for-granted' meanings that people have of the world. These meanings are likely to differ between different social groups in society so that categories are contested by different groups with conflicting interests. Categorization then is not simply a perceptual and cognitive process, but an inherently political and ideological activity. Categories become the site of struggle between and within different interest groups in society (Thompson, 1984).

Textbox 8.2

Realism versus relativism

In this chapter and elsewhere, we have argued against equating ideology with false ideas or distorted knowledge and stereotypes as false beliefs (Augoustinos, 1999; Augoustinos & Walker, 1998). This issue is inextricably linked to the enduring debates over realism and relativism that have been played out within social psychology and indeed within critical discursive psychology. Many critical psychologists who subscribe to the view that knowledge and ideas are primarily socially constructed have also felt it necessary to not abandon realism altogether. One of the difficulties with a constructivist approach to reality is its inherent relativism. If there are no true and correct versions of reality, then how can we assess and evaluate the multiple constructions of reality that we come across? Some versions of reality are surely preferable to others, not only morally and politically, but, in some cases, epistemologically (see Eagleton, 1991). Surely, substantiating the truth or falsity of a statement, such as 'women are inferior to men,' is an important way to undermine oppressive and discriminatory views and practices.

Epistemological relativists like Wetherell and Potter, however, do not see any inherent dangers with a relativist approach. They argue:

> The refusal to privilege some types of account on epistemological grounds – relativism, as it is often called – should not be seen as a morally or politically vacuous stance, or as rhetorically ineffective. There is still the imperative to establish the claims of some version over others ... We do not, therefore see any contradiction between a view of discourse as constitutive and a view of discourse as ideological – where commitment to studying ideology is also a commitment to the critique of some positions, some of the ways in which power is exercised and some forms of argumentative practice. (1992, p. 69)

One provocative article by Edwards, Ashmore and Potter (1995), entitled 'Death and furniture: The rhetoric, politics, and theology of bottom line arguments against relativism', caused quite a storm when it first appeared. Read this article and work through some of its implications about making claims about 'reality'.

> **Textbox 8.2   (Continued)**
>
> Consider and discuss the following issues.
>
> - What kinds of devices, rhetorics and strategies can people use to bolster their claims about the nature of reality?
> - What do claims about reality allow speakers to do?
> - What consequences can such claims have?
> - Is it possible to argue for a particular position without resorting to claims about truth and reality?
> - What does a relativist epistemology make possible in understanding knowledge and social reality?
> - What new and creative ways of producing knowledge and understanding are enabled by a relativist epistemology?
> - What are the disadvantages associated with a relativist position?
> - Are realists, even critical realists, just plain morally and philosophically lazy?

Perhaps the most interesting insight that discursive psychology has shed on the everyday use of ideology is the flexible and even contradictory ways in which liberal and social reformist principles are combined in discourse to legitimate and justify existing power relations. For example, several of the studies we have presented demonstrate how participants speak approvingly of the principles of equal opportunity, but this is usually qualified by the use of a specific *liberal* definition of equality. Individuals must earn their way legitimately by participating competitively within the existing system of meritocracy. 'Everyone should be treated equally' is a pervasive self-sufficient rhetorical argument that is used to argue against reformist policies such as affirmative action (Augoustinos, Tuffin & Every, 2005). Respondents typically argue that past injustices which have resulted in inequitable outcomes should not be righted by such 'unfair' policies that transgress the liberal principle of treating everyone the same, and besides, the present generation should not bear the brunt of past historical mistakes. In the case of 'race' and culture, in particular, the solution to existing inequities is to progress towards a better and more integrated society where all groups are united under one 'national' identity (e.g., Augoustinos et al., 2002; Riley, 2002; Wetherell & Potter, 1992; Wetherell et al., 1987). Again here we are reminded of the inherent flexibility of liberalism, a philosophical outlook which can construct both an egalitarian version of reality and one which rationalizes, justifies and legitimates unequal and oppressive outcomes between groups.

Consistent with the discursive approach, Billig (1987, 1996) has argued that traditional social psychology has failed to study the argumentative nature of human thinking; more specifically, the everyday use of rhetoric to criticize, justify and persuade. Every person is a rhetorician of some sort. Arguing, criticizing, blaming, justifying, are all common features of everyday life. According to Billig, the study of rhetoric is linked to the study of common sense, for one of the most effective means by which to argue and persuade is to present one's viewpoint as 'common sense', 'natural' and 'obvious'. Moreover, for Billig, ideology is located in common sense itself, that which is taken for granted and which appears to be self-evident, natural and true. As for Gramsci and Moscovici, the stock of common sense from which people draw upon every day to understand the world is an important repository of knowledge and reasoning. It is not inferior knowledge and reasoning, as many psychologists have assumed, but it is historically contingent. Unlike the image of the naïve and limited thinker central to cognitive social psychology:

> The image of the subject in the rhetorical approach is very different. The rhetorical subject is a thinking and arguing subject. In this image, ideology, far from precluding thought, provides the resources for thinking in ordinary life and about ordinary life. Yet, in so doing, ideology can restrict the scope of thinking by setting the agenda for what is common-sensically thought and argued about. It is by adopting a historical and critical approach that this dimension of ideology can be examined, in order to see how its contingent history reaches down into the present micro-process of psychological thinking. In this sense, the rhetorical subject is subject to ideology, but not in a blind and unthinking manner. (Billig & Sabucedo, 1994, p. 128)

For Billig, ideology can also be located in the process of argumentation itself. The inconsistencies, contradictions, gaps in knowledge, what is said as opposed to what is never mentioned, are aspects of argumentation which reflect the parameters within which ideology operates.

Importantly, Billig and discursive psychologists have argued that ideological components of common sense are not articulated in a highly consistent and integrated way. In contrast to cognitive accounts which look for coherent and consistent traces of ideology in consciousness, discursive and rhetorical accounts emphasize the fragmentary, fluid and flexible nature of ideology. In *Ideological Dilemmas*, Billig et al. (1988) point to the ways in which people apply contradictory themes in different contexts. Such inconsistencies and contradictions highlight the inherent dilemmatic quality of ideological thinking. People do not necessarily accept values uncritically and without conscious deliberation. Contradictory themes such as individualism/collectivism are expressed and articulated in variable and flexible ways in everyday life. As Susan Condor (1990) points out, people may not simply endorse or reject dominant views, but, rather, develop complex configurations of thought in which some dominant ideological elements find expression in conjunction with individual and group-based understandings.

Ideology as material practices

In addition to cognition and discourse, ideology may be reflected in the material practices that constitute everyday life. Gramsci's notion of hegemony emphasized that ideology was not only a 'system of ideas' but also referred to 'lived, habitual social practices[s]' (Eagleton, 1991, p. 15): everyday practices and rituals realized through contemporary social institutions such as the family, schools, the legal and political systems. For example, everyday economic practices such as banking, working, selling and buying may all contribute to legitimating the existing relations of production. Participating in a competitive educational system legitimates meritocracy, while traditional labour arrangements in the home perpetuate and reinforce patriarchal relations. Hegemony may also be exercised in more obvious ways by the dissemination of certain values and ideas by the mass media. Althusser (1971) emphasized the materialist base of ideology, grounding it to practices within contemporary institutions such as the family, schools, legal, political and state structures. For Althusser, ideology 'is a particular organisation of signifying practices which goes to constitute human beings as social subjects, and which produces the lived relations by which such subjects are connected to the dominant relations of production in a society' (Eagleton, 1991, p. 18). While maintaining traces of economic determinism, Althusser argues that ideology does not simply reflect the nature of our 'lived relations', but that these lived relations themselves constitute our social identities. Ideology here is not just our beliefs, representations, discourses, but more like the behavioural and social practices that we engage in every day as we live out our lives. Moreover, Althusser suggests that our lived relations are largely unconscious and affective in nature. In this way ideology becomes a spontaneous, unconscious and affective way of responding to our lived relations, a way of being which has a strong affinity to the recent work on automaticity in social cognition. This reflects Althusser's rather determinist view that ideology is pervasive, inescapable, a view which, some would argue, underestimates the reflexive capacities of people to think and behave outside ideology.

In locating ideology in our behavioural and social practices, we need also to consider Foucault's view that relations of power and dominance are more likely to be maintained and perpetuated by the forms of our everyday micro-practices, rather than by our beliefs and cognitions (Fraser, 1989). Because the concept of ideology has often been associated with the Marxist notion of false consciousness, Foucault did not use the term 'ideology' in his analyses of modern power. Instead, he referred to dominant signifying and behavioural practices which sustained and legitimated relations of dominance as 'discourses' (Foucault, 1972). Indeed, it is this Foucauldian notion of 'discourse' that is adopted by many critical discursive psychologists, such as Ian Parker (2002), in their approach to the analysis of discourse (see Chapter 2). The conceptualization of ideology as constituting material rather than cognitive practices is also entirely consistent with discursive research which analyses the discursive resources and repertoires used in text and talk to construct and represent reality (see previous section). As forms of social practices, text and talk are material practices, and thus differentiating them from non-linguistic practices is not always productive (see Wetherell, 1999).

As we discussed in Chapter 2, Foucault (1972) was primarily interested in the ways in which certain disciplines of knowledge were constructed historically, and in how the expertise they conferred on their practitioners allows the exercise of power through knowledge. Foucault argued that those with recognized 'scientific' knowledge (particularly social science knowledge) exercise power by regulating the behaviour and subjectivities of individuals through the social practices they proscribe. Foucault's notion of power is not one of coercion or repression. He argues that modern power is achieved largely through the self-regulation and self-discipline of individuals to behave in ways which are largely consistent with dominant discourses about what it is to be human. These discourses shape and mould our subjectivities, the people we become. For example, dominant psychological discourses about the self for a large part of this century have extolled the virtues of logical, rational thought, cognitive order and consistency, emotional stability and affective control, moral integrity, independence and self-reliance. These humanist discourses are powerful in that they have contributed to the shaping of certain behavioural practices, modes of thought and institutional structures which function to produce people possessing these valued qualities. Moreover, institutions and practices have emerged which rehabilitate, treat and counsel those who fail to become rational, self-sufficient, capable and emotionally stable individuals. Thus, psychology, as a body of knowledge and a 'scientifically' legitimated discipline, shapes and prescribes what it is to be a healthy and well-adjusted individual (Rose, 1996).

Chapter Summary

We have argued in this chapter that there has been a dearth of social psychological work on the role and influence of ideology on what passes as everyday knowledge and practice, and the ways in which ideology shapes and structures social reality for the ordinary person. We adopted a specific definition of ideology which referred to beliefs, values, representations, discourses, interpretative repertoires and behavioural practices which contribute to the legitimation and reproduction of existing institutional arrangements, power and social relations within a society. Asymmetries of power are not only socio-economic in nature but are related also to gender, 'race' and ethnicity. The task for a social psychological theory of ideology is to understand the interface between social, economic and historic structural forces and the everyday functioning of individuals and groups. This can be contrasted with social cognitive theories which conceptualize thinking as primarily an individual phenomenon and also with some social theories which have the tendency to view people as being completely constituted and dominated by ideology. The study of ideology needs to be contextualized within a framework that sees the individual as being in a dialectical relationship with society, capable not only of reproducing the established social order but also of producing resistance and change.

The study of ideology, however, will require social psychologists to engage in wider debates about the nature of contemporary western culture and society. Critical theory, feminist social theory, and postmodernism are intellectual movements which may contribute usefully to the future development of a social psychological theory of ideology. Furthermore, any efforts to study ideology must avoid the functionalist trap of simply seeking to explain the stability and reproducibility of social systems. The dynamics of challenge and resistance – the situations in which dominant representations or discourses become undermined or overhauled – needs to become an integral conceptual and empirical focus for the study of ideology. In this way we can achieve Moscovici's vision of studying 'social life in the making' (1988, p. 219). We believe that social psychology's contribution to the study of ideology is perhaps its most difficult, but greatest, challenge. We hope that this challenge is taken up by the next generation of social psychologists.

Further Reading

Eagleton, T. (1991). *Ideology*. London: Verso.

Hall, S. (1996). The problem of ideology: Marxism without guarantees. In D. Morley & H. K. Chen (Eds.), *Stuart Hall: Critical dialogues in cultural studies*. London: Routledge.

Jost, J. T., & Major, B. (Eds.). (2001). *The psychology of legitimacy: Emerging perspectives on ideology, justice, and intergroup relations*. Cambridge: Cambridge University Press.

Van Dijk, T. A. (1998). *Ideology: A multidisciplinary approach*. London: Sage.

Part
Three

9 Conclusion

In this text, we have considered each of four foundational theoretical perspectives – the social cognitive, social identity, social representations, and discursive perspectives. We then described and critiqued how each of these perspectives addresses a series of topics – social perception, attitudes, attributions, self and identity, prejudice, and ideology. In doing so, and with the aim of identifying a path towards integration across these perspectives, we have endeavoured to highlight many points of commonality, as well as difference, among the perspectives.

We maintain the premise that a theoretically adequate social psychology must integrate the different positions afforded by the social cognitive, social identity, social representations, and discursive perspectives. We also assert that, currently, each of these perspectives is, in its own way, limited. These limitations may be conceptual, methodological, or epistemological. In terms of the politics of the academy, the social cognitive tradition is prime among the four perspectives. This approach dominates the mainstream journals and conferences, secures most of the available research funds and, in a way, defines the discipline by being the prototype of the category 'social psychology'. The other perspectives must each, in its own way, define itself in relation to this social cognitive mainstream. But even within the social cognitive mainstream there are significant voices of discontent. Gilbert (1998) articulates concerns about the intellectual limitations ensuing from social cognition's commitment to experimentation over other methods and its recent dalliance with cognitive neuroscience. An 'unrelenting passion for the tidy experimental paradigms' (Gilbert, 1998, p. 117) is not only a clear disappointment, but also a dead-end in terms of what it can contribute to a full understanding of what Gilbert calls personology. He also doubts that cognitive neuroscience is likely to be the 'level of analysis at which social psychology can make its most profound contribution' (p. 119). We agree and moreover lament that many social psychologists are heading down this reductionist path. It will be a sad day indeed when the Understandascope – which provides a rich and colourful kaleidoscope of our cognitive, cultural, discursive and ideological resources – is traded in for the fMRI machine. The use of functional magnetic resonance imaging to identify complex social phenomena in brain activity, such as stereotyping and prejudice, poses more questions than it answers.

Perhaps a little strangely, Gilbert (1998) takes us back to a future that was articulated half a century ago. Gustav Ichheiser was a contemporary of Fritz Heider, and, like Heider, was an Austrian Jew who fled wartime Europe to the safer climate of the United States. Ichheiser (1941, 1943, 1949) developed a sophisticated analysis of attribution, including specification of what Ross later called the fundamental attribution error. Whereas Heider developed an analysis of perception and attribution based on intra- and inter-individual processes, Ichheiser clearly saw attribution as an ideological process, depending on, and reproducing, the tenets of rampant individualism (see also Guilfoyle, 2000).

Returning to the point of integration across the four foundational perspectives, we suggest that there are at least three broad issues about which the four perspectives differ. We also suggest that these issues remain as intellectual challenges for the whole of social psychology, at least partly because none has been fully engaged with and resolved by the discipline. Unless and until social psychology resolves these issues, a fully integrated social psychology will remain elusive.

The Individual *and* Society

Social psychology is an interstitial discipline, existing between psychology and sociology. Writ large, psychology focuses its theoretical attention on the individual *qua* individual, abstracted from any social context. Psychology has only a superficial sense of the social and of 'society'. On the other hand, sociology writ large focuses its theoretical attention on society and its institutions, and has only a superficial sense of the individual. Harking back to the metaphor we tortured in Chapter 1, social psychology, as the bastard child of both psychology and sociology, ought to be ideally positioned to understand in a deep, rather than superficial, sense what it means to be a *social* individual. It doesn't.

The sense of *social* in social psychology is impoverished. Typically, the individual and the social are considered in abstract isolation and separation from one another. This is clear in Gordon Allport's famous, and still widely accepted, definition of social psychology as:

> The attempt to understand how the thought, feeling, and behavior of individuals are influenced by the actual, imagined, or implied presence of others. (1985, p. 3)

As we mentioned in Chapter 1, this definition disallows the possibility of the simultaneous constitution of the individual and the social. It forces a separation, arguably dialectic, between the individual and the social. This separation is often reproduced – for example, in a chapter on 'the social being in social psychology', Taylor (1998) persists with headings such as 'the individual in the cultural setting' and 'the individual in biological and evolutionary context'. It is useful, sometimes, to talk of individuals *in* settings and contexts, but conceptually the discipline needs to overcome this dichotomy, to find a way of theorizing the setting and the context *in* the individual as much as the other way round, and of not thinking that one can be construed outside of, or apart from, the other.

It is clear, we hope, from all the research discussed in this book, that the individual cannot be properly and fully understood in abstract isolation from the social. Even in social cognitive experiments on the automatic activation of stereotypes (e.g., Macrae et al., 1994), the social cannot be removed; it is always present in the goal orientations the participants bring to the judgement task in the experiment, in the gender or the race of the experimenter, in the relationship between the experimenter and the participant and in the institutional context of that relationship, and in the socially constructed meaning of the stimulus material (words, pictures of faces, etc.). Even in the most minimal of social groups constructed in the laboratory, the minimal group of Tajfel et al. (1971), the group has meaning because of the network of social relationships in which participants are inextricably implicated. This all goes beyond the 'imagined or implied presence of others' suggested by Allport's definition, to suggest that social psychology's understanding of 'sociality' is under-theorized. We suspect that significant theoretical mileage can be gained for the discipline by developing a more adequate understanding of 'sociality'.

Levels of Analysis

Many of the different studies we have considered throughout the book may seem to be unrelated, or at best only tangentially related, to one another. Part of the reason for this, we suggest, is that those different studies are articulated at the different levels of conceptual and empirical analysis identified by Doise (1986):

- intraindividual
- interindividual
- intergroup
- collective.

The four different foundational perspectives addressed in this book operate primarily at these different levels of analysis: the social cognitive perspective typically at the intraindividual level; the social identity perspective at the intergroup level; the social representations perspective at the intergroup and ideological levels; and the discursive perspective at the interindividual, inter-group, and ideological levels. Intraindividual analyses are anathema to social representations and to discursive researchers; intergroup and ideological analyses are anathema to social cognitive researchers. These differences, we suggest, do not *necessarily* connote fundamental incompatibilities, though. The task confronting an integrated social psychology is to articulate the inter-relationships in theory and research across different levels, rather than to assert by fiat that research at one or another level is inferior.

The experiments by Macrae et al. (1994) were formulated, conceptually and empirically, at the intraindividual level. The results say something about stereotyping and prejudice. In contrast, the work by Wetherell and Potter (1992) was formulated at the level of identifying shared discursive and ideo-logical resources and has strong overtones at the collective level. The results say something about stereotyping and prejudice. Although neither Macrae et al. nor Wetherell and Potter would consider the research by the other as terribly insightful, it is none the less the case that Macrae et al. produced interesting results that mean something. It is hard to see how they can just be dismissed as meaningless or totally irrelevant. Similarly, Wetherell and Potter produced interesting results that mean something. It is hard to see how they can just be dismissed as meaningless or totally irrelevant. The intellectual task facing the discipline is to develop an integrative framework which can accommodate, which can make sense of, the results of the research done by

Macrae et al. *and* by Wetherell and Potter. The discipline is a long way from such an articulated integration.

Realist v. Constructivist Epistemologies

All four perspectives share a common view of the object of their research and theorizing – namely, that humans actively construct their social environment. The perspectives differ in how they suggest humans do this. More fundamentally, they differ in how they understand their own construction of knowledge. The social cognitive and social identity perspectives, and to an extent the social representations perspective, too, rest on a realist philosophy of science which suggests that it is possible to build a theoretical knowledge of the world which resembles 'truth'. In other words, they assert that some theoretical accounts can be judged to be more or less 'true' than others. The discursive perspective does not accept that the veracity of different theoretical accounts can be assessed, and differences between different theoretical accounts arbitrated, by recourse to empirical data. Rather, one account prevails over another because of the vicissitudes of the social and political processes of negotiating shared understandings of the world, not because of its greater truth value.

This is a difficult issue with no simple answers. What is clear, though, is that social psychology cannot proceed without a more thorough and more adequate analysis of 'truth' and 'reality'. A major agenda for social psychology has always been trying to produce social change (see the next section), and that is largely shared across the four different perspectives. It is difficult to develop theory or research oriented to social change without a clear sense of what it is that is to be changed. It is also difficult to engage in the business of social change without having an account of which research is 'better'. It may well be the case that one theoretical or empirical account of a social issue prevails because of the social and political processes of negotiating shared understandings rather than because of the veracity of the data, but the data themselves are also an important part of the way in which understandings are negotiated.

Social Change

As a discipline, social psychology has always had a fairly strong liberal bent. This is evident in various ways. For example, the Society for the

Psychological Study of Social Issues (SPSSI) was established in 1936 as a society of psychologists dedicated to understanding social issues and implementing programmes for social change. SPSSI is still a vibrant, active, and international association. One of the most influential figures in the development of North American social psychology, and in the development of SPSSI, is Kurt Lewin. Lewin is famous for, among other things, developing the idea of action research. Such research involves social scientists tackling social problems as defined by community members, using social scientific knowledge, in a collaborative manner, designed to engineer desired social change, and with theoretical as well as practical gain. There is an explicit interplay between so-called 'pure', theoretically driven, research, on the one hand, and 'applied', problem-oriented research on the other.

A further way in which the liberal bent of social psychology can be witnessed is through the development of the subdiscipline of 'applied social psychology'. Textbooks in this area readily attest to the kind of social problems addressed by applied social psychologists – how to get people to litter less, use fewer natural resources, donate blood, be less bigoted, make better decisions when serving on juries, engage in safe sex practices, and so on.

When we think about the ways in which social psychology orients itself to the issue of producing social change, we see clearly that it has a set of aims which are politically liberal – no one does research on how to encourage consumption of natural resources, or how to be less tolerant. More subtly, no one does research explicitly on how to promote individualism, which may well have the same consequences for resource-consumption behaviour or for tolerance and intolerance. The goals of social psychology are clearly, unashamedly, liberal. To the extent that these goals are ever disputed within the discipline, it is to assert that they are not radical enough, and never that they should be replaced by a politically conservative set of goals.

Whenever social psychologists engage in applying their work to attempt to resolve some social issue, they must also accept an explicit value and political orientation. Even when they don't, when they engage in putatively basic, theoretical work, that work still has an implicit value and political orientation. Often, when left unacknowledged or unexamined, though, that orientation is conservative or regressive in its consequences.

The most telling example of the conservative consequences of the unacknowledged political nature of social psychological theorizing is the overwhelming emphasis on individualism within the discipline. As we suggested in Chapter 8, by focusing, for example, on the individual as the site of stereotyping, the discipline ignores broader, arguably more powerful, forces in the production of intergroup inequality. Because social psychology deals, by definition, with people and groups, and with the relationships between people and between groups, it is, necessarily and unavoidably, political. Indeed, we as authors of this book are not immune from such a statement. It applies to our research. It applies to our teaching. And it applies to this text.

Also, and somewhat paradoxically, research which explicitly claims to be politically oriented to social change can be conservative or reactionary in its (unintended) consequences. Intention is no guarantee of outcome. Some of the research in the discursive tradition perhaps can be seen in this light. Discursive psychology, more than most areas of psychology, is oriented to issues of social justice and change. However, in avoiding going beyond the text, in avoiding the reification of anything outside talk-in-interaction, there is a danger that we are left with no understanding of what it is that is to be changed, since 'it' lies outside of the interactional moment.

In writing this book we hope we have challenged you, the reader, whether you are a student or a colleague, not just by presenting some difficult material that takes some effort to understand, but also by confronting your own epistemological and political beliefs and assumptions. We have deliberately tried to change *you*; in doing so we have, of course, changed ourselves. The Understandascope is as much a mirror as a telescope.

'The philosophers have only interpreted the world, in various ways; the point is to change it.' (Marx, 1846, in Marx and Engels, 1846/1947)

Glossary

Information-processing model

A model which represents people as recipients and processors of information. Social experience and action are seen to be the result of the way in which new social information is perceived and assimilated with already existing information

Naïve scientist

Metaphor of the person actively trying to make sense of his or her surroundings by forming and testing hypotheses about the world

Cognitive miser

Metaphor of the person as a conserver of cognitive resources through the use of efficient, but not necessarily accurate, cognitive short cuts

Motivated tactician

Metaphor of social actors as having a range of information-processing strategies which are deployed flexibly and strategically according to their personal goals and situational requirements

Perceptual-cognitivism

An emphasis on the ways in which social information is perceived, encoded, stored and retrieved as a basis for social experience and social action

Mental representation

A mental object (such as a thought, belief, attitude) that refers to (represents) a real object (such as a person, concept, or object). The way in which objects are stored and acted on in the mind

Automaticity

Accessing or categorizing of information that occurs outside of conscious awareness and control

Controlled processes	Deliberate, conscious, strategic processing of information
Personal identity	The part of one's identity that is derived from individual experiences, characteristics and capacities
Social identity	The part of one's identity that is derived from the social groups and categories to which one belongs, together with the value attached to such groups
Interindividual behaviour	Behaviour that occurs between people who are are interacting on the basis of their personal identities
Intergroup behaviour	Behaviour that occurs between people who are interacting on the basis of their social identities
Minimal group	A group created in the laboratory that has no features other than membership
Social categorization	The process of identifying the self and/or others as members of a particular social category, emphasizing within-category similarities and between-category differences
Accentuation effect	An increase in perceived intercategory differences that follows categorization
Self-evaluation	Judgements made about the self by comparison with some standard (other people, personal goals, etc.)
Self-enhancement	The tendency to make comparisons that are favourable to the self
Intergroup social comparison	Comparison and evaluation of two (or more) social groups on some dimension

Intergroup differentiation	The perception of differences between groups. SIT and SCT argue that identifying as a member of a group motivates people to engage in intergroup differentiation
Superordinate level	In SCT this is the overarching level of categorization in which people think of themselves and other people as members of the same group (e.g. 'humankind')
Intermediate level	In SCT this is the group level of categorization in which people think of themselves and others in terms of their social identities (e.g., 'men' and 'women')
Subordinate level	In SCT this is the personal level of categorization in which people will think of themselves and others in terms of their personal identities
Depersonalized	In SCT, a state in which one's social identity takes over from one's personal identity
Self-stereotype	The application of the stereotype of one's group to one's self. Occurs in depersonalization
Social representations	Socially and culturally shared understandings of social objects that provide taken-for-granted, common-sense knowledge of the world
Anchoring	A process by which unfamiliar objects or concepts are understood in terms of their relations to existing social representations
Objectification	A process by which abstract ideas and concepts become associated with tangible, concrete instances which then come to represent them
Personification of knowledge	The linking of an idea or concept to a person or group, which then comes to represent it (e.g., Freud and psychoanalysis)

Figuration	The process by which an abstract concept is made memorable and accessible by association with a representative image
Ontologizing	The process by which a non-physical object is imbued with physical reality (e.g., the mind becomes understood as a material object)
Reified universe	The scientific world, in which expert knowledge is acquired through the controlled application of logical thought and scientific method
Consensual universe	The everyday world, in which expert knowledge has been transformed into common-sense social representations.
Figurative nucleus	The simplified and culturally accessible form to which complex ideas are reduced as they are transferred from the reified to the consensual universe
Central core	The defining elements of a social representation. Changes to the central core of a social representation involve changes to the representation itself
Periphery	The periphery of a social representation contains ideas, images and exemplars that enrich the representation, but that are not essential to its nature. Peripheral aspects of a social representation can change over time without affecting the central nature of the representation itself
Themata	Areas or themes around which elements of the central core of a social representation are contradictory or inconsistent

Realist epistemology

Approach to knowledge which argues that objects have a reality that is independent of their representation

Social constructionism

An approach to knowledge which regards all representations as being created through and contingent on socio-cultural meanings and practices. 'Knowledge' (or our understanding of 'what things are') is understood as a cultural product, and not a transparent representation of the things it allegedly represents

Discourse

Language in use, including text and talk

Talk-in-interaction

Analysis of talk is oriented to the interactional context in which it occurs. Usually refers to talk that is 'naturally occuring' (such as radio talk-back, everyday conversation, therapy session, etc.): that is, talk that is not produced for the purpose of being studied

Interpretive repertoires

Metaphors, arguments and terms that are often used together to describe particular kinds of events, actions or groups of people

Meta-contrast ratio

The ratio of between-group variance to within-group variance on a salient dimension. In SCT, the meta-contrast ratio determines the level at which categorization will occur

Prototypicality

The extent to which a particular category member displays the 'central tendency', or average, of the category members

References

Abelson, R. (1981). Psychological status of the script concept. *American Psychologist, 36*, 715–729.

Abercrombie, N., Hill, S., & Turner, B. S. (Eds.) (1990). *Dominant ideologies.* London: Unwin Hyman.

Aboud, F. (1988). *Children and prejudice.* Oxford: Blackwell.

Abrams, D., & Hogg, M. A. (1988). Comments on the motivational status of self-esteem in social identity and intergroup discrimination. *European Journal of Social Psychology, 18*, 317–334.

Abrams, D., & Hogg, M. A. (Eds.) (1990a). *Social identity theory: Constructive and critical advances.* Hemel Hempstead: Harvester Wheatsheaf.

Abrams, D., & Hogg, M. A. (1990b). The context of discourse: Let's not throw out the baby with the bathwater. *Philosophical Psychology, 3*, 219–225.

Abramson, L. Y., Seligman, M. E. P., & Teasdale, J. D. (1978). Learned helplessness in humans: Critique and reformulation. *Journal of Abnormal Psychology, 87*, 49–74.

Abric, J. (1976). *Jeux conflits et représentations sociales.* PhD thesis, Université de Provence.

Abric, J. C. (1984). A theoretical and experimental approach to the study of social representation. In R. M. Farr and S. Moscovici (Eds.), *Social representation* (pp. 169–183). Cambridge/Paris: Cambridge University Press/Maison des Sciences de l'Homme.

Abric, J. C. (1993). Central system, peripheral system: Their functions and roles in the dynamics of social representations. *Papers on Social Representations, 2*, 75–128.

Adams, H. E., Wright, L. W., & Lohr, B. A. (1996). Is homophobia associated with homosexual arousal? *Journal of Abnormal Psychology, 105*, 440–445.

Adorno, T. W., Frenkel-Brunswik, E., Levinson, D. J., & Sanford, R. N. (1950). *The authoritarian personality.* New York: Harper & Row.

Agger, B. (1991). Critical theory, poststructuralism and postmodernism: Their sociological relevance. *Annual Review of Sociology, 17*, 105–131.

Ajzen, I. (1988). *Attitudes, personality, and behavior.* Milton Keynes: Open University Press.

Ajzen, I. (1989). Attitude structure and behavior. In A. R. Pratkanis, S. J. Breckler and A. G. Greenwald (Eds.), *Attitude structure and function* (pp. 241–274). Hillsdale, NJ: Erlbaum.

Ajzen, I. (1991). The theory of planned behavior. *Organizational Behavior and Human Decision Processes, 50*, 1–33.

Ajzen, I., & Fishbein, M. (1980). *Understanding attitudes and predicting behavior.* Englewood Cliffs, NJ: Prentice Hall.

Ajzen, I., & Madden, T. J. (1986). Prediction of goal-directed behavior: Attitudes, intentions, and perceived behavioral control. *Journal of Experimental Social Psychology, 22*, 453–474.

Ajzen, I., Timko, C., & White, J. B. (1982). Self-monitoring and the attitude-behavior relation. *Journal of Personality and Social Psychology, 42,* 426–435.

Alcoff, L. M. (2003). Identities: Modern and postmodern. In L. M. Alcoff & E. Mendieta (Eds.), *Identities: Race, class, gender, and nationality* (pp. 1–8). Oxford: Blackwell.

Alexander, M. J., & Higgins, E. T. (1993). Emotional trade-offs: How social roles influence self-discrepancy effects. *Journal of Personality and Social Psychology, 65,* 1259–1269.

Allansdottir, A., Jovchelovitch, S., & Stathopoulou, A. (1993). Social representations: The versatility of a concept. *Papers on Social Representations, 2,* 3–10.

Allport, F. H. (1924). *Social psychology.* New York: Houghton Mifflin.

Allport, G. W. (1935). Attitudes. In C. Murchison (Ed.), *A handbook of social psychology* (pp. 798–844). Worcester, MA: Clark University Press.

Allport, G. W. (1943). The ego in contemporary psychology. *Psychological Review, 50,* 451–478.

Allport, G. W. (1954). *The nature of prejudice.* Reading, MA: Addison-Wesley.

Allport, G. W. (1985). The historical background of social psychology. In G. Lindzey & E. Aronson (Eds.), *Handbook of social psychology* (Vol. 1, 3rd ed., pp. 1–49). New York: Random House.

Altemeyer, R. W. (1981). *Right-wing authoritarianism.* Winnipeg, MB: University of Manitoba Press.

Altemeyer, R. W. (1988). *Enemies of freedom: Understanding right-wing authoritarianism.* San Francisco, CA: Jossey-Bass.

Altemeyer, R. W. (1996). *The authoritarian specter.* Cambridge, MA: Harvard University Press.

Altemeyer, R. W. (1998). The other authoritarian personality. *Advances in Experimental Social Psychology, 30,* 47–91.

Althusser, L. (1971). Ideology and ideological state apparatuses. In L. Althusser (Ed.), *Lenin and philosophy and other essays.* London: New Left Books.

Andersen, S. M., & Klatzky, R. L. (1987). Traits and social stereotypes: Levels of categorization in person perception. *Journal of Personality and Social Psychology, 53,* 235–246.

Andersen, S. M., Klatzky, R. L., & Murray, J. (1990). Traits and social stereotypes: Efficiency differences in social information processing. *Journal of Personality and Social Psychology, 59,* 192–201.

Anderson, C. A., & Lindsay, J. (1998). The development, perseverance and change of naïve theories. *Social Cognition, 16,* 8–30.

Antaki, C. (1985). Ordinary explanation in conversation: Causal structures and their defence. *European Journal of Social Psychology, 15,* 213–230.

Antaki, C. (1994). *Explaining and arguing: The social organization of accounts.* London: Sage.

Antaki, C., Condor, S., & Levine, M. (1996). Social identities in talk: Speakers' own orientations. *British Journal of Social Psychology, 35,* 473–492.

Antaki, C., & Widdicombe, S. (Eds.) (1998). *Identities in talk.* London: Sage.

Apostle, R. A., Glock, C. Y., Piazza, T., & Suelze, M. (1983). *The anatomy of racial attitudes.* Berkeley, CA: University of California Press.

Armitage, C. J., & Connor, M. (2001). Efficacy of the theory of planned behaviour: A meta-analytic review. *British Journal of Social Psychology, 40,* 471–499.

Aronson, E. (1968). Dissonance theory: Progress and problems. In R. P. Abelson, F. Aronson, W. J. McGuire, T. M. Newcomb, M. J. Rosenberg & P. H. Tannenbaum (Eds.), *Theories of cognitive consistency: A sourcebook* (pp. 5–27). Chicago, IL: Rand-McNally.

Aronson, E. (1989). Analysis, synthesis, and the treasuring of the old. *Personality and Social Psychology Bulletin, 15*, 508–512.

Aronson, E., Wilson, T. D., & Akert, R. M. (1994). *Social psychology: The heart and the mind*. New York: HarperCollins.

Au, T. K. (1986). A verb is worth a thousand words: The causes and consequences of interpersonal events implicit in language. *Journal of Memory and Language, 25*, 104–122.

Augoustinos, M. (1991). Consensual representations of the social structure in different age groups. *British Journal of Social Psychology, 30*, 193–205.

Augoustinos, M. (1993). The openness and closure of a concept: Reply to Allansdottir, Jovchelovitch & Stahopoulou. *Papers on Social Representations, 2*, 26–30.

Augoustinos, M. (1995). Social representations and ideology: Towards the study of ideological representations. In U. Flick and S. Moscovici (Eds.), *The psychology of the social: Language and social knowledge in social psychology* (pp. 200–217). Reinbek: Rowohlt.

Augoustinos, M. (1999). Ideology, false consciousness and psychology. *Theory and Psychology, 9*, 295–312.

Augoustinos, M. (2001). Social categorisation: Towards theoretical integration. In K. Deaux & G. Philogène (Eds.), *Representations of the social: Bridging theoretical traditions* (pp. 201–216). Oxford: Blackwell.

Augoustinos, M., Ahrens, C., & Innes, J. M. (1994). Stereotypes and prejudice: The Australian experience. *British Journal of Social Psychology, 33*, 125–41.

Augoustinos, M., LeCouteur, A. & Soyland, J. (2002). Self-sufficient arguments in political rhetoric: Constructing reconciliation and apologising to the Stolen Generations. *Discourse and Society, 13*, 105–142.

Augoustinos, M., & Quinn, C. (2003). Social categorization and attitudinal evaluations: Illegal immigrants, refugees or asylum seekers. *New Review of Social Psychology, 2*, 29–37.

Augoustinos, M. & Tuffin, K. & Every, D. (2005). New racism, meritocracy and individualism: Constraining affirmative action in education. *Discourse and Society, 16*, 315–40.

Augoustinos, M., Tuffin, K., & Rapley, M. (1999). Genocide or a failure to gel? Racism, history and nationalism in Australian talk. *Discourse and Society, 10*, 351–378.

Augoustinos, M., & Walker, I. (1995). *Social cognition: An integrated introduction*. London: Sage.

Augoustinos, M., & Walker, I. (1998). The construction of stereotypes within psychology: From social cognition to ideology. *Theory and Psychology, 8*, 629–652.

Austin, J. L. (1962). *How to do things with words*. Oxford: Oxford University Press.

Banaji, M. R., & Greenwald, A. G. (1994). Implicit stereotyping and prejudice. In M. P. Zanna and J. M. Olson (Eds.), *The psychology of prejudice: The Ontario symposium* (Vol. 7, pp. 55–76). Hillsdale, NJ: Erlbaum.

Bandura, A. (1989a). Human agency in social cognitive theory. *American Psychologist, 44*(9), 1175–1184.

Bandura, A. (1989b). Self-regulation of motivation and action through internal standards and goal systems. In L. A. Pervin (Ed.), *Goal concepts in personality and social psychology* (pp. 19–85). Hillsdale, NJ: Erlbaum.

Bargh, J. A. (1984). Automatic and conscious processing of social information. In R. S. Wyer, Jr and T. K. Srull (Eds.), *Handbook of social cognition* (Vol. 3, pp. 1–44). Hillsdale, NJ: Erlbaum.

Bargh, J. A. (1989). Conditional automaticity: Varieties of automatic influence in social perception and cognition. In J. S. Uleman and J. A. Bargh (Eds.), *Unintended thought* (pp. 3–51). New York: Guilford Press.

Bargh, J. A. (1994). The four horsemen of automaticity: Awarenesss, intention, efficiency, and control in social cognition. In R. S. Wyer, Jr and T. K. Srull (Eds.), *Handbook of social cognition* (Vol. 1, pp. 1–40). Hillsdale, NJ: Erlbaum.

Bargh, J. A. (1997). The automaticity of everyday life. In R. S. Wyer, Jr (Ed.), *Advances in social cognition* (Vol. 10, pp. 1–61). Mahwah, NJ: Erlbaum.

Bargh, J. A. (1999). The cognitive monster: The case against controllability of automatic stereotype effects. In S. Chaiken & Y. Trope (Eds.), *Dual process theories in social psychology* (pp. 361–382). New York: Guilford Press.

Bargh, J. A., Chaiken, S., Govender, R., & Pratto, F. (1992). The generality of the automatic attitude activation effect. *Journal of Personality and Social Psychology, 62,* 893–912.

Bargh, J. A., Chaiken, S., Raymond, P., & Hymes, C. (1996). The automatic evaluation effect: Unconditional automatic attitude activation with a pronunciation task. *Journal of Experimental Social Psychology, 32,* 104–128.

Bargh, J. A., & Chartrand, T. L. (1999). The unbearable automaticity of being. *American Psychologist, 54,* 462–479.

Bargh, J. A., Chen, M., & Burrows, L. (1996). Automaticity of social behaviour: Direct effects of trait construct and stereotype priming on action. *Journal of Personality and Social Psychology, 71,* 230–244.

Bartlett, F. (1932). *Remembering.* Cambridge: Cambridge University Press.

Baudrillard, J. (1983). *Simulations* (trans. P. Foss, P. Patton and P. Beitchman). New York: Semiotext(e).

Baumeister, R. F. (1998). The self. In D. Gilbert, S. T. Fiske & G. Lindzey (Eds.), *Handbook of social psychology* (Vol. 1, 4th ed., pp. 680–740). New York: McGraw-Hill.

Bell, D. (1960). *The end of ideology: On the exhaustion of political ideas in the fifties.* New York: Free Press of Glencoe.

Bem, D. (1967). Self-perception: An alternative interpretation of cognitive dissonance phenomena. *Psychological Review, 74,* 183–200.

Bem, D. (1970). *Beliefs, attitudes, and human affairs.* Belmont, CA: Brooks/Cole.

Bem, D. (1972). Self-perception theory. In L. Berkowitz (Ed.), *Advances in experimental social psychology* (Vol. 6, pp. 1–62). New York: Academic Press.

Bem, S. L. (1981). Gender schema theory: A cognitive account of sex typing. *Psychological Review, 88,* 354–64.

Bennett, W. L. (1977). The growth of knowledge in mass belief studies: An epistemological critique. *American Journal of Political Science, 21,* 465–500.

Bentler, P., and Speckart, G. (1979). Models of attitude–behavior relations. *Psychological Review, 86,* 452–64.

Berger, P. and Luckmann, T. (1967). *The social construction of reality: A treatise in the sociology of knowledge.* Chicago, IL: Aldine.

Bettencourt, B. A., Dorr, N., Charlton, K., & Hume, D. (2001). Status differences and intergroup bias: A meta-analytic examination of the effects of status stability, status legitimacy and group permeability. *Psychological Bulletin, 127,* 520–542.

Billig, M. (1976). *Social psychology and intergroup relations.* London: Academic Press.

Billig, M. (1982). *Ideology and social psychology.* Oxford: Blackwell.

Billig, M. (1987). *Arguing and thinking: A rhetorical approach to social psychology.* Cambridge: Cambridge University Press.

Billig, M. (1988). Social representation, objectification and anchoring: A rhetorical analysis. *Social Behaviour, 3,* 1–16.

Billig, M. (1991). *Ideology, rhetoric and opinions*. London: Sage.

Billig, M. (1995). *Banal nationalism*. London: Sage.

Billig, M. (1996). *Arguing and thinking*. Cambridge: Cambridge University Press.

Billig, M. (1999). Whose terms? Whose ordinariness? Rhetoric and ideology in conversation analysis. *Discourse and Society, 10*, 543–582.

Billig, M., Condor, S., Edwards, M., Middleton, D., & Radley, A. (1988). *Ideological dilemmas: A social psychology of everyday thinking*. London: Sage.

Billig, M. and Sabucedo, J. (1994). Rhetorical and ideological dimensions of common sense. In J. Siegfried (Ed.), *The status of common sense in psychology*. New York: Ablex.

Blair, I. V, & Banaji, M. R. (1996). Automatic and controlled processes in gender stereotyping. *Journal of Personality and Social Psychology, 70*, 1142–1163.

Blair, I. V., Ma, J. E., & Lenton, A. P. (2001). Imagining stereotypes away: The moderation of implicit stereotypes through mental imagery. *Journal of Personality and Social Psychology, 81*, 828–841.

Blommaert, J., & Verschueren, J. (1993). The rhetoric of tolerance or, what police officers are taught about migrants. *Journal of Intercultural Studies, 14*, 49–63.

Blommaert, J., & Verschueren, J. (1998). *Debating diversity: Analyzing the discourse of tolerance*. New York: Routledge.

Bobo, L. (1983). Whites' opposition to busing: Symbolic racism or realistic group conflict? *Journal of Personality and Social Psychology, 45*, 1196–1210.

Bocock, R. (1986). *Hegemony*. Chichester: Ellis Horwood.

Bodenhausen, G. V. (1988). Stereotypic biases in social decision making and memory: Testing process models of stereotype use. *Journal of Personality and Social Psychology, 55*, 726–737.

Bodenhausen, G. V., Kramer, G. P., & Susser, K. (1994). Happiness and stereotypic thinking in social judgment. *Journal of Personality and Social Psychology, 66*, 621–632.

Bodenhausen, G. V., & Macrae, C. N. (1998). Stereotype activation and inhibition. In R. S. Wyer, Jr (Ed.), *Stereotype activation and inhibition: Advances in social cognition* (Vol. 11, pp. 1–52). Mahwah, NJ: Erlbaum.

Boldero, J., & Francis, J. (2002). Goals, standards and the self: Reference values serving different functions. *Personality and Social Psychology Review, 6*, 232–241.

Bond, M. (1983). Cross-cultural studies of attribution. In M. Hewstone (Ed.), *Attribution theory: Social and functional extensions*. Oxford: Blackwell.

Bond, M., Leung, K., & Wan, K. C. (1982). How does cultural collectivism operate? The impact of task and maintenance on reward distribution. *Journal of Cross-Cultural Psychology, 13*, 186–200.

Bower, G. H., & Gilligan, S. G. (1979). Remembering information related to one's self. *Journal of Research in Personality, 13*, 420–432.

Bowlby, J. (1973). *Separation: Anxiety and anger* (Attachment and loss, Vol. 2). New York: Basic Books.

Branscombe, N. R., Ellemers, N., Spears, R., & Doosje, B. (1999). The context and content of social identity threat. In N. Ellemers, R. Spears & B. Doosje (Eds.), *Social identity: Context, commitment, content* (pp. 35–58). Oxford: Blackwell.

Breakwell, G., & Canter, D. (Eds.) (1993). *Empirical approaches to social representations*. Oxford: Oxford University Press.

Breakwell, G. M., & Millward, L. J. (1997). Sexual self-concept and sexual risk taking. *Journal of Adolescence, 20*, 29–41.

Breckler, S. J. (1984). Empirical validation of affect, behavior, and cognition as distinct components of attitude. *Journal of Personality and Social Psychology, 47,* 1191–1205.

Brewer, M. B. (1988). A dual process model of impression formation. In T. K. Srull and R. S. Wyer, Jr (Eds.), *Advances in social cognition* (Vol. 1, pp. 1–36). Hillsdale, NJ: Erlbaum.

Brewer, M. B. (1991). The social self: On being the same and different at the same time. *Personality and Social Psychology Bulletin, 17,* 475–482.

Brewer, M. B., & Brown, R. J. (1998). Intergroup relations. In D. T. Gilbert, S. T. Fiske and G. Lindzey (Eds.), *Handbook of social psychology* (Vol. 2, 4th ed., pp. 554–594). New York: McGraw Hill.

Brewer, M. B., & Campbell, D. T. (1976). *Ethnocentrism and intergroup attitudes: East African evidence.* New York: Halsted.

Brewer, M. B., Dull, V., & Lui, L. (1981). Perceptions of the elderly: Stereotypes as prototypes. *Journal of Personality and Social Psychology, 41,* 656–670.

Brewer, M. B., & Silver, M. (1978). Ingroup bias as a function of task characteristics. *European Journal of Social Psychology, 8,* 393–400.

Brewin, C. R. (1986). Internal attribution and self-esteem in depression: A theoretical note. *Cognitive Therapy and Research, 10,* 469–475.

Brown, J. D., Collins, R. L., Schmidt, G. W., & Brown, D. (1988). Self-esteem and direct versus indirect forms of self-enhancement. *Journal of Personality and Social Psychology, 55,* 445–453.

Brown, R. (1965). *Social psychology.* New York: Macmillan.

Brown, R. (1986). *Social psychology* (2nd ed.). New York: Macmillan.

Brown, R. J. (1988). *Group processes: Dynamics within and between groups.* Oxford: Blackwell.

Brown, R. J. (1995). *Prejudice: Its social psychology.* Oxford: Blackwell.

Brown, R. J. (2000). Social identity theory: Past achievements, current problems and future challenges. *European Journal of Social Psychology, 30,* 745–778.

Brown, R., & Fish, D. (1983). The psychological causality implicit in language. *Cognition, 14,* 237–273.

Bruner, J. S. (1957). On perceptual readiness. *Psychological Review, 64,* 257–263.

Bruner, J. S. (1958). Social psychology and perception. In E. E. Maccoby, T. M. Newcomb and E. L. Hartley (Eds.), *Readings in social psychology* (pp. 85–94). New York: Henry Holt.

Bruner, J. S., Goodnow, J. J., & Austin, G. (1956). *A study of thinking.* New York: Wiley.

Brunstein, J. C., Schultheiss, O. C., & Grassman, R. (1998). Personal goals and emotional well-being: The moderating role of motive dispositions. *Journal of Personality and Social Psychology, 75,* 494–508.

Burman, E. (1990). Differing with deconstruction: A feminist critique. In I. Parker & J. Shotter (Eds.), *Deconstructing social psychology* (pp. 208–220). London: Routledge.

Burman, E. (1991) What discourse is not. *Philosophical Psychology, 4,* 325–342.

Burnstein, E., & Vinokur, A., (1977). Persuasive argumentation and social comparison as determinants of attitude polarization. *Journal of Experimental Social Psychology, 13,* 537–560.

Bushman, B. J., & Baumeister, R. F. (1998). Threatened egotism, narcissism, self-esteem and direct and displaced aggression: Does self-love or self-hate lead to violence? *Journal of Personality and Social Psychology, 75,* 219–229.

Campbell, D. T. (1967). Stereotypes and the perception of group differences. *American Psychologist, 22,* 817–829.

Cano, I., Hopkins, N., & Islam, M. R. (1991). Memory for stereotype-related material – a replication study with real-life groups. *European Journal of Social Psychology, 21,* 349–357.

Cantor, N., & Kihlstrom, J. F. (1987). *Personality and Social Intelligence.* Englewood Cliffs, NJ: Prentice-Hall.

Cantor, N., & Mischel, W. (1977). Traits as prototypes: Effects on recognition memory. *Journal of Personality and Social Psychology, 35,* 38–48.

Cantor, N., & Mischel, W. (1979). Prototypes in person perception. *Advances in Experimental Social Psychology, 12,* 4–47.

Cantor, N., Norem, J., Langston, C., Zirkel, S., Fleeson, W., & Cook-Flannagan, C. (1991). Life tasks and daily life experience. *Journal of Personality, 59,* 425–451.

Cantor, N., Norem, J. K., Niedenthal, P. M., Langston, C. A., & Brower, A. M. (1987). Life tasks, self-concept ideals, and cognitive strategies in a life transition. *Journal of Personality and Social Psychology, 53,* 1178–1191.

Caplan, N., & Nelson, S. D. (1973). On being useful: The nature and consequences of psychological research on social problems. *American Psychologist, 28,* 199–211.

Cartwright, D. (1979). Contemporary social psychology in historical perspective. *Social Psychology Quarterly, 42,* 82–93.

Carver, C. S., & Scheier, M. F. (1981). *Attention and self-regulation: A control theory approach to human behavior.* New York: Springer-Verlag.

Carver, C. S., & Scheier, M. F. (1982). Control theory: A useful conceptual framework for personality-social, clinical and health psychology. *Psychological Bulletin, 92,* 111–135.

Carver, C. S., & Scheier, M. F. (1990). Origins and functions of positive and negative affect: A control-process view, *Psychological Review, 97,* 19–35.

Chaiken, S., & Bargh, J. A. (1993). Occurrence versus moderation of the automatic attitude activation effect: Reply to Fazio. *Journal of Personality and Social Psychology, 64,* 759–765.

Chaiken, S., & Trope, Y. (Eds.) (1999). *Dual-process theories in social psychology.* New York: Guilford Press.

Chamberlain, C. (1983). *Class consciousness in Australia.* Sydney: George Allen & Unwin.

Chen, M., & Bargh, J. A. (1997). Non-conscious behavioral confirmation processes: The self-fulfilling nature of automatically-activated stereotypes. *Journal of Experimental Social Psychology, 33,* 541–560.

Christie, R., & Jahoda, M. (Eds.) (1954). *Studies in the scope and method of the authoritarian personality.* Glencoe, IL: Free Press.

Clark, K. B., & Clark, M. P. (1947). Racial identification and preference in Negro children. In T. Newcomb and E. L. Hartley (Eds.), *Readings in social psychology* (pp. 169–178). New York: Holt.

Codol, J.-P. (1984). On the system of representations in an artificial social situation. In R. M. Farr and S. Moscovici (Eds.), *Social representations* (pp. 239–253). Cambridge/Paris: Cambridge University Press/Maison des Sciences de l'Homme.

Cohen, C. E. (1981). Person categories and social perception: Testing some boundaries of the processing effects of prior knowledge. *Journal of Personality and Social Psychology, 40,* 441–452.

Condor, S. (1988). 'Race stereotypes' and racist discourse. *Text, 8,* 69–89.

Condor, S. (1990). Social stereotypes and social identity. In D. Abrams and M. Hogg (Eds.), *Social identity theory: Constructive and critical advances* (pp. 230–249). Hemel Hempstead: Harvester Wheatsheaf.

Condor, S. (2000). Pride and prejudice: Identity management in English people's talk about 'this country'. *Discourse and Society, 11*, 175–205.

Converse, P. E. (1964). The nature of belief systems in mass publics. In D. E. Apter (Ed.), *Ideology and discontent* (pp. 206–261). New York: Free Press.

Conway, M. (1992). Developments and debates in the study of human memory. *The Psychologist, 5*, 439–461.

Cooley, C. H. (1902). *Human nature and the social order.* New York: Scribner's.

Costall, A., & Still, A. (Eds.) (1987). *Cognitive psychology in question.* Brighton: Harvester.

D'Agostino, P. R. (2000). The encoding and transfer of stereotype driven inferences. *Social Cognition, 18*, 281–291.

Darley, J. M., & Gross, P. H. (1983). A hypothesis-confirming bias in labeling effects. *Journal of Personality and Social Psychology, 44*, 20–33.

Dasgupta, N., & Greenwald, A. G. (2001). On the malleability of automatic attitudes: Combating automatic prejudice with images of admired and disliked individuals. *Journal of Personality and Social Psychology, 81*, 800–814.

Davies, B., & Harré, R. (1990). Positioning: The discursive production of selves. *Journal for the Theory of Social Behavior, 20*, 43–64.

Deaux, K. (1992). Personalizing identity and socializing self. In G. M. Breakwell (Ed.), *Social psychology of identity and the self-concept* (pp. 9–33). San Diego, CA: Surrey University Press.

Deaux, K. (1993). Reconstructing social identity. *Personality and Social Psychology Bulletin, 19*, 4–14.

Deaux, K., & Emswiller, T. (1974). Explanations of successful performance on sex-linked tasks: What is skill for the male is luck for the female. *Journal of Personality and Social Psychology, 29*, 80–85.

Deaux, K., & Philogène, G. (Eds.) (2001). *Representations of the social: Bridging theoretical traditions.* Oxford: Blackwell.

Deaux, K., Reid, A., Mizrahi, K., & Ethier, K. A. (1995). Parameters of social identity. *Journal of Personality and Social Psychology, 68*, 280–291.

de Rosa, A. S. (1987). The social representations of mental illness in children and adults. In W. Doise and S. Moscovici (Eds.), *Current issues in European social psychology* (Vol. 2, pp. 47–138). Cambridge/Paris: Cambridge University Press/Editions de la Maison des Sciences de l'Homme.

Devine, P. G. (1989a). Stereotypes and prejudice: Their automatic and controlled components. *Journal of Personality and Social Psychology, 56*, 5–18.

Devine, P. G. (1989b). Automatic and controlled processes in prejudice: The role of stereotypes and personal beliefs. In A. R. Pratkanis, S. J. Breckler and A. G. Greenwald (Eds.), *Attitude structure and function* (pp. 181–212). Hillsdale, NJ: Erlbaum.

Devine, P. G. (2001). Implicit prejudice and stereotyping: How automatic are they? Introduction to the special section. *Journal of Personality and Social Psychology, 81*, 757–759.

Devine, P. G., & Ostrom, T. M. (1988). Dimensional versus information-processing approaches to social knowledge: The case of inconsistency management. In D. Bar-Tal and A. W. Kruglanski (Eds.) *The social psychology of knowledge* (pp. 231–261). Cambridge: Cambridge University Press.

Dijksterhuis, A., & van Knippenberg, A. (1998). The relation between perception and behavior or how to win a game of Trivial Pursuit. *Journal of Personality and Social Psychology, 74*, 865–877.

Doise, W. (1978). *Individuals and groups: Explanations in social psychology*. Cambridge: Cambridge University Press.

Doise, W. (1986). *Levels of explanation in social psychology*. Cambridge: Cambridge University Press.

Doise, W. (2001). Human rights studied as normative social representations. In K. Deaux & G. Philogène (Eds.), *Representations of the social: Bridging theoretical traditions* (pp. 96–112). Oxford: Blackwell.

Doise, W., Clemence, A., & Lorenzi-Cioldi, F. (1993). *The quantitative analysis of social representations*. Hemel Hempstead: Harvester Wheatsheaf.

Doise, W., Deschamps, J. C., & Meyer, G. (1978). The accentuation of intracategory similarities. In H. Tajfel (Ed.), *Differentiation between social groups* (pp. 159–168). London: Academic Press.

Doise, W., & Sinclair, A. (1973). The categorization process in intergroup relations. *European Journal of Social Psychology, 3*, 145–187.

Doise, W., Spini, D., & Clemence, A. (1999). Human rights studied as social representations in a cross-national context. *European Journal of Social Psychology, 29*, 1–29.

Donaghue, N. (1999). *Dynamic self-discrepancies*. Unpublished doctoral thesis, University of Melbourne, Victoria.

Donaghue, N., & Fallon, B. J. (2003). Gender role self-stereotyping and the relationship between equity and satisfaction in close relationships. *Sex Roles, 48*, 217–230.

Donaghue, N., & Ho, W. (2005). Cultural differences in the pursuit of ideal and ought goals: Comparing nationality and self-construal as moderators of subjective well-being. Manuscript submitted for publication.

Doosje, B., & Ellemers, N. (1997). Stereotyping under threat: The role of group identification. In R. Spears, P. J. Oakes, N. Ellemers and S. A. Hasam (Eds.), *The social psychology of stereotyping and group life* (pp. 257–272). Oxford: Blackwell.

Dornbusch, S. M. (1987). Individual moral choices and social evaluations: A research odyssey. *Advances in Group Processes, 4*, 271–307.

Dovidio, J. F., Brigham, J. C., Johnson, B. T., & Gaertner, S. L. (1996). Stereotyping, prejudice, and discrimination: Another look. In C. N. Macrae, C. Stangor, & M. Hewstone (Eds.), *Stereotypes and stereotyping* (pp. 276–319). New York: Guilford Press.

Dovidio, J. F., Evans, N., & Tyler, R. (1986). Racial stereotypes: The contents of their cognitive representations. *Journal of Experimental Social Psychology, 22*, 22–37.

Dovidio, J. F., & Gaertner, S. L. (Eds.) (1986). *Prejudice, discrimination, and racism*. New York: Academic Press.

Dovidio, J. F., Kawakami, K., & Gaertner, S. L. (2002). Implicit and explicit prejudice and interracial interaction. *Journal of Personality and Social Psychology, 82*, 62–68.

Dovidio, J. F., Kawakami, K., Johnson, C., Johnson, B., & Howard, A. (1997). On the nature of prejudice: Automatic and controlled process. *Journal of Experimental Social Psychology, 33*, 514–540.

Drew, P., & Holt, E. (1989). Complainable matters: The use of idiomatic expressions in making complaints. *Social Problems, 35*, 398–417.

Duckitt, J. (1988). Normative conformity and racial prejudice in South Africa. *Genetic, Social, and General Psychology Monographs, 114*, 413–437.

Duckitt, J. (1991). The development and validation of a modern racism scale in South Africa. *South African Journal of Psychology, 21*, 23–39.

Duckitt, J. (1992). *The social psychology of prejudice*. New York: Praeger.

Duckitt, J. (2001). A dual-process cognitive-motivational theory of ideology and prejudice. In M. P. Zanna (Ed.), *Advances in experimental social psychology* (Vol. 33, pp. 41–113). San Diego, CA: Academic Press.

Durant, J., Bauer, M. W., & Gaskell, G. (1998). *Biotechnology in the public sphere: A European sourcebook.* London: Science Museum Publications.

Durkheim, E. (1898). Représentations individuelles et représentations collectives. *Revue de Metaphysique et de Morale, VI,* 273–302.

Duval, S., & Wicklund, R. A. (1973). Effects of objective self-awareness on attributions of causality. *Journal of Experimental Social Psychology, 9,* 17–31.

Duveen, G., & de Rosa, A. S. (1992). Social representations and the genesis of social knowledge. *Papers on Social Representations, 1,* 94–108.

Duveen, G., & Lloyd, B. (Eds.) (1990). *Social representations and the development of knowledge.* Cambridge: Cambridge University Press.

Eagleton, T. (1991). *Ideology.* London: Verso.

Eagly, A. H., & Chaiken, S. (1993). *The psychology of attitudes.* Fort Worth, TX: Harcourt Brace Jovanovich.

Eagly, A. H., & Chaiken, S. (1998). Attitude structure and function. In D. T. Gilbert, S. T. Fiske & G. Lindzey (Eds.), *Handbook of social psychology* (4th ed., pp. 269–322). New York: McGraw-Hill.

Edley, N. (2001). Unravelling social constructionism. *Theory and Psychology, 11,* 433–441.

Edley, N., & Wetherell, M. (1995). Imagined futures: Young men's talk about fatherhood and domestic life. *British Journal of Social Psychology, 38,* 181–194.

Edwards, D. (1991). Categories are for talking: On the cognitive and discursive bases of categorization. *Theory and Psychology, 1,* 515–542.

Edwards, D. (1997). *Discourse and cognition.* London: Sage.

Edwards, D., Ashmore, M., & Potter, J. (1995). Death and furniture: The rhetoric, politics, and theology of bottom line arguments against relativism. *History of the Human Sciences, 8,* 25–49.

Edwards, D., & Potter, J. (1992). *Discursive psychology.* London: Sage.

Edwards, D., & Potter, J. (1993). Language and causation: A discursive action model of description and attribution. *Psychological Review, 100,* 230–241.

Eiser, J. R. (1994). *Attitudes, chaos, and the connectionist mind.* Oxford: Blackwell.

Ellemers, N. (1993). The influence of socio-cultural variables on identity management strategies. *European Review of Social Psychology, 4,* 27–57.

Ellemers, N., Spears, R., & Doosje, B. (2002). Self and social identity. *Annual Review of Psychology, 53,* 161–186.

Elms, A. C. (1975). The crisis of confidence in social psychology. *American Psychologist, 30,* 967–976.

Emler, N., Ohana, J., & Dickinson, J. (1990). Children's representations of social relations. In G. Duveen and B. Lloyd (Eds.), *Social representation and the development of knowledge* (pp. 47–69). Cambridge: Cambridge University Press.

Emmons, R. A. (1986). Personal strivings: An approach to personality and subjective well-being. *Journal of Personality and Social Psychology, 51,* 1058–1068.

Emmons, R. A. (1996). Striving and feeling: Personal goals and subjective well-being. In J. A. Bargh and P. M. Gollwitzer (Eds.), *The psychology of action: Linking motivation and cognition to behavior* (pp. 314–337). New York: Guilford Press.

Erdley, C. A., & D'Agostino, P. R. (1988). Cognitive and affective components of automatic priming effects. *Journal of Personality and Social Psychology, 54,* 741–747.

Erikson, R. S., Luttbeg, N. R., & Tedin, K. L. (1980). *American public opinion: Its origins, content, and impact* (2nd ed.). New York: Wiley.

Essed, P. (1991a). Knowledge and resistance: Black women talk about racism in the Netherlands and the USA. *Feminism & Psychology, 1*, 201–219.

Essed, P. (1991b). *Understanding everyday racism: An interdisciplinary theory* (Sage series on race and ethnic relations, Vol. 2). Thousand Oaks, CA: Sage.

Etaugh, C., & Brown, B. C. (1975). Perceiving the causes of success and failure of male and female performers. *Developmental Psychology, 11*, 103.

Exline, J. J. & Lobel, M. (1999). The perils of outperformance: Sensitivity about being the target of a threatening upward comparison. *Psychological Bulletin, 125*, 307–337.

Eysenck, H. J. (1975). The structure of social attitudes. *British Journal of Social and Clinical Psychology, 14*, 323–331.

Eysenck, H. J., & Wilson, G. D. (Eds.) (1978). *The psychological basis of ideology.* Lancaster: MTP Press.

Farr, R. (1989). The social and collective nature of representations. In J. Forgas and J. M. Innes (Eds.), *Recent advances in social psychology: An international perspective* (pp. 157–166). North Holland: Elsevier.

Farr, R. (1990). Social representations as widespread beliefs. In C. Fraser and G. Gaskell (Eds.), *The social psychological study of widespread beliefs.* Oxford: Clarendon Press.

Farr, R. M. (1996). *The roots of modern social psychology 1872–1954.* Oxford: Blackwell.

Farr, R., & Anderson, A. (1983). Beyond actor/observer differences in perspective: Extensions and applications. In M. Hewstone (Ed.), *Attribution theory: Social and functional extensions* (pp. 45–64). Oxford: Blackwell.

Fazio, R. H. (1989). On the power and functionality of attitudes: The role of attitude accessibility. In A. R. Pratkanis, S. J. Breckler and A. G. Greenwald (Eds.), *Attitude structure and function* (pp. 153–179). Hillsdale, NJ: Erlbaum.

Fazio, R. H. (1993). Variability in the likelihood of automatic attitude activation: Data reanalysis and commentary on Bargh, Chaiken, Govender, and Pratto (1992). *Journal of Personality and Social Psychology, 64*, 753–758.

Fazio, R. H., & Olson, M. A. (2003). Attitudes: Foundations, functions, and consequences. In M. A. Hoff and J. Cooper (Eds.), *The Sage handbook of social psychology* (pp. 139–160). London: Sage.

Fazio, R. H., & Olson, M. A. (2003). Implicit measures in social cognition: Their meaning and uses. *Annual Review of Psychology, 54*, 297–327.

Fazio, R. H., Sanbonmatsu, D. M., Powell, M. C., & Kardes, F. R. (1986). On the automatic activation of attitudes. *Journal of Personality and Social Psychology, 50*, 229–238.

Fazio, R. H., & Williams, C. J. (1986). Attitude accessibility as a moderator of the attitude–perception and attitude–behavior relations: An investigation of the 1984 presidential election. *Journal of Personality and Social Psychology, 51*, 505–544.

Fazio, R. H., & Zanna, M. P. (1978a). Attitudinal qualities relating to the strength of the attitude–behavior relationship. *Journal of Experimental Social Psychology*, 393–408.

Fazio, R. H., & Zanna, M. P. (1978b). On the predictive validity of attitudes: The roles of direct experience and confidence. *Journal of Personality, 46*, 223–243.

Fazio, R. H., & Zanna, M. P. (1981). Direct experience and attitude–behavior consistency. In L. Berkowitz (Ed.), *Advances in experimental social psychology* (Vol. 14, pp. 161–202). New York: Academic Press.

Fazio, R. H., Zanna, M. P., & Cooper, J. (1977). Dissonance and self-perception: An integrative review of each theory's proper domain of application. *Journal of Experimental Social Psychology, 13*, 464–479.

Feagin, J. R. (1972). Poverty: We still believe that God helps those who help themselves. *Psychology Today, 6*, 101–129.

Feather, N. T. (1978). Reactions to male and female success and failure at sex-linked occupations: Effects of sex and socio-economic status of respondents. *Australian Journal of Psychology, 30*, 21–40.

Feather, N. T. (1985). Attitudes, values and attributions: Explanations of unemployment. *Journal of Personality and Social Psychology, 98*, 876–889.

Feather, N. T., & Simon, J. G. (1975). Reactions to male and female success and failure in sex-linked occupations: Impressions of personality, causal attributions, and perceived likelihood of different consequences. *Journal of Personality and Social Psychology, 31*, 20–31.

Feldman-Summers, S., & Kiesler, S. B. (1974). Those who are number two try harder: The effects of sex on attributions of causality. *Journal of Personality and Social Psychology, 30*, 864–855.

Ferguson, L. (1973). Primary social attitudes of the 1960s and those of the 1930s. *Psychological Reports, 33*, 655–664.

Festinger, L. (1950). Informal social communication. *Psychological Review, 57*, 271–282.

Festinger, L. (1954). A theory of social comparison processes. *Human Relations, 7*, 117–140.

Festinger, L. (1957). *A theory of cognitive dissonance.* Stanford, CA: Stanford University Press.

Fishbein, M., & Ajzen, I. (1975). *Belief, attitude, intention, and behavior: An introduction to theory and research.* Reading, MA: Addison-Wesley.

Fiske, S. T. (1982). Schema-triggered affect: Applications to social perception. In M. S. Clark and S. T. Fiske (Eds.), *Affect and cognition: The 17th Annual Carnegie Symposium on Cognition* (pp. 56–78). Hillsdale, NJ: Erlbaum.

Fiske, S. T. (1992). Thinking is for doing: Portraits of social cognition from Daguerreotypes to Laserphoto. *Journal of Personality and Social Psychology, 63*, 877–839.

Fiske, S. T. (1998). Stereotyping, prejudice, and discrimination. In D. T. Gilbert, S. T. Fiske & G. Lindzey (Eds.), *Handbook of social psychology* (Vol. 2, 4th ed., pp. 357–411). New York: McGraw-Hill.

Fiske, S. T. (1999). Preface. In J.-M. Monteil & P. Huguet, *Social context and cognitive performance: Towards a social psychology of cognition* (p. v). Hove, East Sussex: Taylor & Francis.

Fiske, S. T. (2004). *Social beings: A core motives approach to social psychology.* New York: Wiley.

Fiske, S. T., & Dyer, L. M. (1985). Structure and development of social schemata: Evidence from positive and negative transfer effects. *Journal of Personality and Social Psychology, 48*, 839–852.

Fiske, S. T., Kinder, D. R., & Larter, W. M. (1983). The novice and the expert: Knowledge-based strategies in political cognition. *Journal of Experimental Social Psychology, 19*, 381–400.

Fiske, S. T., Lin, M., & Neuberg, S. L. (1999). The continuum model: Ten years on. In S. Chaiken & Y. Trope (Eds.), *Dual-process theories in social psychology* (pp. 231–254). New York: Guilford Press.

Fiske, S. T., & Neuberg, S. L. (1990). A continuum of impression formation, from category-based to individuating processes: Influences of information and motivation on attention and interpretation. In M. P. Zanna (Ed.), *Advances in experimental social psychology* (Vol. 23, pp. 1–74). New York: Academic Press.

Fiske, S. T., & Pavelchak, M. (1986). Category-based versus piecemeal-based affective responses: Developments in schema-triggered affect. In R. M. Sorrentino & E. T. Higgins (Eds.), *Handbook of motivation and cognition: Foundations of social behavior* (pp. 167–203). New York: Guilford Press.

Fiske, S. T., & Taylor, S. E. (1984). *Social cognition.* Reading, MA: Addison-Wesley.

Fiske, S. T., & Taylor, S. E. (1991). *Social cognition* (2nd ed.). New York: McGraw-Hill.

Fleming, D. (1967). Attitude: The history of a concept. In D. Fleming and B. Bailyn (Eds.), *Perspectives in American history* (Vol. 1, pp. 285–365). Cambridge, MA: Charles Warren Center for Studies in American History.

Fletcher, G. J. O., & Ward, C. (1988). Attribution theory and processes: A cross-cultural perspective. In M. H. Bond (Ed.), *The cross-cultural challenge to social psychology* (pp. 230–244). Newbury Park, CA: Sage.

Forsterling, F. (1985). Attributional retraining: A review. *Psychological Bulletin, 3,* 495–512.

Forsterling, F. (2001). *Attribution: An introduction to theories, research and applications.* London: Psychology Press.

Foucault, M. (1970). *The order of things: An archeology of the human sciences.* London: Tavistock.

Foucault, M. (1972). *The archeology of knowledge.* London: Tavistock.

Foucault, M. (1977). *Discipline and punish: The birth of the prison* (trans. A. M. SheridanSmith). London: Allen Lane.

Foucault, M. (1980). *Power/knowledge: Selected interviews and other writings 1972–77* (trans. C. Gordon). Hemel Hempstead: Harvester Wheatsheaf.

Foucault, M. (1986). *History of sexuality, Vol. 3: The care of the self.* New York: Random House.

Foucault, M. (1988). Technologies of the self. In L. H. Martin & P. Hutton (Eds.), *Technologies of the self: A seminar with Michel Foucault* (pp. 16–49). Amherst, MA: University of Massachusetts Press.

Fraser, C., & Gaskell, G. (Eds.) (1990). *The social psychological study of widespread beliefs.* Oxford: Clarendon Press.

Fraser, N. (1989). *Unruly practices: Power, discourse and gender in contemporary social theory.* Minneapolis, MN: University of Minnesota Press.

Freud, S. (1925). *Collected Papers.* London: Hogarth.

Fukuyama, F. (1992). *The end of history and the last man.* London: Hamish Hamilton.

Furnham, A. (1982a). Why are the poor always with us? Explanations for poverty in Britain. *British Journal of Social Psychology, 21,* 311–322.

Furnham, A. (1982b). Explanations for unemployment in Britain. *European Journal of Social Psychology, 12,* 335–352.

Furnham, A. (1982c). The perception of poverty amongst adolescents. *Journal of Adolescence, 5,* 135–147.

Gaertner, S. L., & Dovidio, J. F. (1977). The subtlety of white racism, arousal and helping behavior. *Journal of Personality and Social Psychology, 35,* 691–707.

Gaertner, S. L., & Dovidio, J. (1986). The aversive form of racism. In J. Dovidio & S. L. Gaertner (Eds.), *Prejudice, discrimination and racism* (pp. 61–89). New York: Academic Press.

Gaertner, S. L., & McLaughlin, J. P. (1983). Racial stereotypes: Associations and ascriptions of positive and negative characteristics. *Social Psychology Quarterly, 46,* 23–40.

Garland, H., & Price, K. H. (1977). Attitudes towards women in management and attributions for their success and failure in a managerial position. *Journal of Applied Psychology, 62,* 29–33.

Gartrell, C. D. (2002). The embeddedness of social comparisons. In I. Walker & H. J. Smith (Eds.), *Relative deprivation: Specification, development, integration* (pp. 164–184). New York: Cambridge University Press.

Gaskell, G. (2001). Attitudes, social representations, and beyond. In K. Deaux and G. Philogène (Eds.), *Representations of the social: Bridging theoretical traditions* (pp. 228–241). Oxford: Blackwell.

Gaskell, G., & Fraser, C. (1990). The social psychological study of widespread beliefs. In C. Fraser and G. Gaskell (Eds.), *The social psychological study of widespread beliefs* (pp. 3–24). Oxford: Clarendon Press.

Geertz, C. (1975). On the nature of anthropological understanding. *American Scientist, 63,* 47–53.

Gergen, K. J. (1965). Interaction goals and personalistic feedback as factors affecting the presentations of self. *Journal of Personality and Social Psychology, 1,* 413–424.

Gergen, K. J. (1967). Multiple identity: The healthy, happy human being wears many masks. *Psychology Today, 5,* 15–39.

Gergen, K. J. (1973). Social psychology as history. *Journal of Personality and Social Psychology, 26,* 309–320.

Gergen, K. J. (1985). The social constructionist movement in modern psychology. *American Psychologist, 40,* 266–275.

Gergen, K. J. (1991). *The saturated self.* New York: Basic Books.

Gergen, K. J. (1993). *Refiguring self and psychology.* Hampshire: Dartmouth.

Gergen, K. J. (1994). *Realities and relationships: Soundings in social construction.* Cambridge, MA: Harvard University Press.

Gergen, K. J. (1999). *An invitation to social construction.* London: Sage.

Gibbons, F. X. (1978). Sexual standards and reactions to pornography: Enhancing behavioral consistency through self-focused attention. *Journal of Personality and Social Psychology, 36,* 976–987.

Gibson, J. J. (1979). *The ecological approach to visual perception.* Boston, MA: Houghton Mifflin.

Gilbert, D. T. (1989). Thinking lightly about others: Automatic components of the social inference process. In J. S. Uleman and J. A. Bargh (Eds.), *Unintended thought* (pp. 189–211). New York: Guilford Press.

Gilbert, D. T. (1995). Attribution and interpersonal perception. In A. Tesser (Ed.), *Advanced social psychology* (pp. 99–147). New York: McGraw-Hill.

Gilbert, D. T. (1998). Ordinary personology. In D. Gilbert, S. T. Fiske & G. Lindzey (Eds.), *Handbook of social psychology* (Vol. 2, 4th ed., 89–150). New York: McGraw-Hill.

Gilbert, D. T., & Hixon, J. G. (1991). The trouble of thinking: Activation and application to stereotypic beliefs. *Journal of Personality and Social Psychology, 60,* 509–517.

Gilbert, D. T., & Malone, P. S. (1995). The correspondence bias. *Psychological Bulletin, 117,* 21–38.

Gilbert, D. T., Pelham, B. W., & Krull, D. S. (1988). On cognitive busyness: When person perceivers meet persons perceived. *Journal of Personality and Social Psychology, 54,* 733–740.

Gilbert, G. M. (1951). Stereotype persistence and change among college students. *Journal of Abnormal and Social Psychology, 46,* 245–254.

Gilbert, N., & Mulkay, M. (1984). *Opening Pandora's box*. Cambridge: Cambridge University Press.

Gilroy, P. (1987). *'There ain't no black in the Union Jack': Politics of race and nation*. London: Routledge.

Glick, P., & Fiske, S. T. (1996). The ambivalent sexism inventory: Differentiating hostile and benevolent sexism. *Journal of Personality and Social Psychology, 70*, 491–512.

Glick, P., & Fiske, S. T. (1997). Hostile and benevolent sexism: Measuring ambivalent sexist attitudes towards women. *Psychology of Women Quarterly, 21*, 119–135.

Goffman, E. (1963). *Stigma: Notes on the management of spoiled identity*. Englewood Cliffs, NJ: Prentice Hall.

Goffman, E. (1981). *Forms of talk*. Oxford: Blackwell.

Goldberg, D. T. (1993). *Racist culture*. Oxford: Blackwell.

Goldberg, D. T. (1996). Racial formation in contemporary American national identity. *Social Identities, 2*, 169–91.

Goldberg, D. T. (1999). Racial subjects: Writing race in America. *Canadian Journal of Sociology, 24*, 434–36.

Gonzales, M. H., Burgess, D. J., & Mobilio, L. J. (2001). The allure of bad plans: Implications of plan quality for progress towards possible selves and postplanning energization. *Basic and Applied Social Psychology, 23*, 87–108.

Gramsci, A. (1971). *Selections from the prison notebooks* (trans. Q. Hoare and G. Nowell Smith). London: Lawrence & Wishart.

Graumann, C. F. (1986). The individualization of the social and the desocialization of the individual: Floyd H. Allport's contribution to social psychology. In C. F. Graumann and S. Moscovici (Eds.), *Changing conceptions of crowd mind and behavior* (pp. 97–116). New York: SpringerVerlag.

Graumann, C. F. (1996). Psyche and her descendents. In C. F. Graumann & K. J. Gergen (Eds.), *Historical dimensions of psychological discourse* (pp. 83–100). New York: Cambridge University Press.

Greenberg, J., & Rosenfield, D. (1979). Whites' ethnocentrism and their attributions for the behaviour of blacks: A motivational bias. *Journal of Personality, 47*, 643–657.

Greenberg, J., Solomon, S., Pyszczynski, T., Rosenblatt, A., Burling, J., Lyon, D., Simon, L., & Pinel, E. (1992). Why do people need self-esteem? Converging evidence that self-esteem serves an anxiety-buffering function. *Journal of Personality and Social Psychology, 63*, 913–922.

Greenwald, A. G., & Banaji, M. R. (1995). Implicit social cognition: Attitudes, self-esteem, and stereotypes. *Psychological Review, 102*, 4–27.

Greenwald, A. G., Banaji, M. R., Rudman, C. A., Farnham, S. D., Nosek, B. A., & Mellot, D. S. (2002). A unified theory of implicit attitudes, stereotypes, self-esteem, and self-concept. *Psychological Review, 100*, 3–25.

Greenwald, A. G., McGhee, D. E., & Schwartz, J. L. K. (1998). Measuring individual differences in implicit cognition: The implicit association test. *Journal of Personality and Social Psychology, 74*, 1464–1480.

Greenwald, A. G., & Pratkanis, A. R. (1984). The self. In R. S. Wyer, Jr, & T. K. Srull (Eds.), *Handbook of social cognition* (Vol. 3, pp. 129–178). Hillsdale, NJ: Erlbaum.

Grice, H. P. (1975). Logic and conversation. In P. Cole & J. L. Morgan (Eds.), *Syntax and semantics III: Speech acts* (pp. 41–55). New York: Academic Press.

Guerin, B. (1993). Subtle gender bias in the abstractness of verbs and adjectives. Paper presented at the Meeting of Australian Social Psychologists, Newcastle, NSW.

Guilfoyle, A. (2000). *The challenge and the promise: A critical analysis of prejudice in intergroup attribution research.* Unpublished PhD dissertation, Murdoch University.

Hall, S. (1986a). The problem of ideology: Marxism without guarantees. *Journal of Communication Inquiry, 10,* 28–44.

Hall, S. (1986b). Variants of liberalism. In J. Donald and S. Hall (Eds.), *Politics and ideology* (pp. 34–69). Milton Keynes: Open University Press.

Hall, S. (1989). Introduction. In S. Hall & M. Jacques (Eds.), *New times: The changing face of politics in the 1990s* (pp. 11–20). London: Lawrence & Wishart.

Hall, S. (1992). New ethnicities. In J. Donald & A. Rattansi (Eds.), *'Race', culture and difference* (pp. 252–260). London: Sage.

Hall, S. (1996). The problem of ideology: Marxism without guarantees. In D. Morley & H. K. Chen (Eds.), *Stuart Hall: Critical dialogues in cultural studies.* London: Routledge.

Hamilton, D. L. (1979). A cognitive-attributional analysis of stereotyping. In L. Berkowitz (Ed.), *Advances in experimental social psychology* (Vol. 12, pp. 53–81). New York: Academic Press.

Hamilton, D. L., Devine, P. G., & Ostrom, T. M. (1994). Social cognition and classic issues in social psychology. In P. G. Devine, D. L. Hamilton, & T. M. Ostrom (Eds.), *Social cognition: Impact on social psychology* (pp. 1–13). San Diego, CA: Academic Press.

Hamilton, D. L., & Sherman, J. W. (1994). Stereotypes. In R. S. Wyer, Jr, and T. K. Srull (Eds.), *Handbook of social cognition* (Vol. 2, 2nd ed., pp. 1–68). Hillsdale, NJ: Erlbaum.

Hamilton, D. L., Stroessner, S. J., & Driscoll, D. D. (1994). Social cognition and the study of stereotypes. In P. G. Devine, D. L. Hamilton, & T. M. Ostrom (Eds.), *Social cognition: Impact on social psychology* (pp. 291–321). San Diego, CA: Academic Press.

Hamilton, D. L., & Trolier, T. K. (1986). Stereotypes and stereotyping: An overview of the cognitive approach. In J. Dovidio & S. Gaertner (Eds.), *Prejudice, discrimination and racism* (pp. 127–163). Orlando, FL: Academic Press.

Hare-Mustin, R. T., & Maracek, J. (1988). The meaning of difference: Gender theory, postmodernism and psychology. *American Psychologist, 43,* 455–464.

Harré, R., & Van Langenhove, L. (1999). Reflexive positioning: Autobiography. In R. Harré, L. Van Langenhove & L. Berman (Eds.), *Positioning theory: Moral contexts of intentional action* (pp. 60–73). Oxford: Blackwell.

Hasher, L., & Zacks, R. T. (1979). Automatic and effortful processes in memory. *Journal of Experimental Psychology: General, 108,* 356–388.

Haslam, S. A. (1997). Stereotyping and social influence: Foundations of stereotype consensus. In R. Spears, P. J. Oakes, N. Ellemers & S. A. Haslam (Eds.), *The social psychology of stereotyping and group life* (pp. 119–143). Oxford: Blackwell.

Haslam, S. A., & Turner, J. C. (1992). Context-dependent variation in social stereotyping 2: The relationship between frame of reference, self-categorization and accentuation. *European Journal of Social Psychology, 22,* 251–278.

Haslam, S. A., & Turner, J. C. (1995). Context-dependent variation in social stereotyping 3: Extremism as a self-categorical basis for polarized judgement. *European Journal of Social Psychology, 25,* 341–371.

Haslam, S. A., Turner, J. C., Oakes, P. J., McGarty, C., & Hayes, B. K. (1992). Context-dependent variation in social stereotyping 1: The effects of intergroup relations as mediated by social change and frame of reference. *European Journal of Social Psychology, 22,* 3–20.

Haslam, S. A., van Knippenberg, D., Platow, M. J., & Ellemers, N. (2003). *Social identity at work: Developing theory for organizational practice.* New York: Psychology Press.

Hastie, R., & Park, B. (1986). The relationship between memory and judgment depends on whether the judgment task is memory-based or on-line. *Psychological Review, 93,* 258–268.

Hastorf, A., & Cantril, H. (1954). They saw a game: A case study. *Journal of Abnormal and Social Psychology, 49,* 129–34.

Heider, F. (1944). Social perception and phenomenal causality. *Psychological Review, 51,* 358–74.

Heider, F. (1958). *The psychology of interpersonal relations.* New York: Wiley.

Heider, F., & Simmel, M. (1944). An experimental study of apparent behavior. *American Journal of Psychology, 57,* 243–249.

Henriques, J., Hollway, W., Urwin, C., Venn, C., & Walkerdine, V. (1984). *Changing the subject: Psychology, social regulation and subjectivity.* London: Methuen.

Henriques, J., Hollway, W., Urwin, C., Venn, C., & Walkerdine, V. (1998). *Changing the subject: Psychology, social regulation and subjectivity* (2nd ed.). London: Routledge.

Hepburn, A. (2003). *An introduction to critical social psychology.* London: Sage.

Herek, G. M. (1986). The instrumentality of attitudes: Toward a neofunctional theory. *Journal of Social Issues, 42,* 99–114.

Herek, G. M. (1987). Can functions be measured? A new perspective on the functional approach to attitudes. *Social Psychology Quarterly, 50,* 285–303.

Herzlich, C. (1973). *Health and illness: A social psychological analysis.* London: Academic Press.

Hewstone, M. (Ed.). (1983). *Attribution theory: Social and functional extensions.* Oxford: Blackwell.

Hewstone, M. (1985). On common-sense and social representations: A reply to Potter and Litton, *British Journal of Social Psychology, 24,* 95–97.

Hewstone, M. (1986). *Understanding attitudes to the European Community: A social-psychological study in four member states.* Paris/Cambridge: Maison des Sciences de l'Homme/Cambridge University Press.

Hewstone, M. (1988). Causal attribution: From cognitive processes to collective beliefs. *The Psychologist: Bulletin of the British Psychological Society, 1,* 323–327.

Hewstone, M. (1989a). *Causal attribution: From cognitive processes to collective beliefs.* Oxford: Blackwell.

Hewstone, M. (1989b). Représentations sociales et causalité. In D. Jodelet (Ed.), *Les représentations sociales* (pp. 252–274). Paris: Presses Universitaires de France.

Hewstone, M. (1990). The 'ultimate attribution error'? A review of the literature on inter-group causal attribution. *European Journal of Social Psychology, 20,* 311–335.

Hewstone, M., & Augoustinos, M. (1995). Social attributions and social representations. In U. Flick and S. Moscovici (Eds.), *The psychology of the social: Language and social knowledge in social psychology* (pp. 78–99). Reinbek: Rowohit.

Hewstone, M., & Brown, R. J. (1986). *Contact and conflict in intergroup encounters.* Oxford: Blackwell.

Hewstone, M., Hopkins, N., & Routh, D. A. (1992). Cognitive models of stereotype change: (1) Generalization and subtyping in young people's views of the police. *European Journal of Social Psychology, 22,* 219–234.

Hewstone, M., Jaspars, J., & Lalljee, M. (1982). Social representations, social attribution and social identity: The intergroup images of 'public' and 'comprehensive' schoolboys. *European Journal of Social Psychology, 12,* 241–269.

Hewstone, M., Johnston, L., & Aird, P. (1992). Cognitive models of stereotype change: (2) Perceptions of homogeneous and heterogeneous groups. *European Journal of Social Psychology, 22,* 235–249.

Hewstone, M., Rubin, M., & Willis, H. (2002). Intergroup bias: Social prejudice. *Annual Review of Psychology, 53,* 575–604.

Hewstone, M., & Ward, C. (1985). Ethnocentrism and causal attribution in Southeast Asia. *Journal of Personality and Social Psychology, 48,* 614–623.

Higgins, E. T. (1987). Self-discrepancy: A theory relating self and affect. *Psychological Review, 94,* 319–340.

Higgins, E. T. (1995). Emotional experiences: The pains and pleasures of distinct self-regulatory systems. In R. D. Kavanaugh, B. Z. Glick & S. Fein (Eds.), *Emotions: The G. Stanley Hall symposium.* Hillsdale, NJ: Erlbaum.

Higgins, E. T. (1996a). Knowledge activation: Accessibility, applicability, and salience. In E. T. Higgins & A. W. Kruglanski (Eds.), *Social psychology: Handbook of basic principles* (pp. 133–168). New York: Guilford Press.

Higgins, E. T. (1996b). The 'self-digest': Self-knowledge serving self-regulatory functions. *Journal of Personality and Social Psychology, 71,* 1062–1083.

Higgins, E. T. (1997). Beyond pleasure and pain. *American Psychologist, 52,* 1280–1300.

Higgins, E. T. & Bargh, J. A. (1987). Social cognition and social perception. *Annual Review of Psychology, 38,* 369–425.

Higgins, E. T., Bond, R. N., Klein, R., & Strauman, T. (1986). Self-discrepancies and emotional vulnerability: How magnitude, accessibility, and type of discrepancy influence affect. *Journal of Personality and Social Psychology, 51,* 5–15.

Higgins, E. T., Klein, R., & Strauman, T. (1985). Self-concept discrepancy theory: A psychological model for distinguishing among different aspects of depression and anxiety. *Social Cognition, 3,* 51–76.

Higgins, E. T., Roney, C. J., Crowe, E., & Hymes, C. (1994). Ideal versus ought predilections for approach and avoidance: Distinct self-regulatory systems. *Journal of Personality and Social Psychology, 66,* 276–286.

Higgins, E. T., & Tykocinski, O. (1992). Self-discrepancies and biographical memory: Personality and cognition at the level of psychological situation. *Personality and Social Psychology Bulletin, 18,* 527–535.

Higgins, E. T., Van Hook, E., & Dorfman, D. (1988). Do self-attributes form a cognitive structure? *Social Cognition, 6,* 177–207.

Hilgard, E. R. (1980). The trilogy of mind: Cognition, affection, and conation. *Journal of the History of the Behavioral Sciences, 16,* 107–117.

Hilton, D. J. (1990). Conversational processes and causal explanation. *Psychological Bulletin, 107,* 65–81.

Himmelfarb, S. (1993). The measurement of attitudes. In A. H. Eagly and S. Chaiken (Eds.), *The psychology of attitudes* (pp. 23–87). Fort Worth, TX: Harcourt Brace Jovanovich.

Hirschfeld, L. (1997). The conceptual politics of race: Lessons from our children. *Ethos, 25,* 63–92.

Hoffman, C., & Hurst, N. (1990). Gender stereotypes: Perception or rationalization? *Journal of Personality and Social Psychology, 58,* 197–208.

Hogan, R. T., & Emler, N. P. (1978). The biases in contemporary social psychology. *Social Research, 45*, 478–534.

Hogg, M. A. (2000). Social processes and human behavior: Social psychology. In K. Pawlik & M. R. Rosenzweig (Eds.), *International handbook of psychology* (pp. 305–327). London: Sage.

Hogg, M. A. (2001). A social identity theory of leadership. *Personality and Social Psychology Review, 5*, 184–200.

Hogg, M. A., & Abrams, D. (1988). *Social identifications: A social psychology of intergroup relations and group processes.* London: Routledge.

Hogg, M. A., & Abrams, D. (2003). Intergroup behavior and social identity. In M. A. Hogg & J. Cooper (Eds.), *Handbook of social psychology* (pp. 407–431). London: Sage.

Hogg, M. A., & Turner, J. C. (1987). Intergroup behaviour, self-stereotyping and the salience of social categories. *British Journal of Social Psychology, 26*, 325–340.

Hogg, M. A., Turner, J. C., & Davidson, B. (1990). Polarized norms and social frames of reference: A test of self-categorization theory of group polarization. *Basic and Applied Social Psychology, 11*, 77–100.

Horney, K. (1950). *Neurosis and Human Growth.* New York: Norton.

Howard, J. W., & Rothbart, M. (1980). Social categorization and memory for in-group and out-group behavior. *Journal of Personality and Social Psychology, 38*, 301–10.

Hraba, J., Hagendoorn, L., & Hagendoorn, R. (1989). The ethnic hierarchy in the Netherlands: Social distance and social representation. *British Journal of Social Psychology, 28*, 57–59.

Hunter, J. A., Stringer, M., & Watson, R. P. (1991). Intergroup violence and intergroup attribution. *British Journal of Social Psychology, 30*, 261–266.

Huston, A. (1983). Sex typing. In P. H. Mussen (Ed.), *Handbook of child psychology: Socialization, personality and social development* (Vol. 4, 4th ed., pp. 387–467). New York: Wiley.

Ibanez, T., & Iniguez, L. (Eds.) (1997). *Critical social psychology.* London: Sage.

Ichheiser, G. (1941). Real, pseudo, and sham qualities of personality: An attempt at a new classification. *Character and Personality, 9*, 218–226.

Ichheiser, G. (1943). Misinterpretations of personality in everyday life and the psychologist's frame of reference. *Character and Personality, 12*, 145–160.

Ichheiser, G. (1949). *Misunderstandings in human relations: A study in false social perception.* Chicago, IL: University of Chicago Press.

Idson, L. C., & Mischel, W. (2001). The personality of familiar and significant people: The lay perceiver as a social-cognitive theorist. *Journal of Personality and Social Psychology, 80*, 585–596.

Innes, J. M., & Fraser, C. (1971). Experimenter bias and other possible biases in psychological research. *European Journal of Social Psychology, 1*, 297–310.

Isenberg, D. J. (1986). Group polarization: A critical review and meta-analysis. *Journal of Personality and Social Psychology, 50*, 1141–1151.

Jahoda, G. (1988). Critical notes and reflections on 'social representations'. *European Journal of Social Psychology, 18*, 195–209.

James, W. (1890/1952). *The principles of psychology.* Chicago: Encyclopaedia Britannica.

James, W. (1892). *Psychology.* New York: Henry Holt & Company.

Jameson, F. (1991). *Postmodernism: Or the cultural logic of late capitalism.* Durham, NC: Duke University Press.

Jaspars, J. M. F. (1986). Forum and focus: A personal view of European social psychology. *European Journal of Social Psychology, 16*, 3–15.

Jaspars, J., & Fraser, C. (1984). Attitudes and social representations. In R. M. Parr & S. Moscovici (Eds.), *Social representations* (pp. 101–123). Cambridge/Paris: Cambridge University Press/Maison des Sciences de l'Homme.

Jellis, V., & Gaitan, A. (2003). Making sense of 9/11: Argumentative dialogues with the media. Paper presented at the 2nd International Conference on Critical Psychology, Bath, UK.

Joffe, H. (1999). *Risk and 'the other'*. New York: Cambridge University Press.

Joffe, H. (2003). Risk: From perception to social representation. *British Journal of Social Psychology, 42*, 55–73.

Johnson, C. (1992a). Fragmentation versus Fukuyama: An essay on the unexpected longevity of grand narratives. Paper presented to the Annual Conference of the Australian Sociological Association, Adelaide, South Australia.

Johnson, C. (1992b). Applying Habermas to Australian political culture. *Australian Journal of Political Science, 27*, 55–70.

Johnston, L., & Hewstone, M. (1992). Cognitive models of stereotype change: (3) Subtyping and the perceived typicality of disconfirming group members. *Journal of Experimental Social Psychology, 28*, 360–386.

Jones, E. E. (1985). Major developments in social psychology during the past five decades. In G. Lindzey and E. Aronson (Eds.), *Handbook of social psychology* (Vol. 1, 3rd ed, pp. 47–107). New York: Random House.

Jones, E. E. (1998). Major developments in five decades of social psychology. In D. T. Gilbert, S. T. Fiske & G. Lindzey (Eds.), *Handbook of social psychology* (Vol. 1, 4th ed., pp. 3–57). Boston, MA: MacGraw-Hill.

Jones, E. E., & Davis, K. E. (1965). From acts to dispositions: The attribution process in person perception. In L. Berkowitz (Ed.), *Advances in experimental social psychology* (Vol. 2, pp. 219–266). New York: Academic Press.

Jones, E. E., & Harris, V. A. (1967). The attribution of attitudes. *Journal of Experimental Social Psychology, 3*, 1–24.

Jones, E. E., & Nisbett, R. E. (1972). The actor and the observer: Divergent perceptions of the causes of behavior. In E. E. Jones, D. E. Kanouse, H. H. Kelley, R. E. Nisbett, S. Valins & B. Weiner (Eds.), *Attribution: Perceiving the causes of behavior* (pp. 79–94). Morristown, NJ: General Learning Press.

Jost, J. T. (1995). Negative illusions: Conceptual clarification and psychological evidence concerning false consciousness. *Political Psychology, 16*, 397–424.

Jost, J. T., & Banaji, M. R. (1994). The role of stereotyping in system-justification and the production of false consciousness. *British Journal of Social Psychology, 33*, 1–27.

Jost, J. T., Banaji, M. R., & Nosek, B. A. (2004). A decade of system justification theory: Accumulated evidence of conscious and unconscious bolstering of the status quo. *Political Psychology, 25*, 881–919.

Jost, J. T., & Hunyady, O. (2002). The psychology of system justification and the palliative function of ideology. *European Review of Social Psychology, 13*, 111–153.

Jost, J. T. & Kramer, R. M. (2002). The system justification motive in intergroup relations. In D. M. Mackie and E. R. Smith (Eds.), *From prejudice to intergroup emotions: Differentiated reactions to social groups* (pp. 227–245). New York: Psychology Press.

Jost, J. T., & Major, B. (Eds.) (2001). *The psychology of legitimacy: Emerging perspectives on ideology, justice, and intergroup relations*. Cambridge: Cambridge University Press.

Judd, C. M., & Park, B. (1993). Definition and assessment of accuracy in social stereotypes. *Psychological Review, 100*, 109–128.

Kahneman, D., & Tversky, A. (1972). Subjective probability: A judgment of representativeness. *Cognitive Psychology, 3*, 430–454.

Kahneman, D., & Tversky, A. (1973). On the psychology of prediction. *Psychological Review, 80*, 237–251.

Kaplan, K. J. (1972). On the ambivalence-indifference problem in attitude theory and measurement: A suggested modification of the semantic differential technique. *Psychological Bulletin, 77*, 361–372.

Kashima, Y., Siegal, M., Tanaka, K., & Kashima, E. S. (1992). Do people believe behaviours are consistent with attitudes? Towards a cultural psychology of attribution processes. *British Journal of Social Psychology, 31*, 111–124.

Kashima, Y., & Triandis, H. C. (1986). The self-serving bias in attributions as a coping strategy. *Journal of Cross-Cultural Psychology, 17*, 83–97.

Katz, D. (1960). The functional approach to the study of attitudes. *Public Opinion Quarterly, 6*, 248–268.

Katz, D., & Braly, K. (1933). Racial stereotypes in one hundred college students. *Journal of Abnormal and Social Psychology, 28*, 280–290.

Katz, I., & Glass, D. C. (1979). An ambivalence-amplification theory of behaviour toward the stigmatized. In G. Austin & S. Worschel (Eds.), *Social psychology of intergroup relations* (pp. 55–70). Monterey, CA: Brooks/Cole.

Katz, I., & Hass, R. G. (1988). Racial ambivalence and American value conflict: Correlational and priming studies of dual cognitive structures. *Journal of Personality and Social Psychology, 55*, 893–905.

Katz, I., Wackenhut, J., & Hass, R. G. (1986). Racial ambivalence, value duality and behavior. In J. F. Dovidio & S. L. Gaertner (Eds.), *Prejudice, discrimination and racism* (pp. 35–59). San Diego, CA: Academic Press.

Kawakami, K., & Dion, K. L. (1993). The impact of salient self-identities on relative deprivation and action interpretations. *European Journal of Social Psychology, 23*, 525–540.

Kawakami, K., & Dion, K. L. (1995). Social identity and affect as determinant of collective action: Toward an integration of relative deprivation and social identity theories. *Theory and Psychology, 5*, 551–577.

Kawakami, K., Dion, K. L., & Dovidio, J. F. (1998). Racial prejudice and stereotype activation. *Personality and Social Psychology Bulletin, 24*, 407–416.

Kawakami, K., & Dovidio, J. F. (2001). Implicit stereotyping: How reliable is it? *Personality and Social Psychology Bulletin, 27*, 212–225.

Kelley, H. H. (1967). Attribution theory in social psychology. In D. Levine (Ed.), *Nebraska Symposium on Motivation* (Vol. 15, pp. 192–238). Lincoln, NE: University of Nebraska Press.

Kelley, H. H. (1972). Causal schemata and the attribution process. In E. E. Jones, D. E. Kanouse, H. H. Kelley, R. E. Nisbett, S. Valins and B. Weiner (Eds.), *Attribution: Perceiving the causes of behavior* (pp. 151–174). Morristown, NJ: General Learning Press.

Kelley, H. H. (1973). The processes of causal attribution. *American Psychologist, 28*, 107–128.

Kelley, H. H., & Michela, J. (1980). Attribution theory and research. *Annual Review of Psychology, 31*, 457–501.

Kerlinger, F. N. (1984). *Liberalism and conservatism: The nature and structure of social attitudes.* Hillsdale, NJ: Erlbaum.

Kihlstrom, J. F., & Cantor, N. (1984). Mental representations of the self. *Advances in Experimental Social Psychology, 17*, 1–47.

Kihlstrom, J. F., & Klein, S. B. (1994). The self as a knowledge structure. In R. W. Wyer & T. K. Srull (Eds.), *Handbook of Social Cognition* (Vol. 1, 2nd ed., pp. 153–208). Hillsdale, NJ: Erlbaum.

Kinder, D. R., & Sears, D. O. (1981). Prejudice and politics: Symbolic racism versus racial threats to the good life. *Journal of Personality and Social Psychology, 40*, 414–431.

Kinder, D. R., & Sears, D. O. (1985). Public opinion and political action. In G. Lindzey and E. Aronson (Eds.), *Handbook of social psychology* (Vol. 2, 3rd ed., pp. 659–741). New York: Random House.

King, G. W. (1975). An analysis of attitudinal and normative variables as predictors of intentions and behavior. *Speech Monographs, 42*, 237–244.

Kothandapani, V. (1971). Validation of feeling, belief, and intention to act as three components of attitude and their contribution to prediction of contraceptive behavior. *Journal of Personality and Social Psychology, 19*, 321–333.

Kovel, J. (1970). *White racism: A psychohistory*. New York: Pantheon Books.

Krech, D., Krutchfield, R. S., & Ballachey, E. L. (1962). *Individual in society: A textbook of social psychology*. New York: McGraw-Hill.

Krosnick, J. A. (1989). Attitude importance and attitude accessibility. *Personality and Social Psychology Bulletin, 15*, 297–308.

Kruks, S. (2001). *Retrieving experience: Subjectivity and recognition in feminist politics*. Ithaca, NY: Cornell University Press.

Kuhn, M. H. (1960). Self-attitudes by age, sex, and professional training. *Sociological Quarterly, 9*, 39–55.

Kuhn, M. H., & McPartland, T. S. (1954). An empirical investigation of self-attitudes. *Sociological Review, 19*, 68–76.

Kuiper, N. A. (1978). Depression and causal attributions for success and failure. *Journal of Personality and Social Psychology, 36*, 235–246.

Kunda, Z., & Sanitioso, R. (1989). Motivated changes in the self-concept. *Journal of Experimental Social Psychology, 25*, 272–285.

Kwan, V. S. Y., Bond, M. H., & Singelis, T. M. (1997). Pancultural explanations for life satisfaction: Adding relationship harmony to self-esteem. *Journal of Personality and Social Psychology, 73*, 1038–1051.

Lakoff, G. (1987). *Women, fire and dangerous things: What categories reveal about the mind*. Chicago, IL: University of Chicago Press.

Lakoff, G., & Johnson, M. (1980). *Metaphors we live by*. Chicago, IL: University of Chicago Press.

Lalljee, M., & Abelson, R. P. (1983). The organization of explanations. In M. Hewstone (Ed.), *Attribution theory: Social and functional extensions* (pp. 65–80). Oxford: Blackwell.

Lalljee, M., Brown, L. B., & Ginsburg, G. P. (1984). Attitudes: Dispositions, behaviour or evaluation? *British Journal of Social Psychology, 23*, 233–244.

Lalljee, M., Watson, M., & White, P. (1982). Explanations, attributions and the social context of unexpected behaviour. *European Journal of Social Psychology, 12*, 17–29.

Langer, E. J. (1989). *Mindfulness*. Reading, MA: Addison-Wesley.

LaPiere, R. T. (1934). Attitudes vs. actions. *Social Forces, 13*, 230–237.

Larrain, J. (1979). *The concept of ideology*. London: Hutchinson.

Larrain, J. (1983). *Marxism and ideology.* London: Macmillan.

Lash, S., & Urry, J. (1987). *The end of organised capitalism.* Cambridge: Polity.

Latour, B. (1991). The impact of science studies on political philosophy. *Science, Technology and Human Values, 16,* 3–19.

Lau, R. R., & Russell, D. (1980). Attributions in the sports pages. *Journal of Personality and Social Psychology, 39,* 29–38.

Leach, C. W., Snider, N., & Iyer, A. (2002). 'Poisoning the consciences of the fortunate': The experience of relative advantage and support for social equality. In I. Walker & H. J. Smith (Eds.), *Relative deprivation: Specification, development and integration* (pp. 136–163). New York: Cambridge University Press.

LeCouteur, A., & Augoustinos, M. (2001). Apologising to the Stolen Generations: Argument, rhetoric and identity in public reasoning. *Australian Psychologist, 36,* 51–61.

Lepore, L., & Brown, R. (1997). Category and stereotype activation: Is prejudice inevitable? *Journal of Personality and Social Psychology, 72,* 275–287.

Lepper, G. (2000). *Categories in text and talk.* London: Sage.

Lerner, M. (1980). *The belief in a just world: A fundamental delusion.* New York: Plenum Press.

Lerner, M., & Miller, D. (1978). Just world research and the attribution process: Looking back and ahead. *Psychological Bulletin, 85,* 1030–1051.

Levine, R. A., & Campbell, D. T. (1972). *Ethnocentrism: Theories of conflict, ethnic attitudes, and group behavior.* New York: Wiley.

Lewin, K. (1946). Action research and minority problems. *Journal of Social Issues, 2,* 34–46.

Lewin, K. (1951). *Field theory in social science.* New York: Harper.

Lewinsohn, P. M., Mischel, W., Chaplin, W., & Barton, R. (1980). Social competence and depression: The role of illusory self-perceptions. *Journal of Abnormal Psychology, 89,* 203–212.

Lewis, A. (1990). Shared economic beliefs. In C. Fraser & G. Gaskell (Eds.), *The social psychological study of widespread beliefs* (pp. 192–209). Oxford: Clarendon Press.

Lewis, Y. (2003). The self as a moral concept. *British Journal of Social Psychology, 42,* 225–237.

Leyens, J. P., & Dardenne, B. (1996). Basic concepts and approaches in social cognition. In M. Hewstone, W. Stroebe and G. M. Stephenson (Eds.), *Introduction to social psychology: A European perspective.* Oxford: Blackwell.

Leyens, J. P., Yzerbyt, V., & Schadron, G. (1994). *Stereotypes and social cognition.* London: Sage.

Lippmann, W. (1922). *Public opinion.* New York: Harcourt, Brace.

Lipset, S. (1960). *Political man.* London: Heinemann.

Little, B. R. (1983). Personal projects: A rationale and method for investigation. *Environment and Behavior, 15,* 273–309.

Little, B. R. (1989). Personal projects analysis: Trivial pursuits, magnificent obsessions, and the search for coherence. In D. M. Buss & N. Cantor (Eds.), *Personality psychology: Recent trends and emerging directions,* (pp. 15–31). New York: Springer-Verlag.

Litton, I., & Potter, J. (1985). Social representations in the ordinary explanation of a 'riot'. *European Journal of Social Psychology, 15,* 371–388.

Livingston, R. W., & Brewer, M. B. (2002). What are we really priming? Cue-based versus category-based processing of facial stimuli. *Journal of Personality and Social Psychology, 82,* 5–18.

Locke, V., & Johnston, L. (2001). Stereotyping and prejudice: A cognitive approach. In M. Augoustinos & K. J. Reynolds (Eds.), *Understanding the psychology of prejudice, racism, and social conflict*. London: Sage.

Locke, V., MacLeod, C., & Walker, I. (1994). Automatic and controlled activation of stereotypes: Individual differences associated with prejudice. *British Journal of Social Psychology, 33*, 29–46.

Locke, V., & Walker, I. (1999). Stereotypes, processing goals and social identity: Inveterate and fugacious characteristics of stereotypes. In D. Abrams & M. A. Hogg (Eds.), *Social identity and social cognition* (pp. 164–182). Oxford: Blackwell.

Locksley, A., Borgida, E., Brekke, N., & Hepburn, C. (1980). Sex stereotypes and social judgment. *Journal of Personality and Social Psychology, 39*, 821–831.

Long, K., & Spears, R. (1997). The self-esteem hypothesis revisited: Differentiation and the disaffected. In R. Spears, P. J. Oakes, N. Ellemers & S. A. Haslam (Eds.), *The social psychology of stereotyping and group life* (pp. 296–317). Oxford: Blackwell.

Lord, C. G., Lepper, M. R., & Ross, L. (1979). Biased assimilation and attitude polarization: The effects of prior theories on subsequently considered evidence. *Journal of Personality and Social Psychology, 37*, 2098–2109.

Lowery, B. S., Hardin, C. D., & Sinclair, S. (2001). Social influence effects on automatic racial prejudices. *Journal of Personality and Social Psychology, 81*, 842–855.

Lukes, S. (1973). *Individualism*. Oxford: Blackwell.

Lukes, S. (1975). *Émile Durkheim, his life and work: A historical and critical study*. Harmondsworth: Penguin.

Lyotard, J.-F. (1984). *The postmodern condition: A report on knowledge* (trans. G. Bennington and B. Massumi). Manchester: Manchester University Press.

McArthur, L. Z., & Post, D. L. (1977). Figural emphasis and person perception. *Journal of Experimental Social Psychology, 13*, 520–535.

McCauley, C., & Stitt, C. L. (1978). An individual and quantitative measure of stereotypes. *Journal of Personality and Social Psychology, 36*, 929–940.

McClosky, H. (1964). Consensus and ideology in American politics. *American Political Science Review, 58*, 361–382.

McConahay, J. B. (1982). Self-interest versus racial attitudes as correlates of anti-busing attitudes in Louisville: Is it the buses or the blacks? *Journal of Politics, 44*, 692–720.

McConahay, J. B. (1986). Modern racism, ambivalence, and the modern racism scale. In J. F. Dovidio & S. L. Gaertner (Eds.), *Prejudice, discrimination, and racism* (pp. 91–125). New York: Academic Press.

McCreanor, T. (1997). When racism stepped ashore: Antecedents of anti-Maori discourse in Aotearoa. *New Zealand Journal of Psychology, 26*, 36–44.

McDougall, W. (1921). *The group mind*. Cambridge: Cambridge University Press.

McGarty, C. (1999). *Categorization in social psychology*. London: Sage.

McGarty, C. (2002). Stereotype formation as category formation. In C. McGarty, V. Y. Yzerbyt & R. Spears (Eds.), *Stereotypes as explanations: The formation of meaningful beliefs about social groups* (pp. 16–57). New York: Cambridge University Press.

McGarty, C., & Penny, R. E. C. (1988). Categorization, accentuation and social judgement. *British Journal of Social Psychology, 22*, 147–157.

McGarty, C., Turner, J. C., Hogg, M. A., David, B., & Wetherell, M. S. (1992). Group polarization as conformity to the prototypical group member. *British Journal of Social Psychology, 31*, 1–20.

McGarty, C. Yzerbyt, V. Y., & Spears, R. (Eds.) (2002). *Stereotypes as explanations: The formation of meaningful beliefs about social groups*. New York: Cambridge University Press.

McGuire, W. J. (1973). The yin and yang of progress in social psychology. *Journal of Personality and Social Psychology, 26,* 446–456.

McGuire, W. J. (1985). Attitudes and attitude change. In G. Lindzey & E. Aronson (Eds.), *Handbook of social psychology* (Vol. 2, 3rd ed., pp. 136–314). New York: Random House.

McGuire, W. J., & McGuire, C. V. (1982). Significant others in self-space: Sex differences and developmental trends in the self. In J. Suls (Ed.), *Social psychological perspectives on the self* (pp. 71–96). Hillsdale, NJ: Erlbaum.

McLellan, D. (1986). *Ideology.* Milton Keynes: Open University Press.

Mackie, D. M. (1986). Social identification effects in group polarization. *Journal of Personality and Social Psychology, 50,* 720–728.

Macpherson, C. B. (1962). *The political theory of possessive individualism: Hobbes to Locke.* Oxford: Clarendon Press.

Macrae, C. N., & Bodenhausen, G. V. (2000). Social cognition: Thinking categorically about others. *Annual Review of Psychology, 51,* 93–120.

Macrae, C. N., Bodenhausen, G. V., Milne, A. B., & Castelli, L. (2001). On disregarding deviants: Exemplar typicality and person perception. In H. D. Ellis & C. N. Macrae (Eds.), *Validation in psychology.* New Brunswick, NJ: Transaction Publishers.

Macrae, C. N., Bodenhausen, G. V., Milne, A. B., Thorn, T. M. J., & Castelli, L. (1997). On the activation of social stereotypes: The moderating role of processing objectives. *Journal of Experimental Social Psychology, 33,* 471–489.

Macrae, C. N., Milne, A. B., & Bodenhausen, G. V. (1994). Stereotypes as energy saving devices: A peek inside the cognitive toolbox. *Journal of Personality and Social Psychology, 66,* 37–47.

Macrae, C. N., Stangor, C., & Hewstone, M. (1996). *Foundations of stereotypes and stereotyping.* New York: Guilford Press.

Manicas, P. T., & Secord, P. F. (1983). Implications for psychology of the new philosophy of science. *American Psychologist, 38,* 399–413.

Mann, J. F., & Taylor, D. M. (1974). Attributions of causality: Role of ethnicity and social class. *Journal of Social Psychology, 94,* 3–13.

Manstead, A. S. R., Proffitt, C., & Smart, J. L. (1983). Predicting and understanding mothers' infant-feeding intentions and behavior: Testing the theory of reasoned action. *Journal of Personality and Social Psychology, 44,* 657–671.

Maracek, J., & Metee, D. R. (1972). Avoidance of continued success as a function of self-esteem, level of esteem-certainty, and responsibility for success. *Journal of Personality and Social Psychology, 22,* 98–107.

Marcus, G. E., Tabb, D., & Sullivan, J. L. (1974). The application of individual differences scaling in the meaurement of political ideologies. *American Journal of Political Science, 18,* 405–420.

Markova, I. (2000). The individual and society in psychological theory. *Theory and Psychology, 10,* 107–116.

Markus, H. (1977). Self-schemata and processing information about the self. *Journal of Personality and Social Psychology, 35,* 63–78.

Markus, H., & Kitayama, S. (1991). Culture and the self: Implications for cognition, emotion, and motivation. *Psychological Review, 98,* 224–253.

Markus, H., & Kunda, Z. (1986). Stability and malleability of the self-concept. *Journal of Personality and Social Psychology, 51,* 858–866.

Markus, H., & Nurius, P. (1986). Possible selves. *American Psychologist, 41,* 954–969.

Markus, H., & Wurf, E. (1987). The dynamic self-concept: A social psychological perspective. *Annual Review of Psychology, 38,* 299–337.

Marsh, H. W. (1993). Relations between global and specific domains of self: The importance of individual importance, certainty, and ideals. *Journal of Personality and Social Psychology, 65,* 975–992.

Marx, K., & Engels, F. (1846/1947). *The German ideology.* New York: International Publishers.

Mead, G. H. (1934/1962). *Mind, self, and society.* Chicago, IL: University of Chicago Press.

Menon, T., Morris, M. W., Chiu, C., & Hong, Y. (1999). Culture and the construal of agency: Attribution to individual versus group dispositions. *Journal of Personality and Social Psychology, 76,* 701–717.

Mepham, J. (1972). The theory of ideology in capital. *Radical Philosophy, 2,* 12–19.

Messick D. M. & Mackie D. M. (1989). Intergroup relations. In M. R. Rosenzweig (Ed.), *Annual Review of Psychology* (Vol. 40, pp. 45–81). Palo Alto, CA: Annual Reviews.

Michotte, A. E. (1963). *The perception of causality.* New York: Russell & Russell.

Miller, D. T. (1976). Ego involvement and attributions for success and failure. *Journal of Personality and Social Psychology, 34,* 901–906.

Miller, J. G. (1984). Culture and the development of everyday social explanation. *Journal of Personality and Social Psychology, 46,* 961–978.

Milner, D. (1981). Racial prejudice. In J. C. Turner & H. Giles (Eds.), *Intergroup behaviour* (pp. 102–143). Oxford: Blackwell.

Minard, R. (1952). Race relations in the Pocahontas coal fields. *Journal of Social Issues, 8,* 29–44.

Mischel, W. (1968). *Personality and assessment.* New York: Wiley.

Moliner, P., & Tafani, E. (1997). Attitudes and social representations: A theoretical and experimental approach. *European Journal of Social Psychology, 27,* 687–702.

Moloney, G., Hall, R., & Walker, I. (2005). Social representations and themata: The construction and functioning of social knowledge about donation and transplantation. *British Journal of Social Psychology.*

Moloney, G., & Walker, I. (2000). Messiahs, pariahs and donors: The development of social representations of organ donation. *Journal for the Theory of Social Behaviour, 30,* 203–227.

Moloney, G., & Walker, I. (2002). Talking about transplants: The dialectical nature of the dilemma. *British Journal of Social Psychology, 41,* 299–320.

Monteith, M. J., Sherman, J. W., & Devine, R. F. (1998). Suppression as a stereotype control strategy. *Personality and Social Psychology Review, 2,* 63–82.

Morris, M. W., Menon, T., & Ames, D. R. (2001). Culturally conferred conceptions of agency: A key to social perception of persons, groups, and other actors. *Personality and Social Psychology Review, 5,* 169–182.

Morris, M. W., & Peng, K. (1994). Culture and cause: American and Chinese attributions for social and physical events. *Journal of Personality and Social Psychology, 67,* 949–971.

Moscovici, S. (1961). *La Psychoanalyse, son image et son public.* Paris: Presses Universitaires de France.

Moscovici, S. (1981). On social representations. In J. P. Forgas (Ed.), *Social cognition: Perspectives on everyday understanding* (pp. 181–209). London: Academic Press.

Moscovici, S. (1982). The coming era of representations. In J.-P. Codol and J.-P. Leyens (Eds.), *Cognitive analysis of social behaviour.* The Hague: Martinus Nijhoff.

Moscovici, S. (1984). The phenomenon of social representations. In R. M. Farr and S. Moscovici (Eds.), *Social representations* (pp. 3–69). Cambridge/Paris: Cambridge University Press/Maison des Sciences de l'Homme.

Moscovici, S. (1985). Comment on Potter and Litton. *British Journal of Social Psychology, 24*, 91–92.

Moscovici, S. (1988). Notes towards a description of social representations. *European Journal of Social Psychology, 18*, 211–250.

Moscovici, S. (1989). Des représentations collectives aux représentations sociales: Éléments pour une histoire. In D. Jodelet (Ed.), *Les représentations sociales* (pp. 62–86). Paris: Presses Universitaires de France.

Moscovici, S. (1994). Social representations and pragmatic communication. *Social Science Information, 33*, 163–177.

Moscovici, S. (1998). The history and actuality of social representations. In U. Flick (Ed.), *The psychology of the social* (pp. 209–247). Cambridge: Cambridge University Press.

Moscovici, S. (2001). Why a theory of social representations? In K. Deaux & G. Philogène (Eds.), *Representations of the social: Bridging theoretical traditions* (pp. 8–36). Oxford: Blackwell.

Moscovici, S., & Hewstone, M. (1983). Social representations and social explanation: From the 'naïve' to the 'amateur' scientist. In M. Hewstone (Ed.), *Attribution theory: Social and functional extensions* (pp. 98–125). Oxford: Blackwell.

Moscovici, S. & Perez, J. A. (1997). Representations of society and prejudice. *Papers on Social Representations, 6*, 27–36.

Mullen, B., Brown, R., & Smith, C. (1992). Ingroup bias as a function of salience, relevance and status: An integration. *European Journal of Social Psychology, 22*, 103–122.

Mullen, B., & Hu, L. (1989). Perceptions of ingroup and outgroup variability: A meta-analytic integration. *Basic and Applied Social Psychology, 25*, 525–559.

Mullin, B., & Hogg, M. A. (1998). Dimensions of subjective uncertainty in social identification and minimal intergroup discrimination. *British Journal of Social Psychology, 37*, 345–365.

Mummendey, A., Otten, S., Berger, U. & Kessler, T. (2000). Positive-negative asymmetry in social discrimination: Valence of evolution and salience of categorization. *Personality and Social Psychology Bulletin, 26*, 1258–1270.

Myrdal, G. (1944). *An American dilemma: The negro problem and modern democracy.* New York: Harper & Row.

Nairn, R., & McCreanor, T. (1990). Insensitivity and hypersensitivity: An imbalance in Pakeha discourse on Maori/Pakeha accounts of racial conflict. *Journal of Language and Social Psychology, 9*, 293–308.

Nairn, R. G., & McCreanor, T. N. (1991). Race talk and common sense: Patterns in Pakeha discourse on Maori/Pakeha relations in New Zealand. *Journal of Language and Social Psychology, 10*, 245–262.

Neely, J. H. (1991). Semantic priming effects in visual word recognition: A selective review of current findings and theories. In D. Besner & G. W. Humphries (Eds.), *Basic processes in reading: Visual word recognition* (pp. 264–336). Hillsdale, NJ: Erlbaum.

Nelkin, D., & Lindee, M. S. (1995). *The DNA mystique: The gene as a cultural icon.* New York: Freeman.

Nelson, T. D. (2002). *The psychology of prejudice.* Boston, MA: Allyn & Bacon.

Nerlich, B., Dingwall, R., & Clarke, D. D. (2002). The book of life: How the completion of the Human Genome Project was revealed to the public. *Health, 6*, 445–469.

Nesdale, D. (2001). Development of prejudice in children. In M. Augoustinos & K. J. Reynolds (Eds.), *Understanding prejudice, racism and social conflict* (pp. 57–72). London: Sage.

Newman, L. S., & Uleman, J. S. (1989). Spontaneous trait inference. In J. S. Uleman & J. A. Bargh (Eds.), *Unintended thought* (pp. 52–74). New York: Guilford Press.

Newman, L. S., & Uleman, J. S. (1993). When are you what you did? Behavior identification and dispositional inference in person memory, attribution, and social judgment. *Personality and Social Psychology Bulletin, 19*, 513–525.

Nicholls, J. G. (1975). Causal attribution and other achievement-related cognitions: Effects of task outcome, attainment value, and sex. *Journal of Personality and Social Psychology, 31*, 379–389.

Nisbett, R. E. (2003). *The geography of thought: How Asians and Westerners think differently … and why.* New York: Free Press.

Nisbett, R. E., Caputo, C., Legant, P., & Maracek, J. (1973). Behavior as seen by the actor and by the observer. *Journal of Personality and Social Psychology, 27*, 154–164.

Nisbett, R., & Ross, L. (1980). *Human inference: Strategies and shortcomings of social judgement.* Englewood Cliffs, NJ: Prentice Hall.

Nisbett, R., & Wilson, T. (1977). Telling more than we can know: Verbal reports on mental processes. *Psychological Review, 84*, 231–259.

Oakes, P. J. (1987). The salience of social categories. In J. Turner, M. A. Hogg, P. J. Oakes, S. D. Reicher and M. S. Wetherell (Eds.), *Rediscovering the social group: A self-categorization theory* (pp. 117–141). Oxford: Blackwell.

Oakes, P. J., & Haslam, S. A. (2001). Distortion v. meaning: Categorization on trial for inciting intergroup hatred. In M. Augoustinos & K. J. Reynolds (Eds.), *Understanding the psychology of prejudice, racism and social conflict* (pp. 179–194). London: Sage.

Oakes, P. J., Haslam, S. A., & Turner, J. C. (1994). *Stereotyping and social reality.* Oxford: Blackwell.

Oakes, P. J., & Reynolds, K. J. (1997). Asking the accuracy question: Is measurement the answer? In R. Spears, P. J. Oakes, N. Ellemers & S. A. Haslam, (Eds.), *The social psychology of stereotyping and group life* (pp. 51–71). Oxford: Blackwell.

Oakes, P. J., Turner, J. C., & Haslam, S. A. (1991). Perceiving people as group members: The role of fit in the salience of social categorizations. *British Journal of Social Psychology, 30*, 125–144.

Onorato, R. S., & Turner, J. C. (2004). Fluidity in the self-concept: The shift from personal to social identity. *European Journal of Social Psychology, 34*, 257–278.

Opton, E. M., Jr (1971). It never happened and besides they deserved it. In N. Sanford & C. Comstock (Eds.), *Sanctions for evil* (pp. 49–70). San Francisco, CA: Jossey-Bass.

Orne, M. T. (1969). Demand characteristics and the concept of design controls. In R. Rosenthal & R. L. Rosnow (Eds.), *Artifact in behavioral research* (pp. 143–179). New York: Academic Press.

Ostrom, T. M. (1969). The relationship between the affective, behavioral, and cognitive components of attitude. *Journal of Experimental Social Psychology, 5*, 12–30.

Ostrom, T. M. (1994). Foreword. In R. S. Wyer (Ed.), *Handbook of social cognition: Basic principles* (pp. vii–xii). Hillsdale, NJ: Erlbaum.

Oyserman, D., & Markus, H. (1991). Possible selves in balance: Implications for delinquency. *Journal of Social Issues, 46*, 141–157.

Parker, I. (1990). Discourse: Definitions and contradictions. *Philosophical Psychology, 3*, 189–204.

Parker, I. (1991). *Discourse dynamics: Critical analyses for social and individual psychology*. London: Routledge.

Parker, I. (Ed.). (2002). *Critical discursive psychology*. Basingstoke: Palgrave Macmillan.

Parker, I., & Spears, R. (Eds.) (1996). *Psychology and society: Radical theory and practice*. London: Pluto Press.

Pedersen, A., & Walker, I. (1997). Prejudice against Australian Aborigines: Old-fashioned and modern forms. *European Journal of Social Psychology, 27*, 561–587.

Peevers, B. H., & Secord, P. F. (1973). Developmental changes in attributions of descriptive concepts to persons. *Journal of Personality and Social Psychology, 27*, 120–128.

Pendry, L. F., & Macrae, C. N., (1996). What the disinterested perceiver overlooks: Goal-directed social categorization. *Personality and Social Psychology Bulletin, 22*, 249–256.

Pepitone, A. (1976). Toward a normative and comparative biocultural social psychology. *Journal of Personality and Social Psychology, 34*, 641–653.

Pepitone, A. (1981). Lessons from the history of social psychology. *American Psychologist, 36*, 972–985.

Perdue, C. W., Dovidio, J. F., Gurtman, M. B., & Tyler, R. B. (1990). Us and them: Social categorization and the process of intergroup bias. *Journal of Personality and Social Psychology, 59*, 475–486.

Petersen, A., (2001). Biofantasies: Genetics and medicine in the print news media. *Social Science and Medicine, 52*, 1255–1268.

Peterson, C., & Seligman, M. E. P. (1984). Causal explanations as a risk factor for depression: Theory and evidence. *Psychological Review, 91*, 347–374.

Pettigrew, T. F. (1958). Personality and socio-cultural factors in intergroup attitudes: A cross-national comparison. *Journal of Conflict Resolution, 2*, 29–42.

Pettigrew, T. F. (1959). Regional differences in anti-Negro prejudice. *Journal of Abnormal and Social Psychology, 59*, 28–36.

Pettigrew, T. F. (1961). Social psychology and desegregation research. *American Psychologist, 16*, 105–112.

Pettigrew, T. F. (1964). *A profile of the American Negro*. Princeton, NJ: Van Nostrand.

Pettigrew, T. F. (1967). Social evaluation theory. In D. Levine (Ed.), *Nebraska Symposium on Motivation* (pp. 241–311). Lincoln, NE: University of Nebraska Press.

Pettigrew, T. F. (1979). The ultimate attribution error: Extending Allport's cognitive analysis of prejudice. *Personality and Social Psychology Bulletin, 5*, 461–476.

Pettigrew, T. F., Jackson, J. S., Ben Brika, J., Lemain, G., Meertens, R. W., Wagner, U., & Zick, A. (1998). Outgroup prejudice in Western Europe. In W. Stroebe & M. Hewstone (Eds.), *European review of social psychology* (Vol. 8, pp. 241–273). Chichester: John Wiley.

Pettigrew, T. F., & Meertens, R. W. (1995). Subtle and blatant prejudice in Western Europe. *European Journal of Social Psychology, 25*, 57–75.

Petty, R. E., & Cacioppo, J. T. (1996). *Attitudes and persuasion: Classic and contemporary approaches*. Boulder, CO: Westview Press.

Philogène, G. (1994). African American as a new social representation. *Journal for the Theory of Social Behaviour, 24*, 89–109.

Philogène, G. (1999). *From Black to African American: A new social representation*. Westport, CT: Greenwood-Praeger.

Philogène, G., & Deaux, K. (2001). Introduction. In K. Deaux & G. Philogène (Eds.), *Representations of the social: Bridging theoretical traditions* (pp. 3–7). Oxford: Blackwell.

Pill, R., & Stott, N. C. H. (1985). Choice or chance: Further evidence on ideas of illness and responsibility for health. *Social Science and Medicine, 20*, 981–991.

Potter, J. (1996). *Representing reality*. London: Sage.

Potter, J. (1998). Discursive social psychology: From attitudes to evaluations. In W. Stroebe & M. Hewstone (Eds.), *European review of social psychology*, (Vol. 9, pp. 233–266). Chichester: John Wiley.

Potter, J. (2000). Post-cognitive psychology. *Theory and Psychology, 10*, 31–37.

Potter, J., & Billig, M. (1992). Re-presenting representations – Discussion of Raty and Snellman. *Papers on Social Representations, 1*, 15–20.

Potter, J., & Litton, I. (1985). Some problems underlying the theory of social representations. *British Journal of Social Psychology, 24*, 81–90.

Potter, J., & Wetherell, M. (1987). *Discourse and social psychology: Beyond attitudes and behaviour*. London: Sage.

Potter, J., & Wetherell, M. (1998). Social representations, discourse analysis, and racism. In U. Flick (Ed.), *The psychology of the social* (pp. 138–155). Cambridge: Cambridge University Press.

Potter, J., Wetherell, M., Gill, R., & Edwards, D. (1990). Discourse: Noun, verb or social practice? *Philosophical Psychology, 3*, 205–217.

Pountain, D., & Robins, D. (2000). *Cool rules: Anatomy of an attitude*. London: Reaktion Books.

Pratkanis, A. R. (1989). The cognitive representation of attitudes. In A. R. Pratkanis, S. J. Breckler, & A. G. Greenwald (Eds.), *Attitude structure and function* (pp. 71–98). Hillsdale, NJ: Erlbaum.

Pratkanis, A. R., & Greenwald, A. G. (1989). A sociocognitive model of attitude structure and function. In L. Berkowitz (Ed.), *Advances in experimental social psychology* (Vol. 22, pp. 245–285). New York: Academic Press.

Pratto, F. (1999). The puzzle of continuing group inequality: Piecing together psychological, social and cultural forces in social dominance theory. *Advances in Experimental Social Psychology, 31*, 191–263.

Pratto, F., Sidanius, J., Stallworth, L. M., & Malle, B. F. (1994). Social dominance orientation: A personality variable predicting social and political attitudes. *Journal of Personality and Social Psychology, 67*, 741–763.

Pratto, F., Stallworth, L. M., & Sidanius, J. (1997). The gender gap: Differences in political attitudes and social dominance orientation. *British Journal of Social Psychology, 36*, 49–68.

Pratto, F., Stallworth, L. M., Sidanius, J., & Siers, B. (1997). The gender gap in occupational role attainment: A social dominance approach. *Journal of Personality and Social Psychology, 72*, 37–53.

Puchta, C., & Potter, J. (2003). *Focus group practice*. London: Sage.

Quattrone, G. A. (1982). Overattribution and unit formation: When behaviour engulfs the person. *Journal of Personality and Social Psychology, 42*, 593–607.

Quinn, K., Macrae, N., & Bodenhausen, G. (2003). Stereotyping and impression formation: How categorical thinking shapes person perception. In M. Hogg & J. Cooper (Eds.), *The Sage handbook of social psychology* (pp. 87–109). London: Sage.

Rapley, M. (1998). 'Just an ordinary Australian': Self-categorization and the discursive construction of facticity in 'new racist' political rhetoric. *British Journal of Social Psychology, 37*, 325–344.

Ratzlaff, C., Matsumoto, D., Kouznetsova, N., Raroque, J., & Ray, R. (2000). Individual psychological culture and subjective well-being. In E. Diener & E. M. Suh (Eds.), *Culture and subjective well-being* (pp. 37–59). Cambridge, MA: MIT Press.

Reeves, F. (1983). *British racial discourse*. New York: Cambridge University Press.

Regan, D. T., & Fazio, R. H. (1977). On the consistency between attitudes and behavior: Look to the method of attitude formation. *Journal of Experimental Social Psychology, 13*, 38–45.

Reicher, S., & Hopkins, N. (1996a). Seeking influence through characterizing self-categories: An analysis of anti-abortionist rhetoric. *British Journal of Social Psychology, 35*, 297–311.

Reicher, S., & Hopkins, N., (1996b). Self-category constructions in political rhetoric: An analysis of Thatcher's and Kinnock's speeches concerning the British miners' strike (1984–5). *European Journal of Social Psychology, 26*, 353–371.

Reicher, S., & Hopkins, N. (2001). *Self and nation: Categorization, contestation and mobilization*. London: Sage.

Reicher, S., Hopkins, N., & Condor, S. (1997). Stereotype construction as a strategy of influence. In R. Spears, P. J. Oakes, N. Ellemers, & S. A. Haslam (Eds.), *The social psychology of stereotyping and group life* (pp. 94–118). Oxford: Blackwell.

Reid, A., & Deaux, K. (1996). Relationships between social and personal identities: Segregation or integration? *Journal of Personality and Social Psychology, 65*, 317–338.

Reynolds, K. J., & Turner, J. C. (2001). Prejudice as a group process: The role of social identity. In M. Augoustinos & K. J. Reynolds (Eds.), *Understanding prejudice, racism, and social conflict*. London: Sage.

Richards, G. (1997). *'Race', racism and psychology: Towards a reflexive history*. London and New York: Routledge.

Riley, S. C. E. (2002). Constructions of equality and discrimination in professional men's talk. *British Journal of Social Psychology, 41*, 443–461.

Ring, K. (1967). Experimental social psychology: Some sober questions about some frivolous values. *Journal of Experimental Social Psychology, 3*, 113–123.

Rojahn, K., & Pettigrew, T. (1992). Memory for schema-relevant information: A meta-analytic resolution. *British Journal of Social Psychology, 31*, 81–109.

Rosch, E. (1975). Cognitive reference points. *Cognitive Psychology, 7*, 532–547.

Rosch, E. (1978). Principles of categorization. In E. Rosch and B. B. Lloyd (Eds.), *Cognition and categorization* (pp. 27–48). Hillsdale, NJ: Erlbaum.

Rose, N. (1989). *Governing the soul: The shaping of the private self*. New York: Routledge.

Rose, N. (1996). *Inventing ourselves: Psychology, power and personhood*. Cambridge: Cambridge University Press.

Rosenberg, M. J., & Hovland, C. I. (1960). Cognitive, affective, and behavioral components of attitudes. In C. I. Hovland & M. J. Rosenberg (Eds.), *Attitude organization and change* (pp. 1–14). New Haven, CT: Yale University Press.

Rosenthal, R. (1969). Interpersonal expectations: Effects of the experimenter's hypothesis. In R. Rosenthal & R. L. Rosnow (Eds.), *Artifact in behavioral research* (pp. 181–277). New York: Academic Press.

Ross, L. (1977). The intuitive psychologist and his shortcomings: Distortions in the attribution process. In L. Berkowitz (Ed.), *Advances in experimental social psychology* (Vol. 10, pp. 173–220). New York: Academic Press.

Ross, L., Amabile, T. M., & Steinmetz, J. L. (1977). Social roles, social control, and social perception processes. *Journal of Personality and Social Psychology, 35,* 485–494.

Ross, L., & Lepper, M. R. (1980). The perseverance of beliefs: Empirical and normative considerations. In R. A. Schweder (Ed.), *New directions for methodology of behavioral science: Fallible judgment in behavioral research.* San Francisco, CA: Jossey-Bass.

Ross, L., & Nisbett, R. E. (1991). *The person and the situation: Perspectives of social psychology.* New York: McGraw-Hill.

Rothbart, M. (1981). Memory processes and social beliefs. In D. Hamilton (Ed.), *Cognitive processes in stereotyping and intergroup behavior* (pp. 145–182). Hillsdale, NJ: Erlbaum.

Rothbart, M., Evans, M., & Fulero, S. (1979). Recall for confirming events: Memory processes and the maintenance of social stereotypes. *Journal of Experimental Social Psychology, 15,* 343–355.

Ruble, D. N., Feldman, N. S., Higgins, E. T., & Karlovac, M. (1979). Locus of causality and use of information in the development of causal attributions. *Journal of Personality, 47,* 595–614.

Rudman, L. A., Ashmore, R. D., & Gary, M. L. (2001). 'Unlearning' automatic biases: The malleability of implicit prejudice and stereotypes. *Journal of Personality and Social Psychology, 81,* 856–868.

Rumelhart, D. E. (1984). Schemata and the cognitive system. In R. S. Wyer, Jr & T. K. Srull (Eds.), *Handbook of social cognition* (Vol. 1, pp. 161–188). Hillsdale, NJ: Erlbaum.

Rumelhart, D. E., & Norman, D. A. (1978). Accretion, tuning and restructuring: Three modes of learning. In J. W. Cotton & R. Klatzky (Eds.), *Semantic factors in cognition.* Hillsdale, NJ: Erlbaum.

Ruvolo, A. P., & Markus, H. R. (1992). Possible selves and performance: The power of self-relevant imagery. *Social Cognition, 10,* 95–124.

Sacks, H. (1992). *Lectures on conversation.* G. Jefferson (Ed.). Oxford: Blackwell.

Sacks, H., Schegloff, E. A., & Jefferson, G. (1974). A simplest systematics for the organization of turn-taking for conversation. *Language, 50,* 696–735.

Sampson, E. E. (1975). On justice as equality. *Journal of Social Issues, 31,* 45–64.

Sampson, E. E. (1977). Psychology and the American ideal. *Journal of Personality and Social Psychology, 35,* 767–782.

Sampson, E. E. (1981). Cognitive psychology as ideology. *American Psychologist, 86,* 730–743.

Sampson, E. E. (1988). The debate on individualism: Indigenous psychologies of the individual and their role in personal and societal functioning. *American Psychologist, 43,* 15–22.

Sampson, E. E. (1993). Identity politics: Challenges to psychology's understanding. *American Psychologist, 48,* 1219–1230.

Scarborough, E. (1990). Attitudes, social representations, and ideology. In C. Fraser & G. Gaskell (Eds.), *The social psychological study of widespread beliefs* (pp. 99–117). Oxford: Clarendon Press.

Schank, R. C., & Abelson, R. P. (1977). *Scripts, plans, goals and understanding: An inquiry into human knowledge structures.* Hillsdale, NJ: Erlbaum.

Schegloff, E. A. (1968). Sequences in conversational openings. *American Anthropologist, 70,* 1075–1095.

Schegloff, E. A. (1997). Whose text? Whose context? *Discourse and Society, 8,* 165–187.

Schlenker, B. R., & Leary, M. R. (1982). Audiences' reactions to self-enhancing, self-denigrating, and accurate self-presentations. *Journal of Experimental Social Psychology, 18,* 89–104.

Schlenker, B. R., & Miller, R. S. (1977). Egocentrism in groups: Self-serving biases or logical information processing? *Journal of Personality and Social Psychology, 35,* 755–764.

Schmidt, C. F. (1972). Multidimensional scaling of the printed media's explanations of the riot of the summer of 1967. *Journal of Personality and Social Psychology, 24,* 59–67.

Schmitt, M. T., Branscombe, N. R. (2003). Response – Will the real social dominance theory please stand up? *British Journal of Social Psychology, 42,* 215–219.

Schmitt, M. T., Branscombe, N. & Kappen, D. M. (2003). Attitudes toward group-based inequality: Social dominance or social identity? *British Journal of Social Psychology, 42,* 161–186.

Schneider, W., & Shiffrin, R. M. (1977). Controlled and automatic human information processing: I. Detection, search, and attention. *Psychological Review, 84,* 1–66.

Schuman, H., Steeh, C., Bobo, L., & Krysan, M. (1997). *Racial attitudes in America: Trends and interpretation,* (rev. ed.). Cambridge, MA: Harvard University Press.

Schwartz, S. H. (1978). Temporal instability as a moderator of the attitude–behavior relationship. *Journal of Personality and Social Psychology, 36,* 715–724.

Schwartz, S. H., & Tessler, R. C. (1972). A test of a model for reducing measured attitude–behavior discrepancies. *Journal of Personality and Social Psychology, 24,* 225–236.

Sears, D. O. (1988). Symbolic racism. In P. A. Katz & D. A. Taylor (Eds.), *Eliminating racism: Profiles in controversy* (pp. 53–84). New York: Plenum Press.

Sears, D. O., & Kinder, D. R. (1971). Racial tensions and voting in Los Angeles. In W. Z. Hirsch (Ed.), *Los Angeles: Viability and prospects for metropolitan leadership* (pp. 51–88). New York: Praeger.

Sears, D. O., & McConahay, J. B. (1973). *The politics of violence: The new urban blacks and the Watts riot.* Boston, MA: Houghton Mifflin.

Secord, P. F. (1959). Stereotyping and favorableness in the perception of negro faces. *Journal of Abnormal and Social Psychology, 59,* 309–315.

Secord, P. F., Bevan, W., & Katz, B. (1956). The negro stereotype and perceptual accentuation. *Journal of Abnormal and Social Psychology, 53,* 78–83.

Semin, G. R. (1985). The 'phenomenon of social representations': A comment on Potter and Litton. *British Journal of Social Psychology, 24,* 93–94.

Semin, G. R. (1989). Prototypes and social representations. In D. Jodelet (Ed.), *Les représentations sociales* (pp. 239–251). Paris: Presses Universitaires de France.

Semin, G. R., & Fiedler, K. (1988). The cognitive functions of linguistic categories in describing persons: Social cognition and language. *Journal of Personality and Social Psychology, 54,* 558–568.

Semin, G. R., & Fiedler, K. (1989). Relocating attributional phenomena within a language cognition interface: The case of actors' and observers' perspectives. *European Journal of Social Psychology, 19,* 491–508.

Shavitt, S. (1989). Operationalizing functional theories of attitude. In A. R. Pratkanis, S. J. Breckler & A. G. Greenwald (Eds.), *Attitude structure and function* (pp. 311–338). Hillsdale, NJ: Erlbaum.

Shavitt, S. (1990). The role of attitude objects in attitude functions. *Journal of Experimental Social Psychology, 26,* 124–148.

Sheppard, B. H., Hartwick, J., & Warshaw, P. R. (1988). The theory of reasoned action: A meta-analysis of past research with recommendations for modifications and future research. *Journal of Consumer Research, 15*, 325–343.

Sherif, C. W., Sherif, M., & Nebergall, R. E. (1965). *Attitude and attitude change: The social judgment-involvement approach*. Philadelphia, PA: Saunders.

Sherif, M. (1966). *In common predicament: Social psychology of intergroup conflict and cooperation*. Boston, MA: Houghton Mifflin.

Sherif, M., Harvey, O. J., White, B. J., Hood, W., & Sherif, C. (1961). *Intergroup conflict and cooperation: The Robbers Cave experiment*. Norman, OK: University of Oklahoma Institute of Intergroup Relations.

Sherif, M., & Sherif, C. W. (1956). *An outline of social psychology* (rev. ed.). New York: Harper & Row.

Sherman, J. W., Lee, A. Y., Bessenoff, G. R., & Frost, L. A. (1998). Stereotype efficiency reconsidered: Encoding flexibility under cognitive load. *Journal of Personality and Social Psychology, 75*, 589–606.

Shrauger, J. S. (1975). Responses to evaluation as a function of initial self-perceptions. *Psychological Bulletin, 82*, 581–596.

Shweder, R. A., & Bourne, E. J. (1982). Does the concept of the person vary cross-culturally? In A. J. Norsello & G. M. White (Eds.), *Cultural conceptions of mental health and therapy* (pp. 97–137). Boston, MA: Reidel.

Sidanius, J. (1993). The psychology of group conflict and the dynamics of oppression: A social dominance perspective. In S. Iyengar & W. McGuire (Eds.), *Explorations in political psychology*. Durham, NC: Duke University Press.

Sidanius, J., Devereux, E., & Pratto, F. (1992). A comparison of symbolic racism theory and social dominance theory as explanations for racial policy attitudes. *Journal of Social Psychology, 132*, 377–395.

Sidanius, J., & Pratto, F. (1993). The inevitability of oppression and the dynamics of social dominance. In P. Sniderman & P. Tetlock (Eds.), *Prejudice, politics, and the American dilemma* (pp. 173–211). Stanford, CA: Stanford University Press.

Sidanius, J., & Pratto, F. (1999). *Social dominance: An intergroup theory of social hierarchy and oppression*. New York: Cambridge University Press.

Sidanius, J. & Pratto, F. (2003). Commentary – Social dominance theory and the dynamics of inequality: A reply to Schmitt, Branscombe & Kappen and Wilson & Liu. *British Journal of Social Psychology, 42*, 207–213.

Sidanius, J., Pratto, F., & Bobo, L. (1996). Racism, conservatism, affirmative action and intellectual sophistication: A matter of principled conservatism or group dominance? *Journal of Personality and Social Psychology, 70*, 476–490.

Sinclair, L., & Kunda, Z. (1999). Reactions to a black professional: Motivated inhibition and activation of conflicting stereotypes. *Journal of Personality and Social Psychology, 77*, 885–904.

Slugoski, B. R., Lalljee, M., Lamb, R., & Ginsburg, G. P. (1993). Attribution in conversational context: Effect of mutual knowledge on explanation-giving. *European Journal of Social Psychology, 23*, 219–238.

Smetana, J. G., & Adler, N. E. (1980). Fishbein's value x expectancy model: An examination of some assumptions. *Personality and Social Psychology Bulletin, 6*, 89–96.

Smith, E. R. (1998). Mental representation and memory. In D. T. Gilbert, S. T. Fiske & G. Lindzey (Eds.), *Handbook of social psychology* (Vol. 1, 4th ed., pp. 391–445). New York: McGraw-Hill.

Smith, M., & Walker, l. (1991). Evaluating the British version of the Attitudes toward Women Scale. *Australian Journal of Psychology, 43*, 7–10.

Smith, M., & Walker, I. (1992). The structure of attitudes to a single object: Adapting Criterial Referents Theory to measure attitudes to 'woman'. *British Journal of Social Psychology, 31*, 201–214.

Smith, M. B. (1947). The personal setting of public opinions: A study of attitudes toward Russia. *Public Opinion Quarterly, 11*, 507–523.

Smith, M. B., Bruner, J. S., & White, R. W. (1956). *Opinions and personality.* New York: Wiley.

Sniderman, P. M., & Tetlock, P. E. (1986a). Symbolic racism: Problems of motive attribution in political analysis. *Journal of Social Issues, 42*, 129–150.

Sniderman, P. M., & Tetlock, P. E. (1986b). Interrelationship of political ideology and public opinion. In M. G. Hermann (Ed.), *Political psychology: Contemporary problems and issues* (pp. 62–96). San Francisco, CA: Jossey-Bass.

Snyder, M., & Kendzierski, D. (1982). Acting on one's attitudes: Procedures for linking attitude and behavior. *Journal of Experimental Social Psychology, 18*, 165–183.

Snyder, M., & Swann, W. B. (1978). Behavioral confirmation in social interaction: From social perception to social reality. *Journal of Experimental Social Psychology, 14*, 148–162.

Snyder, M., Tanke, E. D., & Berscheid, E. (1977). Social perception and interpersonal behavior: On the self-fulfilling nature of social stereotypes. *Journal of Personality and Social Psychology, 35*, 656–666.

Sousa, E., & Leyens, J.-P. (1987). *A priori* versus spontaneous models of attribution: The case of gender and achievement. *British Journal of Social Psychology, 26*, 281–292.

Spears, R., Jetten, J., & Doosje, B. (2002). The (il)legitimacy of ingroup bias: From social reality to social resistance. In J. T. Jost & B. Major (Eds.), *The psychology of legitimacy: Emerging perspectives on ideology, justice and intergroup relations* (pp. 332–362). New York: Cambridge University Press.

Spence, J. T., & Helmreich, R. (1972). The Attitudes Toward Women Scale: An objective instrument to measure attitudes toward the rights and roles of women in contemporary society. *JSAS Catalog of Selected Documents in Psychology, 2*, 66.

Stacey, B. G. (1982). Economic socialization in the pre-adult years. *British Journal of Social Psychology, 21*, 159–173.

Stangor, C., & Lange, J. E. (1994). Mental representations of social groups: Advances in understanding stereotypes and stereotyping. In M. P. Zanna (Ed.), *Advances in experimental social psychology* (Vol. 26, pp. 357–416). San Diego, CA: Academic Press.

Stangor, C., & McMillan, D. (1992). Memory for expectancy-congruent and expectancy-incongruent information: A review of the social and social-developmental literatures. *Psychological Bulletin, 111*, 42–61.

Stangor, C. & Schaller, M. (1996). Stereotypes as individual and collective representations. In C. N. Macrae, M. Hewstone, & C. Stangor (Eds.), *Foundations of stereotypes and stereotyping* (pp. 3–37). New York: Guilford Press.

Stephan, W. G. (1977). Stereotyping: The role of ingroup–outgroup differences in causal attribution for behavior. *Journal of Social Psychology, 101*, 255–266.

Stephan, W. G. (1985). Intergroup relations. In G. Lindzey & E. Aronson (Eds.), *The handbook of social psychology* (Vol. 2, 3rd ed., pp. 599–658). New York: Random House.

Stephan, W. G., & Stephan, C. W. (1985). Intergroup anxiety. *Journal of Social Issues, 41*, 157–175.

Stephan, W. G., & Stephan, C. W. (1993). Cognition and affect in stereotyping: Parallel interactive networks. In D. M. Mackie & D. L. Hamilton (Eds.), *Affect, cognition and stereotyping: Interactive processes in group perception* (pp. 111–136). San Diego, CA: Academic Press.

Stone, W. F., Lederer, G., & Christie, R. (Eds.) (1993). *Strength and weakness: The authoritarian personality today.* New York: Springer-Verlag.

Stone, W. F., & Schaffner, P. E. (1988). *The psychology of politics.* New York: Springer-Verlag.

Storms, M. D. (1973). Videotape and the attribution process: Reversing actors' and observers' points of view. *Journal of Personality and Social Psychology, 27,* 165–175.

Strauman, T. J. (1996). Stability within the self: A longitudinal study of the structural implications of self-discrepancy theory. *Journal of Personality and Social Psychology, 71,* 1142–1153.

Strauman, T. J., & Higgins, E. T. (1987). Automatic activation of self-discrepancies and emotional syndromes: When cognitive structures influence affect. *Journal of Personality and Social Psychology, 53,* 1004–1014.

Strauman, T. J., Vookles, J., Berenstein, V., Chaiken, S., & Higgins, E. T. (1991). Self-discrepancies and vulnerability to body dissatisfaction and disordered eating. *Journal of Personality and Social Psychology, 53,* 1004–1014.

Stryker, S. and Statham, A. (1985). Symbolic interaction and role theory. In G. Lindzey and E. Aronson (Eds.), *Handbook of social psychology* (Vol. 1, 3rd ed., pp. 311–378). New York: Random House.

Sullivan, H. S. (1953). *The interpersonal theory of psychiatry.* New York: Norton.

Svenson, O. (1981). Are we all less risky and more skillful than our fellow drivers? *Acta Psychologica, 47,* 143–148.

Swann, W. B. (1985). The self as architect of social reality. In B. R. Schlenker (Ed.), *The self and social life* (pp. 100–125). New York: McGraw-Hill.

Swann, W. B. (1987). Identity negotiation: Where two roads meet. *Journal of Personality and Social Psychology, 53,* 1038–1051.

Swann, W. B., & Read, S. J. (1981). Self-verification processes: How we sustain our self-conceptions. *Journal of Experimental Social Psychology, 17,* 351–370.

Sweeney, P. D., Anderson, K., & Bailey, S. (1986). Attributional style in depression: A meta-analytic review. *Journal of Personality and Social Psychology, 50,* 974–991.

Swim, J. K., Aikin, K. J., Hall, W. S., & Hunter, B. A. (1995). Sexism and racism: Old-fashioned and modern prejudices. *Journal of Personality and Social Psychology, 68,* 199–214.

Swim, J. K., & Sanna, L. J. (1996). He's skilled, she's lucky: A meta-analysis of observers' attributions for women's and men's successes and failures. *Personality and Social Psychology Bulletin, 22,* 507–519.

Tafarodi, R. W. (1998). Paradoxical self-esteem and selectivity in the processing of social information. *Journal of Personality and Social Psychology, 74,* 1181–1196.

Taguieff, P.-A. (1998). *La couleur et le sang: doctrine racists à la française.* Paris: Édition Mille et une Nuits.

Tajfel, H. (1969a). Cognitive aspects of prejudice. *Journal of Social Issues, 25,* 79–97.

Tajfel, H. (1969b). Social and cultural factors in perception. In G. Lindzey & E. Aronson (Eds.), *Handbook of social psychology* (Vol. 3, 2nd ed., pp. 315–394). Reading, MA: Addison-Wesley.

Tajfel, H. (1970). Experiments in intergroup discrimination. *Scientific American, 223*, 96–102.

Tajfel, H. (1972). Experiments in a vacuum. In J. Israel and H. Tajfel (Eds.), *The context of social psychology: A critical assessment* (pp. 69–119). London: Academic Press.

Tajfel, H. (1974). Social identity and intergroup behaviour. *Social Science Information, 13*, 65–93.

Tajfel, H. (1976). Against biologism. *New Society, 29*, 240–242.

Tajfel, H. (Ed.) (1978). *Differentiation between social groups: Studies in the social psychology of intergroup relations*. London: Academic Press.

Tajfel, H. (1981a). *Human groups and social categories: Studies in social psychology*. Cambridge: Cambridge University Press.

Tajfel, H. (1981b). Social stereotypes and social groups. In J. C. Turner & H. Giles (Eds.), *Intergroup behaviour* (pp.144–167). Oxford: Blackwell.

Tajfel, H. (1982). Social psychology of intergroup relations. *Annual Review of Psychology, 33*, 1–39.

Tajfel, H., & Billig, M. (1974). Familiarity and categorization in intergroup behaviour. *Journal of Experimental Social Psychology, 10*, 159–170.

Tajfel, H., Billig, M. G., Bundy, R. P., & Flament, C. (1971). Social categorization and intergroup behaviour. *European Journal of Social Psychology, 1*, 149–178.

Tajfel, H., Sheikh, A. A., & Gardner, R. C. (1964). Content of stereotypes and the inference of similarity between members of stereotyped groups. *Acta Psychologica, 22*, 191–201.

Tajfel, H., & Turner, J. C. (1979). An integrative theory of intergroup conflict. In W. G. Austin and S. Worchel (Eds.), *The social psychology of intergroup relations* (pp. 33–48). Monterey, CA: Brooks/Cole.

Tajfel, H., & Turner, J. C. (1986). The social identity theory of intergroup relations. In S. Worchel and W. G. Austin (Eds.), *Psychology of intergroup relations* (pp. 7–24). Monterey, CA: Brooks/Cole.

Tajfel, H., & Wilkes, A. L. (1963). Classification and quantitative judgement. *British Journal of Psychology, 54*, 101–114.

Tangney, J. P., Niedenthal, P. M., Covert, M. V., & Hill-Barlow, D. H. (1998). Are shame and guilt related to distinct self-discrepancies? A test of Higgins' (1987) hypotheses. *Journal of Personality and Social Psychology, 75*, 256–268.

Tate, C., & Audette, D. (2001). Theory and research on 'Race' as a natural kind variable in psychology. *Theory and Psychology, 11*, 495–520.

Taylor, D. M., & Brown, R. J. (1979). Towards a more social social psychology. *British Journal of Social and Clinical Psychology, 18*, 173–180.

Taylor, D. M., & Jaggi, V. (1974). Ethnocentrism and causal attribution in a South Indian context. *Journal of Cross-Cultural Psychology, 5*, 162–171.

Taylor, S. E. (1982). Social cognition and health. *Personality and Social Psychology Bulletin, 8*, 549–562.

Taylor, S. E. (1998). The social being in social psychology. In D. T. Gilbert, S. T. Fiske & G. Lindzey (Eds.), *Handbook of social psychology* (Vol. 1, 4th ed., pp. 58–95). New York: McGraw-Hill.

Taylor, S. E., & Crocker, J. (1981). Schematic bases of social information processing. In E. T. Higgins, C. P. Herman and M. P. Zanna (Eds.), *Social cognition: The Ontario symposium* (Vol. 1, pp. 89–134). Hillsdale, NJ: Erlbaum.

Taylor, S. E., & Fiske, S. T. (1975). Point of view and perceptions of causality. *Journal of Personality and Social Psychology, 32*, 439–445.

Taylor, S. E., & Fiske, S. T. (1978). Salience, attention, and attribution: Top of the head phenomena. In L. Berkowitz (Ed.), *Advances in experimental social psychology* (Vol. 11, pp. 249–288). New York: Academic Press.

Taylor, S. E., Fiske, S., Etcoff, N. L., & Ruderman, A. J. (1978). Categorical and contextual bases of person memory and stereotyping. *Journal of Personality and Social Psychology, 36*, 778–793.

Taylor, S. E., Neter, E., & Wayment, H. A. (1995). Self-evaluation processes. *Personality and Social Psychology Bulletin, 21*, 1278–1287.

Terborg, J. R., & Ilgen, D. R. (1975). A theoretical approach to sex discrimination in traditionally masculine occupations. *Organizational Behavior and Human Performance, 13*, 352–376.

Terry, D. J., & Hogg, M. A. (1996). Group norms and the attitude-behaviour relationship: A role for group identification. *Personality and Social Psychology Bulletin, 22*, 776–793.

Terry, D. J., & Hogg, M. A. (Eds.) (1999). *Attitudes, behaviour, and social context: The role of norms and group membership*. Hillsdale NJ: Erlbaum.

Terry, D. J., Hogg, M. A., & McKimmie, B. M. (2000). Attitude-behaviour relations: The role of ingroup norms and mode of behavioural decision-making. *British Journal of Social Psychology, 39*, 337–361.

Terry, D. J., Hogg, M. A., & White, K. M. (1999). The theory of planned behaviour: Self-identity, social identity and group norms. *British Journal of Social Psychology, 38*, 225–244.

Tesser, A. (1986). Some effects of self-evaluation maintenance on cognition and action. In R. M. Sorrentino & E. T. Higgins (Eds.), *Handbook of motivation and cognition: Foundations of social behavior* (pp. 435–464). New York: Guilford Press.

Tesser, A. (1988). Toward a self-evaluation maintenance model of social behavior. In L. Berkowitz (Ed.), *Advances in experimental social psychology* (Vol. 21, pp. 181–227). New York: Academic Press.

Tesser, A. (2000). On the confluence of self-esteem maintenance mechanisms. *Personality and Social Psychology Review, 4*, 290–299.

Thomas, W. I., & Znaniecki, F. (1918–20). *The Polish peasant in Europe and America* (5 vols). Boston, MA: Badger.

Thompson, J. B. (1984). *Studies in the theory of ideology*. Cambridge: Polity Press.

Thurstone, L. L. (1928). Attitudes can be measured. *American Journal of Sociology, 38*, 529–554.

Tougas, F., Brown, R., Beaton, A. M., & Joly, S. (1995). Neosexism: Plus ça change, plus c'est pareil. *Personality and Social Psychology Bulletin, 21*, 842–850.

Triandis, H. C. (1995). *Individualism and collectivism*. Boulder, CO: Westview Press.

Triplett, N. (1898). The dynamogenic factors in pacemaking and competition. *American Journal of Psychology, 9*, 507–533.

Trope, Y., & Gaunt, R. (2003). Attribution and person perception. In M. A. Hogg & J. Cooper (Eds.), *Handbook of social psychology* (pp. 190–210). London: Sage.

Tuffin, K. (2005). *Understanding critical social psychology*. London: Sage.

Turnbull, W., & Slugoski, B. (1988). Conversational and linguistic processes in causal attribution. In D. Hilton (Ed.), *Contemporary science and natural explanations:*

Commonsense conceptions of causality (pp. 66–93). New York: New York University Press.

Turner, J. C. (1985). Social categorization and the self-concept: A social-cognitive theory of group behavior. In E. J. Lawler (Ed.), *Advances in group processes: Theory and research* (Vol. 2, pp. 77–122). Greenwich, CT: JAI Press.

Turner, J. C. (1999). Some current issues in research on social identity and self-categorization theories. In N. Ellemers, R. Spears & B. Doosje (Eds.), *Social identity: Context, commitment, content* (pp. 6–34). Oxford: Blackwell.

Turner, J. C., Hogg, M. A., Oakes, P. J., Reicher, S. D., & Wetherell, M. S. (1987). *Rediscovering the social group: A self-categorization theory*. Oxford: Blackwell.

Turner, J. C., & Oakes, P. J. (1989). Self-categorization theory and social influence. In P. B. Paulus (Ed.), *Psychology of group influence* (2nd ed., pp. 233–275). Hillsdale, NJ: Erlbaum.

Turner, J. C. & Reynolds, J. K. (2003). Commentary – Why social dominance theory has been falsified. *British Journal of Social Psychology, 42*, 199–206.

Tykocinski, O., Higgins, E. T., & Chaiken, S. (1994). Message framing, self-discrepancies, and yielding to persuasive messages: The motivational significance of psychological situations. *Personality and Social Psychology Bulletin, 20*, 107–115.

Uleman, J. S. (1999). Spontaneous versus intentional inferences in impression formation. In S. Chaiken & Y. Trope (Eds.), *Dual-process theories in social psychology* (pp. 141–160). New York: Guilford Press.

Vallone, R. P., Ross, L., & Lepper, M. R. (1985). The hostile media phenomenon: Biased perception and perceptions of media bias in coverage of the 'Beirut Massacre'. *Journal of Personality and Social Psychology, 49*, 577–585.

Van Dijk, T. A. (1991). *Racism and the Press*. London: Routledge.

Van Dijk, T. A. (1992). Discourse and the denial of racism. *Discourse and Society, 3*, 87–118.

Van Dijk, T. A. (1993). *Elite Discourse and Racism*. Newbury Park, CA: Sage.

Van Dijk, T. A. (1998). *Ideology: A multidisciplinary approach*. London: Sage.

Vaughan, G. M. (1978a). Social categorization and intergroup behaviour in children. In H. Tajfel (Ed.), *Differentiation between social groups: Studies in the social psychology of intergroup relations* (pp. 339–360). London: Academic Press.

Vaughan, G. M. (1978b). Social change and intergroup preferences in New Zealand. *European Journal of Social Psychology, 8*, 297–314.

Verkuyten, M. (1997). Discourses of ethnic minority identity. *British Journal of Social Psychology, 36*, 565–586.

Verkuyten, M. (1998). Personhood and accounting for racism in conversation. *Journal for the Theory of Social Behaviour, 28*, 147–167.

Verkuyten, M. (2005). Accounting for ethnic discrimination: A discursive study among minority and majority group members. *Journal of Language and Psychology, 24*, 66–92.

Wagner, W., & Kronberger, N. (2001). Killer tomatoes! Collective symbolic coping with biotechnology. In K. Deaux & G. Philogène (Eds.), *Representations of the social: Bridging theoretical traditions* (pp. 147–164). Oxford: Blackwell.

Wagner, W., Kronberger, N., Gaskell, G., Allum, N., Allansdottir, A., Cheveigne, S., Dahinder, U., Diego, C., Montali, L., Mortensen, A., Pfenning, U., & Rusanen, T. (2001). Nature in disorder: The troubled public of biotechnology. In G. Gaskell &

M. Bauer (Eds.), *Biotechnology 1996–2000: The years of controversy*. London: National Museum of Science and Industry.

Wagner, W., Kronberger, N., & Seifert, F. (2002). Collective symbolic coping with new technology: Knowledge, images, & public discourse. *British Journal of Social Psychology, 41*, 323–343.

Wagner, W., Valencia, J., & Elejabarrieta, F. (1996). Relevance, discourse and the 'hot' stable core of social representations: A structural analysis of word associations. *British Journal of Social Psychology, 35*, 331–351.

Walker, I., & Smith, H. J. (2002). *Relative deprivation: Specification, development, integration*. New York: Cambridge University Press.

Watson, R. (1997). Some general reflections on 'categorization' and 'sequence' in the analysis of conversation. In S. Hester & P. Eglin (Eds.), *Culture in action: Studies in membership categorization analysis* (pp. 49–76). Washington, DC: University Press of America.

Weary, G. (1981). Role of cognitive, affective, and social factors in attribution biases. In J. H. Harvey (Ed.), *Cognition, social behavior, and the environment* (pp. 213–225). Hillsdale, NJ: Erlbaum.

Weber, R., & Crocker, J. (1983). Cognitive processes in the revision of stereotypic beliefs. *Journal of Personality and Social Psychology, 45*, 961–977.

Wegner, D. M., & Bargh, J. A. (1998). Control and automaticity in social life. In D. T. Gilbert, S. T. Fiske & G. Lindzey (Eds.), *Handbook of social psychology* (Vol. 1, 4th ed., pp. 446–496). New York: McGraw-Hill.

Weiner, B. (1985). 'Spontaneous' causal thinking. *Psychological Bulletin, 97*, 74–84.

Weiner, B. (1986). *An attributional theory of motivation and emotion*. New York: Springer-Verlag.

Wetherell, M. (1982). Cross-cultural studies of minimal groups: Implications for the social identity theory of intergroup relations. In H. Tajfel (Ed.), *Social identity and intergroup relations* (pp. 207–240). Cambridge: Cambridge University Press.

Wetherell, M. (1998). Positioning interpretive repertoires: Conversation analysis and post-structuralism in dialogue. *Discourse and Society, 9*, 387–412.

Wetherell, M. (1999). Psychology and Marxism: A commentary. *Theory and Psychology, 3*, 399–407.

Wetherell, M. (2001). Debates in discourse research. In M. Wetherell, S. Taylor & S. J. Yates (Eds.), *Discourse theory and practice: A reader*. London: Sage.

Wetherell, M., & Edley, N. (1998). Negotiating hegemonic masculinity: Imaginary positions and psycho-discursive practices. *Feminism & Psychology, 9*, 335–356.

Wetherell, M., & Potter, J. (1992). *Mapping the language of racism: Discourse and the legitimation of exploitation*. Hemel Hempstead: Harvester Wheatsheaf.

Wetherell, M., Stiven, H., & Potter, J. (1987). Unequal egalitarianism: A preliminary study of discourses concerning gender and employment opportunities. *British Journal of Social Psychology, 26*, 59–71.

Wheeler, L. (1991). A brief history of social comparison theory. In J. Suls & T. A. Wills (Eds.), *Social comparison: Contemporary theory and research* (pp. 3–21). Hillsdale, NJ: Erlbaum.

Wicker, A. W. (1969). Attitudes versus actions: The relationship of verbal and overt behavioral responses to attitude objects. *Journal of Social Issues, 25*, 41–78.

Wiley, M. G., Crittenden, K. S., & Birg, L. D. (1979). Why a rejection? Causal attributions of a career achievement event. *Social Psychology Quarterly, 42,* 214–222.

Wilkinson, S., & Kitzinger, C. (Eds.) (1996). *Representing the other: A 'Feminism and Psychology' reader.* London: Sage.

Williams, G. A. (1960). Gramsci's concept of hegemony. *Journal for the History of Ideas, XXI,* 586–599.

Willig, C. (1999). Beyond appearances: A critical realist approach to social constructionist work in psychology. In D. Nightingale & J. Cromby (Eds.), *Psychology and social constructionism: A critical analysis of theory and practice.* MiltonKeynes: Open University Press.

Willig, C. (2001). *Introducing qualitative research in psychology: Adventures in theory and method.* MiltonKeynes: Open University Press.

Wilson, T. D., Kraft, D., & Dunn, D. S. (1989). The disruptive effects of explaining attitudes: The moderating effect of knowledge about the attitude object. *Journal of Experimental Social Psychology, 25,* 379–400.

Wilson, T. D., & Linville, P. W. (1985). Improving the performance of college freshmen with attributional techniques. *Journal of Personality and Social Psychology, 49,* 287–293.

Wilson, M. S. & Liu, J. H. (2003a). Social dominance orientation and gender: The moderating role of gender identity. *British Journal of Social Psychology, 42,* 187–198.

Wilson, M. S. & Liu, J. H. (2003b). Response – Social dominance theory comes of age, and so must change: A reply to Sidanius & Pratto and Turner & Reynolds. *British Journal of Social Psychology, 42,* 221–223.

Wittenbrink, B., Judd, C. M., & Park, B. (2001). Spontaneous prejudice in context: Variability in automatically activated attitudes. *Journal of Personality and Social Psychology, 81,* 815–827.

Wittgenstein, L. (1953). *Philosophical investigations.* Oxford: Blackwell.

Wundt, W. (1897). *Outlines of psychology.* New York: Stechert.

Yzerbyt, V. Y., & Rocher, S. (2002). Subjective essentialism and the emergence of stereotypes. In C. McGarty, V. Y. Yzerbyt, & R. Spears (Eds.), *Stereotypes as explanations: The formation of meaningful beliefs about social groups* (pp. 38–66). Cambridge: Cambridge University Press.

Yzerbyt, V. Y., Rocher, S., & Schadron, G. (1997). Stereotypes as explanations: A subjective essentialistic view of group perception. In R. Spears, P. J. Oakes, N. Ellemers, & S. A. Haslam (Eds.), *The social psychology of stereotyping and group life* (pp. 20–50). Oxford: Blackwell.

Zajonc, R. B. (1980). Feeling and thinking: Preferences need no inferences. *American Psychologist, 35,* 151–175.

Zanna, M. P., Olson, J. M., & Fazio, R. H. (1980). Attitude–behavior consistency: An individual difference perspective. *Journal of Personality and Social Psychology, 38,* 432–440.

Zanna, M. P., & Rempel, J. K. (1988). Attitudes: A new look at an old concept. In D. Bar-Tal & A. W. Kruglanski (Eds.), *The social psychology of knowledge* (pp. 313–384). Cambridge: Cambridge University Press.

Zuckerman, M. (1979). Attribution of success and failure revisited, or: The motivational bias is alive and well in attribution theory. *Journal of Personality, 47,* 245–287.

Zurcher, L. (1977). *The mutable self: A self concept for social change.* Beverly Hills, CA: Sage.

Index

This index is in word by word order. References in **bold** refer to the glossary. First and second authors of single and two-author works are included, but only first authors of multi-author works.